Embassy to Tamerlane, 1403-1406

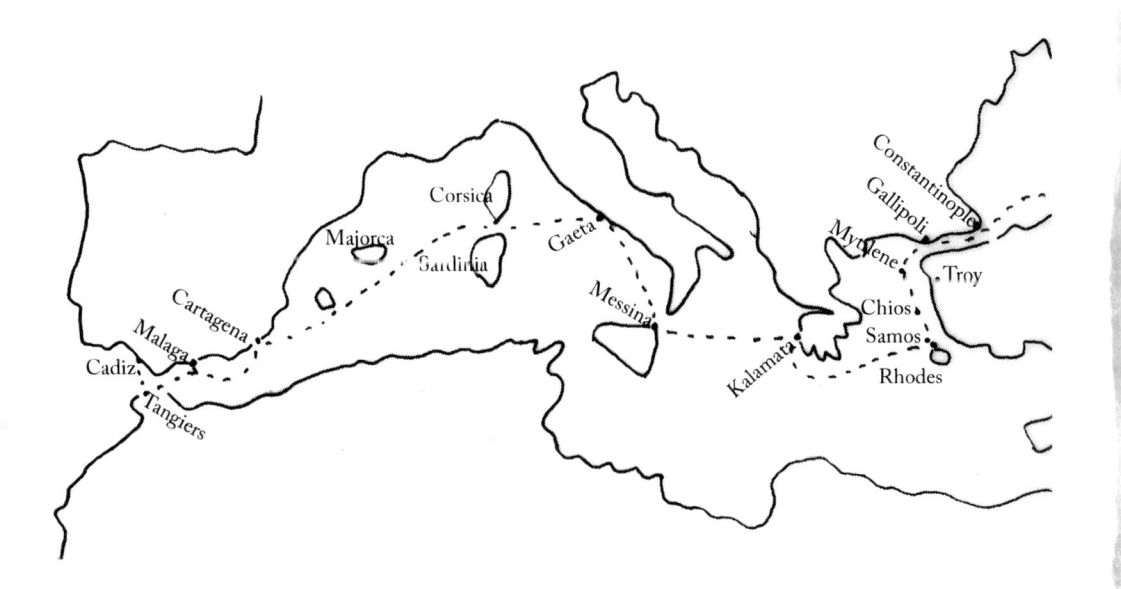

The Route Out

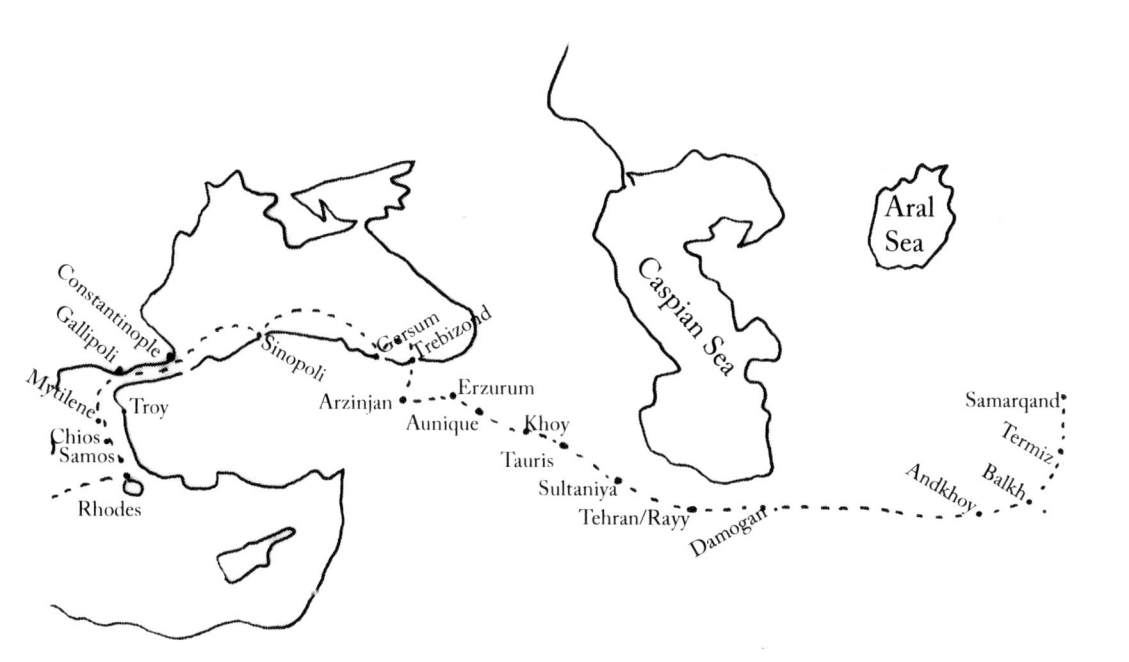

Travellers in the Wider Levant:
Series Editors: Caroline Stone and Paul Lunde

1. Travels in the Levant
    Pierre Belon
2. Letters written during a ten years' residence at the Court of Tripoli
    Miss Tully
3. Embassy to Tamerlane
    Ruy Gonzáles de Clavijo
4. Russian Travellers to India and Persia
    Fedot Kotov and others
5. Barefoot through Mauretania
    Odette du Puigaudeau
6. Narrative of the British Mission to Theodore
    Hormuzd Rassam
7. Ismailia
    Sir Samuel W. Baker

Embassy to Tamerlane, 1403-1406

Ruy Gonzáles de Clavijo

translated by Guy Le Strange

with a new Introduction
by
Caroline Stone

Hardinge Simpole

Hardinge Simpole Ltd,
The Roan,
Kilkerran,
KA19 8LS,
Scotland,
United Kingdom

http://www.hardingesimpole.co.uk
admin@hardingesimpole.co.uk

First published in this edition 2009

Copyright © Hardinge Simpole 2009
Introduction © Caroline E.M. Stone 2009
Cover photograph Tiles from the Salón de Embajadores, Reales Alcázares, Sevilla, © Alexander Stone Lunde 2009.

ISBN-10   1 84382 198 2 Paperback
ISBN-13   978 1 84382 198 4 Paperback

All rights reserved. No part of this publication may be reproduced, stored in a retrieval system, or transmitted in any form or by any means, electronic, mechanical, photocopying, recording or otherwise, without the prior permission of the publishers.

Contents

The Route Out – Map	*ii–iii*
Introduction, 2008	*ix*
Preface	*xxiii*
Detailed Contents	*xxvii*
Introduction	*xxxi*
Chapter I	1
Chapter II	19
Chapter III	37
Chapter IV	53
Chapter V	69
Chapter VI	85
Chapter VII	102
Chapter VIII	121
Chapter IX	137
Chapter X	155
Chapter XI	170
Chapter XII	188
Chapter XIII	206
Chapter XIV	225
Chapter XV	245
Chapter XVI	268
Chapter XVII	287
Notes	*305*
Appendix	*343*
Index	*345*
The Route Back – Map	*362–362*

Acknowledgements

I should like to thank the Golden Web Foundation for its financial support during the preparation of this volume, undertaken as part of the Civilizations in Contact Project, Cambridge.

Caroline Stone

Introduction – 2008

The original Introduction and notes to this edition of Clavijo's *Embassy to Tamerlane* are extremely informative and so it is only necessary to add a few additional remarks on the context of Clavijo's world and diplomatic embassies. Further information, with contemporary sources and extensive bibliography, including mss., is to be found in the Spanish edition by Francisco López Estrada, *Embajada a Tamorlán*, Madrid 1999, pp.53-70 and, at greater length, in the original edition of 1943, pp.i-lxxviii.

Ruy Gonzáles de Clavijo - Life

On one of the richly decorated marble tombs in the church of San Francisco in Madrid, the inscription read:

"Here lies the honourable knight, Ruy González de Clavijo, whom God pardon. He was chamberlain to the king Don Henry, of happy memory, and to Don John, his son. The king, Don Henry, sent him on an embassy to Tamerlane, and he died on the 2nd of April, in the year of our Lord 1412."

Very little is known about the life of Ruy González de Clavijo. Although he is mentioned in a number of histories and poems, it is almost always in the context of his embassy. He was from Madrid, not then the capital, of good family, although not of the highest nobility, and a member in some capacity of the royal household – *camerero* or, according to Argote de Molina, *maestresala*. He was clearly trusted by the king, whose will he witnessed, and who left him an annual pension of 10 000 *maravedis*. Named as one of the remarkable men of Madrid in *De Varones Illustres*, he was singled out as an excellent orator - *noble orador* - and much respected by his peers.

Clavijo was wealthy enough to rebuild the chapel where he was eventually buried and to have a house fine enough to be used by a member of the royal family; neither survives today. Even the documentation relating to the church of San Francisco, which might have shed light on the fate of Clavijo's tomb, was burned during the Civil War. However, Clavijo's unusually detailed descriptions of the architecture both at Constantinople and Samarqand, the structure and decoration of Timur's tents, and the layout of his gardens, suggest that the subject was one of personal interest to him. Numerous miniatures, particularly from Shiraz and Herat, painted during the Timurid period, corroborate Clavijo's accounts of architecture, tents and scenery, as well as banquets and costumes.

He exchanged poems with his wife, Mayor Arias, on the subject of his journey, and these verses also preserve a few details of his household.[1] Mayor Arias' poem in particular has considerable merit. It is not certain whether Clavijo had children – Argote de Molina thought not - although one poem implies the existence of a daughter, Maria, and Gonzalo Fernández de Oviedo, writing a couple of generations after Clavijo, mentions a son, Pedro, as having had masses said for his parents.

The Embassy to Timur: the Narrative

It is not known why Clavijo was chosen for this important embassy and the method by which the account was composed, presumably at the king's request, has been much discussed. It is generally assumed that it was written up from notes immediately after his return, across the summer of 1406, before the death of Enrique III in December, possibly with contributions from his fellow ambassadors. Clavijo's diary of his journey was edited and printed in Seville in 1582, apparently from the original manuscript, by Argote de Molina (1549-1596), a Spanish scholar of the reign of Philip II, together with a life of Timur and other material relating to him. It provides a fascinating sequel to the longer and more famous travels of Marco Polo, who followed a similar route more than a century earlier.

The *Embassy* is not, however, merely an official report. Clavijo's descriptions of places and events are lively and memorable. He talks of meals and social events and occasionally uses colloquial expressions that are still to be heard in Spain today. As might be expected, he went to considerable trouble to unravel the complex political situations in the different places he found himself and a good deal of what he reports is in fact correct – a major achievement in view of the linguistic problems involved.

Enrique III of Castile

Enrique III (b.1379, reigned 1390-1406) came to throne at a particularly tumultuous period, in the aftermath of the Black Death. The Great Schism, which not only divided the Catholic Church but split Europe politically, was almost coterminous with his life, for much of which the Hundred Years War was also raging. Spain itself had only just emerged from a civil war, in the course of which Pedro I (b.1334, reigned 1350-1369) was murdered by his half-brother Enrique II (b.c.1333, reigned 1369-1379), who usurped the throne; fighting with the Muslim kingdom of Granada continued sporadically.

The Ottoman Turks were also expanding rapidly into the Balkans and the two disastrous defeats of the Christians, at Kosovo in 1389 and Nicopolis in 1394, led to well-founded fears of a new Muslim invasion of Europe. The Ottoman Sultan, Bayazid, had already boasted that before long his horses would be eating barley off the altar of St Peter's at Rome and the European monarchs were more than anxious to make alliances with any rulers in the East who might be sympathetic to their resistance to the Ottomans. There had always been much confusion in the West about the religious affiliation of the Mongols and their successors and this was increased by the legends of Prester John[2], the powerful Christian monarch whom it was believed would come to the aid of Christendom. Clavijo's embassy therefore fits into a series of attempts to make contact with and gain the good-will of rulers beyond the confines of Europe.

Enrique was a positive and active ruler, with broad interests, and many of his numerous diplomatic missions across Europe were aimed at negotiating truces or compromises. Several Chronicles refer to them and, certainly, this is how he is recalled in one completed in 1491:

"...he [Enrique III] so wished to know of foreign matters, that he sent gentlemen of his court not only to the Christian kings and to Prester John of the Indes, but even to the great Sultan of Babilonia and Egypt and to Timur Beg, which in our language means the Iron Lord, and to Murad, the Grand Turk. And also to the kings of Tunis and Fez and Morocco and other great kings and Moorish lords, that he might acquire information about their lands and states and customs. He spent great sums on this, the result no doubt of his nobleness of heart, for it is very fitting that great princes should seek to know about their counterparts."[3]

His attempts to extend Spain's diplomatic relations and investigate the possibility of negotiations with the Ottomans[4] led to two of his ambassadors being present before Ankara in 1402 when Timur (c. 1336-1405, known to the west as Tamerlane) defeated the Turkish sultan, Bayazid, and took him captive. The Spanish ambassadors were treated with the utmost courtesy by the conqueror and, accompanied by an envoy from Timur, Muhammad al-Caxi (al-Kashi, from the city of Kesh, Timur's home town, although variant spellings have suggested al-Ghazi), returned to the court of Spain with letters and presents of jewels and women for the king "according to his custom".

Timur took the opportunity of sending back to Europe two young women, one of a noble Greek family, the other related to the royal house of Hungary, whom he had liberated when he captured Bayazid. It seems both were beauties and their romantic adventures have survived in ballads - most notably in a poem by Francisco Imperial, a Genoese gentleman resident in Seville - as have their very modest expense accounts, preserved in the Municipal Archives. According to Gil González Dávila, they married the ambassadors who rescued them, and he gives the inscription dated 1435 from the tomb of the Hungarian, Doña Catalina, who married Sanchez de Palazuelos, known as "Tamorlan" because of his exploits.[5] The story of the marriage of the Greek, Doña Angelina, to the other ambassador, Payo Gómez de Sotomayor, seems to have been a popular legend rather than fact.

Enrique III, impressed by Timur's civility, was anxious to obtain his support against the Turks who were threatening Europe. Timur's arrival had served to relieve the siege of Constantinople by Bayazid in 1395 (the city ultimately fell in 1453) and the king decided to send a return embassy to him at Samarqand, headed by Clavijo.

"His highness the king, having received the letters and presents and heard the good words which Timur Beg had sent .... ordered that another present and ambassadors should be dispatched to Timur to increase the friendship which he had shown ....and because the mission is very arduous and the journey very long, it is necessary to put in writing an account of all the places and countries through which the ambassadors passed, and the things which happened to them, lest they be forgotten..."

Advice for Diplomats

On numerous earlier missions, one of Enrique's most trusted ambassadors had been Pero López de Ayala, who also wrote a number of major works, including *Crónicas Españolas* - chronicles of the kings he had served - which can be considered the first Renaissance historical work in Spanish, and his *Libro Rimado de Palacio*.[6] By 1400, Ayala had essentially retired and perhaps would have been considered too valuable to be risked on such a journey, but it is possible that he was consulted on the choice of Clavijo as ambassador. His lines in the *Libro Rimado* on the importance of good envoys are pertinent and Clavijo surely fulfilled the conditions as well as any man (see Appendix for Spanish text):

"I shall speak of nine things by which you may know the great power of the king and recognize it: three concern far lands and six the kingdom, as you will see.

If his ambassadors are sent out in good order, excellent knights and truly learned scholars, well equipped and well escorted, then they will make a memorable impression on those who see them.

This is certainly some very great prince, they will say, who has sent an embassy that does him so much credit; even he who did not see it will later come to hear of it and its great fame will not be forgotten."

Reading the *Embassy to Tamerlane*, something of Clavijo's personality comes through, in spite of the lack of intimate details. His great interest in architecture has already been mentioned. His lack of bigotry is also striking. Persecutions of the Jewish community had wracked Spain ten years earlier, the war against Granada was on-going, Ottoman conquest and colonization were threatening Europe and were a major reason for the embassy, yet

Clavijo reflects none of this and can comment on the abandoned Christian villages and desecrated churches – admittedly Orthodox rather than Catholic - with an objectivity unusual for the period. This is all the more remarkable in that Spain at this date was still in the process of liberating itself from its Muslim occupiers. Clavijo views wars betweens Venetians and Genoese, Turks and Tatars, Byzantines and Ottomans as all equally regrettable, but part of the world's political scenery and there is a remarkable lack of censoriousness, religious, political and social.

He was clearly devout and describes the relics and religious treasures of Constantinople in great detail, as would have been expected by his audience, but there is something unmedieval in his approach and he lays no great stress on miracles and wonders, although other writers describing his embassy added the expected marvels that he largely failed to provide[7].

This is not altogether surprising. The influence of the Renaissance and Humanist ideas were beginning to make itself felt in Castile, again in considerable part through Ayala. He spent much of his early life in Avignon, then a great centre of classical studies, and subsequently made many texts and translations, both ancient and modern, available in Spain. It is not known whether Clavijo ever joined his compatriots there, but when Ayala went to Avignon on an embassy in 1394, he found some 200 Spaniards studying law in the city, among them 61 Castilians.

As regards the second and third verses, referring to the envoys' qualifications and equipment, it is also interesting that, in spite of various raids made on their stores and demands for gifts, the embassy managed to get almost their full complement of official presents to Timur, implying that they were indeed well equipped and well escorted. Even on the return journey, after being caught up at Tabriz in the dynastic fighting that followed Timur's death, they were still in a position to give out the traditional golden robes of honour as they crossed the Caucasus, a few days before embarking for Constantinople.

Argote de Molina cites correspondence with Timur and copies of letters from Timur have survived[8]; unfortunately there are no details of the letter that the envoys presented to him - but doubtless it conformed to Ayala's standards:

"The second point to be considered is the letter that brings his message, handsome in appearance, truthful in content, written in the best style, carefully closed and sealed with a fine seal, and complete with day, month and era."

Coinage

"If when you see his coins, they are well made, of gold and silver, round and well minted, the metal pure and everything well done, then this is the third sign of high nobility."

The subject of money raised in verse 4 quoted above is also interesting. It is estimated that in 1391 what is now Spain had more than 130 types of coins, because of the extremely volatile political situation and the fact that the money in circulation had not been systematically called in and reminted. It was Pedro I of Castile who first created the handsome silver coin, which from its inscription *numus regalis* came to be known as a *real*. It was divided into 3 *maravedis*. Under Pedro's half-brother and murderer, Enrique II, the currency was severely debased. A second reform, re-establishing the silver content of Pedro's *real* and attempting to unify the coinage, was made in 1391 by Enrique III. It is not surprising that Ayala should have had the subject of coinage clearly in mind and especially as a reflection of the ruler's power. Clavijo makes a number of references to prices, coins and money, since one of the aims of his book was surely to provide information on trade and general conditions for future envoys or travellers to the area.[9]

Another subject that Clavijo discusses, and was probably part of his brief, is communications. He was to have problems with this repeatedly, as he tried to get news of Timur's whereabouts, for example his efforts at Rhodes, where even the Knights were very short of up-to-date information. The problem worked both ways. On June 10th, 1405, the Archbishop of Seville wrote to Enrique III from Genoa:

"Moreover, my Lord, Your Honour should know that everywhere we have been and from all [the ships we have] encountered on the sea, the captain and I [have made every] effort to obtain reliable news of your ambassadors to Tamerlane, but we have [learned] nothing certain."[10]

It is, therefore, hardly surprising that Clavijo should have been so interested in and impressed by the efficiency of Timur's communications system and road network – even if he was somewhat shocked at the casual way post-horses were ridden to death. Merely possessing a horse was the mark of a gentleman in his world, whereas on the steppes herds were numbered in tens of thousands and hence expendable.

Embassies and Ambassadors[11]

There has been some discussion as to who actually made up the Embassy. Clearly Fray Alfonso Páez de Santa Maria, a learned theologian qualified as a "doctor bien letrado", but little more is known of him, or of the unlucky Gómez de Salazar, who died on the way out to Samarqand. It is apparent from a number of remarks that Clavijo makes they were "bien aconpañados" although the exact number of attendants is unclear. Unfortunately nothing more is known of Timur's envoy, Mohammad al-Caxi, whom the Spanish ambassadors had to dress in European clothes while going through Ottoman territory to protect him from the Turks with whom Timur was at war.

The whole question of embassies and ambassadors at this period is of considerable interest and Enrique III was not the only monarch anxious to extend his contacts into relatively unknown regions. Timur himself more often operated by direct military action than diplomacy and his gesture in the direction of the ruler of Castile was an unusual one, although curiously enough he had had an earlier contact with Spain.

In 1364, the great historian and political theorist, Ibn Khaldun[12], himself of Andalusian origin, had been on a mission to Seville to negotiate with Pedro I on behalf of the Kingdom of Granada, an experience of importance for the development of his political thought. He was perhaps received in the newly built Hall of the Ambassadors in the Royal Palace at Seville, which Clavijo too must surely have known. In 1400, Ibn Khaldun was sent to Damascus, this time to negotiate with Timur, and his conversations with him, especially on historical topics, make up some of the most interesting pages of his *Autobiography*.[13] Timur questioned Ibn Khaldun closely about western lands and asked him for a written report on North Africa and Spain, probably with a view to eventual conquest, rather than from academic curiosity.

It is much to be regretted that Clavijo was not able to take up the invitation of Timur's successor, Shah Rukh, to visit him at Herat. Shah Rukh and his remarkable wife, Jauhar Shad, patronized music, architecture and book production, as well as scholarship, and created a very lively and international cultural environment, centred on their capital, in complete contrast to Timur's grandiose schemes and forced compliance at Samarqand and Kesh. They also made considerable use of diplomatic contacts, among other things to defuse the long-threatened war with China.[14] Both Chinese and Central Asian accounts of these embassies have survived and it would have been extremely interesting to have had Clavijo's impressions of a court so very different to that of Timur's at Samarqand.[15]

Clavijo's embassy was mentioned in a number of contemporary sources, for its own merits, but also as part of the fascination with Timur that swept Europe and continued into the 16th century, giving rise to numerous plays and poems in almost every European language. This was because Timur was such an outstanding figure, and the combination of an exotic "world conqueror" and the, perhaps mythical, rags to riches tale of his origins had great appeal, but also because he was perceived, at least briefly, as a possible saviour of Europe from the Ottoman menace.

In the East too, Clavijo's embassy was not forgotten. Sharif al-Din Ali Yazdi who died in 1454, wrote in his biography of Timur - the *Zafar-namah* - or Book of Victory:

"He [Timur] next visited the garden of Dilen Shah, where he received an ambassador from one of the greatest sovereigns of Europe, who brought him a number of rare and curious things and offered magnificent gifts of great value. Particularly, there were hangings on which the Europeans had worked portraits, with such skill and delicacy that if one were to compare them to the famous paintings that the artist, Mani, set down long ago on the cloth of Artene, Mani would blush to see his works appearing so inferior..."[16]

In a manuscript of the *Zafar-namah* written at Tabriz in 1529, there is a miniature of European Ambassadors before Timur, with the son of the Ottoman Sultan Murad I. The envoys' dress is somewhat approximate, but from their hats, trousers and reddish hair and beards, the artist's intentions are clear.[17]

A fellow Spaniard, Pero Tafur, whose travels cover the years 1435-9, when writing of the Kaffa region, also mentions Clavijo's embassy:

"By this route the ambassadors of King Enrique travelled when they went to the court of Timur-Beg. I was told by Don Alfonso Fernandez de Mesa that from there to the farthest point they reached was as far as from Kaffa to Castile, but that they went straight there and back and saw many strange things by the way, and at the court of Timur-Beg, as they assert."[18]

Two hundred years after his embassy to Timur, Clavijo was mentioned by another remarkable figure, a Persian prince who came as an ambassador to Europe, converted to Christianity and stayed on in Spain. He set down a history of Persia and an account of his own travels, in which he refers to Clavijo's embassy.[19]

Samarqand

Clavijo description of Samarqand is extremely important, as he caught the city just at the moment when it was being transformed by Timur from an important trade centre on the Silk Road to the magnificent capital of his vast empire. Clavijo's descriptions of the forced demolitions, high speed building and Timur's frequent changes of plan, all of which put great pressure on the architects, as well as his techniques for recruiting reluctant labour, may partly explain why some of Timur's largest buildings both at Samarqand and Kesh collapsed after relatively short life spans. The city of Samarqand, whch was to become symbolic of exoticism and luxury in the West, is a major protagonist in Clavijo's account, so it is perhaps worth saying a little about it.

The city lies, with mountains on three sides, on the south bank of the Zarafshan River, in an area made fertile by irrigation. Its main importance was due to its position on the Silk Road, since it was where routes from China, India, Iran and the West intersected and goods, ideas, and innovations were exchanged. Trade was its main source of wealth, although Samarqand also came to be known for its manufactured goods, notably paper and textiles.

Built on the site of the ancient Afrasiab, probably founded c. 7th c. B.C., Maracanda, the capital of Sogdiana, is first mentioned in accounts of Alexander's campaigns in the East. According to Strabo, he razed it to the ground. Subsequently, the city came under Persian domination, but for most of its early history it belonged to the Graeco-Bactrian world, maintaining links with the West. Between the end of the Classical period and the beginning of the Islamic, there are few sources for the history of Samarqand other than Chinese, indicating its importance for contacts between China and western lands.

Samarqand was conquered by the Muslim armies in 711-712 and the city's first mosque was built. At this time the population was apparently in the process of converting from Buddhism to Nestorian Christianity, while still including substantial Zoroastrian and Jewish minorities. The process of Islamization was not completed until about A.D. 1500.

The city was of great military importance for the Muslim expansion beyond the Oxus and from the 9th century on, Samarqand was the commercial centre of Transoxania. Paper-making seems to have been introduced by Chinese craftsmen captured at the Battle of Talas in A.D. 751, and *Samarqandi* paper was soon being exported all over the Islamic world. The technique spread west, gradually increasing access to books and learning and contributing to higher literacy rates. Samarqand was also a major slave market, exporting captives from Inner Asia and Chinese territory to the Islamic heartlands.

By the 11th century, Samarqand was a centre of culture and learning as well as trade. It had come under the control of Turkish-speaking tribes, and its political history is extremely complex. In 1200, it was one of the largest cities in the east, with more than 500,000 inhabitants. Twenty years later it was attacked by the Mongols under Genghiz Khan and was devastated. The population was reduced by 75% or 80% and the city was left a shadow of its former glory.

With typical resilience, Samarqand had recovered sufficiently by 1296 for Marco Polo to write: "...a noble city, adorned with beautiful gardens...in which are produced all the fruits that man can desire..."

Timur chose Samarqand as his capital and from 1370 rebuilt the city in the area that had previously been the southern suburbs. The ruins of the earlier town are still visible and known as Afrasiyab. At this date, Samarqand expanded rapidly, as Clavijo describes, and was endowed with magnificent mosques, *madrasas*, tombs, gardens and bazaars. Timur brought in the finest craftsmen and scholars from the lands that he had conquered to add lustre to the city.

One of Timur's descendents, Ulugh Beg (d. 1449), further enriched the city architecturally and in addition built an observatory, the best in the world at that date.

Samarqand became one of the major intellectual centres of Asia.

The city also continued to be a trade nexus of great importance, with slaves, silk, textiles, paper, weapons, luxury goods, food -stuffs and live stock passing through its bazaars. Another of Timur's descendents, Babur, the founder of the Mughul Dynasty of India, who ruled Samarqand briefly as a boy in 1497, describes it at some length in his memoirs.

Notes

[1] See D.S. Severin in *Homenaje a Hans Flasche*, Stuttgart, 1991 pp. 553-560 for text and discussion of Mayor Arias' poem.
[2] Francisco Alvares, *The Prester John of the Indies*, ed. Charles Beckingham, Hakluyt, C.U.P., 1961
[3] Diego Rodríguez de Almela, *Compendio historial de la crónicas de España*, ms de la Biblioteca Nacional de Madrid; *Compilación o Compendio de todas las Crónicas de España*, Ch.xxxi, p.721 cited in López Estrada p.26/ xlv. One version reads: "Este rey don Enrrique terçero deseó saber las cosas e novedades de otros reynos e Enbió muchos Enbaxadores e Cavalleros de su Casa por los reynos delos xristianos e delos infieles; así al preste Juhan, señor delas indias como al gran soldán de bauilonia y al tamurbeque e al morato e a otros muchos príncipes..."

[4] The 17th c. historian, Gil González Dávila, even gives an account, on no very reliable authority, of an ambassador from the Ottoman court arriving at Valencia to ask for Spanish help against Timur - *Historia de la vida y hechos del rey Enrique III de Castilla* ,1638, p.185: " "…un caso sucedido este año digno de ser admirado…Llegó a la costa de Valencia vn Moro que se llamaua Mohamet Abdalá, que se hallo en la gran batalla que tuuieron el poder de aquellos famosos Bárbaros Tamorlán y Bayaceto; era natural de Alexandría y venía con embaxada a pedir y suplicar al Rey don Henrique le prestasse el poderío de sus armas contra la potencia del que entonces quería tener y auassallar al mundo porque dezía: qve assí como no aví más qve vn Sol en el cielo, no avía más qve un poder y vna corona en la tierra."

[5] See López Estrada, 1943, pp.lxi – lxiii and xlix - lix.

[6] Pero López de Ayala, *Libro rimado de palacio*, ed. Kenneth Adams, Madrid, 1993.

[7] López Estrada, 1943 p.lxix et al.

[8] López Estrada, 1943, p.xxiv and liii and in the French National Archives Series J, 937, File II/7, letters between Timur and Charles VI of France, 1402 - 3 www.archivesnationales.culture.gouv.fr

[9] It is extremely difficult to estimate the real value of coinage in the past, but the note below attempts to update the valiant attempt made by the original translators. These are very rough approximations to give some idea of buying power, calculated with www.eh.net rather than any detailed knowledge of the coinage:
  Silver real = c.£3.50 (e.g. in Ch.VII and notes)
  Real de a ocho = c.£28
  Asper = c.30p (Byzantine coin weighing c. 1 gr)
  Tanga = 2 silver reales = c.£7 (e.g. Ch.XII - coin common at Delhi perhaps introduced to Central Asia in the wake of Timur's conquests)
  Ducat = c.£40+ (in Ch.XVII the price of two sheep. The term was used for a number of coins; perhaps here the Venetian gold ducat so possibly weighing c.3 gr)
  Meri = c. £1.75

It should be remembered that at this date, unlike today, the gold:silver ratio stood somewhere in the order of 10:1, as opposed to c.55+:1 (2008)

Gil González Dávila in Ch.lxxxi of his *Historia* gives an extremely interesting list of prices for basic food stuffs, cloth etc. cited in López Estrada 1943, pp.xlii-xliv

[10] L. Suárez Fernández, *Castilla…*, Madrid, CSIC, 1960, p558: "Otrosí, Señor, sepa la vuestra merçed que por todos los lugares por do so venido e por todod los [navíos que hemos] encontrado en la mar, yo e el patrón [pusimos toda] nuestra diliencia por saber nuevas çiertas de vuestros embax[adores] al Taborlán, e non las avemos [savido] que fuesen ciertas…"

[11] For an extremely detailed account of Spain's diplomatic relations see M.A. Ochoa Brun, *Historia de la diplomacia española*, Madrid c.1990, esp. vols I and II

[12] *Ibn Jaldún El Mediterráneo en siglo XIV : Auge e declive de los imperios*, Exhibition Catalogue, Seville, 2006 and Ibn Khaldun C. Stone, *Ibn Khaldun*, Saudi Aramco World, Sept/Oct, 2006 or on-line at www.aramcoworld.com

[13] Walter Joseph Fischel, *Ibn Khaldun and Tamerlane*, Berkeley, U. of California Press, 1952

[14] C. Stone, *The Diplomacy of the Sons*, SAW, May/June, 2006 see above.

[15] Sally K Church, *Chen Cheng and his Diplomatic Missions to Herat* (forthcoming)

[16] Sharif al-Din Ali Yazdi, *Zafar-namah* tr. Pétis de la Croix, as Cherefeddin Ali Yazdi, *Histoire de Timur-Bec*, Paris 1722, vol iv, pp.178-9

[17] An illustration in the *Zafar-nama*, life of Timur, by Sharif al-Din Ali Yazdi from a ms. *in the* Gulistan Palace Library, Tehran folio 520, reproduced in Basil Gray, Persian Painting, London , (1963) 1995, p132.

[18] *Travels of Pero Tafur*, tr. And ed. Malcolm Letts, London, 1926, p.135.

[19] *Relaciones de Don Iuan de Persia…* Valladolid 1604 and *Don Juan of Persia…* tr and ed. G. Le Strange, London, 1926. "…Y echa de se ver que podemos poner en el número de los Reyes Persas al gran Tanburlán, pues en su muerte a la qual se hallaron los Embajadores Españoles que auia embiadole en correspondencia de otros Don Enrique Tercero, Rey de Castilla: dize Ruy Gonçalez de Clauijo, uno de los embaxadores y el que escriuió la relación de aquella misma embaxada…"

Preface

THE Hakluyt Society in 1859 brought out a translation of Clavijo's Embassy by Mr. Clements Markham F.G.S. (as he then was) which had merit considering the date of its publication. Sixty-nine years ago Samarqand and Bukhara were still Central Asian Khanates, no good maps were available of Persia or Asia Minor, and the Byzantine topography of Constantinople was where Ducange had left it in the 17th century. Since 1859 that topography has been set right by Van Millingen, the route from Constantinople to Samarqand has been travelled over and described abundantly, the history of the time of Timur is fairly well known, and Sir Clements Markham whom I met a year before his death agreed that his translation required to be brought up to date, only regretting that he himself was too old to undertake it.

The Spanish text from which the present translation has been made is that edited in 1881 with a Russian version by I. Sreznevski and published at St. Petersburg by the Imperial Academy of Sciences. In my ignorance of Russian I have been unable to profit by this translation; but the Russian preface prefixed by Sreznevski has, by the kindness of my friend Dr. Ellis H. Minns, been read over to me in English. From this it appears that the Russian editor was unaware of the existence in the Madrid National Library of an early 15th century manuscript of Clavijo's narrative, also secondly of a late 16th century copy of some early MS. now lost from which the Editio Princeps of 1582 was printed. From the former if carefully collated better readings would ensue for a number of the proper names of persons and places mentioned by Clavijo.

Examining Clavijo's narrative it will be found that in the printed text (as in the older Madrid manuscript) the dates are always spelt out in full, *e.g.* "lunes el quince del mes de mayo," but the day of the week and the given day of the month in some cases do not agree with the calendar: for instance here that Monday was the 20th. It seems likely that the mistakes which so frequently occur are due to the fact that in the original draft supplied by Clavijo to his copyist (who produced that MS.) the day of the month was by him written for brevity in the Roman figures. In this case we may suppose he wrote XX, which the copyist mistook and reading XV, wrote down as "quince," the 15th day. Or indeed Clavijo himself during his long journey may easily have fallen into error as to the day of the month. In any case the day of the week is less likely to be wrong, since of course in the Moslem as in the Christian calendar the week days are identical. The day of the week therefore is retained in the translation and the day of the month when altered is printed with the rectified figure in square brackets. When a sentence is given in brackets this has been added to the translation in place of a foot-note.

Our chief problem however, is in the transliteration given by Clavijo of Turki and Persian personal names. Many of these my learned friend the late Professor Khanikoff had already elucidated and I have followed Sreznevski for the balance left over. The place names with our excellent maps are generally easy to identify, but some names of the villages along the high-road from Trebizond to Samarqand, also some harbours on the Black Sea I have been unable to give otherwise than in the spelling of Clavijo. In some cases I could myself correct Sreznevski from my own recollection, for between Tabriz and Serrakhs in 1887 and 1888 I travelled along Clavijo's route. In the translation I give all personal and place names in the form commonly used in our English transliteration, while the spelling peculiar to Clavijo is inserted in brackets in the Index.

In my ignorance of Armenian, for the identification

of Surmari (Surmalu) I have to thank Mr. A. G. Ellis for the references embodied in a note to Chapter VII on that important mediæval city, which Clavijo is, I believe, the only traveller to describe in the age prior to its final destruction. Further I wish to record my indebtedness to Mr. J. B. Trend who while in Madrid found and examined for me both the manuscripts of the Biblioteca Nacional, collating some passages that I wished to have verified. It is remarkable, as already said, that Streznevski makes no mention of these manuscripts, and it is evident from Mr. Trend's careful examination that the copy made for the Editio Princeps was not collated with the earlier 15th century manuscript. It is greatly to be desired therefore that a new edition of the text should be undertaken by a competent Spanish scholar, more especially as now, thanks to Sreznevski, nearly all the proper names of places and persons have been identified, and could be added in brackets properly transliterated and following the very erroneous form set down in ignorance by Clavijo.

Contents

Introduction   xxix

Events in the Near East about the year 1400 -- Sultan Báyazid and the Emperor Manuel -- The battle of Nicopolis -- Marshal Boucicault -- Early wars of Timur -- The battle of Angora -- Henry III of Castile and Leon -- Embassy of Clavijo -- The voyage to Constantinople -- By the Black Sea to Trebizond -- Across Persia -- The Egyptian envoy : Giraffe and Ostriches -- Post-roads and post-riders -- Passage of the Desert and across the Oxus -- Samarqand: Timur and his government -- Homeward -- Death of Timur -- Prince Omar: later history -- Clavijo and the account of his Embassy -- Publication, manuscripts and editions

Chapter I : Cadiz to Rhodes   1

The lord Timur Beg -- The two Castilian envoys -- Timur's ambassador to Henry III of Castile and Leon -- That king's embassy to Timur -- Clavijo and his companions set out by sea for Constantinople -- Malaga -- Iviza -- Gaeta and King Ladislas -- The storm, Messina -- Arrival at Rhodes

Chapter II : Rhodes to Pera   19

Rhodes, the Grand Master absent on an expedition against the Turks -- Threat of Timur against Syria and Egypt -- Voyage to Chios : Mitylene : the young Emperor John, and his father-in-law Gallilusio -- Troy and its remains -- The Dardanelles -- Gallipoli and the Turkish fleet -- The Sea of Marmora -- Arrival at Constantinople

Chapter III : Constantinople   37

Audience with the Emperor Manuel -- Church of St John the Baptist in Pera -- St Mary Peribleptos -- St John of the Studion -- The Hippodrome, with the Obelisk and the Serpent Column -- Santa Sophia

Chapter IV : Constantinople   53

The Church of St George at the Mangana -- News of the defeat of the Genoese by the Venetians -- The Church of St Mary of Blachernæ and the Anemas Tower -- The relics in the Church of St John the Baptist in Pera -- The Church of St Mary Hodegetria and her picture painted by St Luke -- The history of the Emperor John Palæologus, his sons and grandson -- The great Cistern -- The Church of the Holy Apostles and the Aqueduct -- The Walls and Port of Constantinople -- Pera -- The monasteries and their relics

Chapter V : Pera to Trebizond   69
The great storm and shipwreck in the Black Sea -- Return to Pera for the winter -- March 1404 set out for Trebizond -- The voyage along the southern coast of the Black Sea

Chapter VI : Trebizond to Arzinján   85
Manuel II Emperor of Trebizond -- Court officials -- The city of Trebizond -- Rites in the Armenian and Greek Churches -- Journey down to Arzinján -- Cabasica the robber-chief of Dorile -- Reception by the Governor of Arzinján -- The story of Taharten and Sháh 'Ali -- The banquet and wine drinking

Chapter VII : Arzinján to Khoy   102
The city of Arzinján -- Taharten, prince of Arzinján, threatened by Sultan Báyazid appeals to Timur -- Timur raids the Turkish lands, and captures Sívás -- He invades Syria -- Returns to Asia Minor: the battle of Angora -- As to the death of Sultan Murád at Kosovo -- Journey from Arzinján to Erzerum -- The Dervishes of Delilárkent -- Mount Ararat -- Mákú and the Christians-Khoy

Chapter VIII : Khoy to Sultaniyah   121
Khoy : the Egyptian Ambassador -- The Giraffe -- The city of Tabriz -- Zanján the city of Darius -- Sultáníyah and its commerce -- Reception by Prince Mírán Sháh : his history

Chapter IX : Sultaniyah to Níshápúr   137
Sultáníyah to Tehrin : Bábá Sheykh -- The ruins of Ray -- The Horde of Timur's son-in-law -- The gerfalcons -- Fírúzkúh -- Dámghán, towers of skulls -- Bustám and Jájarm -- The system of post-horses established by Timur : riding night and day -- Isfaráyin

-- Níshápúr and the Kurdish nomads -- Death of Gómez de Salazár -- The turquoise mines

Chapter X : Níshápúr to the Oxus   155
Meshed and the tomb of the Imám Rezá -- Journey through the desert -- How the Tartars treat the Persians -- The Merv oasis on the Murgháb river -- The Chagatays -- Balkh and the Oxus

Chapter XI : The Oxus to Samarqand   170
The passage of the Oxus -- Tirmiz -- The custom of presents -- The Iron Gates of Samarqand and those near Derbend -- The city of Kesh : its Mosque and Palace -- The early history of Timur -- The Chagatay Clan -- Journey from Kesh to Samarqand

Chapter XII : Samarqand   188
Arrival at Samarqand -- First audience of Timur -- The Ambassador from China -- The palaces and gardens of Samarqand -- The feasts and wine drinking of the Tartar -- The great camp of the Horde outside Samarqand -- The Embassy from the borders of Cathay -- A special feast with the Grand Doorkeeper

Chapter XIII : Samarqand   206
The Camp of the Horde outside Samarqand -- The Pavilion of State in the Enclosure -- The great round tent -- The feast given by the Princess Khánzádeh -- Drinking bouts and drunkenness -- Clavijo for himself refuses wine -- The marriage feast of Timur's grandson -- His Highness's methods of justice -- His grandson Prince Pir Muhammad -- How Timur conquered India

Chapter XIV : Samarqand   225
The robes of the Great Khanum -- The eight wives of Timur -- The marriage of his grandsons -- The elephants -- The Great Khanum's feast -- The treasures of her tent -- The portable Mosque -- Badakhshán and the ruby mines -- The chapel and burial place of Prince Muhammad Sultán -- The last audience to the ambassadors given by Timur

Chapter XV : Samarqand   245

The new bazaar in Samarqand; and the Mosque of the Great Khanum's mother -- Illness of Timur: report of his death -- Description of the city of Samarqand -- The orchards and corn-lands -- Fat-tailed sheep : cheap prices -- Artisans and craftsmen brought from all conquered lands to settle in Samarqand -- The great markets for merchandise and foodstuffs -- The new Emperor of China and his Embassy - The citadel of Samarqand -- The armourers and their armour -- The tribe of Amazons -- Judges and justice -- Toktamish and Idiku -- The armies of Timur

Chapter XVI : Samarqand to Tabriz   268

Bukhárá -- The Oxus valley -- Desert sands -- Bávard -- The Well of the Wind near Dámghán -- Shahraqán to Qazvín -- Great fall of snow -- On to Tabriz -- Journey thence to Qarabágh in order to visit Prince Omar -- Confusion following on the death of Timur being reported -- The death of Prince Yahán Sháh -- Events in Samarqand where Prince Khalíl seizes his father's treasure -- Prince Omar imprisons his brother Abu Bakr -- Futile negotiations: Prince Mirán Sháh dispossessed of his rights

Chapter XVII : Tabriz to Seville   287

The Ambassadors are plundered: they protest -- The Georgians raid Armenia and defeat the Moslems -- Prince Abu Bakr escapes from prison joining his father and they proceed to Samarqand -- Prince Omar in his camp at Vian receives the Spaniards and dismisses them on their homeward journey -- They set out with the Turkish Ambassadors for Trebizond -- Qara Yúsuf chief of the Black Sheep Turkomans -- Turning aside the Ambassadors make their way to Aláshkert -- How Christian Armenia fell to the power of the Moslems -- Ani the old capital of Armenia -- Journey to Trebizond -- Constantinople to Genoa -- Savona to Cadiz

Notes   *305*
Appendix   *347*
Index   *349*

Introduction

"We take the Golden Road to Samarqand."

– J. E. Flecker.

To understand the scope and the passage of Clavijo's famous embassy to Timur, some details of contemporary events in Constantinople and Western Asia may best be summarized in the following pages, which farther will relieve repetition in the notes to the Translation.

In the year 1400 the princes of Europe sympathetically were much bestirred, fearing the imminent fall of Constantinople and the extinction of the Eastern Empire. The Ottoman Sultan Bázayíd (otherwise Bajazet) was already in possession of almost the whole of what subsequently became Turkey in Europe. The Emperor Manuel still was lord of Constantinople, but beyond the city walls possessed a mere strip of territory along the north coast of the Sea of Marmora, and extending to the Black Sea, a strip some fifty miles in length but under thirty in breadth. Four years before (September 1396) an immense composite crusading army under the leadership of the Count of Nevers (a cousin of king Charles VI of France) had marched against the Turks to the support of king Sigismund of Hungary. But the Christians had been completely routed by Sultan Báyazíd at Nicopolis on the lower Danube, an immense number of them had been killed, a lesser number made prisoners (who later had to be ransomed at heavy cost), and Europe in terror, the Emperor Manuel now shut up in Constantinople, all were waiting to learn what the Sultan next would do.

From their capital established at Brusa the Turkish Sultans, past and present, had fomented many conspiracies at the Imperial Court. The father of Manuel had been the Emperor John Palæologus (1341-1391) and Manuel's elder brother

Andronicus had at an early age been proclaimed Emperor elect.[1] In the days of Báyazíd's father Sultan Murád (1360 to 1389) his eldest son Sávaji had made a conspiracy with Andronicus whereby these two young princes had purposed to dethrone their respective fathers. The conspiracy miscarried, Sávaji was put to death which brought his younger brother Báyazíd later to be Sultan, and Andronicus (in company with his young son John) was shut up in the Constantinople State prison, the celebrated Tower of the Anemas. As a result Manuel his younger brother then became heir-apparent and co-Emperor. But in Constantinople after two years the tables were turned by a palace plot. The Emperor John Palæologus and Manuel found themselves in the Anemas Tower, while Andronicus (with John the younger) assumed the purple. Kaleidoscopic changes again ensued; the old Emperor and Manuel after two years' detention managed to make their escape from durance and regained power: Andronicus was outlawed and banished. Later, however, with John the younger, he was established in the government of Selymbria, a city on the Sea of Marmora, a few miles west of Constantinople, and the peace lasted some years.

In 1391 the old Emperor John Palæologus died, and shortly afterwards his son Andronicus, who had lately retired to a monastery, followed him to the tomb, but leaving John the younger as a pretender to the throne, for his uncle Manuel had now succeeded and been acknowledged Emperor in the room of John Palæologus. Prince John's pretensions were supported by Sultan Báyazíd who since 1389 was reigning in succession to his father Murád; and after his victory at Nicopolis (1396) was intermittently threatening Constantinople by blockade. The imminence of the peril finally roused Europe. Marshal Boucicault in command of a Christian army took ship sailing for the Ægean, where in 1399 he forced the Turkish grip on the Dardanelles. An army of over 2000 French men-at-arms was successfully landed and relieved Constantinople, Báyazíd's galleys having to retire. After a year, however, the Turks returned to the blockade, Boucicault in despair made his escape from Constantinople, taking the Emperor Manuel with him, and sailed for Venice, whence the two came on to France, where the Emperor pleaded the cause of Eastern Christendom. Before leaving Constantinople Manuel had come to terms with his nephew Prince John (the Young Emperor as Clavijo calls him) whom he left as his deputy in charge of the capital, during his absence. From the year 1400 to1402 the Emperor Manuel passed his days seeking in vain for help, voyaging through Italy and France, also coming over to England where he was entertained by Henry IV of Lancaster, but no aid was forthcoming. After these two years spent in disappointment Manuel had finally to make his way back to the East, landing first in Greece whence, impotently, he watched the events that were going forward in his capital every day falling further into the power of Báyazíd camped at its gates.

A change however was at hand, and the Turk, hitherto victorious, was soon to face the Tartar hosts of Timur (known to Europe as Tamerlane) who was advancing across Asia Minor against him, whereby the fate of Constantinople came to be delayed half a century till 1453 and in the reign of Báyazíd's great-grandson Sultan Muhammad the Conqueror. Timur who was born about 1335 by conquest of all rivals had become lord of Samarqand in 1369.[2] In 1380 Persia was invaded and succumbed, in 1390 Qipchaq and Muscovy were overrun, in 1398 north-western India was ravaged and plundered. Then in 1400 and at the age of sixty-five Timur began to turn his attention to the affairs of Western Asia. On setting out against the Ottoman Sultan in Asia Minor and against the Mamluk Sultan of Egypt who was lord of Syria, Timur first overran the Christian kingdom of Georgia.

Thence turning south (while on his way through plundering many provinces of Anatolia) he appeared suddenly in Syria, where the Tartars stormed Aleppo and then sacked Damascus in January 1401. Turning next eastward by July Timur was at Baghdad which suffered the fate of Damascus, and early in 1402 he was back in Asia Minor marching with his countless hordes westward. He reached Angora early in July, and on the 20th of that month the fateful battle was fought. At Angora the Ottoman Turks were totally defeated by Timur's Tartars, and Báyazíd a captive is said to have been carried with him eastward by his conqueror in an iron cage. Báyazíd died miserably in March 1403, and Constantinople for the next half century was thus spared to Christendom. Timur departing, Manuel immediately returned to his capital: while the Young Emperor (John) retired into exile and took up his quarters in the island of Mitylene where he married the daughter of Gattilusio the Genoese lord of the same. Of John the Younger and his claims to the empire, and his subsequent adventures, Clavijo gives a long account, for the Spaniards put in to Mitylene on their way to Constantinople and heard much gossip.

From the time when early in the year 1400 Timur had appeared in Georgia his proceedings must have been watched with increasing interest by the princes of Europe, for all eyes as already said had long been fixed on the affairs progressing in the Near East. In Spain at that date Henry III was king of Castile and Leon. His wife was a daughter of John of Gaunt; another of whose daughters was the queen of John the Great of Portugal. Hence, to look forward, the nephew of the king of Castile was young Prince Henry the future Navigator (so-called) at that time a boy of ten, but whose initiative afterwards brought about the rounding of the Cape to India; while it was Henry III's grand-daughter Isabella who sent Columbus voyaging to America. As regards the

Spanish Peninsula at the beginning of the 15th Century the Moorish king of Granada was still master of the sea-board from Gibraltar to a point somewhat west of Cartagena, and his dominions stretched back north nearly to the bank of the upper Guadalquivir. Aragon, the north-western quarter of Spain, was an independent kingdom governed by Martin I, whose sister queen Eleanor was the mother of Henry III of Castile.

To return to the events of the year 1402, we learn from Clavijo that at Eastertide Henry III, who was anxious for authentic news, had despatched two envoys into the Levant to report on what was going forward, and so it came about that during the summer they, having reached the Ægean and landing, presented themselves before Timur in his camp outside Angora, where they were graciously received. After the great victory of the 20th July Timur set out to march in his leisurely fashion back to Samarqand, intending to sojourn that winter season in the plains of Qarabágh that are in eastern Georgia. However before leaving Angora Timur saw fit to despatch a return embassy to Spain with many rich gifts for king Henry,[3] his envoys being shown the way westward by the Spaniards now on their homeward journey: and this led in due course to the famous embassy of Clavijo and his fellow ambassadors. These profited by the companionship of the Tartar envoy and followed Timur, hoping to come up with him in Georgia, but being delayed by winter weather ultimately had to seek him in Samarqand. The Spanish ambassadors were three in number, the king's Chamberlain Clavijo, the friar Alfonso Paez and an officer of the royal guard named Gómez de Salazar. They bore with them many royal gifts from their king for Timur, among the rest a mew of gerfalcons for which Spain at that time was celebrated. The embassy travelled with many attendants: some of whom as will be related left their bones in Persia, where too Gómez de Salazar succumbed to the hardships of travel dying at Níshápúr on the outward journey.

Clavijo set out to travel to Samarqand somewhat over a century after Marco Polo had shown in his famous book how Central Asia could be come to. From Spain to Samarqand the journey ran over seventy degrees of longitude going nearly due east, never far from the fortieth parallel of latitude. Journeying diligently but in a leisurely fashion the embassy reached Samarqand from Cadiz in a little under fifteen months, having many delays and a stoppage of five months in Constantinople. The journey home proved to be nearly as long, owing to a halt of six months in Tabriz. From Cadiz to Trebizond outward and homeward, the journey was by sea, some 2,500 miles each way. Their ship was a Carrack, as used then in the Mediterranean, a three masted vessel with a high poop, square rigged forward, and with a huge lateen sail on the after mast. From Rhodes to Constantinople a smaller ship had to serve, spoken of as a Fusta, or Barque, and for the voyage across the Black Sea to Trebizond the ship they took was a Galliot, a vessel of a single mast with a great lateen sail used when the wind was fair, and oars - many banks of rowers - taken to when the wind was contrary.

Of the city of Constantinople Clavijo has left us a most important description. The date was half a century before the destruction wrought by the Turkish conquest, and of the seven great churches which he has carefully described, two only are still standing - Santa Sophia and the former church of St John the Baptist in Studion now become the Mosque of the Mír Akhor. The appreciation shown by the Spaniards for Holy Relics was of course consonant with the taste of the age. In many of the churches a variety of sacred bones was submitted to their respectful gaze, and Clavijo found no difficulty in crediting the authenticity of the Lance of Longinus, still marked with the Blood, red and fresh as at the time of the Crucifixion. Further he was shown the Sop given to Judas, the Rod of Scourgings and the Seamless Vestment (the same is yet preserved at Treves as the Holy Coat). Lastly the far famed portrait of Our Lady painted by the hand of St Luke; and numerous pieces of the wood of the True Cross, of course, were not wanting duly enshrined in gold. At Constantinople the ambassadors were lodged at Pera, but were received in audience by the Emperor Manuel at the great palace of the Blachernae in Stambul, as the capital of the Eastern Empire had already come to be called. Of this palace no stone remains standing, the site alone being marked by foundations of walls now covered by later Turkish constructions.

Leaving Constantinople in November the season proved to be too late, and the galliot in which they sailed was wrecked in the Black Sea almost in sight of the mouth of the Bosporus. Returning therefore the ambassadors passed the winter in Pera, and to this four months' delay in their journey is due Clavijo's description of Samarqand. Had they reached Trebizond as at first arranged in November, they would during December easily have come to the Qarabágh Plains, bordering the lower reaches of the river Araxes, where they would have found Timur in winter quarters. Since, however, they only managed to start from Trebizond at the end of the following April, Timur had already set out on his homeward march, and the embassy had to travel across the whole breadth of Persia to Transoxiana, and thus we have the very notable and important description left by Clavijo of Timur and his court at home in Samarqand. For the sea voyage from Constantinople to Trebizond the ambassadors in their galliot coasted the southern shore of the Euxine, putting in for the night wherever possible to some friendly harbour. The Genoese had several ports in occupation, though most were in the hands of the Ottoman Turks, and in some places

Timur was represented by a feudatory governor or petty prince. Among these last was to be counted the Christian Emperor of Trebizond. Independently of Constantinople, Emperors had ruled in Trebizond since early in the 13th century when Alexis Comnenus, to escape the tyranny of the Latin occupation of the capital, had established his dynasty assuming the empire of this territory. Here the ambassadors now came ashore, for at Trebizond began the long land journey of near to 3000 miles before they could come up with Timur in Samarqand.[5]

From Trebizond the first stage went due south to Arzinján on the Western Euphrates, the way passing over a succession of mountain ranges. Beside the rugged path the hill tops were here and there crowned by the strongholds of robber-chiefs who exacted a toll from all travellers. These men recognized allegiance to no over-lord, they fought one with another or in combination against the Turk immigrants, and thrived on the booty that they could collect by force or fraud. From Arzinján onwards travelling changed very much for the better, the government established by Timur was in force, and his lieutenants obedient to the authorized demands of the returning Tartar ambassador (travelling with the Spaniards), provided abundant hospitality and all help to further them on the way. To any one who has travelled through Persia in recent years, it will be most striking how little the circumstances of the road have altered in the last five centuries. Change the names of persons, and Clavijo's diary might almost pass for a book of travel of the present century: the place names are mostly the same and the stages over the long route are those that a traveller by mule or horse caravan would come to night after night. At Khoy to the north of the Urúmíyah Lake, where the Spaniards entered Persia, they came up with an ambassador from the Sultan of Egypt, sent to compliment Timur. He too was bringing many gifts, among the rest several ostriches, also a giraffe, an animal, of course, new to Clavijo who describes the beast in detail. The Egyptian Embassy travelled onward with the Spaniards all the way from Khoy to Samarqand carrying along the giraffe and the ostriches, and these we are happy to learn came in safe and sound to their journey's end to live peacefully doubtless in Samarqand.

To the S.E. of Khoy the great city of Tabriz was at this time the commercial capital of Persia: it is situated where the trade route from Central Asia meets the caravan road from the west coming through Asia Minor from the Black Sea ports. In early Mongol times it had been also the political capital of Persia, but Timur latterly had transferred the seat of government from Tabriz to Sultáníyah, where his deputy now resided. From Tabriz the way led across the table land of the northern provinces of Persia and the ambassadors in due course came on to Sultáníyah, where they paid their respects to Prince Mírán Sháh the eldest of Timur's surviving sons. He had till very recently been governor general of Northern Persia, but had now been superseded in his command for reasons that Clavijo refers to and explains later in his narrative. From Sultáníyah across fertile plains Tehrán was reached, where the local governor made them a feast, and where for the first time they tasted horse-meat, a delicacy they were destined to appreciate on many occasions. By special orders received from Timur they next had to make their way up from the plains round and about Tehrán, travelling into the foothills of the Elburz range, in order to visit a Tartar grandee who was son-in-law to Timur, and whom they found encamped in the Lár valley under the southern slope of Mount Demavend. From here crossing many passes they went on, coming to the great fortress of Fírúzkúh – 'Turquoise Mountain'- and descending from thence regained the upland plains once more at Dámghán, rejoining the caravan high-road from Tehrán to Meshed.

At this latter city it is to be noted that they were allowed freely to visit the sanctuary and tomb of the Imám Rezá. The present Shí'ah intolerance of admitting Christians to visit mosques and shrines throughout Persia was then unknown: for this strict sequestration has only been made the rule since the Safavi kings came in a century after the days of Timur, since which time Persia has become thoroughly orthodox after the pattern of the Shí'ahs. During their long ride from Tabriz to Samarqand, through the territories of Timur's government, what greatly impressed the Castilians - for Clavijo refers to the matter more than once - was the system of relays of post-horses kept up at government expense. This was the Yam (Mongol) or Chapar (Persian) establishment of post-riders and post-houses, by use of which (a sufficient stable of animals being kept in readiness) the government messengers rode out night and day on their missions. If needful the horses of all private individuals might be, and were to be, commandeered by the Yamchís, or post-riders. We are told that even a prince, Timur's own son, might have to give up his horse at the demand of the messenger carrying despatches. The Spaniards, as envoys to Timur, were always supplied with needful mounts at the successive stations passed, where from one to three hundred horses might be found, kept ready to be saddled at a moment's notice. On a much reduced scale this is still the order and custom that obtains at this present day on the post-roads traversing the great distances of the Persian kingdom.

Further, as already remarked, from the moment of entering the territories ruled over by Timur the Spanish ambassadors were accounted his guests, and copious rations of meat and bread were at all points supplied gratis, with abundant wine. In this connexion Clavijo takes occasion to notice how brutally the Tartars treated the Persian peasants. The guides and the various officers from the Court, sent to meet and conduct the ambassadors, everywhere enforced their demands with the whip and a shower of blows. As they journeyed forward from time to time - in the towns especially - the Spaniards were presented with robes of honour of gold brocade (kincob) and occasionally a horse would be given them for their own, and these gifts (as Clavijo remarks) came in usefully later on, when they in turn were expected to present their guides at parting with farewell offerings.

On coming to Meshed the Spaniards were warned to make due preparations for the next stage, namely over the waterless desert which has to be crossed before coming to the Oxus. Leaving the Meshed valley they mounted the low pass in the mountain range to the eastward coming down into the stony tract that stretches thence to Serrakhs (or its neighbourhood), where they must have been ferried over the river Tejend. This flows parallel with the Murgháb river to the eastward, where lies the settlement of Merv: and Serrakhs is separated from Merv by about 110 miles of the waterless Qara Qum, the desert of the Black Sands. This long tract they passed in much distress of thirst. From Merv eastwards the road is fairly supplied with wells, and coming to the Oxus bank they crossed the great river immediately to the north of ancient Balkh, and so entered Transoxiana the homeland of Timur. Coming to this district Clavijo notes the fact of a change of language. Persian, which he had heard spoken up to now, gave place to what he names as Mongol, but which in fact was Eastern Turkish, the dialect at the present day commonly called Chagatay Turkí, and spoken throughout Central Asia. Travelling north from Tirmiz on the right bank of the Oxus, the Spaniards came to Kesh, the birth-place of Timur, and the burial-place of his father the Khán Teragay. Here Clavijo expatiates on the beauty of the newly built mosque and the palace adorned with tiles of the kind familiar to him in Spain, made by the Moors,

xli

known as Azulejos (Blue Tiles), as still to be admired on the walls of the Alhambra. In blue and gold with many other colours these formed the patterned panellings of the walls in the Kesh palace, and the workmanship of the Tartar artificers, as Clavijo notes, would indeed have done credit to the best workmen of Paris, a curiously early tribute to French superiority in the handicrafts.

From Kesh, after some delay, the embassies from Egypt and Spain both finally came on to Samarqand, where after a suitable pause, they were received in audience by Timur. At the age of seventy he had just taken to himself his eighth wife, and he was so blind that the envoys had to be led close up to his seat, in order to be clearly distinguished to his failing sight. At Samarqand both embassies were entertained hospitably during the following three months, many festivals and feastings being in progress to celebrate the nuptials of various princes and princesses the grand-children of his Highness. The Spaniards were next shown the sights, and duly admired the many palaces and the splendid gardens, but what most astonished them was the view of the great camping grounds of the Horde outside the city limits. Here Clavijo estimates that 50,000 tents were pitched, all in ordered lines of streets, where commodities of every kind were on sale. The tents were of two kinds, one raised on poles with guy-ropes, the other kind not braced with ropes but having thin poles interlacing thrust between the material of the tent walls, as is the case with the Kirgiz kibitkas of the present day. But the glory of the camp was the State Pavilion of Timur, a huge composite tent standing in its Enclosure, a wide area surrounded by canvas walls that shut out intrusion. The whole arrangement is very completely described by Clavijo in every detail, and it may be noted that a century before his time Marco Polo has much to relate of similar quarters at the camp of Kubilai Khán. Further there were many other

Enclosures with their canvas walls, to guard from public view the space within occupied by many tents or pavilions where each of Timur's wives had her separate establishment. The splendour of these royal tents amazed Clavijo, most were of crimson brocade, some were lined with costly furs to keep out the heat of summer and the cold of winter. One such had a lining entirely of priceless ermine skins.

In Samarqand city the ambassadors visited the Mosques and the so-named Cross Palace where they were shown Timur's bedroom. Although he was too feeble to sit his horse and had to be carried abroad in his litter, Timur was perpetually out seeing to the buildings in progress. He presided at all the feasts, ate enormous meals of roast horse, and sat drinking wine from dawn to dark, often continuing all night at his potations, as on more than one occasion mentioned. Justice was dispensed out of hand, and Clavijo records that with the Tartars it was considered more honourable to be hanged than to be beheaded, thus contrary, as he notes, to the usage of Spain. The fourteen great elephants that Timur had brought back from his Indian campaign of the year 1399 performed tricks at the festivals, and the appearance of an elephant, since none had presumably been seen in Spain, is minutely described. In short the ambassadors were very nobly entertained and Timur's administration in peace and war is shrewdly set forth with commentary by the observant envoy. The result of all this feasting was that in the late autumn Timur fell ill, and his intimate attendants thought he was about to die. It proved a premature alarm for he got better again, but not to involve the foreign ambassadors in the turmoils of a disputed succession, the Spaniards with the Egyptians were urged to depart in peace, and not to wait for any farewell audience of his Highness, who (the attendant lords said) could or would not again see them. This was disappointing to their dignity, and Clavijo for one vigorously protested at the supposed affront, complaining above all that no letter in reply to that of his master the king of Castile was forthcoming from Timur. All remonstrance, however, proved unavailing, they had to yield to pressure, and in company with the Egyptian ambassador, and others from Turkey, Clavijo and his companion set forth homeward bound from Samarqand in the last days of November 1404.

The return journey in the earlier part followed another route, the first stage was down the rich valley of the Zarafshan river to Bukhara and beyond this city they re-crossed the Oxus. The sandy tract come to here was narrower than that between Merv and Tirmiz crossed three months before on the outward march, and they reached the limits of Khurásán and cultivation at Báverd, at present known as Abiverd. This was at Christmastide 1404 and the new year as then reckoned began next day. Following on the caravan rejoined the outward route at Jájarm, and thence with short variations in the stages reached Tabriz on the last day of February 1405. Here a delay of nearly six months occurred. As has been set forth, when they were leaving Samarqand Timur was already ill, supposed indeed to be dying, but he had partially recovered and after a rest of a month early in January of the new year had insisted on starting the campaign that was to effect the conquest of China. His illness however returned upon him, and after crossing the Jaxartes he died at Otrar in the middle of February. The post-riders (already spoken of) would have brought the news to Tabriz and all north-western Persia before February had run out.

Timur's grandson Prince Omar was at this period Governor General of Persia residing at Tabriz, but at the moment he was still in his winter quarters encamped with his Horde on the pastures of Qarabágh a couple of hundred miles north of Tabriz. Thither, to go to him, the ambassadors had been summoned, on arrival, to pay him their respects: but the news of Timur's death threw all Western Asia into turmoil for many were the heirs presumptive and pretenders to the vast inheritance. Clavijo gives a vivid account of the civil war between the sons and grandsons and the nephew of Timur, Jahán Sháh, the Commander-in-Chief of his armies, and of their struggle for power some details in explanation will be added presently. To continue the account of the homeward journey we find it was not till the 27th of August that the ambassadors managed to get away from Tabriz, after much plundering of baggage and some ill-treatment at the hands of the Tartar officials. On the 17th of September they reached Trebizond and embarked for Constantinople, which was safely reached in twenty-five days by sea passage. Thence in a Genoese carrack they took ship for Genoa where they came to port on the 3rd of January 1406. After four weeks' delay here, spent in making a visit to the Spanish Anti-pope at Savona, on the 1st of February they finally took passage from Genoa, and on the 1st of March landed at San Lúcar at the mouth of the Guadalquivir, whence they rode in to Seville. The journey had lasted some three months short of three years, but of this long period (as already explained) there had been an unavoidable delay in Constantinople, a lengthy sojourn in Samarqand, and a second enforced delay at Tabriz: amounting in sum to over fifty weeks, so that they had been actually on the road, travelling by sea and land, for somewhat over a hundred weeks, going from Spain to Samarqand and back.

The account which Clavijo gives of Timur and his family, and of Court life at Samarqand is curious: no other such account having come down to us. Timur was at the time in his seventieth year and in bad health, worn out by the fatigues of his constant campaigns. He prided himself on being a very orthodox Moslem, but at his many feasts much forbidden wine was drunk; and Clavijo remarked that on these occasions his guests came to be mostly the worse

xlv

for liquor. Nothing surprised the Grand Khánum, Timur's chief wife, more than the fact that Clavijo himself would drink no wine. His colleague Alfonso Paez, the Master in Theology, had no reserves, and at one banquet Timur with his own hand, as we are told, handed him a cup of wine, which according to etiquette the Master had to swallow at a draught. On this and other like occasions the ladies of the court were always present, and Clavijo reports that he met eight of Timur's wives. At this date only two of his sons were yet alive Sháh Rukh and Mírán Sháh, the latter relegated to exile in Western Persia, but several grandsons came and went during the period that the Spaniards were in residence at Samarqand; and the wife of Mírán Sháh who was living at her father-in-law's court gave the ambassadors a splendid banquet. Horses roasted whole provided the guests with meat, while three thousand jars of wine were set round alternating with skins full of cream sweetened with sugar. These feasts would often last the day through and long into the following night, and the women took their full share of meat and drink. The ambassadors saw Timur frequently, and at the first audience after three obeisances had to remain kneeling before him, until commanded to rise and take seats on the ground.

Timur died, as already said, two months after the ambassadors had left Samarqand and his will was then promptly set aside. His eldest and favourite son (Jahángír) had died thirty years before, leaving a son, Pír Muhammad, to whom his grandfather had willed the succession, but his uncles and cousins agreed it were certainly better to take it from him. To understand what followed the genealogical table[6] (given in the Notes) should be consulted and it may later serve to make clear the references to divers members of Timur's family, as their names occur in the course of Clavijo's narrative. As mentioned above, at the time of his death only two of Timur's many sons were living: Sháh Rukh who ruled at Herat, and ultimately succeeded to the Empire; and Mírán Sháh who was the father of three sons; two Omar and Abu Bakr by one wife, and a third Khalíl Sultán - the son of the widow of that elder brother (Jahángír) who had died thirty years before. This half-brother (Khalíl) was not on good terms with the other two, but his mother had long been Timur's favourite daughter-in-law and she lived at Samarqand. Of the other two princes (grandsons) Omar Mirza the elder was governor general in Western Persia, while Abu Bakr presided over his father's government at Baghdad in the 'Iráq province, for Mírán Sháh was incapacitated by ill-health or feeblemindedness. Timur further had a nephew of whom we hear a good deal, Jahán Sháh Mirza, the son of his sister, and again he had a daughter married to a great noble who lived at Ray, where the ambassadors had been his guests, and whose name was Sulaymán Mirza.[7]

In the disputes over the succession all these princes had their part, all being personally known to Clavijo. Timur's two sons, the princes Sháh Rukh and Mírán Sháh, were, as will be noted only half-brothers: Jahán Sháh was their first cousin, and Sulaymán Mirza their brother-in-law. The other princes mentioned were all of the next generation. The beginning of the struggle for empire is graphically sketched by Clavijo. As was to be expected the outlying provinces immediately fell off. The Ottoman Turks regained independence, and the Mamlúk Sultan of Egypt once more became lord of Syria, but Persia and Transoxiana remained true to the descendants of Timur. After a bloody struggle and many deaths, Sháh Rukh established his power as lord paramount at Samarqand, and till the day of his death (1447) ruled not unwisely in his father's home possessions. His brother and his nephews failed to make good any claim they had to the sovereignty.

To return to Clavijo. The Spanish ambassadors getting home safely in the spring of 1406 proceeded in due course from Seville north to Alcalá de Henares where they found king Henry III in residence. What report as to politics in the Near East and the Levant Clavijo brought to his master is nowhere stated: but it must have been unfavourable as regards the condition of things at Constantinople. The new Ottoman Sultan (the son of Sultan Báyazíd) had now nothing to fear from the Tartar lord of Samarqand, and the Emperor of Constantinople had everything to fear in the immediate future from the Turk, though it proved to be still near the half century before Constantinople fell.

Of the junior ambassador, the Master in Theology Fray Alfonso Paez de Santa Maria, nothing further is known, but of Clavijo there is a short biographical article in Latin by Nicholas Antonio (1617-1684) and another in Spanish by José Alvarez y Baena.[8] The date of Clavijo's birth is nowhere given, but it is stated that he served from youth as chamberlain to king Henry III. In December 1406, the year of his homecoming, his name occurs as one of the witnesses to that king's Will signed at Toledo. After Henry's death, in the following year, Clavijo retired from court and proceeded to build for himself a sumptuous alabaster and marble sepulchre in the chapel he founded in the Convent of San Francisco at Madrid. Here he was buried in 1412, and Baena transcribes the mortuary inscription in full, but in continuation reports that Clavijo's tomb here was destroyed at the close of the fifteenth century in order to bury in this same chapel the body of Juana of Portugal, widow of king Henry IV of Castile and Leon. This princess was the celebrated mother of La Beltraneja, who claimed the throne on the death of Henry IV, surnamed the Impotent, said not to have been her father, and who was dispossessed by her aunt Isabella the Catholic. The original marbles of Clavijo's tomb were subsequently used to decorate the entrance gate to the new buildings. At a later date in 1760 the Convent was pulled down and no trace now remains of these monuments. Baena states that Clavijo had his house in Madrid on the spot later (namely in the 18th century) occupied by the church called the Capilla del Obispo, situate in the parish of San Andrés. It is added that Clavijo's house had been so sumptuous as to serve later as the palace of the Infante Don Enrique de Aragon, brother-in-law of Queen Maria of Aragon a daughter of king Henry III. Clavijo therefore in life and in death, till later dispossessed, had been very suitably housed.

Clavijo wrote the narrative of the famous Embassy shortly after 1406, so that the manuscript was made public, by copyists, rather more than half a century before the invention of printing. Many copies doubtless were then made, for the book became popular, and one of these copies fortunately is preserved among the MSS. of the Biblioteca Nacional at Madrid. It was however unfortunately never completed by the scribe, it lacks the title-sheet, and ends abruptly in the paragraph describing the arrival, on the homeward journey of the Ambassadors, at Messina. This copy is in a clear 15th century hand, there are 154 folios written in double column and on both sides of the page. As was customary at that time contractions are freely used. It was not from this MS. however, but from one unfortunately now not to be found, that for the purpose of printing the book in 1582 Argote de Molina took a copy, and this copy is preserved likewise in the Madrid National Library, having formed part of the collections made by the late Don Pascual de Gayangos, who bequeathed it to the nation by his will.[9] The book printed in 1582 is the Editio Princeps and is at the present time exceedingly rare. In 1782 Antonio de Sancha brought out the second edition, an almost exact reprint in a quarto volume published at Madrid, of which the first portion gives the *Cronica de Don Pedro Niño*: and this is the text Sir Clements Markham translated. Basing his work on these two editions, the Russian scholar I. Sreznevski in 1881 republished the Spanish text, giving also a Russian translation followed by an annotated index, in Russian and in French.[10] It was then, at length, that the many problems presented by Clavijo's faulty Castilian transliteration of Persian and Turkish place names, and names of persons, were at last adequately discussed and elucidated, and from the information supplied in the French Index the notes to the present translation have been compiled.

Chapter I

Cadiz to Rhodes

THE life and acts of the great Tamerlane, with a description of the lands that are under his dominion and rule, written by Ruy González de Clavijo, chamberlain to his highness the very great and noble king Don Henry, third of that name, sovereign lord of Castile and Leon. This together with an itinerary wherein is described all that fell out during the embassy despatched by his highness the said king to his lordship that said potentate, who is otherwise known as Timur Beg, in the year of the Incarnation one thousand four hundred and three.[1]

The great lord Timur Beg[2] having brought to naught the lord of Samarqand [the Chagatay Khán Suyurghatmish in the year 1371 took to himself that empire, whereby his dominion and rule were established as forthwith will be explained. For he then proceeded to conquer the whole land of Mongolia which same includes the empire of Samarqand, and next the land of India the Less. Then next he conquered all the country and empire of Khurásán which is a mighty lordship, and following this conquered and brought under his sway the whole country of the Tájiks[3] [who are Persians] with the lordship of the city which is called Ray. Following this again he subdued bringing under his rule the whole of Persia, and Media with the lordships of Tabríz and Sultáníyah. Next he conquered the lands of Gílán and Derbend together with Armenia the Less and Arzinján with Erzerúm and Avník. Then he brought under his sway and government Mardín with the country of Georgia, which last marches with Armenia aforesaid. Then Timur overcame in battle the lord of India the Less taking from him the greater part of his territory: while on the other quarter he sacked the city of Damascus, taking possession also of Aleppo, and lastly occupied all Mesopotamia with Baghdad.

Again he overran and ravaged various other countries and kingdoms, gaining many battles and making many conquests until at last he came against the Turkish Sultan Báyazíd surnamed Ilderim [the Thunderbolt] who was one of the greatest and most potent sovereigns that the world has seen. In his lands of Turkey Timur brought him to battle nearby a certain castle and city which is called Angora. In that battle Timur conquered taking the Turkish Sultan prisoner, him and one of his sons. Now it fell out that present at the time of that battle were two ambassadors come from the high and mighty lord Don Henry by the grace of God King of Castile and Leon - whom God preserve - and the names of these two men were Payo de Sotomayor and Hernan Sánchez de Palazuelos. These two had been sent by King Henry to enquire and report as to the power and might pertaining on the one hand to this Timur Beg and on the other hand to the Turkish Sultan Ilderim, and to make note as to the number of the following and multitude of those peoples whom either party could bring against his rival, and thus to report which of the two parties would be most like to gain in the struggle.

It came about that after this battle of Angora the lord Timur had notice of the presence of these ambassadors, namely Payo and Herman Sánchez, and holding in respect the King of Castile he paid them much honour carrying them with him in his train and entertaining them very nobly. Then learning from them all details as to the power of that high and mighty lord the King of Castile, and of the great esteem in which he was held among the other kings of Christendom, he gave them in charge many gifts for their lord the king, whereby to gain his friendship. And shortly after his great victory at the battle of Angora Timur determined to send an ambassador of his own to Castile with Letters from him and a great present especially to mark his amity. This [Tartar] ambassador was a certain Chagatay noble called[4] Hajji Muhammad, who had in his charge the Letter from Timur with the gifts sent by him to our king, and coming to Spain to the court of King Henry the ambassador delivered to his highness all that Timur Beg had laid charge on him, namely with the Letter the gifts and the jewels, and the women [the Christian captives taken from the Turks at Angora] whom Timur now sent back to Spain for safe keeping.[5] Then King Henry having received these Letters and presents, and having come to know the purpose which Timur had written to him in these Letters and the message brought by his ambassador, also of the great affection which Timur bore him, determined on his side to despatch a counter embassy with gifts thus to increase the affection that was between him and Timur Beg.

Our king therefore proceeded to appoint as his envoys in the new embassy these three, to wit Fray Alfonso Paez de Santa Maria, who was Master in Theology, Ruy González de Clavijo and Gómez de Salazar one of his Royal Guard, and to them his highness confided his Letters and princely gifts. Now this embassy being most arduous and sent to very distant countries it has appeared to me necessary and suitable that all the places that we visited should be set down in writing when describing the countries that we passed through, with the happenings that befell us then and there throughout. For these things being thus written and recounted and made known, to the best of our ability in what follows, they shall not fall to oblivion and be lost. Therefore in the name of God, in whose hands all things rest, and to the honour of the most Blessed Virgin Mary His mother, I began to write this account from the day when we, the ambassadors reached Port St Mary over against Cadiz. Here we had intent of embarking in a carrack[6] on which we should set sail, and returning home in our company was that ambassador from the lord Timur who had been sent to our king as already stated above. Monday the 21st of May of the year of our Lord 1403 we the ambassadors, as aforesaid, arrived at the Port St Mary, and on that same day we despatched certain provisions that were brought with us to be taken across [the bay of Cadiz] and carried aboard the carrack in which we were to sail, these provisions being in addition to what had just been sent in charge of certain of our servants, and already embarked, coming from Seville and Jerez. The following day Tuesday the 22nd of May we, therefore, took passage in a barque, and with us went Messer Julian Centurio the captain of that carrack in which we were all to journey together, and we passed across the bay to the harbour of Las Muelas which is at Cadiz where the carrack was lying. Then on Wednesday, next day, we set sail in the carrack, leaving the shores of Spain, the weather being favourable, and by nightfall were off Cape Spartel. On the morrow Thursday the ship had come abreast of Tangier, with the mountains on the Barbary coast; and thence lay across towards Tarifa Point and Ximena and having passed Ceuta came to Algeciras and Gibraltar. Then to Marbella, and past all these coasts we sailed so near that we could perceive clearly the towns lying at the foot of the mountain range which here borders the Straits, for that same day we were up with the hills known as the Sierra de la Fi[guerola].

Friday which was the 25th day of May, when the day dawned clear we found ourselves off Malaga,[7] and cast anchor in this port. Here the ship remained that day also Saturday, Sunday, Monday and Tuesday following, by reason that the captain had to disembark certain jars of olive oil and other merchandise. Malaga city stands in the plain and adjacent to the sea. Within the city circuit is a point of land that juts into the sea whereon is a high built castle standing on a mound, the whole enclosed by a double wall. Outside the town is another castle, greater in size and height, which is known as the Alcazaba, and from that inner castle to the one outside extend double walls running together throughout. Below and outside the town, and where another headland is jutting out into the sea, there are the dockyards and arsenal: and beyond these again an enclosing wall starts that goes back from the sea front with many towers in its circuit. This wall encircles many fine orchards belonging to the city; and beyond these far at the back rises a high mountain range on the slopes of which lie many homesteads, with vineyards and orchards. Along the strand between the sea-shore and the city wall are built stores that are warehouses for merchandise, and the town itself is very densely populated.

    The following Wednesday which was the [30th] of May the carrack made sail from Malaga, coasting along the shore below the mountain range, whose slopes were beset with cornlands vineyards and orchards. Next we came to Velez Malaga, a high built castle standing on the mountain flank, and then passed Almuñecar, a town lying down by the shore of the sea, and by nightfall we were in sight of and sailing under the range of the Sierra Nevada. Next day Thursday the ship was abreast of Cape Palos, which is off Cartagena, and on Friday we doubled Cape Martin at the base of a high mountain range which is of the province of Catalonia [in the kingdom of Aragon]. Saturday at dawn we were abreast of an uninhabited island that is called Formentera, and already were in sight of the island of Ibiza, and coming up with it passed all that Saturday with Sunday, Monday and Tuesday following lying off and on the coast unable to double the headland to reach the port, for the wind was at all times contrary. On that Tuesday night however at last we made the port [of Ibiza], and this day was the 5th of June. Here the captain discharged much cargo that he had brought, and took other cargo aboard, loading up with salt, and the ship lay here from the Tuesday of our arrival all Wednesday, Thursday and Friday being unable to get away, for a head wind was blowing against us. Indeed it was not till Wednesday the 13th of June that we were able to set sail. But then both the following days Thursday and Friday it fell calm so that we made but little way.

Ibiza is but a small island being five leagues in the length by three in the breadth. On the same day that the ship reached the island we three ambassadors landed, and the governor, who is in charge, being thereto appointed by the king of Aragon, ordered a lodging forthwith to be prepared for us. Further he sent down men and horses to bring us up to the town. The whole island is a mass of high mountains, with the lower slopes covered by pine forests. The chief town is very populous and stands on a great hillock which overlooks the sea. The town is enclosed by three walls, and in the space between every two they have built many houses. There is a castle, with high towers and an encircling wall, on the summit of the hill within the town at the point above the sea, and facing the castle is the church, opposite, which has a very lofty tower that, so to speak, matches the castle. Beyond outside the town and the castle there is further another outer town wall. Throughout the island of Ibiza are found many salt-pans where much salt is produced, of a very fine quality. This is gathered at the close of the summer season, being produced by the evaporation of the sea water that has been let in. These salt-pans give a good revenue, for yearly many ships come hither from the Levant, and load up with cargoes of this salt.

Within the town limits there stands a tower, wherein are many chambers, which is known as the Tower of Avicenna:[8] for they say that Avicenna was a native of this island of Ibiza. In the town walls and on their towers may be seen many marks of the cannon-balls which the late king Don Pedro IV of Aragon discharged against this place when he was laying siege to the island [to eject the Barbary Moors].

On the following Saturday which was the [16th] of June

we were at the hour of none [three p.m.] coasting the island of Majorca, so near indeed that we could perfectly perceive the folk on the country-side, and by Sunday following were passing an island that is called Cabrera, where there is a small castle. Monday and Tuesday we made very little way because the wind was light, but that Wednesday we were abreast of the island of Minorca, and thence sailing on entered the Gulf of Lyons. Thursday, Friday and Saturday we passed crossing that Gulf, and profited by good weather so that by Sunday, which was St John's Day [the 24th of June] we had come up with an island which is called Linera [or Asinara to the N.W. of Sardinia] which is of the dominion of the Viceroy of Aragon [who is the governor of Sardinia]. On Monday at dawn we found ourselves sailing through the strait between the two islands of Corsica and Sardinia; and on the island of Corsica stands a castle that bears the name of Bonifacio which belongs to a certain Genoese lord: while opposite on the island of Sardinia is another castle that is called Longosardo which belongs to the Catalans [and is of Aragon]. These two castles, aforesaid, of those islands of Corsica and Sardinia, stand on the sea-shore and face each other as though to guard the strait, which parting these islands is very narrow and dangerous of navigation. This passage here is known as the Mouths or Strait of Bonifacio.

Tuesday, the next day we sailed near an island that is [off the mainland of Italy, and] called Ponza, which now is uninhabited, though formerly people lived on it; for there used to be here two monasteries, besides many magnificent buildings which are attributed to the poet Virgil. On the mainland, to the left as we passed down leaving the island on the right hand, we saw a high mountain range and this goes by the name of Monte Cassino. Here is seen the castle called San Felice which belongs to king Ladislas [of Naples]. Beyond this passing south we saw another mountain range by the coast, and at its foot next appeared the town of Terracina, which same is in the territory of Rome being but twelve leagues distant from that capital. Occupying the land between the houses of the city of Terracina and the sea beach were many orchards, and among some high trees appeared the buildings of a nunnery, but the nuns had all been carried off captive by the Barbary Moors. Wednesday our voyage was continued and on the following day Thursday which was the [28th] of June we had reached by nightfall the port of Gaeta. Here we found we could anchor so close to the shore that it was possible to lay a gangway to the city wall by which to land. On coming ashore we ambassadors took lodgings in a hostel near by the church of San Francisco outside the town, the carrack remaining here for sixteen days following, while the captain was discharging cargo consigned to certain merchants of the port, and next taking aboard olive-oil in its room.

The city of Gaeta and its harbour both are very fine, though of the latter the entrance is narrow, but it broadens out within. All round the city are high hills on which are built many castles and beautiful houses, all standing within their orchards. On the left hand as one enters the port is seen a lofty hill, crowning the summit of which is a castle, that is a watch-tower, and they say this was built by [the Paladin] Roland, and hence it goes by the name of Orlando's Tower.[9] Running back from this hill is another adjoining it on which the houses of the town are built, these standing down one below the other to the waters of the harbour. Thence houses extend all along the sea beach, with the town wall beyond, against which dash the waves of the sea. [Above the entrance to the harbour, and where on either hand] the wall ends, rise up two towers, the foundations of which stand in the water, and from one tower to the other may be counted as the distance that a catapult can cast its bolt. From the one tower to the other, when necessary, they stretch a chain, behind which the galleys and other ships may lie safely in time of war. On the height, that passes between the hill on which the houses of the city are built and the neighbouring hill of Orlando's Tower, has been erected another tower with many tall turrets and battlements set along a curtain that joins it to the walls of Orlando's Tower. By this fortification the city is protected on its hill slope, while thereby the hill of Orlando's Tower is also safe-guarded from attack.

Gaeta from the sea is likewise well protected, for the waters enclose the promontory on both sides; and they have no fear in war time, for from the heights within the town they can spy enemy ships and prevent them coming into port. Adjoining the fortifications of the town another wall has been built which extends for some distance along the sea front, enclosing within its circuit a high hill, and the same on two sides thus faces the waters of the sea. This hill is covered with vineyards and orchards and olive-yards. Beside and within the wall connecting this hill with the town fortifications there runs a street, built on either hand with houses and shops. On the one hand beside this street stands a church much venerated of the people which bears the name of Saint Mary of the Annunciation, while opposite on the other side of the street is another church which is that of Saint Anthony. Here attached to Saint Mary's Church is the fine Monastery of Saint Francis. At the further end of this street, of which we now speak, the guarding wall runs up the slope of the hill going over and down to the sea-shore on the other side, whereby at the back it entirely encloses that hill. This long wall of fortification has been built in order that in time of war no enemy ship may come to land here, and that the city may be thus safe from surprise.

At the point where this outer wall, enclosing the hill slopes, joins up with the Gaeta town wall there stands the church of the Holy Trinity near by which are various towers, each like a fort, that guard the houses near by. Not far from this church there is a grotto on the hilltop, and it looks as though it had been hewn out artificially. It is, however, natural and the opening into the hill side has a height of some ten fathoms and next penetrates down for fifty paces, the passage being so narrow that only one man at a time can pass in. At the further end is a hermit's cell, which bears the name of the Holy Cross being called Santa Cruz. We were told that there are documents preserved in Gaeta city which state that this grotto opened of itself [the first Good Friday], namely on the very day on which our Lord Jesus Christ suffered death.

The outer city wall of which we have been speaking encloses a great number of beautiful orchard lands occupied by orange and lemon and citron plantations with vineyards and olive-yards. Here there are many country houses having terraced roofs: the whole district being most beautiful to the observer. Then extending beyond this outer city wall begins a long street of houses running beside the sea beach with beautiful buildings and many palaces. These all stand in their orchards which same are irrigated by the mountain streams that here flow in. This street passes all round the bay going back from the city, and at its further end is the township which is called Mola [di Gaeta] which same indeed lies quite two leagues distant from Gaeta city. The whole length of this street of houses is well constructed, being paved throughout: and overhanging it rises the hill slope, which same is occupied by many farms and villages. Standing in the city of Gaeta you may look and admire this well peopled country-side, and it is indeed a marvel of beauty and richness. During the delay of our ship in Gaeta we went to see all these places, that we have spoken of, and further visited beyond the town of Mola another township with a lofty castle. Indeed there were many other such places round and about on the hill slopes descending from the range of mountains at the foot of which on the cape Gaeta city is situated. Lastly on the right hand of the entrance to the port there is built a very high tower for an outlook, and this is known as the Carigliano Tower.

All these cities and lands formerly belonged to the Count of Fondí, but now they are part of the lordship of king Ladislas, who gained possession of them after his war with king Louis.[10] The houses in the city of Gaeta are quite magnificent, and they are built one below the other, coming down the hill slope to the waters of the port. They all have high windows that overlook the sea. The finest quarter of the city is that of the main street which runs level with and beside the beach. The other streets are narrow and high built, being steep and ill to walk in. In the main street there is much business traffic, and all the year round the trade here is constant. At the time when king Ladislas was waging war against king Louis, he had lost the whole of the kingdom of Naples all save this same city of Gaeta, and it was from Gaeta, finally sallying forth, that he conquered and got back the kingdom of Naples to himself. While king Ladislas was living in the city of Gaeta, and having been there married to the Lady Constantia the daughter of Manfred Lord of Chiaramonte, he put her from him, and next (but against her will) married her to a certain one of his vassals the son of Messer Louis of Capua. It is related further that king Ladislas in that church, we have mentioned above, called the Holy Trinity, himself was present at this marriage [of his wife to Messer Louis] and took their hands in the presence of a great concourse of his people there assembled to join them in wedlock, and caused the rite to be performed: further that on the afternoon of these espousals king Ladislas himself taking the hand of that lady, who was or had been his wife, danced with her publicly. Later, they say, she was wont to speak with open scandal of many vile matters, talking loudly in street and market place. King Ladislas had indeed done all this that

11

he did under the advice of Queen Margaret his mother, and afterwards he married the Lady Mary who was the sister of [Janus the last] king of Cyprus. By his first wife the Lady Constantia aforesaid, with whom he had lived in wedlock during one and a half years only, the king had no children, though this lady by her second husband [the Lord of Capua] has since had many sons. But king Ladislas also has a sister, who is called the Lady Joanna, who is married to [William of Hapsburg] who is Duke of Styria and Babenberg, and she is said to be a most beautiful woman.

On Friday which was the 13th of July the carrack made sail leaving Gaeta at midday setting forth further on its voyage. The next day Saturday we were passing beside an island which is named Ischia: and following this another which is called Proceda, but both are uninhabited. That same day too we came abreast of a third island which has inhabitants and is called Capri, forming part of the lordship of Naples: there is here a fine town. We were next off a promontory of the mainland that is named Cape Minerva,[11] and then sailed past two hills noticing between the two a city that is known as Amalfi. On these hills also may be seen various castles, and we learnt that in the town of Amalfi the head of Saint Andrew is preserved. That same day Saturday at the hour of vespers we saw, as though coming down out of the clear sky, two great dark clouds that descending rested on the sea; and immediately the sea rose up to meet them, with a violent rushing noise, the clouds bursting forth in a water-spout. All the heavens became darkened and entirely overcast; but we of the carrack kept our distance therefrom as much as was possible, for had those water-spouts prevailed to catch us up we had certainly foundered.

On the following day Sunday we were sailing between two uninhabited islands that are level land being without hills, and these are called Alicudi and Filicudi: and somewhat further on lying to the left we came near another island, which has a high mountain, and this is known as Stromboli being a volcano whence issues fire and smoke. That night we saw great flames coming from the crater with a thunderous noise. Lying to our right also was another island named Lipari, and this supports a population and belongs to the lordship of king Ladislas. In this island is reserved the Veil of the blessed Saint Agatha. The island of Lipari formerly possessed an active volcano, but through the prayers of Saint Agatha it shortly ceased to vomit smoke and flames, and the same was the case with some neighbouring islands where formerly there were volcanoes. Further at the present day when any island near by begins to pour forth flames they bring out here in Lipari that Veil in procession which prevents the eruption extending to their island, whereupon also that other eruption will cease. On the Monday following in the forenoon as we were sailing by some other uninhabited islands, which are known variously as the Salinas, and Volcanello and Volcano, we perceived that in all these the craters were active, for with loud noise they were pouring forth flames. Next we passed beside two other islands that are uninhabited, and these are called respectively Panarie and Panarelli.

On Tuesday following which was the 17th of July we were becalmed between these two last named islands, and having no wind could make no way. But that night in the third hour as we lay there a great storm began to blow, and the wind being contrary, forced us back on our former course. The storm lasted during that night, and indeed all that following Wednesday it blew fiercely, so that at midday the sails of the carrack from stem to stern all were split and we ran under bare poles, being the while in great peril. All that Wednesday till two hours after nightfall the wind blew, during which time the craters, especially those on the islands of Stromboli and Volcano aforementioned, flamed high in the wind with mighty eruption of smoke and fire and noise. During this storm the captain of our ship coming to us caused litanies to be chanted, we and all the crew imploring the mercy of God: then our prayers being said we saw as we were riding out the storm, a light as of a candle that appeared on the mainyard arm and at the mast head of the carrack, while another light flamed at the end of the bowsprit above the forecastle, and again another light like a candle on the yard-arm over the poop. All these lights [which are St Elmo's Fires] were seen by the crew of the carrack, for they were all called up on deck to witness. The fires were visible but for a short space of time, and then disappeared, during all which season the storm continued to rage.

After a space of time we and the crew turned in to sleep, excepting indeed the captain and some few mariners who had to keep watch. And they being all broad awake, namely the captain and two of his seamen keeping the watch, they heard voices as at a distance, yet seemingly alongside the carrack, as though men were talking. The captain asked his men did they hear those voices, to which they answered Yea, and all that time the storm wind did not cease to howl. At that same period, seeing again that those [St Elmo] lights came back as they had been aforetime, the captain caused all the crew of the carrack to be roused, and to them he related what he and those on watch had heard. For a space of time as is the saying of a mass, those lights remained visible and then went out, after which the storm ceased. As to those lights they say that it is to Fray Pero González of Tuy[12] to whom one should pay one's orisons in time of need for succour.

The next day at dawn we found ourselves back again among the [Lipari] islands, already described and sailing in sight of Sicily, hoping to make way under a fair breeze; but till the following Thursday, perforce continued to cruise about those islands, for it had fallen almost to a calm. On the Friday, however, we were lying abreast of the mainland of Sicily and in sight of a building which is called the Tower of Faro. This stands at the point where you turn [down the straits] towards the bay of Messina when you are making for that port; there is, however, here always a strong current that sets out of the straits, and we having at that time but little wind to carry us forward, were unable to double the point of the Faro.

Thus we failed that day to come to the port of Messina, and that night the wind increased greatly, whereby the pilot, who had come out to us from Messina to take the carrack through the straits and into port, ordered sail to be made turning us back. As we again came abreast of the Faro Tower the carrack struck taking ground, and the rudder became unshipped from its box. We thought now indeed all was lost, but the wind continuing light and the sea not rising, after a spell we managed to get the carrack off the rocks and so gained safety with sea room. Forthwith we let down two anchors: and remained stationary till daylight. When the morning dawned the flood tide began to run, and a breeze sprang up, whereby making sail we reached the port of Messina.

This Tower of Faro stands opposite across the straits to the mainland of Calabria, being on the [N.E.] point of the island of Sicily, and the straits are here so narrow that the sea is but a league across. In the Tower of the Faro by night there is always kept burning the light-house, in order that the ships that go by the straits may be able to find the passage. All the country on the Calabria side as we passed down appeared to be well cultivated and rich in cornlands with many orchards and vineyards. The town of Messina stands beside the sea, and its city wall which is defended by many strong towers rises above the strand. The houses of the town are very finely built of mortared stone, and high, so that the windows of each house overlook the sea being visible therefrom. The chief

15

street of the town runs parallel with the sea front, and the city here has five or six gateways opening to the water-side. At one end of the town there are to be seen many dockyards, while outside the city limits stands the Monastery of Black Friars, known as San Salvador, where the monks order their services according to the Greek rite. Messina further has in its midst a strong castle.

On Monday following which was the [23rd] of July we took our departure from Messina and the wind being favourable sailed down the coast of Sicily having on the right hand the mountain and crater of [Etna called] Mongible.[13] We next passed over towards the coast of Calabria, where the city of Reggio came in sight. After this continuing our voyage the ship was crossing the entrance of the Venetian Gulf [which is the Adriatic] all the next Tuesday, Wednesday and Thursday, and by Friday at nightfall had come to be off Modon on the mainland of [the Morea in] Greece which same is under the lordship of Venice. Thence sailing on we came abreast of the island of Sapienza, and afterwards passed the island of Venetico, and further again another island called Cerne [or Cabrera], at length coming to and doubling Cape San Gallo. Here was to be seen on the mainland a place that is known as Corone. The next morning, Saturday, we were abreast of Cape Maria called Matapan, and beyond is Cape Sant Angelo both these being of the mainland, which is of the lordship of Venice.

Next by midday the ship was off the shore of a well inhabited island called Cetul [or Cerigo], and we took the passage between this island and a high rock that goes by the name of El Lobo [the Wolf, or the Seal]. On the island of Cerigo we noticed a small castle, with very lofty turrets, that crowned a promontory by the sea. Here down by the margin of the strand was a tower that guarded the ascent to this castle, and not far thence, in the curve of the shore, was a plain close to the sea where appeared the remains of a wall and a building in ruins. This they say marks the place where of old a [heathen] temple stood with its sacred image that Paris threw down, at the time when he carried off Helen, he having been despatched by his father King Priam to make war on the Greeks. Our ship on getting clear of the island of Cerigo took her course between three rocks here, that are known as Three, Two and Ace ["Tres, Dos, As"]. On Sunday which was the 29th of July at the hour of tierce [9 a.m.] we were abreast of an uninhabited island which is called Sekilos[14] crowned by high peaks on which falcons breed. We had intended to pass in our carrack between the main island and a certain high rock that was near by, but the current here running very strongly between the two carried us forward, so that we failed to turn the ship's course in time, almost running her aground. While passing thus near these rocks some young falcons that were nesting there were disturbed making a great cry. On this occasion our captain, with some merchants who were on board, also many men of the crew were for the moment so alarmed at the ship's peril that they had stripped to their shirts, but on seeing that we came through in safety, for verily God did vouchsafe to us a proof of His great mercy, all made proof of their gratitude.

On Monday following we found ourselves sailing between two inhabited islands that bear the names respectively of Millo and Ante-Millo: these in past times having formed part of the Dukedom of the Archipelago, but now belonging to the Venetians. The islands are covered with flocks and herds out at pasture. Tuesday and the Wednesday following we lay becalmed between these islands and could make no way: but Thursday we sailed on and came up with three other islands that are accounted as of the Dukedom of the Archipelago, and their names are Nios, Santorin and Therasia. Then by midday we were off another island which is called Naxos and this is of great size and is the capital and seat of the Dukedom. At dawn on Friday following, the 3rd of August, the carrack lay off the inhabited island which is called Kalymnos, and here there were to be noticed many corn lands, and the ship tarried here awhile and then we sailed on towards the neighbouring island which is called Lango [or Kos] the inhabitants of which are men come over from Rhodes, and certain of the Knights of the Order of St John are stationed here in command. While sailing down hither we had the mainland of the Turkish coast to the left hand, passing the island named Nisyros off Cape Krio. This island lies so near the mainland that we did not dare run the passage in between at night-time, fearing lest the carrack should touch ground. Awaiting the daylight therefore we came through and thence sailed past various other islands of the lordship of Rhodes which lie off the Turkish coast and which are known as Piscopi [or Telos], St Nicholas of Carchini and Pimia: and finally at nightfall of that same day, Saturday, brought the carrack to anchor in the port of the city of Rhodes.

Chapter II

Rhodes to Pera

As soon as we had arrived in the port of Rhodes we sent up to know if the Grand Master were there. News was returned that, with certain galleys and a good number of his Knights, the Grand Master in convoy with the carracks and galleys of the Genoese fleet, which was under the command of Marshal Bucicaut, all together had left Rhodes for an expedition against Alexandretta.[1] We therefore the next day, Saturday, on disembarking proceeded up to the great palace at Rhodes to see the Lieutenant, whom the Grand Master had left in his place, and to confer with him. Knowing of our arrival the Lieutenant, with the Brothers who were in residence, came forth to meet us, saying that though their lord the Grand Master was absent, yet to show honour to his highness the King of Castile, they would do all that lay in their power to satisfy our needs. We explained that we had come to land in order to enquire for news of where Timur Beg might then be, and to take counsel as to what we should do. The Lieutenant now gave orders that we should be lodged in the quarters of a certain Knight of the Order that stood near by the church dedicated to the blessed Saint Catharine.

Hither therefore we came Sunday, which was the 5th day of August, remaining there till Thursday the 30th of August: but in all this time we could get no news that was certain. Details of what was going forward were told us by some who had come back from the fleet that was now lying off the coasts of Syria, also an account was brought in by certain pilgrims from Jerusalem: all of which was to the following effect. Timur, they said, yet had it in mind to return against Syria and to subdue the Sultan of Cairo,[2] to whom he was sending his envoys. These envoys, it was reported, had already come and informed the Sultan of Cairo that he must now coin in his mint money with the arms and superscription of Timur, and pay him yearly tribute. Should the Sultan not be willing to do this, then when the summer drought was past and there was no longer lack of rain [for pasture], he Timur - who cared not a jot for that Sultan - would return back to Syria [and conquer Egypt]. This was said to have been the message that had come from Timur to the governor of Jerusalem for proclamation to the people of the land of Egypt: but all accounts were but of hearsay, and therefore we could not reckon on them with any certainty.

While we thus were awaiting information, there came back from the fleet four great Genoese carracks and two other ships bringing news of their recent doings. These reported that the fleet with the Knights on board had steered direct for a castle on the Syrian coast called Kandeli to which they had laid siege during twelve days. But the commander of that fortress had then sallied forth and made an attack on the besiegers, when fifteen of their war horses had been captured and a number of the French and Genoese Knights had been killed. With this ill-success the fleet had sailed away, and coming next to the city of Tripoli of Syria they had proceeded to attack it. The people of this town, to defend themselves, had dammed back a water course near by, and no sooner was it seen that our men had disembarked from their ships than they opened the dam, bringing sudden disaster on our people who had in haste betaken themselves back to their ships. Next a council of war had been held by the commanders of the fleet as to what should be done, and it was determined to the following effect. Since the carracks and other sailing ships of the fleet were swifter than the galleys, these, the former, should sail forth making their way to Alexandretta where they should remain stationary for nine days: while the latter, the galleys, under command of the Knights should proceed on south and attack Beyrut a city on the coast of Syria, which same is the port of Damascus being two days' journey by land distant therefrom.

The carracks therefore had sailed to Alexandretta, while the galleys with the commanders of the fleet had proceeded down to Beyrut which city they had taken by assault and burnt. The carracks after coming to Alexandretta had waited there for the nine days, as agreed, but during that time their captains had received no news from the galleys; meanwhile daily they were losing numbers of the horses that were shipped aboard the carracks, for these beasts were dying for lack of water to drink. Further the men too were more and more put to straits for their victuals, and hence now it was reported that all these ships were immediately coming back to Rhodes. Thus it came about that before we again set forth from Rhodes all the carracks had returned. But as to the movements of the lord Timur, and where he now was in camp, during all this time of our stay we could get no exact information, and so concluded that we must make the journey to Qarabágh, an outlying province of Persia, where, as well known, Timur was wont to pass the winter, and where we should doubtless have certain news, if we found him not.

Rhodes is no very large city, it lies in a plain, close to the sea occupying a peninsula. There is here a great castle standing by itself apart, and walled round and about is the city like a fortress, with a suburb, within and without. The city itself has towers all along its walls, and within are both the palace of the Grand Master and the quarters of the Knights. Also there is here a monastery and a very beautiful church, and a great hospital where they tend the sick. The Knights are not by rule allowed ever to leave the fortress, and can go nowhere outside, unless it be by special permission of the Master. The port of Rhodes is very large and is well protected, being enclosed within the city walls. It has two breakwaters, moles of immense structure, each rising on its own foundation. These jut out into the sea, and between the two is the harbour where ships may lie in safety. On one of the breakwaters they have built fourteen windmills. Outside the city fortress are seen many fine orchards with country houses; here round and about are planted citron, lemon and lime trees, with many others fruit-bearing. The population of the island of Rhodes and of the city is Greek in origin: and for the most part they belong to the Greek church. Rhodes is a great port of call for merchants: they come thither from all parts, and the ships that sail for Alexandretta, or with goods for Jerusalem and other places in Syria will put in at this port, or at least pass in sight of the same. The Turkish mainland of Asia Minor lies so near to Rhodes that it can easily be descried thence. Throughout and about the island there are numerous other towns and castles besides the capital city, which last bears the name of Rhodes as we have said.

Friday which was the 31st day of August we chartered our passage in a ship that should take us to the island of Chios, and the master of the same was a Genoese named Messer Leonardo Gentil. The ship set sail and we left Rhodes, but the winds proved contrary. The voyage from Rhodes to Chios is indeed a dangerous passage, for, on the one hand to the right, the Turkish mainland must be avoided, and our course lay near to it, while on the other hand to the left there are dangers of shipwreck from the numerous islands, some very well populated, others uninhabited. Hence by night the risk is great to sail the course, and in foul weather most dangerous. Now that Friday when we left Rhodes, and Saturday and Sunday and Monday and Tuesday, all that time we had contrary winds, so that our course was by tacking and going about: indeed more than once we failed to double a certain cape here that was off the mainland of Turkey. On the Wednesday which was the 5th of September, we were abreast of the island of Stanchio [or Kos][3] and, as we could make no way by reason of the head-winds, the ship anchored in the harbour of the capital town of this island. Here we remained the whole of that day, watering and taking in provisions of meat. Stanchio island is of the lordship of Rhodes: its chief town, which is very populous, lies in a plain not far from the sea. It possesses a small castle and between the castle and the town lies a great lagoon of sea-water. You enter the castle across a bridge which spans the ditch which is filled by the sea water. All round the town lie orchards and vineyards and country houses. This island is always garrisoned by a hundred Knights of the Order of St John, under a Lieutenant and they hold the castle and the town in force.

Thursday the 6th of September we again set sail, but for the whole of that day the vessel made little way on account of a contrary wind, and the next day Friday it was the same for the like cause. Further it was impossible to make long tacks by reason of the numerous islands that lay on every hand, with the mainland of Turkey over against us and near by. All that day the ship tacked again and again making but little progress, and at midday when we were come near to an island which is known as the Isle of Beasts, the head wind rose to fury driving our vessel towards the shore, so that we feared she would be wrecked. With difficulty we managed to cast anchor, and thus stationary remained safe all that day and the next. This island is totally uninhabited, and it is low ground having no hills. Next on the Sunday following at midday we made sail, and all that afternoon were going by many uninhabited islands; subsequently our course lay past a large well inhabited island which was called Kalymnos, the same being of the lordship of Rhodes. Monday morning at daybreak having been all night stationary we were near where we had been at sundown, but by midday were abreast of a city on the Turkish mainland which is called New Palatia.[4] They told us that it was near this city that Timur had been encamped [some time before the battle of Angora when he conquered the Turkish Sultan Báyazíd] and overran all his lands.

Next Tuesday morning we were lying off a well inhabited island, of the lordship of Rhodes which is called Leros, and seeing that a head wind was blowing, in order not to lose again our distance already come, by being blown back, we hove to and then cast anchor in the port of this island, where later we took in water. In the island of Leros there is a city with a very strong castle, high built, the same surrounded by the houses of the town, but these are ill conditioned. The place is under command of a Knight from Rhodes, and the population is Greek. The Turks, raiding from New Palatia, have lately done much damage in the island: and in the last year the crew from a Turkish galliot landed and carried off the flocks of the inhabitants. They kidnapped too the men who were harvesting the corn, taking them prisoners to Palatia. On Thursday we made sail from Leros and at daybreak were off an uninhabited island called Madrea but where there are good pasture lands for flocks and springs of sweet water. That same day too we passed abreast of another island called El Forno[5] and sailing on came to the island of Patmos, where the population is Greek. The following day we found ourselves off a very large island called Samos of which the people are Turks: and thence we were in sight of the island of Nikaria which is very populous and the lordship thereof is held by a certain Lady, who possesses a galley to her own use: and on this island we noticed many well cultivated lands. That same day many other islands, both great and small, were seen and passed.

The following Saturday which was the 15th of September, and the next day Sunday, we were becalmed among the islands and could make no headway: but at nightfall a breeze sprang up for a short while, so that by the Monday morning we found ourselves off a cape of the Turkish mainland which is called Cape Xanto, and from this point came in sight of the island of Chios. And so that Tuesday in the forenoon at the hour of mass, we entered the port of Chios, and that same day we ambassadors landed, and caused all our baggage in the ship to be brought on shore. The town of Chios is but a small place; indeed the island itself is not of the largest size, and it belongs to the Genoese. Chios town is built on a plain by the sea, and it possesses two suburbs, one on the one hand and the other opposite, and there are round and about many orchard lands and vineyards. The mainland of Turkey stands over against Chios, lying clearly in sight. There are in this island many towns and castles to be seen, and for size Chios may measure one hundred and twenty miles in circuit. On a certain of the trees here, those known as the lentisc tree, the gum mastic is found. The town of Chios has a fine wall round it, strengthened by many towers: but it lies in the plain not on any high hill.

Now while we ambassadors were detained in Chios news came that ['Isá] the eldest son of [Báyazíd] the late Sultan of the Turks whom Timur conquered, was recently dead: he it was who had inherited the Sultanate. His younger brothers all were now waging civil war one with another, for it to be seen who should become lord of that country which is Turkey. We had desired to depart forthwith from Chios but could find no ship ready to sail, and therefore had to stay waiting on that Tuesday the day of our arrival, also Wednesday, Thursday, Friday, Saturday, Sunday, and over till Sunday week following, which came to the 30th of the month of September, when at last a small Spanish ship was found made ready for sea, of which the Genoese, Messer Boquira de Marta was master. On that Sunday aforesaid therefore at midnight they made sail and getting aboard we left the port of Chios, with a fresh following wind. When the day dawned we found ourselves abreast of an inhabited island on the right hand, lying near the Turkish mainland, which is called Mitylene, and there were two other inhabited islands to be seen on the left hand, these being known as Ipsara and Antipsara, and by evening we had come to be off a cape of the Turkish mainland which is called Cape St Mary.[6]

During the night the wind rose and it blew a gale so that some sails were split being carried overboard. Now the Strait known as the Passage of Romania [the Dardanelles] was near by, but the wind was rising and the night very dark, so that we feared to miss the mouth of the strait, wherefore the captain determined to heave to and await the coming of daylight. Shortly before midnight, however, again a squall struck us, whereby, being blown back, we found ourselves at dawn abreast of the island of Merdi, just off the mainland of Turkey. It was then decided that we should make course for the port of Mitylene in order that the ship's sails might be replaced, and a pilot was taken aboard coming from the shore for none among the crew knew those waters. Some time before we came round to the harbour of Mitylene we could see a castle on that island which is called Mollenos, and next beyond this another castle appeared which bears the name of Cuaraca. It was midday when the ship finally anchored in the port of [Kastro] the capital city of Mitylene, and we remained there that day of our arrival, which was Tuesday, also Wednesday, Thursday and Friday, during which time the ship's sails were re-set and a pilot was engaged.

The city of Mitylene is well populated: the houses crown the hill top of a peninsula that juts into the sea, on either hand of which is a harbour. A strong wall, with many towers surrounds the town: and beyond it lies an extensive suburb. This island of Mitylene is 300 miles in circuit, and besides the capital city there are numerous other towns and castles, with their orchards and vineyards. We saw many fine buildings in the neighbourhood of the capital, with some churches, and it appeared to us that in past times this island had had a far greater population than it now possessed. In a plain near by the city, where there are many springs of water among the orchard lands, numerous ruins might be seen of former palaces. In the midst of one palace, standing yet erect, were some forty columns of white marble set as though round a hall, and they say that these columns once adorned a council chamber where the citizens were wont to meet. The population of Mitylene is Greek, and formerly they were subject to the Emperor in Constantinople, but now they are under the government of a Genoese lord, whose name is Messer John Gattilusio. His father [Francesco] had married a daughter of [Adronicus III][7] the former Emperor and it is her son who is now the lord of the Island. Of him they relate a wondrous tale, for they say that one night some twenty years ago the island suffered from a terrible earthquake, when this young prince [Messer John, then a child] with his father and mother and two of his brothers, all were asleep in the chambers of the castle, which same that night collapsed in ruins. All died crushed in the overthrow, save only the child John, who being protected by his cradle escaped. He was found on the following morning alive and unhurt, having fallen in the cradle from the heights on which the castle stood into a vineyard far below. This indeed was a marvellous providence.

Now on that day when we had come on shore at Mitylene we were told news concerning the Young Emperor of Constantinople [Prince John the son of Andronicus] who had been recently deprived of his rights of succession [by his uncle the Emperor Manuel] as will be explained more fully later.[8] This Young Emperor John had married a daughter of Messer John Gattilusio, the lord of Mitylene, and had lived with his father-in-law in recent times in this island. Further we learnt that shortly before our arrival here, the Young Emperor John and his father-in-law Gattilusio had sailed away aboard their two galleys, with convoy of five galliots, with a view to gain possession of Salonika, which city belongs to the Emperor [Manuel] of Constantinople, and the cause that had moved them to make the attempt was as follows. The Young Emperor John in times past had been subject to and lived at the court of the Turkish Sultan Báyazíd,[9] his abode being in the Turkish town of Selymbria. To which place [in 1399] came Marshal Boucicault - who [at a later date] was the Governor of Genoa - in command of ten galleys, and who forcibly carrying him off to Constantinople, had brought about a reconciliation between the Young Emperor and his uncle the Emperor Manuel. The condition of the peace then effected was that Manuel should give his nephew Salonika, in which city he should reign. As to the cause of the quarrel between uncle and nephew, the details of this will be explained in due place presently.

Marshal Boucicault thus having made peace between uncle and nephew, taking the Emperor Manuel in his company, proceeded on his return to France where [to oppose the Turks the Emperor Manuel] pleaded to obtain the aid of the French King, the Young Emperor John being as agreed installed Governor at Constantinople in the room of his uncle, and until the latter should return from France with succour of arms. But while Manuel was thus away in France the Young Emperor had sought and come to terms of amity with Sultan Báyazíd – who was [at Angora], at that date, being on the point of fighting his great battle with Timur. The agreement come to was that if the Turkish Sultan should be the victor [at Angora], he John would then resign to him the city of Constantinople and become his vassal. When, therefore, later the Emperor Manuel had returned to Constantinople [after the Sultan's defeat at Angora] and had learnt the detail of this treason that his nephew had contemplated, he was exceeding wrath with him, commanding that he should never more come into his presence. Thus banished from Constantinople, he then went to live in exile in this island of Stalimene [which is Mitylene]. Further the Emperor Manuel next had deprived John the Young Emperor of his lordship of Salonika, which, as said above, had been promised and granted to him: and its having been now taken from him was the cause why he and his father-in-law Gattilusio had recently set sail hoping to re-capture that city by force of arms.

Now a long time before their departure from Mitylene Gattilusio had despatched his envoy in a galliot to his friend Marshal Boucicault [at Alexandretta] with the following message: that he Boucicault knew well how the Emperor Manuel had long ago promised and granted the city of Salonika to the Young Emperor John for him to live and reign there, but that now the Emperor refused to let him take possession, banishing him to Mitylene: Gattilusio therefore by his messenger implored Boucicault that on sailing from Alexandretta he should give his aid in the capture of Salonika, joining his two friends with the whole [of the Genoese] fleet under his command at the port of Mitylene where he Gattilusio would be in waiting for him. [In the meantime, however, Gattilusio and the Young Emperor had sailed] and now while we were delayed in the port of Mitylene we learnt how that galliot, which had been sent out with the envoy to Boucicault, had returned: but what was the answer brought none knew. Then news had come to hand that Boucicault had sailed back from Alexandretta with his fleet arriving at Rhodes, whence again they had departed, though none knew whither they were bound.

It was after this on the morning of Saturday the 6th of October at break of day that we set sail and left Mitylene, going back by the same way by which we had arrived at [Kastro] city, to wit passing up the strait between the mainland of Turkey and the island, until again we reached Cape St

Mary which is on the Turkish coast. Sunday following we had doubled the cape shortly coming up with an island on our left hand which is now uninhabited, and which is called Tenedos. Further on the left hand over beyond Tenedos was to be seen another island that appeared well populated: it belongs to the Emperor of Constantinople and bears the name of Imbros. The wind at first was contrary that day, or at times entirely failing, but later towards night-fall coming on to blow foul, the ship made little head against its force. The island of Tenedos appearing now near at hand we would fain have come to the port there, but the head wind prevented this, and the current which runs here through the strait was bearing us back. It was therefore deemed prudent to cast anchor that night half way up the narrows lying between the mainland of Turkey and the island of Tenedos. These narrows are indeed the fairway by which ships pass when about to enter the Strait of Romania [which is the Dardanelles]. Here on the right hand of the Straits once stood the mighty and populous city of Troy, and from our anchorage we could see the buildings of the ancient city. The town wall is seen to be pierced at intervals with gateways, and portions of that wall are standing with turrets now in ruin and within are the remains of palaces and other buildings which mark where the city had once stood. Adjacent thereto begins the plain which stretches back from the sea coast going up to the foot-hills of a high mountain range inland. The circuit of ruins of Troy appeared to extend over many miles of country, and at the point above the ancient city rose a high steep hill on the summit of which, it is said, stood the castle known of old as Ilion.

The island of Tenedos which as explained lies over against these ruins, and near by which we were now at anchor, was of old the harbour of Troy, where the Greek ships that came against the city were drawn to land. Then it was that King Priam had peopled this island, founding there a mighty castle that was named Tenedos. This next guarded the Greek ships that came against the city, and at that day doubtless the island supported a large population, though now it remains entirely uninhabited. As soon as our ship had come to anchor a boat was sent ashore to get water and firewood, of both of which the ship stood in need. Some of our attendants also landed in the boat to see the island: and walking about it they came on many vineyards and orchards, with trees near by the springs of water. There were too extensive corn lands, and the vine grew well and abundantly; much game too was to be met with such as partridges and rabbits [or hares]. Our people saw here a great castle in ruins, and we learnt that the reason why the island is now totally uninhabited is this wise.

Some twenty-two years ago the Emperor of Constantinople [John Palæologus, father of the Emperor Manuel] being lord of that island, had promised to grant it to the Genoese, who in return were to come to his succour with their galleys in the war which he, the Emperor, was waging against the Turkish Sultan Murád. But after having thus promised it to the Genoese the Emperor in fact sold it to the Venetians. These last landed here forthwith, occupying the island, which at that date was entirely uninhabited, and proceeded to lay out their town, fortifying it and building the adjacent castle. No sooner did the Genoese hear what the Venetians had done than they loudly proclaimed that the island by right already belonged to them. For, said they, it had been promised to them in gift, and further they, the Genoese, had already assisted the Emperor in the manner stipulated. Hence it was not justice for him thus to sell or give the island to any others, and on this discord ensued between Genoa and Venice. Each city armed its fleet of galleys and warships, the Venetians and the Genoese together coming to Tenedos and in part occupying the island where much destruction was wrought and many lives were lost. Finally, however, terms of peace were negotiated at Venice, when it was agreed that both the Venetian castle and the new township should be dismantled or destroyed, indeed that the island should be depopulated, neither the one party nor the other having occupation or possession. Thus it was that Tenedos has since come to be uninhabited, but those late incidents are the chief cause why at the present moment there is such distrust and enmity between the Venetian and the Genoese people.

It was our wish on the Wednesday following to have made our departure from Tenedos, but we were prevented by reason of a contrary wind which blew that day and all Thursday and Friday and Saturday and Sunday, holding us back. That Sunday in the evening there arrived at the harbour of Tenedos a trading bark, sailing from Constantinople, and we sent to know what had been their last port of call. The answer came that they had just come from Gallipoli[10] a town in the occupation of the Turks, on the mainland of Thrace, and that they now were bound for Chios with a cargo of wheat. Further they reported that the plague was raging in Gallipoli, with a very great mortality. The wind still that day Sunday continuing contrary we unable to depart were detained yet in Tenedos for [three] days.

From the island heights looking to the westward we were able to descry on the distant mainland of Greece a lofty mountain peak that is known as Mount Athos where, as we were informed there was a monastery of Greek monks. All the inhabitants are very holy men, and no woman ever is allowed to come thither, nor indeed any female animal, such as a cat or a dog or any other domestic creature, left peradventure any such might become the mother of offspring. The monks eat no meat, though the place is well stocked and provided and richly endowed. The report given us was that from the sea level to the height, on the mountain top where the monastery is built, is a distance of two days' journey. There are between fifty and sixty minor monasteries on Mount Athos besides this monastery. All the monks there, they said, wear robes that are fashioned of black hair-cloth,[11] and they drink no wine, they eat no meat, they cook with no olive oil and avoid any fish that has red blood. These details we had from certain of the crew of that Greek ship whom we spoke with in Tenedos, for they had sojourned many of them in that holy mountain; and their account was confirmed by the master of our ship and others who had also been there.

At last on Wednesday morning which was the 17th of October the wind being fair, though but light, we took our departure from Tenedos, where for [ten] days past we had lain at anchor, wind-bound in the strait between that island and the mainland of Turkey. On that same Wednesday aforesaid by midday we had come up abreast of a certain uninhabited island called Mambre; but all the following Thursday it fell calm, and we could make no way being therefore unable to pass that island and enter the straits of the Dardanelles which now opened out before us: but the next day Friday the wind blew favourably and at the hour of vespers we made our passage into the channel. At the mouth the Strait of the Dardanelles is so narrow a space that it is but eight miles across, and[12] on the right hand side of the strait lies the land of the Turks. Here at the point of entrance by the seaside, and crowning a high hilltop, is a great castle, with a village below it of considerable size. The castle walls are in ruin and its gateways unclosed, for, as they told us, it might be a year and a half ago eight Genoese galleys had sailed hither, and landing they had taken the castle [from the Turks] by assault, sacking it. This place is known as the Cape or End of the Roads.[13] Of old time, when the Greeks came across the sea to lay siege to and destroy Troy, it was here that the Grecian camp was set. Here too they had dug great trenches to lie between them and Troy, the same being made lest the Trojans in their attack might come to and destroy the Grecian ships. These trenches are seen to be three in number and they lie one behind the other.

On the left hand of the mouth of the Dardanelles and on the mainland of Greece - opposite therefore to the castle just named, and to the right of another which had belonged to the Armenians - there is seen yet another castle on a hill close to the sea beach and this last is known as Xetea.[14] All these castles therefore were supposed to have been built to guard the entrance of the Strait of the Dardanelles. Next a short distance beyond, on the Turkish side, there appeared two huge towers, with a few houses standing round their bases, and the place is now known as Dubeque. It is said that in ancient days settlements of the city of Troy occupied the whole space of country side between this spot and the land down even to Cape St Mary, spoken of previously, which is a plain some sixty miles in extent. That same evening as the sun was going down our ship was off a tower that stood close to the beach on the Grecian side of the straits, and this tower is known as the Tower of Blame.[15]

The next day Saturday we had come to the city called Gallipoli, where there is a castle, and though the city stands on the Grecian bank of the straits none the less it is in the hands of the Turks and belongs now to the eldest son of the late Sultan Báyazíd who is known as Sulayman Chelebi.[16] Here the Turks station their fleet of galleys and other ships where also they have made a great arsenal and dockyard. There were upwards of forty galleys lying here, and the castle of Gallipoli is very strongly garrisoned with troops, to be held in force. This city of Gallipoli was the first place that the Turks took possession of on the European side of the straits, and at the date of its capture it was in the hands of the Genoese. From Gallipoli the Turk country is but ten miles distant, which is the same as three leagues, across the water, and it was through taking Gallipoli that it came about that the Turks subsequently conquered all the Greek lands that they now hold in Thrace: and should they ever come to lose Gallipoli, they would indeed lose all the lands they have conquered in Greece. Since they have come to possess this port, where they station their fleet of galleys, this for them is the passage across from the Turkish home lands both for their troops, and for supplies; and this fortress of Gallipoli is the base by which the Turks hold the Empire of the Greeks in thrall.

The whole length of the Dardanelles strait, from the sea entrance up to the city of Gallipoli, is in fact a very narrow passage having the land of the Greeks on the one hand and the land of the Turks on the other: but beyond Gallipoli this passage broadens out into the Sea [of Marmora]. On the heights above the town of Gallipoli there are two castles and these are called respectively Satorado and Examillo. From these across the strait you may overlook the Turkish country, which appears all hills and valleys, while the country of Thrace on the European side is all plains with corn lands on every hand. As we sailed on the ship was off a promontory on the Turkish side by nightfall which terminates the [peninsula] called Cyzicus. They related that when Timur had conquered Sultan Báyazíd [at Angora], certain of the Turkish troops fleeing from the battle field managed to reach this peninsula hoping to escape slaughter, and they had compassed by digging a trench across the neck of land to turn this peninsula into an island. The next day, Sunday, we were lying off an inhabited island called Marmora: and it is from the quarries here that they get the jasper slabs and marble columns which adorn the churches in Constantinople. That same evening at sundown we were sailing past the shore of an estate belonging to the Emperor which is called Redea, and near here is the island that lies at no great distance from the Turkish coast known as Kolominos. From this point you may see the Bay of Trilla, at which those land who go to Brusa, one of the great cities of the Turks

On Monday at dawn the ship was still at the same spot for it had fallen calm, and all that day and Tuesday what little wind there was blew contrary. We therefore made way slowly approaching the coast of Thrace, and coming finally to anchor some two miles from the shore, found that we were still about fifteen miles distant from Constantinople. Then from here we sent on a messenger to the city of Pera to bespeak lodgements; and to let the Emperor have notice that our embassy was arriving forthwith to visit him. Next on Wednesday the 24th of October we found ourselves constrained to trans-ship all our baggage into a great boat, and bestowing ourselves in the same, all came safely to Pera where arrangements had already been made for lodging us and our people. We had abandoned the ship in this fashion because of the head wind that continued ceaselessly to blow preventing the vessel for a time from making the harbour of Constantinople. No sooner had we arrived than forthwith we took counsel with friends seeking advice as to how the journey onward might best be arranged; for the season was late and the winter was already coming upon us.

Chapter III

Constantinople

ON the following Sunday which was the 28th of October the Emperor [Manuel] sent for us the Ambassadors, and we passed over [the Golden Horn] from Pera to Constantinople in a boat. On landing we found many officers awaiting us, and horses for our accommodation to carry us up to the Palace [of the Blachernæ].[1] Here on arrival we learnt that the Emperor with his attendants had just come from hearing Mass, who forthwith received us very graciously in his private chamber. The Emperor was seated on a raised dais, carpeted with small rugs, on one of which was spread a brown lion skin and at the back was a cushion of black stuff embroidered in gold. After conversing for some considerable time with us, the Emperor at length dismissed us, and we returned to our lodgings, whither later on his Highness sent us a stag, which his huntsmen had just brought in to the palace. With the Emperor at our audience had been present the Empress [Irene] his wife, with three young princes his sons [namely John, Theodore and Andronicus],[2] the eldest of whom may have been eight years old. On the Monday following the Emperor sent to us some gentlemen of his household, and these brought an answer to the various questions concerning matters on which we had spoken with him at our audience.

Tuesday the 30th of October being come we sent to the Emperor a message, saying how much we desired to visit and view the city, as also to attend at the Churches and see the Relics preserved therein, whereby we now besought his Highness of his grace to grant us our desire. Upon hearing which the Emperor sent to be our attendant his son-in-law, namely Messer Ilario [Doria, Patrician] of Genoa, who was husband to the natural daughter of the Emperor [the

37

princess named Zampia Palæologina]. He now therefore was deputed to accompany us, with certain persons of the Imperial household, and show us all that we might wish to see: and the first place that we forthwith proceeded to visit was the Church of St John the Baptist.[3]

This is commonly known as St John in Petra and stands not far distant from the Palace [of the Blachernæ]. Over the outer entrance gate to the church as you approach is seen the figure of St John in mosaic work, very richly wrought and finely portrayed: and next over the gateway is set a lofty cupola,[4] rising above four arches, and under this you pass in order to enter the main building of the church. The walls and the ceiling of this cupola are covered in beautiful mosaic with figures and designs; for this mosaic work is composed in most minute pieces, cubes gilt in fine gold, or enamelled in blue and white and green and red, with many other colours as needed to portray the figures and patterns and the scroll-work there about; whereby the same is indeed very beautiful to see. Passing under this cupola you come to a large court surrounded by porticoes backed by buildings; and here grow cypresses with many other trees. Beyond, near the main entrance to the church stands a fountain under a fine cupola supported on eight columns of white marble, and the trough of the fountain is formed of a block of white stone. The main building of the church is square in plan with a semi-circular apse, while above rises a lofty cupola that is supported on columns of green jasper. Fronting you as you enter are three small chapels, in each of which stands its altar. The high altar is the middle one of the three, and the chapel gates are covered with plates of silver gilt. At the doorway of the chapel of the high altar are four small columns of jasper which are covered crosswise by bands in gilded silver encrusted with divers fine gems. The gateways of all three of the chapels are hung with curtains of silk stuffs on poles running from side to side, and these curtains are set here to be drawn when the priest enters the chapel to say mass, in order that he may not be seen of the congregation.

The ceiling of the nave is everywhere very richly wrought in mosaic work, and we see displayed a figure which is that of God the Father. The walls below are likewise covered with mosaic work coming almost down to the ground level, but below the same are set slabs of green jasper in the wall skirting. The pavement is composed of flags of jasper in many colours set in a variegated scroll pattern. The chapel of the high altar has all round its walls stall seats in carved woodwork very finely wrought, and between each of the seats is set a brazier in brass full of cinders in which any one needing thereto may spit, lest otherwise he might defile the pavement. There are also hanging here many lamps both of silver and of glass.

Very numerous are the relics preserved in this church, but the Emperor himself holds the keys of the chests where for the most part they are guarded. Yet that same day we were shown the left arm of St John the Baptist, the same being of the whole arm length from below the shoulder to the hand, but the limb had been burnt and all that remained intact was but skin and bone. At the elbow joint as also at the wrist was a band of jewels in a gold setting. Further we now learnt this church possessed many other relics, some indeed those pertaining to our Lord Jesus Christ, but these could not be shown us on this day, for the Emperor had gone a-hunting the keys of the reliquaries being left with the Empress his wife, and she had failed to send those for our use. These other reliquaries, however, on a subsequent occasion were fully shown to us, as will be described later. To this Church of St John belongs a monastery, where the monks have their refectory in a great gallery. In the centre place thereof stands for their use a table made of white marble, some thirty paces in length, round which are set divers wooden seats. Further there are one and twenty sideboards made of white stone blocks, which may serve as stands on which to put their dishes of meat. Here too are also three other smaller tables, each of a single stone block. Within the monastery walls we saw many orchards and vineyards: with much else that cannot succinctly be described in this place.

On that same day we further visited the Church of St Mary Peribleptos.[5] Before its gateway stands a great court filled with cypresses, elms, walnut trees and many others. The main building of the church is adorned externally with numerous figures and designs richly wrought after divers fashions in gold and blue and other colours. On the left hand side as you enter the church are several sacred pictures, among the rest a figure representing St Mary our Lady, while to right and left of the same appear the portraits of an Emperor and an Empress. Below the figure of St Mary, being at her feet, are represented thirty castles and cities, each with its name attached inscribed in the Greek character. They say that these various cities and castles are all of the lordship belonging to this church, having been conferred and granted to the same by a certain Emperor whose name was Romanus, and he lies buried elsewhere in the church. Below the figure of St Mary are seen hanging various plates of steel inscribed with the privileges that have been bestowed on this church, sealed with seals in lead and wax, and these privileges are what have been given to this church by each one of these cities and castles aforesaid.

The Church of St Mary has five altars; and in plan it is a square with a semi-circular apse loftily built, and it is very large. Columns of jasper in many colours support the roof; both the walls and the flooring being covered with slabs of jasper. The central nave is inclosed by three aisles [one being the narthex], and a single ceiling covers both nave and aisles, the same very richly wrought in mosaic work. In a corner of the church to the left is seen a great tombstone of red jasper where is buried the aforesaid Emperor Romanus, and they told us that this tomb had formerly been encased in gold and set with many precious stones, but that when some two hundred years ago[6] the Latins were in possession of Constantinople they had plundered this tomb. Farther in the church is seen another tombstone in jasper, which is that of another Emperor.[7] There was shown us here a relic, which is indeed the other arm of the blessed St John the Baptist, the same being the right arm, and it consisted of that limb from the elbow down to the hand. This all appeared to be still quite fresh and perfect, for it is related that when the body of the blessed St John was burnt with fire, his right hand had remained unconsumed and was later preserved: for indeed he had pointed upwards with it crying " Ecce Agnus Dei " [at the Baptism in Jordan]. This relic was enclosed all round with thin rods of gold, but behold the thumb was missing, and the reason that this fingerjoint was wanting, according to the monks, is after this wise.

Of old, in the city of Antioch, when idolatry was practised, there lived there a great dragon, and it was the custom of the people of Antioch to offer once a year to that dragon a living person for him to eat, the same to be chosen by lot, and the one on whom the lot fell could in nowise escape being given for the dragon's eating. Now it is related that on that certain occasion in question the lot had fallen on the daughter of a certain good man [who was yet a pagan], and thus his heart was full of grief, knowing that he could surely not escape from the sacrifice of his daughter's life to the dragon. In his anguish of mind he betook himself to a certain church of Christian monks that was in the city, and to these monks he spoke saying that he had heard how in times past God had wrought miracles at the intercession of St John, and believing the account to be true, he had now come to pay his devotions there, more especially to that arm of St John, the relic they possessed. Further he would now desire of St John that, after the fashion of many other miracles which the Lord God had in the past wrought at his intercession, God would again vouchsafe to manifest the Divine Grace, and grant that this maiden his daughter should not die so dreadful a death, but escape from the peril of being given to the dragon. On this the monks, having compassion for his grief, forthwith brought out to comfort him that arm of St John. He kneeling down made his devotion adoring that Relic, full of sorrow for the plight in store for his daughter; and it came to him to gnaw with his teeth into the thumb on the hand of that glorious Saint, next biting the thumb off, and carrying it away in his mouth, for the monks did not perceive what was being done. Now when the time had come that the girl should be delivered to the dragon, who opening his mouth was about to devour her, that good man her father slyly threw this thumb of the blessed St John the Baptist into the dragon's mouth, and immediately the beast burst himself asunder. Thus was that great miracle wrought, and the good man her father was converted to the faith of our Lord Jesus Christ, becoming a Christian.

In this same church we were next shown a small cross, a palm length long on a stand made of gold; and it had golden rods at the ends of the arms, on which at the cross was set the crucifix, very small in size. The whole lay loose in a carved-wood case that was covered with gold plate, so that the relic could thus be taken in and out. This small cross it is said was made from a piece of the actual wood of the True Cross on which our Lord Jesus Christ suffered death, and it was black in colour. It had been fashioned and cut out at the time when the blessed St Helena, mother of the Emperor Constantine who founded Constantinople, had brought the limbs of the True Cross from Jerusalem, where she had discovered the same by digging in the ground. Further also were shown here the body of the blessed St Gregory, perfectly preserved and whole. Going outside the church we passed through a cloister, very beautifully adorned in mosaic work illustrating the events of sacred history. Among the rest was to be seen here the Jesse Tree showing the descent of the Blessed Virgin Mary, and this so wonderfully displayed and richly wrought that he who sees it never can have seen the like elsewhere. Of and belonging to this church we found many monks in residence, and they showed us all those sights that have been named above; after which they brought us to their refectory. This was a broad high chamber, in the centre of which stood a polished marble table, very beautifully made, Some 35 palms in length. The pavement of the refectory was of white slabs of stone, and at the further end of the chamber we saw two other small tables likewise made of white marble. The ceiling was wrought in mosaic, and the walls also were adorned with mosaic-work pictures displaying incidents of the Gospel Story. The Angel Gabriel was shown as he made his Salutation to the Blessed Virgin Mary; next came the Birth of our Lord Jesus Christ; and next how He went about the world with His disciples, with the various events of His blessed life until His crucifixion and death. About the floor of the refectory were set, here and there, many sideboards in white marble, for the purpose of the serving of dishes and meats. The monastery further had within its precinct a number of houses, where the monks dwelt, all with suitable furnishings. Round and about lay orchards, vineyards with fountains of water, so that it was as though the whole place had been a great township.

Next on that same day we were taken to visit another church of the name of St John which is at the Monastery [of the Studion][8] inhabited by a congregation of monks, under the rule of a prior. The entrance gateway to the convent is very high and richly wrought, this leads on to a great court beyond which stands the main building. This is the church, which is in plan square shaped with a semi-circular apse very high built. The nave is enclosed by three aisles [namely two side aisles and the narthex] the nave and aisles being all under one roof level. The church has seven altars: and the ceiling of both nave and aisles, and the walls likewise, all are adorned with mosaic work extremely richly wrought, displaying the incidents of sacred history. The nave is built on either side with twenty-four columns of green jasper, and the three aisles have galleries, which open into the central nave. In these aisles also there are to be seen twenty-four [dwarf] columns of green jasper [placed for support below the galleries]. As regards the ceiling of the nave as also the surface of the walls, everywhere it is adorned with mosaic work. From the galleries in the aisles you may look down into the central nave, and here in place of [the usual metal grating] there is a stone lattice work that is formed of small pieces of jasper. At the east end beyond the nave is a beautiful chapel wrought, with the most exquisite mosaic, whereon is displayed the figure of the Virgin Mary, for this chapel indeed was built to her honour. Attached to the church is a great chamber used as the refectory, here within stands a large white marble table, and the walls of this refectory display, wrought in mosaic, the story of the Last Supper, showing our Lord Jesus Christ seated at table with His disciples. Further this monastery possesses many suitable outhouses, with orchards and fountains, and various other convenient commodities.

On the same day[9] also we were taken to see a great open space that is called the Hippodrome where it is wont to joust and tilt. This place [at the upper end] is enclosed by pillars of white marble, each so great that at arm's length it would take three men to embrace the shaft; and they are each above two lance lengths in the height. These marble pillars are all set one beside the other in a line, being thirty-seven in number and each stands on a great white block of stone. Above they are connected one with another by a series of low arches, and these support a gallery through which one may walk from end to end having a balustrade with battlements to enclose the one side. The upper work built on these arches is of a height only to come up breast-high, and the whole is constructed of slabs of white marble of which indeed the gallery is built also. This place is thus arranged to serve for the accommodation of the dames and damsels of high degree, when they witness the tilting and jousting in the Hippodrome. Beyond and behind these marble stands, there runs a line of wall, built of marble likewise and on that same level but twenty or thirty paces to the back, where there is a high platform raised on four marble pillars, and here is a marble throne, with many seats all round it. Behind these seats and facing down toward the arena stand four statues in white stone each of the size of a man. It is in this place that the Emperor and Empress take their seats when they witness the jousts and tiltings.[10]

In the arena below and facing these seats [stands the Obelisk which is] set on two huge blocks of marble, each a lance length in the height, perhaps more, placed once above the other. Four cubes of copper placed on the upper level of the topmost block, support [this Obelisk, which is] a fuse shaped monolith tapering towards the top, and its height may be estimated as about six lance-lengths. This great stone stands, as already said, supported on the four copper cubes thus free and detached from the base block below. It is a wonder to imagine how so great a mass of stone, to be thus pointed and finely wrought, can have been quarried, and by what ingenuity and human force it could have been raised and settled in its present place. It is indeed of so great a height that from the sea you may see it long before the city of Constantinople itself comes into view. This monument was erected, it is said, to commemorate a certain great event that had happened to occur, and on the base block that supports it may be seen an inscription recording the event to be commemorated and mentioning the name of [the Emperor Theodosius the Great] who ordered it to be placed here. We noted that this inscription is written in the Greek language, but seeing that it was already late when we were brought hither we failed to await the coming of one who should read it to us and translate its import. They told us however, that it related to that great event which had happened at the time when the Emperor caused the monolith to be set up.

From this point the line of columns surrounding the Hippodrome continues, but beyond the Obelisk none are so tall as those we have described above. All we saw are sculptured and painted [with inscriptions] recording the great deeds and acts of the nobles and mighty men of the past. In this neighbourhood may be seen [the Serpent Column] showing three serpents made in copper or in some other metal, and they are interlaced together as though to form a rope. Each serpent has its head, which rises separate above and apart, with the mouth open. They say that these figures of serpents were set up here to serve for an enchantment, because that in times past there was a plague of serpents and other noisome reptiles who killed many people by their venom. Then a certain Emperor living at that age caused by means of this figure an enchantment to be effected, whereby forthwith and ever after in Constantinople no serpent could harm any one. This Hippodrome is a very large place, and all round encircling it are built in rows benches that rise up one behind the other, and these are made to seat the common folk who come to witness the games. Below these seats they have constructed the lodgings, with chambers opening on to the arena, where those who joust in the tourneys may arm themselves and disarm after the event.

On that same day also we were taken to see the Church called Santa Sophia; and the name Santa Sophia has the signification in Greek as who should say the True Wisdom, namely the Son of God. To this dedication the church was built, and it is the largest, and most honourable, and best endowed of all the churches of Constantinople. Here there are canons resident called by the Greeks Caloyers, who serve the Mass in Santa Sophia which indeed is their Cathedral Church, for the Patriarch of the Greeks has his seat here who is known among them as the Metropolitan. On one side of the Court which fronts the church stand nine great white stone columns, the very largest and stoutest that ever a man saw. Their summits are crowned each with its capital, and they relate that here aforetime had been built on the summit a great chamber where the Patriarch and his clergy were wont to assemble and hold their chapters. In this same Court before the church was a single wonderfully tall column of stone on the top of which stood a great horse, in copper. This was of the bulk of four ordinary horses, and astride it sat the figure of an armed warrior, of copper likewise, with a great plume on his head the shape of the tail of a peacock. We saw that the horse by iron chains from its body was firmly attached to the pillar on which it stands, lest it should be shaken loose by the wind and so fall. This great steed is extraordinarily well fashioned, one of its hind legs and a forefoot both are raised in the air as though it were prancing and about to leap down. The warrior on its back has his right arm raised, the hand open, and with the left hand, of the other arm, grasps the reins. In his right hand he holds a round gold ball. Both horse and man are so huge, and the column so tall, that it is indeed a marvel to behold. The figure of the warrior is, they say, the semblance of the great Emperor Justinian, who set it up, and who also built the Church of Santa Sophia, and performed many mighty deeds in his day fighting against the Turks.[11]

The main entrance to the church of Santa Sophia is under an archway which rises above the doorway and is supported on four columns; it is like a little chapel very richly and beautifully wrought. Beyond this comes the great doorway of the church, the door very broad and high, and it is sheathed in bronze. Next comes a closed passage [the outer narthex] in which high up is a gallery, and beyond this again another doorway, the door covered with bronze like the first one, and this leads into the hall [or inner narthex] which is high and broad and its ceiling is of wooden beams. On the left hand of the hall [the inner narthex] opens a broad aisle very beautifully constructed, its walls faced with many slabs of marble and jasper of divers colours; and there is a like aisle from the right side [of the narthex]: both these aisles being under the same ceiling as the hall [of the narthex] which, as we have said, is beyond the inner door of the church. [From the inner narthex] the great nave of the church may be entered through five great and high doorways where each door is covered with bronze plates, but the central doorway is the highest and is the chief gate of entrance. Thus by these you enter the nave of the church, which is square shaped with an apse, the most spacious and the loftiest, and the most beautifully and richly wrought, that I think anywhere in the whole world can be seen. This nave occupies the centre of the building being bounded on three sides by the two aisles and the hall [of the inner narthex] all very high and broad and there are passage ways between all three of them and into the nave. Further these two aisles and the hall [of the inner narthex] have upper galleries [the Gynæceum for the women] which overlook the central nave, so that thence you may listen to and hear the Mass and the Hours. All the three upper-galleries lead one into the other, and their floorings are supported on columns of marble and green jasper, their ceilings visible, looking from the nave.

But the mighty dome that roofs the nave is by far more lofty than the ceilings of the side aisles, and this dome is circular in form and so lofty that a man must have good eyes who would examine it from below. The nave covered by the dome measures 105 paces in the length and 93 in the width, and the dome above is supported on four huge pilasters which are encased in slabs of jasper of many colours. High up spring arches, rising from twelve pilasters of green jasper, all very tall and stout, and these are what support [the dome and the cupolas] of the main building of the church.[12] Of the twelve pilasters the four first named are especially huge, and they stand two on the right hand [of the nave] and two to the left, and are artificially stained with a red colouring matter made from powdered porphyry. As to the ceiling of the great dome it is richly adorned with mosaic work, and here above the high altar is figured very wonderfully an immense picture displaying God the Father, which is wrought in mosaic of many colours. Now the mighty nave is so high, that the figure of God the Father in this picture, as seen from below, appears to be only of ordinary human height. But in fact, as they assert, the two eyes on the divine face stand apart a distance of three palm lengths, though to him who looks up they appear distant one from the other no further than in the face of a man: this because of the immense height at which the picture is set.

In the centre of the floor of the nave rises a sort of pulpit,[13] which is set on four jasper columns, and its sides are covered with jasper slabs of many colours. This pulpit is surmounted by a cupola which is supported on eight pillars of coloured jasper of some considerable size. Here the sermon is preached, and also on feast days they read the Gospel in this place. The whole of the flooring of the nave, and its walls, likewise the walls of the side aisles, all these are covered with numberless great slabs of many coloured jasper. These slabs are well polished, displaying scroll-work and lines that are very beautiful to see. A part of the wall below the archways of the nave is built up with very fine white stone slabs, carved all over with many different figures and designs, and these slabs which are thus ornamented are set in the walls at about a man's height from the floor, while above these the surface of the walling is wrought in most beautiful mosaic work. The upper galleries of the aisles [and narthex] overlook and enclose the nave on every side, all except [at the east end] where is the high altar: and this altar is indeed a wonder to behold. These galleries are each some twenty paces in the breadth,[14] more or less and in the circuit these three galleries together run for a length of 410 paces. The walls of the galleries with the ceilings above them all are faced and adorned in mosaic work that is most beautifully wrought.

In one of the side galleries on the left hand fronting one who should go up there, may be seen a very large white slab of stone which is built into the wall, the centre of many others that surround it. On this slab there appears, formed naturally and not wrought by human art either of sculpture or painting, the perfect figure of the most Blessed Virgin Mary, who holds our Lord Jesus Christ in her arms, while on the further side adjacent is the figure of Saint John the Baptist, His very glorious precursor. These figures as I have said are not drawn or painted with any pigment, nor graven in the stone artificially, but are entirely natural and of its substance; for the stone evidently was formed thus by nature with this veining and marking in it which so clearly depict those Persons whose figures now appear upon its surface. It is said that when unsuspectingly the workmen were quarrying out this piece of stone purposing to bring and set it up in some sacred building, forthwith they suddenly perceived these most wonderful and blessed Figures that were here, and knew it for a great mystery and miracle. Further seeing that Santa Sophia is the greatest church of the city, this slab was ordered to be brought and set up there. These sacred Figures on the stone appear as if standing on the clouds in the clear heaven, indeed it is as though a thin veil were drawn before them; and they are a very marvellous and spiritual manifestation which God Almighty has vouchsafed to grant unto us. Below this wonderful slab there stands an altar within a little chapel, where Mass is said. Near this shrine in the church we were shown a sacred relic, namely the body of a certain Patriarch that was most perfectly preserved, with the bones and the flesh thereon. Further we were here shown the Gridiron on which the blessed Saint Lawrence had been roasted alive.

There are many cellars and cisterns and chambers below ground in Santa Sophia which are wrought in a fashion that is very marvellous to behold, also we saw many houses with other outbuildings round and about, but these for the most part are already falling to decay. The outer walls here are all in ruin, and various doorways that lead into the church have recently been walled up or are blocked by fall of stones. But indeed they say [that of old] the outer circuit of the church buildings enclosed a space that measured ten miles round. There is in Santa Sophia underground an immense cistern, holding much water, and it is stated to be so large that a hundred galleys might easily float in it. All these marvels that we have spoken of, we were shown in this church of Santa Sophia with many others, and they are so innumerable that it were impossible in brief to describe all, or even to enumerate the greater part. Indeed the church is so immense in size, and so wonderful are the sights to be seen there, that spending many hours of time it were impossible to make a complete examination. Even though the visitor should day by day return seeing all he could, yet always on the morrow there would be new sights to view. We may here add that the roof of Santa Sophia is entirely overlaid with sheet lead. Lastly, it is to be understood that the great church is an inviolate sanctuary, where any criminal, whether by birth a Greek or a man of other foreign nation, and whether it may be a theft or a burglary or a murder that he have committed, if he come to take refuge in this church he is perfectly safe from being forcibly taken.

Chapter IV

Constantinople

ON that same day we were taken to see another church which is that of Saint George [at the Mangana].[1] Before the same stands a great court, wherein there are orchards and many houses and the main building of the church lies beyond these. At the church door stands a great font for baptism, very beautifully wrought, and it is surmounted by a cupola supported on eight pillars of white marble that are carved and ornamented with figures. The main building of the church is very lofty, and it is everywhere adorned with mosaic work. There is seen here the figure of our Lord Jesus Christ as He appeared ascending into Heaven. The flooring of the church is a wonder of workmanship being flagged with slabs of porphyry and jasper in many colours, with scroll-work very deftly accomplished. The walls are similarly wrought, and the ceiling immediately inside the doorway displays the figure of God the Father in mosaic work. Further there is here the semblance of the True Cross which an angel points to as it appears up in the clouds of heaven, while the Apostles are seen below, as at the time when the Holy Spirit descended on them in Tongues of Fire. All this is done in mosaic work and very beautifully accomplished. In this same church is to be seen a great tombstone of jasper, which is covered over with a pall of silk, and here lies buried a certain Empress.[2]

We, seeing that the night had now come, went back to our lodgings [in Pera]. It was thereupon arranged we should return next day which was Wednesday coming down from Pera to the Gate called Kynegos [on the Golden Horn].[3] Here we were to meet Messer Ilario, who has been already spoken of, and he with some gentlemen of the Imperial Court would await our coming, with horses for us to ride, and we would then visit the remaining parts of the city, seeing the sights there, and afterwards return to our lodgings in Pera while the attendant gentlemen went back to their own homes. [But all this did not take place] for next day Wednesday aforesaid as we were coming down into Constantinople as had been arranged, we were stopped and turned back, because that morning news had come in to Pera city that certain galleys of the [enemy, namely of the] Venetian Republic, had come out against the fleet of the Genoese armada which had been on its way to make the attack on Alexandretta under command of Marshal Boucicault, and that the Venetians had put the others to the rout [off the Morea] near Modon with very great slaughter, capturing many Genoese galleys. Among the rest they had made prisoner the nephew of Marshal Boucicault, called Chastel Morate. These tidings had caused very great commotion throughout Pera, a number of Venetians resident there had been taken off to prison, and many Venetian ships in the harbour had been seized in reprisal. Among the rest the governors in Pera were laying their embargo on a certain galliot we had been chartering, and aboard which it had been our intention to sail for our forward journey to Trebizond; but the government now asserted they had need and must send out this ship as a despatch boat. To us it was a prime disaster this embargo on our galliot, for the time was getting short before the season when we must set forth, and it was difficult at a moment's notice to find another ship to our purpose. We therefore forthwith set about taking information how the business on which we were bound in the service of our lord and master King Henry should be carried through, and in the first place sent word without delay down to Messer Ilario that it would be impossible for us that day to pass over to Constantinople as had been arranged, but that the next day [Thursday] we would be with him. It was on this same Wednesday that the Emperor coming back from his hunting expedition had sent across to Pera for our eating half a wild boar that he had himself killed.

The following day which was Thursday the 1st of November, as settled, we passed over to Constantinople where we found Messer Ilario awaiting our coming at the Kynegos Gate, with many lords of the Imperial household, and all taking horse they accompanied us as we went to view the Church of Saint Mary [of Blachernæ].[5] This church is within the [Blachernæ] quarter and stands close to a castle [which is the Tower of Anemas] now a ruin, but which formerly had been used as the place where ambassadors [to the Imperial Court] were lodged. We learnt that this Tower indeed had been dismantled by the late Emperor [John Palæologus, father of the Emperor Manuel], because within its walls his elder son [Andronicus] had at one time imprisoned him the Emperor: as we shall further explain on a later page. This church of St Mary was formerly the chapel of the Imperial Palace [of Blachernæ]. It consists, in the main-building of three naves, [or rather a nave and two aisles] the nave being far greater in width and height than the aisles. These last are low built, and have galleries [forming a second floor], from which you may overlook the nave. The roofing of both the aisles and the nave is seen to be supported on great pillars of green jasper, whose bases are formed by blocks of white marble, very skillfully sculptured with figures and designs. The walls in the aisles, up to half their height under the ceiling, are faced with slabs of many coloured jasper, the same being very artificially sculptured in scroll-work of a beautiful design. The ceiling of the central nave is most richly wrought with squared beams of wood joisted together, the whole ceiling of squared beams and joists being thickly gilded in fine gold. Further, though this church is elsewhere in some places out of repair, the gilding and workmanship of the ceiling aforesaid are as fresh and as beautifully preserved as though the same had but recently been completed. In the nave stands a very fine altar, also a pulpit most richly wrought: the whole edifice indeed is splendidly built, rich, and very costly: and the roof outside is entirely covered with a sheeting of lead.

On this same Thursday we were taken later on to see the relics in the church of St John the Baptist [in Pera] which on the previous Tuesday we had not been able to view for lack of the keys. On arrival at the church door we found the monks all arrayed in their vestments to attend us, and they had lighted many torches and tapers: also the keys were to hand. Then chanting their litany and in company with a gentleman of the Imperial Court, in charge of us, all mounted to the tower of the church where the relics were preserved. First the monks brought out a chest, coloured red, which they bore aloft, the while chanting very solemnly their hymn, the torches all aflame, and many thuribles with incense going before. This chest they carried down into the church and placed on a high table which was spread with a silken coverlet. The chest was sealed with two seals of white wax, which guarded two small fastening-hasps of silver, which same locked into the chest. These locks they opened and brought forthwith from within the chest two large dishes of silver-gilt, the which when the relics were exposed to us served for the purpose of their reception. Next they produced from within this chest a great bag, made of white dimity, tied up and closed with a waxen seal. This they broke, and from within produced a small round box of gold. Within this box was preserved [some of] the Sop of bread, which on Holy Thursday at the Last Supper, our Lord Jesus Christ had given to Judas, as a sign pointing to the one who should betray Him: the morsel forsooth being that part which Judas had then been unable to swallow. The relic was wrapped in a piece of red crape-stuff, and it had been sealed up close with two seals of vermilion wax. That morsel of bread was in size about three fingers of a hand across. Next from this same bag they brought forth another gold box, but smaller than the first, and in this golden box was seen enchased in the metal work a small phial that could not be removed therefrom, and which same was made of crystal. In this was preserved some of the Blood of our Lord Jesus Christ, of that which issued from His side, when Longinus wounded Him with the thrust of his lance. Again from this bag they brought forth a third small box made of gold, and the lid of the same was pierced with holes as might be the case with a rasp, and within this box were seen clots of blood. As reported to us this blood once upon a time had flowed from the side of the Image on a crucifix: for a certain Jew in the city of Beyrut had dared to wound the Image, thus to do dishonour to Christ.

Next they drew out from this same bag a crystal phial with its stopper attached to a little gold chain, in the which phial was laid up a small piece of crimson crape-stuff enclosing some of the hairs of the beard of our Lord Jesus Christ, of those that were plucked out by the Jews when they crucified Him. Then again from this bag they brought out a large reliquary in which was kept a piece of the stone slab upon which the body of our Lord Jesus Christ had been laid when taken down from the Cross. Also from this said reliquary was produced a square chest made of silver and gilt, measuring about two and a half palms across. This chest was sealed with six seals that were set on six double hasps that were of silver and round in form, these being to close the lock from which hung down a silver key. They now opened this chest and took from it a board covered with gold plate on which was fixed the lance-point of the Spear with which Longinus pierced the side of our Lord Jesus Christ. It was a thin blade, of iron very sharp pointed, and the sheathing was hollow where the wood of the haft fitted in. In length this spear-head might measure a palm and two fingers, and at the sharp point of the blade was to be seen the mark of the Blood as fresh as though the Spear had but just made the wound it did in the body of our Lord Jesus Christ. The width of the blade across was about two fingers, and this sacred relic was set enchased in that board which was, as already said, covered with gold plate. The surface of the steel of the lance-head is not bright, on the contrary it is dulled as though it had been constantly in use. Further again enchased on that same board is a piece of the Rod with which they struck our Lord Jesus Christ on the head when He stood before Pilate. This piece was about a palm and a half in length. Further again encased on this board below the Point of the Spear and the Rod just mentioned, was a morsel of the Sponge used when the gall and vinegar were given to our Lord God Jesus Christ on the Cross.

In this same chest of silver gilt containing the board here described was preserved the Vestment of the Lord God Jesus Christ for which the servants of Pilate cast lots. This Vestment was folded up and sealed with seals, lest those who come to be shown it should cut therefrom pieces to carry away as relics, as indeed had been done by some aforetime. One of the sleeves of the Vestment was laid outside the remaining part that was folded and sealed up: and the Vestment was seen to have been lined with dimity of a red colour, that was like a crape-stuff. This sleeve laid outside was rather narrow and made after the fashion of those that can be unbuttoned at the wrist at will, and where it was cleft as high as the elbow there were buttons, three in number and small, being those that are made of twisted cord, but the sleeve-stuff was lacking in eyeholes to button into. These buttons and the sleeve, and as much of the Vestment as might be seen, all appeared of a dark red hue or it might be verging on rose colour, thus rather than otherwise. The material of the Vestment seemed to be not woven but wrought together with the needle, for the threads seemed to be trebly twisted. At the same time while we were thus being taken round and having these sacred relics displayed to us, some of the folk of the city and various honourable gentlemen, knowing of our visit, came also in our company, where, at the sight of the relics, they fell to making their prayers and orations, many weeping in their joy.

That same day also we went to visit a Convent of Noble Dames that was called Omnipotens. In the church here we were shown a sculptured slab of marble, of many colours, that was nine palms in the length, and they say that on this slab was laid the body of our Lord Jesus Christ when He was taken down from the Cross. On this slab are visible the very tears shed by the three Marys and by St John, tears which were shed when our Lord Jesus Christ was crucified, and these tears now appear as though they had been frozen after falling on the stone.

Further again in the city of Constantinople there is a very holy church called Santa Maria de la Dessetria [otherwise the Hodegetria].[6] It is but a small church where are established certain Canons, and these religious men eat no meat, neither do they drink any wine, they partake of nothing cooked with olive-oil, not any flesh of fish in which there is blood. The main building of this church is most beautifully adorned with mosaic-work: and they keep here a Picture representing the Blessed Virgin Mary, set in a fine carved frame, and the same it is said was drawn and painted with his very own hand by the glorious and blessed Saint Luke. This Picture they reported to us has done, and does daily do, many miracles. The Greeks here profess great devotion to this Picture: and keep the festival thereof very magnificently. The Picture is painted on a wooden board, square in shape and six palms high by the like across. The board stands supported on two feet, and the painting itself is now covered over by a silver plate in which are enchased numerous emeralds, sapphires, turquoises and great pearls with other precious stones. The Picture is preserved for safety in an iron chest. Every Tuesday is its feast-day when a great concourse of folk assembles, clerics and lay persons who are of pious mind. These with many of such as are clerics from the other churches of the city, when they have said the Hours, piously take the Picture out from this church and carry it to a court near by. As it goes forth it is found to be so heavy that it requires three or four men to carry it, using straps of leather, attached to cramping-irons, by which the frame must be supported. When it is thus brought forth it is set up in the middle of that court where all present make their prayers and devotions with sobbing and wailing. This being done there comes forth an old man, who prays before this image of Our Lady, and then he lifts up the Picture and carries it off, as though it were of but a trifling weight, and all by himself he bears it in the procession that returns forthwith to the church. Indeed it is a miracle how one man can possibly thus lift so great a weight as is the burden of the frame. They say that to no others is it possible thus alone to lift and carry it save to this particular man [and his brothers]. But this man is of a family any of whom can do so, for it has pleased God to vouchsafe this power to them one and all. On certain feast-days of the year they carry this Picture with great solemnities to Santa Sophia, thus to display it for the great devotion in which the people hold the same.

In this church [of the Hodegetria] is buried the Emperor [Andronicus, elder brother of the present Emperor Manuel and] father of the Young Emperor [John already spoken of] who is now in exile living away from Constantinople, but who they say has legal right to be Emperor, though indeed he it was who would have traitorously brought Constantinople and the Empire to ruin.[7] He who is now reigning as Emperor in Constantinople is named by the Greeks (Chirmanoli or)

Chitmanoli, that is to say Manuel, and his elder brother [Andronicus] was emperor before him and at his death had left a son [John whom we call the Young Emperor. Now this Andronicus] had been disobedient, he had rebelled against his father [the Emperor John Palæologus] and would have dethroned him. At that time the Turkish Sultan was Murád the father of Sultan Báyazíd - whom Timur so lately overcame - and at that time the eldest son of Sultan Murád [whose name was Sávají] also was disobedient rebelling against his father. The son of the Emperor and the son of the Sultan therefore came together in a conspiracy which should have dethroned respectively their fathers, they intending then to seize on the empire and the sultanate. The Sultan and the Emperor became allies, now, to put down their sons, and marching against the conspirators came up with them and captured them in the castle of Gallipoli, the same that at this present moment is in the hands of the Turk. It had been agreed between the Emperor and the Sultan that when they should have made prisoners of these rebels, each respectively should blind the eyes of his son, and that the castle of Gallipoli should be demolished, thus to make an example to any who should in the future rebel. When the rebels were captured this castle was demolished and the Turk immediately proceeded to put out his son's eyes: but the Emperor had compassion on his son and would not tear out his eyes, but he ordered him to be thrown into a deep dark prison, and with red-hot basins caused him to be [partially] blinded.

Then after a period of the imprisonment had elapsed he consented that the wife of his son [Andronicus] should visit him in his prison, who using certain remedies brought back in part the sight to his eyes. One day when she was with her husband [Andronicus] in the prison, she perceived a great snake coming forth from a hole in the wall and then go back again. She describing this to her husband, he told his wife to lead him to the place where the snake had disappeared, and waiting till it came forth again killed it with his hands. It was said to have been of a most marvellous bigness. They afterwards showed the snake to his father the Emperor [John Palæologus] who coming to know the circumstances of the case was taken with compassion for his son's state and released him from his imprisonment. But this prince [Andronicus] after a season returned again to his rebellion, and this time succeeded in taking his father prisoner. The Emperor was kept for a season in durance, until later certain of his lords managed to set him free. On this his son [Andronicus] fled, when his father [as has been already written] caused the tower of that prison in which he had been shut up to be demolished. The Emperor then disinherited his elder son [Andronicus], by testament leaving the empire after his demise to the younger brother [of Andronicus] who is the Emperor Manuel now reigning. His elder brother [Andronicus] however had left a son called Demetrius[8] [otherwise John]: and he, some say, has a just claim to the empire, and should reign conjointly [with his uncle Manuel]. In the result latterly the two have come to an accommodation, after this wise, that each should at present bear the name of Emperor, but that after the demise of the Emperor Manuel the Emperor [Demetrius otherwise John] alone should hold the sovereignty. Further when both these Emperors shall have passed to his rest the empire shall descend to the son of Manuel and after him to the son of [John otherwise Demetrius]: and thus alternately in turn each shall succeed, but I deem it for a surety that neither the one Prince nor the other will carry out the present compact.

There is to be seen in Constantinople a very beautiful cistern, which is called the Cistern of Muhammad; it is domed in cement, and this roofing is supported from below by marble columns. These are arranged to form six naves, and the ceiling rests on 490 of the aforesaid columns, all very stout in size. Much water can be stored in this place, sufficient to supply the need of a great number of folk.[9] The city of Constantinople is enclosed within a stout and lofty wall, defended by many strong high towers. This wall runs from three angles [thus making a triangle] and from angle to angle the length of the wall is six miles, so that the whole outer circuit measures 18 miles, to wit six leagues. On two sides this wall faces the Sea [of Marmora and the Golden Horn], on the third side it is of the land. At the angle furthest from the Sea [of Marmora, and overlooking the Golden Horn] is a height on which is built the Imperial Palaces [of Blachernæ]. Though the circuit of the walls is thus very great and the area spacious, the city is not throughout very densely populated. There are within its compass many hills and valleys where corn fields and orchards are found, and among the orchard lands there are hamlets and suburbs which are all included within the city limits. The most populous quarter of the city is along the lower level by the shore towards the point that juts into the Sea [of Marmora]. The trading quarter of the city is down by the gates which open on the strand [of the Golden Horn] and which are facing the opposite gates which pertain to the city of Pera: for it is here that the galleys and smaller vessels come to port to discharge their cargoes: and here by the strand it is that the people of Pera meet those of Constantinople and transact their business and commerce.

Everywhere throughout the city there are many great palaces, churches and monasteries, but most of them are now in ruin. It is however plain that in former times when Constantinople was in its pristine state it was one of the noblest capitals of the world. They say even now that it holds within its circuit 3,000 churches, great and small. Within its area are many fountains and wells of sweet water. In that part of the town which lies adjacent below the Church of the Holy Apostles,[10] there stretches from hill to hill, rising above the houses and orchards the Aqueduct [of Valens], and this carries water that is used to irrigate all those orchards. In a street that leads to a gate - of those that open out towards Pera - is seen the Exchange, and in the midst of the roadway here stand the Stocks firmly built on the ground, where are set those convicted of heinous crime and about to be imprisoned: or those who have contravened the laws and ordinances of the city authorities, namely, for instance, those who sell bread and meat with false weight. All such are exposed in the Stocks, where they remain night and day at the mercy of the rain and the wind, none allowed to succour them. Along the strand by the water side [of the Golden Horn] outside the city wall and facing Pera there are innumerable warehouses and shops for the sale of all sorts of goods. Hither the traders bring and store the merchandise that comes in from overseas. Constantinople as has been said stands by the Sea [of Marmora] and two sides of the triangle of its plan lie along the shore. Facing Constantinople lies the city of Pera, and in between the two is the port [of the Golden Horn]. Thus we may say that Constantinople is similar to Seville, while Pera is like Triana [the suburb of Seville on the west bank of the Guadalquivir] with the port and ships lying between the two. The Greeks do not know the city by the name of Constantinople, as we are wont to call it, but name it commonly Estombol.[11]

The city of Pera is but a small township, but very populous. It is surrounded by a strong wall and has excellent houses, all well built. It is occupied by the Genoese, and is of the lordship of Genoa, being inhabited by Greeks as well as Genoese. The houses of the town stand on the sea-shore and lie so close on the sea that between its waters and the town wall there is barely the space of the width of a carrack's deck; but it may be a little more. The wall here runs along the strand for some length, but then mounts up the steep of the hill, to where on the summit stands a very high tower, which guards and overlooks the town.[12] However this hill where the tower stands is not so high but what it is overtopped by another hill spur to the right of it, and the same lies at the back outside of Pera. This outer higher hill spur is where the Sultan [Báyazíd] had his camp when he was blockading Pera and Constantinople [in 1399]. His attack was from hence, and his engines of war were set up here against the city which thus on two separate occasions he besieged both by land and by sea. On the one occasion the siege lasted six months, and on the land side 400,000 of his men were encamped while from the sea sixty galleys and other ships blockaded the port. The Turks however were unable to effect an entry, not even into any suburb did they come, so well was the city defended. Indeed for so great a nation as are the Turks, it is strange how unskilful they are in their siege operations, and on this occasion they entirely failed.

The arm of the sea [which is the Golden Horn] that runs up dividing Pera from Constantinople is narrow, being [less than] a mile which is a third of a league across at the mouth. This is esteemed the port for both cities, and it is I opine the most safe and the finest harbour in the whole world. It is a safe anchorage from the winds of all four quarters, and any ships that come in there are safe too from the attack of all enemy ships, for these can in nowise come to them, provided of course that Pera and Constantinople are of one mind to hold the port. The water here is clear and deep so that the largest ships of the navy, indeed great carracks, can come up close to the city wall, when a gangway may be thrown to the shore, as though it were but a boat landing from a galley. Opposite Constantinople [across the Bosporus] lies the Turkish territory, and quite near, for here over against the city stretches a plain fronting on the Sea [of Marmora] which is called Skutari. Many barks constantly pass daily going from Constantinople and Pera across to the Turk country at Skutari. [The Golden Horn already described] runs up in a long curve for the distance of half a league all along dividing Pera from Constantinople. The city of Pera came first into the possession of the Genoese after the following fashion.[13] They agreed to buy from a certain Emperor of Constantinople a plot of land at this place, as much as, it was said, a bull's hide, cut into strips, might enclose. As soon as they had founded their city and built its houses, they went on to build craftily two city walls that should enclose the two adjacent suburbs beyond the town; and this was accomplished at their hands forcefully rather than by right or consent of the Emperor. Pera however does none the less still belong to the Emperor, it is his coinage which alone is current there, and he has jurisdiction over the whole township.

The Genoese call their town Pera, but the Greeks name it Galata. Before the Genoese city came to be founded, there were already buildings made where it was wont to collect the flocks at pasture in these fields. Here they were milked and the milk brought over to Constantinople for sale: and for this reason they called the place Galata, for this word signifies the Milking Place in Spanish, since in Greek " Gala " means "milk." It is now about ninety-six years past that Pera was first founded.

There are in Pera two monasteries, both very beautifully built and richly furnished. One is dedicated to St Paul, the other to St Francis, and we were taken to visit them. The Monastery of St Francis is magnificent being very richly ornamented. We were shown a great number of relics that are here preserved, detail of the same being as follows. First a reliquary made of crystal very beautifully wrought, and this is supported on a silver gilt pedestal. In this reliquary are found the bones of the blessed St Andrew, also those of the glorious St Nicholas, also the habit of the glorious and blessed St Francis. Next we were shown another reliquary of crystal mounted in silver, in which was preserved a bone of the hip of St Catharine. Further a third crystal reliquary very richly ornamented with precious stones and pearls set in its silver gilt stand, and in this were the bones of the blessed Saint Louis [King] of France, and of Saint Sí of Genoa. Next we inspected a chest very finely fashioned in which were laid the bones of the Holy Innocents: also we were shown the long bone of the arm of St Pantaleone: and likewise the long bone of the arm of St Mary Magdalen, and the like bone of St Luke the Evangelist also three skulls from among those of the decapitated heads of the Eleven Thousand Virgins, with a bone of the body of St Ignatius and a very holy relic of the blessed Virgin Mary. And further we saw here the right arm, lacking the hand, of St Stephen the proto-martyr, which same was very beautifully enchased in a silver setting that was ornamented with pearls and precious stones. We were next shown the right arm, with the hand attached, of St Anne: this was enchased in a setting, but the little finger is lacking, and they relate that the present Emperor Manuel cut it off from the hand in order to keep it among his private relics, and that a lawsuit was now being brought against him in this matter. Further we were shown a great cross in silver-gilt ornamented with precious stones set round with pearls, and in the centre of this cross was to be seen a smaller cross made of the sacred wood of the True Cross. We were next shown a reliquary of crystal richly wrought, in which appeared a bone of the glorious St Basil; further a very rich cross in silver-gilt ornamented with many pearls and in the same were to be seen enchased many relics of various saints. Again there was a reliquary of crystal finely ornamented and within it was seen a silver hand that held upright by two of its fingers a bone of the blessed St Lawrence. A bag covered with silver ornament was here brought out to us, in which are preserved various relics of the blessed St John, and of St Dionysius and of many other Saints: and they relate that these relics were carried away when the Latins took Constantinople, but that the Greek Patriarch afterwards instituted a lawsuit against the Latins and finally brought the relics back. Together with all these holy relies they showed to us here many rich vestments with numerous beautiful chalices and various crosses other than those detailed above. In this monastery of St Francis there lies buried in the choir before the high altar the Grand Marshal of France, whom the Turk took prisoner when he defeated the French [at the battle of Nicopolis][14] when the French were marching on crusade in alliance with the King of Hungary. In the adjacent monastery of St Paul lies buried likewise the Lord of Truxi, with a great many other French knights whom the Turkish [Sultan Báyazíd traitorously] put to death by means of poisonous herbs given them to eat after they had been duly ransomed and the ransom money fully paid over to him.

Chapter V

Pera to Trebizond

WE had sojourned in Pera from that Wednesday [the 24th of October] of our arrival to Tuesday the 13th of November, and all this time we had been unable to hear of any ship or carrack bound for Trebizond in which we could take passage. The winter already was coming on, during which season the Black Sea is very dangerous for navigation, and anxious now to avoid further delay on our journey we concluded to charter on our private account a galliot. The master of this vessel was a certain Genoese seaman whose name was Messer Nicolo Socato, who forthwith mustered his crew and we took in the necessary stores for the voyage, whereby on this same Tuesday aforesaid the galliot proceeded to take her way out from the harbour. That day however we were unable to make sail, some of the rowers not having yet come on board, and a quantity of the ship's stores lacking. The next day Wednesday which was the 14th of November, at the hour of midday mass we at last were ready to sail, and the wind was fair for entering the strait [of the Bosporus] which leads into the Black Sea.

After sailing [for some three hours][1] we had come abreast of a tower standing on the Grecian shore, close to the water's edge, and which bears the name of Therapia. Here we ran into the harbour, in order to fill our water casks: while at the same time we took our dinner. This done we again made sail and very shortly afterwards passed out into the Black Sea between the two castles, crowning each its hill, which stand at the sea gate. Of these castles the one is known as the Qaraol [or Watch-tower] of Greece and the other as the Qaraol of Turkey.[2] The castle on the Greek side we saw is now dismantled and abandoned: but the castle on the Turkish side is fully garrisoned. Here out in the sea between the opposite castles another tower has been constructed rising sheer out of the water, while at the foot of the Castle of Turkey there is a rock on which yet another tower has been built, and a wall encircles the two towers. It is said that in past times a chain was wont to be stretched from the Castle of Greece to that of Turkey for these castles and towers all were built of old days, when the Greeks were masters of the lands on both sides of the Bosporus, and these fortifications were made to guard the mouth of the straits. Thus when any ship or bark would enter the Bosporus to reach Pera or Constantinople, or any ship from those cities was about to sail out into the Black Sea, the wardens, having laid out the chain from one Castle to the other, could prevent the passage of that ship until the dues had been paid. Thus on that same evening [of Wednesday] at the hour of vespers we found ourselves at the entrance of the Black Sea, but the darkness coming on we cast anchor for a spell. The exit here of the strait is very narrow, on the right hand is the land of the Turks, while on the left hand lies Grecian territory. On both sides hereabout by the shore were to be seen many churches all in ruins with other buildings in a like sad condition.

At midnight we set sail from our anchorage entering the Black Sea, and our course lay coasting the land of Turkey. Then by the hour of tierce [at nine o'clock in the forenoon of Thursday] as we were sailing with a fair wind suddenly our lateen yard broke and the crew had immediately to take to the oars. We now landed on the coast to repair the damage, getting off again shortly after midday. Next we came up with and passed a small castle that stood crowning a rock on the Turkish coast, the sea completely surrounding it except for the passage to the castle by a narrow spit, and this castle bore the name of Sekellio. By sunset at the time of Ave Maria we came to the port[3] of Finogia which lies on a small islet of that name, and the place belongs to the Genoese. The authorities in Pera had lately despatched to cruise in the Black Sea two fully armed carracks with orders to keep watch and intercept the Venetian [enemy] ships, now due, sailing home from Tana [the Sea of Azoff] with their cargoes of merchandise, and who would be suspecting no attack. The two Genoese ships had orders to capture these Venetian merchant-men, they not yet having news of the war that had so lately broken out between the two powers. One of the Genoese carracks aforesaid we now found stationed in the port of Finogia, where at nightfall we came to anchor.

The following day Friday we had intended to set sail again, but there was a head wind and so both we and the carrack remained in harbour. In this very small island, where there are no settled inhabitants, only the port of Finogia, there is a castle which indeed includes within its walls almost the whole surface of the rock, which same lies two miles distant from the Turkish coast. This harbour of Finogia not being a very safe anchorage it had been our intention to proceed on to the port of Kirpen some six miles to the eastward where the second of the two Genoese carracks was lying in wait for the Venetian merchantmen. Our boatswain however advised us that it would be better to remain where we were, not setting out yet for the port of Kirpen: we therefore shifted our anchorage coming in closer to the castle. By midnight it blew a great gale and the sea beginning to rise, the boatswain said we should be more comfortable and safer if we came out of the harbour and lay under the shelter of the carrack. He had us to weigh anchor and with their oars our men tried to row the galliot to where that ship was lying, but by reason of the violence of the storm we failed to fetch up alongside of her. The wind was now increasing with constant terrific squalls, and seeing we could not come to where the carrack lay we attempted to get back to our former anchorage in the harbour. But to get back into the port we had left was impossible, and we put out two of our anchors. The storm still continued to increase in fury, our anchors began to drag, and it was evident that surely the galliot would be cast on the rocks of the island: but by the mercy of our Lord God the anchors held ground so that the galliot was kept clear of that rocky point, which had we but touched we had indeed been lost. With this we lay to our anchors, but the gale continuing to rise, the danger of death was upon us. We all betook ourselves to prayer beseeching our Lord God for mercy lest we never should escape. The waves of the sea now rose so high that they broke in over the bulwarks of our ship, the waters pouring out again on the other side, whereby the galliot labouring much began to fill. Then for a time we passengers and the ship's crew lost all hope: we could only place our trust in the mercy of our Lord God. Had it still been daylight we would have hoisted sail and run the ship ashore: but it was night-time and in the darkness we knew not how we lay.

When now the storm was thus at its height the carrack began to move, next parting from her anchors she swiftly bore down straight on our galliot as though about to run us foul. But by the mercy of the Lord God she just passed us by, without collision. Her anchors had failed to hold and she drifted past us borne towards the shore of the island, beam on. Long before daybreak she had gone to pieces here so completely, that no part of her wreck remained. Her crew however had managed in time to launch a boat the carrack carried, and thus getting ashore all saved their lives, though they saved none of their possessions. The wreckage of the carrack's topmast and bowsprit indeed were carried past our galliot and had they struck us we should have been stove in but by the mercy of God and His Mother the lumber of the carrack went by without anywise harming us. But we of the galliot were shipping water to such an extent that though labouring to bale and be free of it we were often on the point of foundering. We managed in the end to keep ourselves afloat till dawn broke, when the wind changed and it blew fair for crossing over to the Turkish coast. We next strove to hoist our lateen sail, though for manning the yard and working the ship few of us were fit to give a hand, and most were so much the nearer death than life that had death come little would any have cared. However at last we managed to get our sail hoisted, and as the dawn came on we were approaching the Turkish coast. This was very early on the Saturday morning, and the people of the carrack who had got ashore on the island, as already said, had of course imagined that we of the galliot all had been drowned by the foundering of our ship. They therefore were amazed when they perceived us getting up our sail, for, as they told us later, they had been sure when the galliot was seen by them to drift away from under the lee of the carrack, that we were about to perish: and expecting the worst they had turned to our Lord God in supplication and He had spared us from death.

Thus it came to pass that we in the galliot approached the Turkish mainland when we all threw ourselves eagerly into the water coming without harm on shore. No sooner had we thus got to land than we set to salving our baggage and the presents for our embassy which our lord the king of Spain had given into our care. These were soon safely got out of the ship and brought ashore. All indeed was thus salved though with much labour and peril, for no sooner had the galliot touched ground than the under-tow sucked her back, when again the waves would throw her on the beach. The crew however who were still on board worked to cast forth our bales, which we others already ashore then caught up. Thus everything that the King had bestowed to our care was saved, but before very long it came about that by the force of the seas the frame of the galliot began to break up. The cargo that had been got ashore we now carried off to a hill near by where it was stored. The boatswain of the galliot next warned us that though we were now safe ashore with the cargo, it were very likely that the Turks, perceiving the case, would come and seize us prisoners, impounding our possessions to carry to their lord the Sultan. And so it nearly came about, for presently some Turks did appear, enquiring who we were, to which answer was given that we were Genoese folk from Pera, and that we were the crew of the carrack which in the past night had foundered in the port. Further it was stated that the cargo of our ship that had just been brought ashore we now purposed to ship aboard the other carrack which at the moment was lying off Kirpen harbour, and we added that if the Turks would supply horses to carry our goods thither we would pay them a goodly hire. To which the Turks answered that we could have horses for the morrow but not for that day, promising to send messengers to the villages round about and thus all should be arranged. Very fortunately for us these matters fell out, for next day great numbers of Turks came with their horses and conveyed us all with the baggage and bales to Kirpen where we knew the other Genoese carrack to be lying. On our arrival we found the carrack anchored in that port, and forthwith sought speech with the commander of the ship, whose name was Messer Ambrose, acquainting him with all that had befallen us, and informing him also as to how the other Genoese carrack had suffered shipwreck. The Commander Ambrose gave us good reception, saying that for the service of his highness the King of Castile we should regard this his carrack that he Ambrose commanded as though it were a Spanish ship and our own. We were now allowed to bring all our baggage aboard her, of which the Commander forthwith took over charge, and he proceeded to assure the Turks who had come with us that we were indeed the crew of the other carrack which had been lost in the storm. Now in the matter of the envoy of Timur Beg who as on a former page it has been stated was our companion travelling with us, this personage we now proceeded to dress up in some of our clothes, as though he were a Spaniard and a Christian gentleman giving out that he was from Pera; for he stood otherwise in great danger, and had the Turks of that place but come to know he was [a Tartar of Timur's people] they would have put him to death instantly. We next came on board the Genoese carrack, and found all our goods and baggage in safety, and we clearly realized the miracle that our Lord God had vouchsafed in our behalf, in that He had mercifully saved our lives in that great storm the like of which for its fury, as the commander of the carrack and his ship master told us they had never seen before, though for twelve years past they had been sailors navigating the waters of the Black Sea.

It was indeed also a wondrous blessing that the Lord God had vouchsafed in our favour thus bringing it about that we and our goods and the gifts entrusted to our care by our lord the King had, as we have seen, come into safe custody, with no part plundered, either by the Turks on land, or by mariners at sea with whom we now had found refuge. Finally, as regards these last, it was great good fortune to have come up with the Genoese carrack in that harbour, for, said the Commander, she had like herself to have been lost and shipwrecked in that great storm. Thus all being well we remained in the port of Kirpen till the following Tuesday waiting for a favourable wind. It was on that day that a certain Turk appeared seeking speech with us the ambassadors, he being the head-man of a village in those parts which was of the lordship of the Sultan. This man said that we had come to and passed through lands belonging to the Sultan his master, carrying with us bales and goods of various kinds on which customs were due to him the representative of the Sultan, and for the same he had now come and that we must give him payment. [We however refused, and] this new demand had come about because these Turks now had found out that we were not Genoese or natives of the city of Pera: and indeed as we learnt had they found us wandering as strangers in their lands they would have made us all captive. Then that same day [Tuesday] the carrack hoisted sail and we set forth to return back again to the city of Pera, where on Thursday following at dawn, which was the 22nd of November we once more found ourselves at anchor. All our goods and the baggage we next brought ashore from the carrack and caused to be carried up to our former lodgings in the town, where all those we met of our acquaintance assured us that, considering the violence of the storm and the place where the galliot was wrecked, it was nothing short of a miracle that we had escaped with our lives.

Forthwith we next set about seeing how we might proceed on our journey, but could find no ship that would venture, at this winter season, to leave port and navigate the Black Sea. Indeed many ships already chartered for Trebizond and with their cargo already aboard, had now not dared to set sail: and some ships that had started before the coming of the great storm had recently come back, whereby all were forced to stay that winter in port awaiting the coming of the spring in the month of March. Now the reason why this great sea is so dangerous, and thus to be feared of mariners, is that the Euxine in form is circular and its circumference measures about 3,000 miles. It has no other entrance thereto or exit therefrom except and only this strait [of the Bosporus] which same passes down near by Pera. Further it is encircled on every hand by ranges of very high mountain peaks, and [safe landing on] its shores is everywhere to seek. Further again many and great rivers flow into this sea, whereby its waters boil and surge circling round; and the winds blow furiously causing the waves to rise while squalls rage over its surface. The storm more especially is when the wind is from the north and north-west which they call the Master-wind, and it sweeps in a tempest across the sea. There is too especially great danger to ships when they are approaching the entrance to the Bosporus, for the mouth of the strait is hard to find: and if the ship do not make the opening of the passage she will certainly go ashore and be lost, as in fact has happened to many a ship at this most dangerous place. And again even though the ship may successfully make the mouth of the strait and come in, yet if one of those terrible squalls of the Master-wind or of the West-wind should come on to blow the ship is in great danger by reason of her having no sea room to leeward [in the Bosporus] and she may easily drift ashore. Indeed it was in this late season that, as we learnt, a ship coming in from Kaffa was thus lost. Later while we were at Constantinople [sojourning that winter] six Venetian galleys came in from Tana [which is the Sea of Azoff] intending to make their passage on homewards as usual [in spite of that war which had broken out between Genoa and Venice]. Seeing the stormy weather the Emperor gave orders that they should be allowed to take shelter in the harbour [of the Golden Horn]. To the captains of the [Genoese] galleys lying in the port he sent saying that he was lord and master [in the Golden Horn], and that since he was at peace both with the Venetians and the Genoese, these last should do the others no hurt. Then the Venetians and Genoese came to a truce for that season, and the Venetian galleys afterwards sailed away without let or hindrance.

Thus therefore, as said, we ambassadors had to stay sojourning in the city of Pera the whole of that winter time, for we could come to no ship to carry us forward. Then at the beginning of the month of March at last it was found possible to charter a galliot, and this, banked with nineteen pair of oars, we caused to be fresh rigged and armed as was incumbent for that voyage, which same ran us in to much expense before the business was brought to its term. Messer Nicholas Pisano and Messer Lorenzo Veneziano were the masters of this galliot and we hastened on the preparations hoping yet to come up with Timur still encamped in his winter quarters [of Qarabágh]. Thus the first ship that left port that spring season for the Black Sea was that same galliot of ours. On Thursday the 20th of March in the year of our Lord 1404 our galliot being ready at last, we got on board that afternoon at the hour of vespers, and in our company there was travelling home, as already mentioned, that [Tartar] Ambassador whom Timur had sent to the king of Castile. That evening however the galliot only took its way as far as the columns which stand about a mile distant from Pera, for here we had to fill for provision our water casks. Friday next day we set sail [and by midday] at the hour of mass we were out [of the Bosporus] and entering the Black Sea, for the wind was fair, and by the hour of vespers that after noon we found ourselves once again off the Castle of Sekellio, where we lay hove-to. Shortly after midnight we again set sail departing thence and by vespers in the afternoon of the following day were off Finogia Island, where in our first galliot we had been wrecked as already narrated. We made no port here keeping far out to sea, and [sometime after] vespers came abreast with the mouth of the river [Sakaria] which here flows out coming down from the Turkish country. We would fain have passed the night going into port, but the harbour being too shallow for safe anchoring, we kept our distance with sea room lying hove-to some distance outside, the weather being calm.

The next day which was Sunday at the hour of vespers we had reached port at a town of the Turk country which goes by the name of Pontoraquia [otherwise Bender Eregli which is Heraclea Pontica] and this city belongs to Prince Sulaymán Chelebi, who is the eldest son of the late Sultan

[Báyazíd]. Here we remained that night; and Monday the next day were unable to get on the wind being contrary. This town of [Bender Eregli] is built over the slopes of several hills that lie close to the sea beach, and on the highest of these hills there is a very strong castle. The city is not very populous, and the people for the most part are Greeks, very few Turks living here. In former times the place formed part of the Greek Empire, but, some thirty years ago, more or less, as they told us, the Emperor [Manuel] had sold the city, at a price of some thousands of ducats, to Sultan Báyazíd father of Prince Sulaymán Chelebi just mentioned. This city was formerly most famous and a very rich township by reason of the excellent harbour that it possessed. It had received its name of Pontora originally from a former Emperor who had founded it, and who was called Ponto; the district round and about here being known as Raquia.[4] The next day Tuesday which was the 25th of March we got under way leaving this port, and by the hour of vespers were off a castle on the Turkish coast, standing close to the water's edge and this was named Rio: but it was ungarrisoned. The harbour lay at the foot of the castle, where we did not enter, for a very great crowd of the Turkish folk on perceiving our galliot had assembled along the sea beach, they supposing that we were raiders come for plunder. We therefore lay at anchor outside, at some distance from the shore, and at midnight we sailed on.

Next forenoon before the hour of midday mass we had reached the mouth of a river which flows into the sea here coming down from the Turkish highlands, being named the Bartan river, and we put in to fill our water casks. At the river mouth we noticed many high rocks, on one of which a tower had been built in order to guard the entrance and to prevent enemy galleys from using it as a harbour. We took our departure in due time that afternoon and came before long to a city that is called Amasera. This town belongs to the

Genoese, though it stands in the land of the Turks. Amasera occupies a very high hill above the coast foreshore, and over against this standing partly in the sea is another hill, as high, which is joined to the former one on which the town is built by a wall which thus surrounds both these hills. From the summit of the one to that of the other a great arch has been built to form a bridge carrying a roadway. The town has two harbours one on either side of that hill in the sea. The town itself is small and its houses are insignificant, but outside the walls may still be seen many important ruins of great buildings with churches and palaces. It is evident that in bygone times the greater part of the ancient city lay outside what is now the town limit: but all these buildings are now in decay. Wednesday the day of our arrival and Thursday following we remained here, and the next day was Good Friday. After the due celebration of the Church Service for that occasion, we took our departure and at vespers had come abreast of a place known as Dos Castellos [the Two Castles].

Next morning Saturday we made sail, but a thick fog came on, and [by nine o'clock] at the hour of tierce, it began to blow a gale. The sea rose, and the waves running very high we feared for our ship, and knew not in the fog whether we stood near the shore or had sea room: for our next port was yet some way on. Therefore we worked our way forward most cautiously, and by the time of midday found ourselves off [the harbour, with] the castle that is called Ineboli which belongs to the Turks. We would now fain have come in to anchor, but could not make the port, and we put out to sea for safety. Then at the hour of vespers the fog again came down thick, and we could nowhere see the line of coast although we had come in and were certain to be very near the land. Night fell and we knew not where we were: the sea beginning to rise. Some asserted that we had passed the port [of Ineboli], while others said for sure it was not so, and while we were hove-to taking counsel what next to do suddenly we heard the barking of a dog. We of the galliot thereupon all began to shout and our hailing was heard by those ashore on guard at the castle of the port, who next proceeded to show a light from the summit of the keep. Thus we knew our galliot had come near the harbour mouth, though we could see nothing but rocks over which the sea was bursting in breakers, and the entrance of the port being unknown to us, we were in great dismay. At command one of our rowers threw himself into the waters and managed to swim ashore, where procuring a lantern he signalled clearly to us so that the galliot at length was brought safely into the harbour. The next day was Easter Sunday and we remained in port for the festival.

Near this city [of Ineboli] there are high hills at the back, and on one of these is built a very strong castle called Cinolis, and it is in the possession of a Moslem lord whose name is Isfandiyár. He is one who holds much land hereabout, for which he pays tribute to Timur, and throughout his government the moneys of Timur are current coin. The lord Isfandiyár was not at the time in residence here, but his lieutenant having word that we were ambassadors going on our way to Timur immediately came down to pay us his compliment, sending us later a sheep, with fowls, bread and wine. Here in the hills that lie round the castle of Cinolis is grown the best timber of any in all the Greek lands, from which cross-bows are fashioned. On the Monday following which was the 31st of March, we took our departure [from Ineboli] and by the hour of vespers found ourselves in the harbour of a town of the Turks which is called Sinope, where we came to anchor. This city belongs to Isfandiyár and on landing we learnt that the lord Isfandiyár was absent, he being away at a city three days distant from Sinope in another part of his dominions, which same is known as Kastamuni. Further we learnt that he was now assembling there some

40,000 troops, with the intent to make war against [Prince Sulaymán Chelebi] son of the late Sultan of Turkey who was now his declared enemy, since he, Isfandiyár, had become a vassal of Timur. Could we now have visited him we would indeed have been most anxious to come to speech with this lord Isfandiyár, for he might well have given us some certain news as to where Timur was to be found at this time, and thus might have given us counsel for the land journey that we had soon to make. The reason why this lord Isfandiyár had recently become a vassal by choice of Timur was this: that the late Sultan Báyazíd - he whom Timur had conquered [at the battle of Angora] - this Báyazíd of old had put to death the father of Isfandiyár, dispossessing him of all his lands; while Timur after his overthrow of Báyazíd had given back all these lands once more to Isfandiyár.

At dawn on Saturday following which was the 5th of April we took our departure [from Sinope], however the wind fell calm so that we did not make our next port but all that night were at sea. On the following day Sunday at the hour of midday mass we found ourselves lying off a town of the Turk country that stands beside the sea and is called Samsún. This city possesses two castles: one of these belongs to the Genoese, while the other with the adjacent harbour and township is in the hands of Prince Sulaymán Chelebi, for which reason we dared not go into port here but kept well out at sea. Thus all the following night we were at sea but the weather was favourable, and next day Monday at the hour of noon we made our port in the harbour of a castle which is called Unieh, seeking shelter here as the wind began to prove contrary. Above the harbour high up on the hill spurs we saw the houses of the town, but this was only a small place, of which the population for the most part were Greeks. On a neighbouring hill summit had been recently built a castle that was accounted of this township, and where, as they told us, here and about was settled a colony of some 300 Turks. Both the town and this castle none the less were of the lordship of a Greek noble who goes by the name of Melaseno, and he pays tribute to Timur. Down in the port, standing by the sea-shore we noticed a number of houses that were smithies, for in these parts the sea casts up on the strand a certain fine black sand, and from this they sift out nodules that are worked up into iron bars.

The next day Tuesday we set forth again but the wind was contrary, and we had soon to take shelter in a harbour of the Turkish dominion that they call Leona.[5] Here was a castle that stood by the sea-shore, crowning a rocky promontory, but now abandoned with no one inhabiting it: they told us some four years before the Genoese had come and raided this place. All this country-side is in the possession of a Turkish lord whose name is Arzamir. That same day of our putting in we sailed from that harbour, shortly coming abrest of another small castle that is built on a height beside the sea, and the name of this is Santo Nicio. Just beyond this we had to cast anchor, for there was a head wind blowing, and here we lay that night, very close to the mouth of a river. All this country-side, with many villages that were visible to us as we sailed by, belonged to that lord Arzamir: we were told that he had under his command some 10,000 or more horsemen, and he paid tribute to Timur. The next day Wednesday we went forward, the wind being favourable for our voyage, but the rain began to fall in torrents, and [by 9 o'clock in the forenoon] at the hour of tierce, we were up with a town that bears the name of Kerasund. It stands on the shore, with its houses built all up a height that overlooks the sea. A strong city wall encircled the whole of this height, enclosing within its limit many orchards with fine fruit trees. Following on that day, by noon-time, we were passing a large town which likewise was built along the sea beach, and is known as

83

Tireboli. It is the first place that is of the jurisdiction on this side of the Emperor of Trebizond.

Shortly afterwards we were off a castle by the shore which is called Kureli, but we entered neither of these harbours for the wind continued fair in favour of our voyage, and by the time of vespers we were up with a castle named Fol, and here we went into port lying the night there. Next morning, which was Thursday we set out again but there was a head wind and the sea very rough, [by 9 o'clock] at the hour of tierce we were off a castle known as Sanfoca, and here we came to anchor, in order to rest our rowers. Later getting off again by the hour of vespers we had put in at a harbour that bears the name of Platana, for by reason of the head wind that was blowing we did not venture to proceed on that evening to reach Trebizond, although that city was now only ten miles further. Thus we remained stationary all that night, the wind blowing foul, and indeed the sea began to rise and rage so fiercely that we feared we should be thrown ashore as our anchors were dragging. The next morning Friday which was the 11th of April we stayed on at this place till the hour of vespers and then set sail finally coming in to the harbour of Trebizond. Now from Pera whence we had set out in our galliot to this city of Trebizond, it is a distance of 960 miles by our reckoning of the way we had come. At this city of Trebizond the Genoese possess a fine castle that stands in the country-side outside the walls of the town, and at this castle on coming to land we took up our lodging, the Genoese folk receiving us very honourably.

Chapter VI

Trebizond to Arzinjan

ON the following day which was Saturday the Emperor called for us ambassadors, sending horses to bring us to his palace.[1] On arrival we found him in a chamber that was off a gallery, where he received us very graciously: and after talking with him for a space we returned to our lodging. At this audience after having speech with the Emperor we were presented to his son, who was a young man some twenty-five years of age. The Emperor is a man well-built, tall and of a stately presence; he and his son were dressed in imperial robes, wearing hats of a very high shape, which had cordings of gold running up the sides with a great plume on the top made of crane feathers; further these hats were trimmed with marten fur. The Emperor's name is Manuel, and his son is called Alexius. They speak of the son too, like his father, as the Emperor; for this is their custom that the eldest son, who is heir to the Empire, yet during the life-time of his father and like him, is called Emperor: and in the Greek tongue the title is Busileus. This Emperor Manuel pays a tribute to Timur and likewise also, to certain Turks who are his neighbours. We were informed that his Empress was related in blood to the Emperor of Constantinople. The young Emperor his son is married to a daughter of a certain nobleman of Constantinople, and he is now the father of two young daughters.

On Sunday, the following day, in the afternoon, when we were resting at our lodging there came to visit us there two lords of high degree who were of the household of the Emperor, and his personal attendants. The title of one of these was Koros, which in Greek is the name for the page who carries the imperial bow before his majesty, and the other noble was called Protevestati, which is as we should say the Lord Treasurer. This last was a personage very high in the favour of his majesty, and throughout the empire naught was done but by his goodwill. They told us that he had been of low estate originally being the son of a baker, he however appeared to us of a noble presence. Further it was related to us that the young Emperor, the son, realizing how much favour his father was wont to show to this man paying no heed whatever to the advice of any of the other nobles of his empire, became jealous and rebelled against his father, demanding that he should exile that person from his presence. The son making war on his father, defeated him, besieging him during three months in the capital, for all the great nobles of the state were his partisans. Matters however in time were accommodated through the influence of Koros the noble first mentioned, who was a friend of the young Emperor and likewise held the confidence of those nobles who had given him their support. In what followed the Emperor his father has suffered much in honour, and in reputation, but he has insisted on keeping about his person that base-born officer the Protevestati.

    The city of Trebizond lies beside the sea, and its encircling wall climbs over the hill slopes at the back of the town. Here there is built a strong castle on a height that is surrounded by its own wall. On the one side of the city flows a small river whose waters pass down through a deep gorge, and this makes Trebizond to be very strongly protected in that quarter. On the other quarter there is a level plain, but the city wall here is strong. All round outside lie the suburbs, with many fine orchards. Here a fine street runs along beside the sea beach, traversing one of the suburbs and this is a sight to see, for in its shops all the goods brought to the city are on sale. Close to the sea stand two castles, girt by strong walls with towers, one belongs to the Venetians the other to the

Genoese, by each of whom respectively their castle was built with the consent of the Emperor. Outside the city there are to be seen many churches and monasteries.

The Armenians have a bishop and a church of their own tongue in Trebizond, though they are a people who are not greatly liked in these parts. Their service resembles in many details that of the Catholics, and in the Mass they consecrate the Elements with the ceremonies these last make use of; but the priest in putting on the stole does not cross it over his breast. Further in reading the Gospel he turns his back on the abbot and faces the congregation. When they come to the consecration of the wine, no water is poured into the chalice. They have confession, and they fast during all the forty days of Lent. On Saturdays generally throughout the year they eat meat, though on Saturday which is Easter eve and every Saturday in Lent they keep the fast. For the most part, fasting, they eat no fish that has red blood in it, nor do they use or cook with any oil or fat. The common folk fast after a like fashion also, eating fish but drinking no wine, and taking their meals daily as often as is wont to them. From Easter to Pentecost every day they eat meat, even on the Fridays. They hold that on the very day on which our Lord Jesus Christ was born, His baptism took place: and in other matters of faith they lack strictly orthodox belief, but these Armenians are a very pious folk and they hear Mass with very great devotion.

The Greeks likewise are a devout people, but in matters of faith they hold to many errors. Of these the first is that for the Host they use leavened bread, and they proceed to consecrate after this wise. They take a loaf that is a hand's breadth across or more, thereon having stamped a seal of the size of a gold doubloon piece of money having certain letters thereto; and they consecrate that portion only. The priest who says Mass is not seen of the congregation for there is a curtain between him and them. As soon as he has consecrated he takes the loaf wrapped in a white cloth and raising it to his head forthwith comes out chanting. Thus he appears before the congregation, who seeing him throw themselves face down on the ground sobbing and beating their breasts, exclaiming that they are not worthy of the sight. Then the priest returns alone to the altar, consuming that sealed portion of the loaf which has been consecrated. As soon as Mass is over he takes what remains of the loaf, and divides it into portions. This is known as Blessed Bread, and forthwith he bestows it among the congregation handing a portion of it to each one present. In the service of the Mass they use no book, nor in any of their churches - save only in Santa Sophia in Constantinople - do they use any bell, but strike a wooden board to mark the more important moments of the ritual. All their priests are married men, they marry however but once, and their brides must be spinsters. Should the wife die, the priest does not marry again, remaining ever a widower, pretending to be very miserable all his latter days lamenting his loss. It is only two days a week namely on Wednesday and on Saturday that they celebrate Mass, and the week that the priest takes duty he has to remain in the church the whole of those days, without once leaving it to return home.

The Greek priests keep their fast during six seasons of the year, during which times they eat no fish that has red blood, nor do they drink wine, and they make use of no oil, also during the same time no priest visits his home. The seasons of fasting are these: the first is from the 1st of August to Saint Mary's Day which falls in the middle of August, the next fast is from the feast of Saint Catharine to Christmastide; the third fast is that we all hold to namely the forty days of Lent; fourthly they fast during twenty-four days in honour of the Twelve Apostles: and next fifteen days in honour of a holy man whom they name saint Demetrius.[2] Throughout the whole year they eat no meat either Wednesdays or Fridays: but on Saturdays they eat meat, also on Wednesdays they spend much time keeping vigil. They would preferably eat meat on a Friday than on a Wednesday: and so may do, but never at any time throughout the whole year on any Wednesday must they touch meat. In point of fact during four Fridays in the year they are wont to eat meat, which days are these:- the Friday of the week preceding Christmas, the Friday of the Carnival week, the Friday preceding Good Friday, and the Friday before Pentecost. The Greeks have fallen into error in the matter of Baptism, and they are also heterodox in many other customs and rites. Thus they have a custom that when any man has lived a life of evil in the world having been a great sinner, when he has come to die they will dress his body in the robes of a certain monastic order and further bestow on him another name, in order that thus the Devil may not perchance know how to recognise him. These and other like strange beliefs they hold, but they are a very religious folk and given to much devoutness. As to their soldiers and warlike arms the Greeks make use of the sword and the bow, the like of what arms the Turks employ, and they ride after the fashion of these last [with a short stirrup].

We made sojourn in this city of Trebizond from the Friday of our arrival which was the 11th of April until Saturday the 26th of the same month, during which time we were seeking and securing horses for our journey by land and obtaining needful equipment for the same. On Sunday the 27th of April therefore, all being ready, we ambassadors set forth and along with us rode the guards whom the Emperor had ordered to accompany us, who should be our guides through his territories. That same night we camped in a dismantled church standing beside a river that is called Pyxites [the Surmeneh-Su] and our road that day was over mountain ranges of no great height. The country here was well populated, and the fields well cultivated, having corn lands irrigated by the streams that flowed down from the hills. The next day Monday we left this place, and the guard which the Emperor had bestowed to accompany us here turned back, for they told us that beyond being now enemy territory they dared go no further. We therefore travelled on by ourselves [with the guides and our servants] and at the hour of vespers passed by without stopping at a castle that we were told belonged to the Emperor, and the name of which was Palima. This castle crowns a high peak and the way up is by steps. Down among the rocks at its foot are built some few houses. Travelling further the journey this day was through fine forests and the road excellent, except in one part where from the height above a land-slide had taken place, blocking the path and damming back a stream. This place we only managed to pass after much trouble and delay: whereby that day's march proved short, for the cause aforesaid. That night we had to camp out in the open. Tuesday, next day, the way led over very high mountains, here there was snow and we had many streams to cross. By nightfall we had come up with a castle called Zegan, built on a high peak. The sole entrance thereto was by a wooden bridge that stretched from a neighbouring rock up to the castle gate. This stronghold was garrisoned by the men of a Greek noble whose name was Cyril Cabasica.

The next morning Wednesday [by nine o'clock] at the hour of tierce we had come to a castle, that stood crowning a height that lay across and blocking our road, the name of which was Cadaca. At the foot of this castle and the height flowed a river, while on the other hand stood a range of bare mountains that none would dare attempt to make his way over. Thus the road through was but a narrow strait passing between the river on the one side and the rock of the castle on the other, and the passage was exceedingly close, one man, or one horse at a time only being able to make way ahead. Hence, though only a few might be on guard in the castle these could easily stop any number going that road: which to cross this mountain range was the only path by which the march could be made. From this stronghold of Cadaca therefore there now came forth a band of men who demanded toll of our party and were intent to levy customs on the baggage that we were carrying along with us [and this we had to pay]. The place belongs indeed to the lord Cabasica, whom we have mentioned above, and there he had quartered his band of brigands and evil folk, for that lord is a man of evil sort and kind. This road indeed by which we had now come is not the one usual for travellers to take unless their company is so numerous as to warrant safe passage, or on the other hand they are prepared to pay a considerable sum as a free gift to the lord Cabasica and his men. Some three leagues on beyond the castle of Cadaca we passed a tower built on a high rock where the passage was again very narrow, and by the hour of vespers we reached another castle called Dorileh which was strongly built, its structure appeared to be but newly completed, and the road we were following ran below it.

We had received notice that the lord of these lands, [namely Cabasica] was at this very time in residence here: we therefore sent up our dragoman to give him information as to who we were, although in fact this lord already knew all that was needful concerning us, news having been sent forward to him as to ourselves and our embassy from the other castles of that territory by which we had already passed. No sooner therefore had we sent in our messenger than a man came forth from the castle on horseback, with a message from the lord enjoining on us immediately to halt: dismounting therefore we proceeded to bestow our baggage in a church which here stood by the road-side. The horseman now informed us that it was needful for all those who passed that way to pay customs to his lord, to whom also a suitable present, of our goods, was deemed fitting, desiring we forthwith would comply. The man further explained that his master had his residence in those mountains for the purpose of maintaining a band of soldiers to make war on the Turks, and that his sole revenue was from this toll levied on those who passed through the country, or from such booty as he could gain by raiding in enemy lands. We on our side however answered proposing that we should go up to the castle to have speech with that lord, and pay him our respects as was due from ambassadors. However those of his people who had now come down to us would in no wise consent to this, saying that there was no need that day for our visit, seeing that the following morning he himself intended to leave his castle and visit us. In sooth the next day Thursday, which was the 1st of May, in the forenoon the lord Cabasica issued from his stronghold, appearing at our camping place, and accompanying him were thirty of his horsemen, armed with their bows and arrows. He was mounted on a fine horse, and he too held in his hand arrows with his bow. He and his men then dismounted and all sat down: he causing us ambassadors to come near and take seat beside him.

He proceeded to explain to us that he lived in that barren land, where indeed we found him now at peace, but that he had continually to defend himself against the Turks who were his neighbours on all sides, against whom he was ever at war. Further he said he and his men had nothing to live on, except it were what they could get given them by those who passed through their country, or what they could come to by plundering the lands of their neighbours, and hence he, Cabasica must now implore of us to give him some aid as a free gift in the form of money or goods. In answer we stated that we were ambassadors and no merchants, being envoys whom our master the King of Spain was sending to the Lord Timur, and that further we carried no goods with us except what we were bearing as gifts to Timur. That [Tartar] ambassador of Timur, who was our travelling companion, here broke in saying that though he well knew the Emperor of Trebizond was the overlord of all that country, he was in fact none the less a vassal potentate tributary to Timur, wherefore it was incumbent on him, Cabasica, that we all should be allowed to pass those borders without let or hindrance. To this Cabasica backed by his men replied that this all might indeed be very true, but that they were in a state only able to exist by what they could obtain in the manner that had been set forth to us; averring that by necessity their stress of wherewithal to eat would cause them even to plunder and raid into the home lands of the Lord Timur. At length and finally therefore we found it was needful for us to come to terms, and seeing no way out of it we produced of our store a piece of scarlet cloth and a silver cup, and the ambassador of Timur gave on his part a piece of lined scarlet stuff of the kind made in Florence, with a roll of fine linen. This however failed to content them and they demanded more. Then we gave them many good words of courtesy but these would not avail: the only answer we got was that we must satisfy the reasonable demands of the lord Cabasica and his men, and mere words would be useless. Therefore in the end we had to purchase from a certain merchant who was travelling in our company a piece of camelot, and this being given to Cabasica he very unwillingly professed himself content. He said he would now be our guard, undertaking that we should reach safely the confines of the Arzinján territory which is of the sovereignty of Timur. He promised to provide us with horses for our riding and sumpter-beasts to carry our baggage: and this being arranged we desired to proceed on our journey. None the less we were hindered by delays and finally at our own charge had to hire horses to carry us forward, and to pay men to be our escort to conduct us to the Arzinján frontier.

It was only on the Friday morning following that we set forth again, and with us went ten horsemen for our guard. At the hour of mass in the forenoon we came to a castle that was built on a high rock, and this stronghold likewise belonged to Cabasica. The garrison of the castle sallying forth now demanded further customs for the baggage we were carrying with us: and after much demur we had to pay. In the early afternoon of that day we came to a valley, where they told us that near by had been built a castle now strongly garrisoned by certain Turks, who were of the tribe of the Chapanli, and these being at war with Cabasica his men were stationed holding this valley to keep watch and ward on them. Our escort therefore ordered us to stay quiet for a space, while they reconnoitred in the country round. Finally we passed the place in safety and by the hour of vespers had reached a village called Alanza that was already in the district of Arzinján. As soon as the ten horsemen of our escort had come to this village they unloaded our baggage from their beasts and took leave of us returning to their master Cabasica. This our last day's journey had been by a very rough road passing over the ridges of high mountains. In the village of Alanza we found a Turkish noble who was headman acting in the name of the Governor of Arzinján; he received us very courteously, allocating lodgings to us, with provisions and all that was necessary to our comfort. It was in this village and from this same Turk we first learnt that Timur had already departed from Qarabágh, where he had wintered, and had set forth on his march into the plains of Sultáníyah in Persia. The following day Saturday which was the 3rd of May we left Alanza coming on to a village where they gave us good reception supplying us with food, also horses were now provided for us which we should ride, and sumpter-beasts for our baggage. That night we slept at a village further on where we had provisions amply supplied with fresh horses promised for the morrow.

Thus it was and all that we needed on every occasion they freely supplied to us, for it is the custom of this country [where we were now come governed by Timur] so to do. Wherever we halted whether passing through by day, or to stay the night, they would bring out carpets from the houses and seat us honourably upon them. Next they would produce a leather mat for a table-cloth, as might be with us a round of [Cordovan] leather such as we call Guadamacir, and this with them is known as a Sofra, and on this they would place bread.[3] Their bread in these villages was indeed of very bad quality, being made after a strange fashion. They take a little flour, knead it and make pan-cakes of the same. Then they take a frying-pan set it on the fire and when it has got hot throw the thin cake of dough into it, which as soon as it is heated and baked through they remove. This was the only bread that they supplied to us in these villages. On the leather mat aforesaid they would place meat in plenty, also bowls of milk and clotted cream with eggs and honey. Thus indeed the best of victuals they supplied to us: in all houses it was the same, and if we had to remain the night they gave us more food than we could possibly eat. In any village where we came, immediately there would appear and stand before us the headman, and thereupon Timur's Envoy who, as said, was with us, would order him to bring food for our needs, further the headman had to supply us with horses to ride and attendants to serve us. And if he did not carry out these commands quickly enough to please that Tartar the Envoy, then he would administer blows with stick and whip that were to us an amazement to witness. Thus the people of all these villages we passed were admonished: and indeed no sooner did they see that Chagatay[4] lord appear than all the folk would seek to hide themselves from him. This name of Chagatay is given to all those who are of the clan or family to which Timur belongs, being thus of the royal lineage and tribe.

To continue: that same day therefore we left the village just mentioned travelling forward: and we noticed that in many of the hamlets passed through there were Armenians who are Christians, the inhabitants there. Next day Sunday the 4th of May we arrived in the city of Arzinján at the hour of vespers. The road we had travelled was bad crossing steep hill ranges and through forests; and near the city much snow had fallen. A goodly company now came forth from the town to see us enter and to give us welcome, but we passed straight to our lodgings which had already been prepared, and that evening the Governor of the city sent in for our rations many dishes of cooked food, with fruit in plenty and wine and bread. Monday morning following by orders of the Governor we were further supplied with a certain sum in ready money, and it was told us that a like sum we should receive day by day, as long as we remained in the town, this being for our necessary expenses. At midday the Governor sent for us to come and see him, horses being provided for us to ride, and a number of men to be our guard. We therefore proceeded to a meadow without the city and there found the Governor seated on a low dais under an awning of silk stuff supported on two poles, rigged by tent ropes. In attendance on him was a large assembly and no sooner had we appeared than several nobles, and others advanced to receive us, and as we were led to where the Governor was seated, he arose giving us his hand. Then he caused us to take seats near him welcoming us very graciously. The Governor was dressed in a robe of blue Zaytún stuff,[5] embroidered in gold thread, and on his head he wore a very high hat, adorned with jewels and other ornament. On the crown of this hat was a golden crest set in a fold, and from this crest depended two tresses of crimson horse-hair each in three plats, and these came down below the neck resting on either side upon the shoulders. This style of head-dress with the horse-hair tresses is the fashion now established by Timur.

The Governor was a man of fine presence and may have been about forty years of age with a brownish-yellow complexion, and he had a black beard. He first enquired of us concerning the health of the King our master, and next to show us honour took a silver cup filled with wine and with his own hand handed it to each of us three ambassadors pledging us to drink the same. The Governor after this handed the cup in turn to each of his attendants present. Each on the cup being offered to him by the Governor stood up, and next kneeling on both knees before him received the cup taking it in both his hands. To receive or hold the cup in one hand would be to show disrespect to the lord Governor: for they hold that from his equals only a man should take the cup in one hand. When therefore any one of them has thus had the cup handed to him by the Governor, receiving it in both his hands he will rise from his knees and retire a pace or two and kneeling again, but taking care never to turn his back to his lord. Next having drunk the wine he must rise and again kneel three times with his right knee on the ground, and further all the wine that was in the cup must have been swallowed, taken at a draught.

After all present had thus been given to drink by the Governor with his own hand, attendants brought up sumpter-beasts bearing cases of wood on their backs, in which with portable stoves victuals were being cooked in copper pots. Next they discharged their beasts, setting the meats on round trays made of tinned iron, each of which was supported on its foot, thus standing clear off the ground. Further they produced about a hundred iron bowls, all these being round in shape and quite deep. In truth these seemed to me not unlike the helmets that our horse-soldiers wear. On each of these trays aforesaid they now proceeded to serve out portions of food, filling the bowls with cooked mutton together with dumplings of forced-meat and rice. Other meats were added thereto, so that each dish was of a different appearance. Upon each bowl, as also under it, on every tray they placed a thin cake of bread: while before the Governor and before each of us three ambassadors over the ground they spread a table-cloth of silk. Then the guests gathered round the bowls and trays of victuals, and seated on the earth all set to to eat, each having his knife to cut with and his wooden spoon to sup with: but before the Governor there stood a servant to carve his meat for him. Two nobles in particular were there present: and these men the Governor now caused to come forward to eat with him from his own dish; and when it came about for them to partake of the rice and soup, they all three gathered round the one bowl using but one spoon amongst them, which when one had done with another would take up, and so sharing together.

While we were all thus eating there arrived a young Turk, a boy about seven years old who was accompanied by some ten men. All were on horseback, and him the Governor received courteously seating the boy next him by his side. This youth was the nephew of that Isfandiyár the lord of Sinope, a very great nobleman of those parts of whom we have already spoken. The boy here present had just arrived back from the camp of Timur, and with him the news came that Timur had issued his commands to Isfandiyár that he should give up the half of his lands to this youth, who was the son of Isfandiyár's sister. At this same time also there had just returned from the camp of Timur two lords who were natives of this city of Arzinján, and these men Timur up to this period had kept as prisoners, but now had set at liberty: the reason for their detention having been as follows. A great noble of the name of Taharten had formerly been lord of Arzinján and all the lands adjacent which form a broad district. Taharten at the time of his death left no legitimate male issue to succeed him, and his wife was the daughter of the Emperor of Trebizond.

Some time however before his death, he had acknowledged to be his son this very lord now the Governor of Arzinján whose guests we now were. He therefore should have succeeded peacefully to the government of Arzinján on the death of his father Taharten, but at first he had been displaced, for a son of Taharten's sister, whose name was Sháh 'Alí,[6] had taken possession of these lands asserting that as Taharten had left no son by his wife, he the son of his sister, was rightful heir being Taharten's legitimate nephew. The two nobles who had just arrived and whom we came to know, had been the partizans of this Sháh 'Alí. Further, as it was related to us, after Timur had conquered the Turkish Sultan [Báyazíd at Angora], he on his return journey eastward had stopped at Arzinján where he had imprisoned Sháh 'Alí and these two nobles his partizans, establishing as ruler in Arzinján our present host the Governor whom we had found here, namely the man whom Taharten had acknowledged to be his son, though illegitimate. Timur, as said, had now released these two nobles, but still kept in captivity Sháh 'Alí, whom indeed he was carrying with him back to Samarqand.

Now as to the cause of the misunderstanding and the war that followed between Timur and the Turkish Sultan Báyazíd and which led to the battle at Angora, the matter primarily in dispute was due to the doings of this very Taharten the former lord and ruler of the lands of Arzinján. This will be fully explained presently, for in fact it is an affair of much moment.

To return: when now we had made an end of this banquet, we took our leave and went to our lodgings leaving the Governor alone with his attendant lords. As it fell night the Governor sent in to us some further provision for our entertainment, namely boiled meats in saucepans, the cooks being despatched along with the same to dish up the courses, and many servants came to wait on us. Tuesday the next day we had no banquet but the Governor sent us the stipulated allowance in cash for our expenses. The next day Wednesday after dinner-time the Governor called for us, and proceeding to him we found, him in his house of residence. He received us in a hall where was a fountain, and present were many of his nobles and other folk also, with minstrels who were playing music before him. The house was very fine, and nobly furnished to suit his state. When he had come in he bowed courteously, causing us to take seats near him, and they then served us with pieces of sugar-candy. The Governor next said that, this day, he and the one of us ambassadors who did not drink wine - and that person was myself Ruy González de Clavijo - should be table companions in drinking, and so forthwith they brought in a great glass cup filled with water only, but flavoured with sugar. The Governor having tasted of this now offered it to me, Clavijo, handing it himself to me, while to all the other guests they served wine.

Immediately they brought meats in abundance and rice and many soups of various kinds and we ate after the fashion previously described. When the meat course was over they served round bowls in which honey had been put, with peaches cured in vinegar, with grapes and capers that had been treated after the like fashion; but the manner of their partaking of these several dishes was most common. All this time the wine was going round and soon there appeared a large cup that might well hold three pints' measure. Receiving this in his hand and this cup was full of wine, the Governor proceeded himself to hand it in turn to certain of his guests among the nobles present. On receiving it each guest so honoured had to empty the cup at a single draught, leaving no wine remaining over, for to have done this same according to their usage would have been ill-mannered. At length after a season the Governor appeared to be weary of thus handing the wine to one after another of his guests, when certain of his nobles proceeded to take in their hand that big cup, which filled with wine was then passed from one to another, and thus before long all present for the most part became the worse for drink. On this day however the Governor himself drank no wine, thus to keep company with and especially honour me Ruy González by so doing: and the name of the Governor, which I have not before mentioned, was Pitalibet. Finally when night fell I with the other two ambassadors, returned together home to our lodgings.

Chapter VII

Arzinján to Khoy

THE city of Arzinján stands in a plain beside a river which is the [Western] Euphrates: and the Euphrates [as is well known] is one of the rivers that had its rise in Paradise. The plain in which the city lies is at the back enclosed by a range of high mountains: and the summits of these now were covered with snow: but below in the valleys there was none. All round and about could be seen villages with their vineyards and plantations, the whole plain being under cultivation for corn lands and vines. On every hand there were very beautiful gardens and orchards. The city itself however is not very large, it is encircled by a wall with towers. Arzinján was built by the Armenians and in the city wall was to be seen in many places carved in stone the sign of the Cross. All the houses of the town have flat terrace roofs, whereby the people can pass from one house to another by the roof as though along a street. The city is very populous, and there are to be seen here many fine thoroughfares and squares. Many official personages live here, of whom most are rich folk, and there are many opulent merchants. Fine mosques are to be seen here, and there are beautiful fountains for the supply of water. The inhabitants are for the most part Greeks and Armenians who are all Christians.

[Now as we shall more fully explain later] at the time when Timur [had first invaded Asia Minor] he had besieged and captured the Turkish city of Sívás, a stronghold belonging to Sultan [Báyazíd] and he laid it in ruins. In reprisal Sultan [Báyazíd] then marched out and took this city of Arzinján [from the Armenian prince Taharten] capturing it by storm. When Timur had afterwards overcome Sultan [Báyazíd at Angora] he recaptured Arzinján and putting a garrison in it made it his own. It is related that after all this had come to pass the Moslem inhabitants of the city sought a quarrel with their Christian fellow citizens, and they made complaint that prince Taharten was ever more favourable to these last than he was to them, seeing that he specially cherished the Christians. Further they asserted that the Christian churches were superior in size to their mosques. On this Timur, it is said, sent for Taharten, reporting, to him the complaint of the Moslems, and in reply Taharten agreed that it was true he especially favoured the Christians throughout his country for they brought him, he said, wealth by their trade. For all answer Timur then gave an order, commanding that a certain priest of the Greek church, who was regarded as a chief among the Christians, should be brought before him. Then by reason of the hatred in which he, Timur, held the Greeks of Constantinople, as also the Genoese of Pera, he forthwith ordered that this priest of the Christians should immediately change his faith and become a Moslem, but to do this that man would by no means consent. Timur on the spot gave orders that all the Christian population of Arzinján should be put to the sword, but prince Taharten now besought him to have mercy, offering if Timur would spare their lives to bring him a gift of 9,000 aspers, and the asper is of the value of half a silver real with us.[1] This sum Taharten having paid on behalf of the citizens Timur relented, but none the less ordered that all the Christian churches should be demolished, and now took possession of the castle [on the southern bank of the river] opposite the city [on the north bank] that bears the name of Camag, delivering it over for safe-keeping to one of his Chagatay lords. This he did seeing that castle was a very strong place being set where it commanded the whole city and guarded all that neighbourhood, for through the lands of Arzinján many caravans carrying much merchandise journey on their way, coming hither from Syria and bound for Turkey.

 Now the causes that led to the Sultan of the Turks having knowledge of the Mongol Tartars and what indeed brought

Timur first into Asia Minor, where he afterwards fought and conquered Sultan Báyazíd, the causes thereof, I say, were these. The lord of the city of Arzinján was at that date as already explained the prince Taharten: and his territories neighboured those of the Turk. The Sultan had lately become most avaricious to possess all that region, and more especially to be master of that strong castle of Camag which Taharten jealously guarded as his own. Sultan Báyazíd thereupon was prompted to send to Taharten a message demanding of him that he should pay tribute, and also that he should deliver into his care that castle of Camag. To this Taharten replied that willingly would he pay tribute, acknowledging the Sultan as his overlord, but that the Castle of Camag he would not deliver over to the Turks. To Taharten the answer shortly came back that it would be for his peace to deliver it up, otherwise he would certainly lose both it and his whole territory. Now prince Taharten had by this time already heard of Timur and his mighty deeds, and how he was engaged waging war in Persia, where all the Persian princes had been subjugated. Taharten therefore sent envoys to Timur, with gifts and letters, beseeching him that he would come to his aid against the Turk, and he offered to place both himself and his territories completely at the disposal and service of Timur. Timur on this despatched an envoy to Sultan Báyazíd with letters in which he informed the Sultan that prince Taharten was become his subject and vassal. Hence for his own honour he, Timur, could not allow aught of dishonour to be done to Taharten or the matter should be requited at the Sultan's hands.

Now Báyazíd had heard naught of Timur until that hour, and he believed that in the whole world none could be his equal, he being the Sultan of the Turks. His wrath at the coming of the Tartar envoy with this letter, therefore, was extreme: and he forthwith replied saying how he marvelled greatly that so foolish a man as Timur could exist: how could he dare send him, the Sultan, any such message? for he the Sultan should do as he would with Taharten, as indeed he would do with every other man in the whole world. Further in order that Timur might no longer be subject to these presumptuous fancies, he, the Sultan, would set out and seek him wheresoever he might happen to be, when he would conquer and make him captive: and would proceed to dishonour Timur's chief wife by taking her to be one of his bond-slaves. On receiving this message Timur determined to give the Sultan a proof of his power in war. He immediately took his departure from the Qarabágh lands where he had been resting in winter quarters, namely in those famous plains which lie [on the north western frontiers] of Persia, and marched at the head of his army down to the city of Arzinján. Thence he crossed into the territories of the Turk, and halted before the city already mentioned which is called Sívás, to which he laid siege. The garrison of Sívás therefore sent for succour to their lord the Sultan, who when he knew that Timur had entered his lands and was laying siege to his city aforesaid was exceeding wrath. He ordered all his troops to muster and the first squadrons that came in he forthwith despatched to Sívás under the command of his eldest son, whose name was Sulaymán Chelebi. This first army to give succour was of 200,000 cavalry and the Sultan himself was to follow with further support. The Turks however were too late to throw their relief into Sívás which Timur had entered before they came up: as you shall see.

Now Timur had accomplished this after a most cruel fashion. He had pressed the siege vigorously and the garrison came to a parley. Terms were agreed, and Timur stipulated that a number of their chief men should come out to him from the city, he promising not to shed their blood; who should bring and deliver over to him a sum in gold and silver. As soon as Timur had got into his possession this money he made it known that he desired speech with those men of the city on a matter that would prove much to their advantage. Many of the chief personages and leaders therefore came out to him from Sívás to attend him, relying on the promises of safe conduct already given, and aware that he had received and accepted the tribute they had sent at his demand. But Timur had now caused a number of deep pits to be dug, and no sooner had he lured them beyond the city gates, than he turned on them saying: he agreed it was most true he had given his word never to shed their blood, but none the less he now was about to cause them to be smothered alive in those pits, and meanwhile his army after storming the gates should enter the city, adding that he and his men being poor folk must needs then sack the town. That of which he had spoken Timur immediately proceeded to do: first the chief men of Sívás were buried alive, next the city was stormed and given over to sack, and this being done the walls were breached, and most of the houses of the town levelled to the ground. Timur then moved off, and that same day the Tartars having gone, Sulaymán Chelebi the Sultan's son appeared before the gates with his army of two hundred thousand horses. Finding that Sívás was but a heap of ruins and failing to catch up with Timur, the prince must needs await the coming of his father.

Timur meanwhile was marching down on his way to invade [Syria and] the lands of the Mamlúk Sultan of Egypt. On the road thither he met certain tribes of the White Tartars [known as the Aq Quyunlu, of the White Sheep Clan]: these being a migratory folk without settled abode. Timur immediately attacked and overcame them, making the whole tribe prisoners of war together with their chief. The clan indeed numbered some fifty thousand in all, men and women, but Timur none the less forced them immediately to march on and accompany him down into Syria. On arrival in those parts he laid siege to the city of Damascus with the people of which he was exceeding wrath, they having not only refused the tribute money demanded of them, but held prisoners the envoys Timur had sent to them to receive the same. Without delay Damascus was taken by storm and the city was sacked; after which no small number of the master craftsmen of Damascus were assembled and despatched under guard to Samarqand [to be settled and work their trades living there]. In their company Timur now sent the men of the White Sheep Tartars, also a number of the inhabitants of Sívás whom he had carried off into captivity, and among these last were found many Armenian Christians natives of the Sívás countryside. From Syria Timur now marched back into Persia, intending to spend the summer-time on the plains of Alátáq in Upper Armenia, and it was at this date that Sultan Báyazíd made his attack on the city of Arzinján [as has been spoken of above] being prompted thereto by his fury and the wrath that he nurtured against that prince Taharten who had brought on him the dishonour [of what Timur had wrought in Sívás]. The Sultan immediately invested Arzinján taking it by assault, where the wife of Taharten became his prisoner, but he ordered her to be set free, also commanding that no harm should be done the city. The Sultan thereafter betook himself back whence he had come: but his people murmured saying that he had shown but little prudence, seeing that he ought on his part to have destroyed Arzinján even as Timur had destroyed Sívás.

At this season Báyazíd and Timur, each severally having retired to his own lands proceeded to send envoys the one to the other, but without coming to any accord of peace. It was at this period that [Manuel] the Emperor of Constantinople and the Genoese lords who were settled in Pera sent messages to Timur saying that if he were about to do battle with the Turk they would give him aid with men and galleys. They promised for sure forthwith, or in brief delay, to arm their ships of war and station them [in the Dardanelles] so that the Turkish troops who already were over in Greece [and European Turkey] should not be able to pass back into Asia Minor: and thereby he, Timur, would the better be able to deal with the Sultan. Further the Greeks sent and promised Timur a subsidy in money. The Turk therefore now found himself at enmity both with the Emperor of Constantinople and with Timur, and no accommodation having been effected between the two Moslem princes [the Turk and the Tartar] each began to assemble his forces for battle. In these happenings indeed Timur was of the two much the more astute and the better prepared for war. He marched out from Persia invading the Sultan's country, taking the same road along which he had passed on the previous campaign, namely through the Arzinján lands to the city of Sívás. Sultan Báyazíd having news that Timur was thus in occupation of his provinces, immediately set aside the business he had in hand and betook himself first to Angora where was a strong castle and where already he had stored his munitions of war and supplies. Then at the head of all his host Báyazíd set out in haste to come up with Timur on the march, but the latter no sooner knew what the Turkish Sultan intended than he forthwith left the line of road he was following and turned off to the left hand south among the mountains. Báyazíd coming up where he thought to find Timur, now became aware that the latter had changed his route, and rashly imagined that this was done to escape him, in short that Timur had now taken to flight. He therefore followed on after him with all possible speed, but for eight days Timur held on his passage through that mountainous region, keeping ahead and skilfully avoiding engagement with the Turks. Then Timur turned back into the plains, marching direct on Angora where Báyazíd had left his baggage and munitions, and the Sultan realized that his enemy had escaped him by his guile. In vain by forced marches he sought to catch up with him before he should arrive at the castle of Angora. The Sultan indeed with his weary troops at the last moment came up with Timur who had led him thus by devious ways with intent to exhaust him. Then that battle was fought, and Báyazíd overcome was taken prisoner as has been already related.

Meanwhile the Emperor of Constantinople and the Genoese of Pera in place of holding to the pact that they had made with Timur, had allowed the Turkish troops that were in Europe to pass over [across the Dardanelles] into Asia Minor, and after the battle had aided these same Turks in their flight from Angora to return back for safety to European Turkey, the Greeks carrying them across in their ships. It was indeed for this treachery, as he deemed it, that Timur was at enmity with the Greeks, and ever afterwards treated the Christian folk throughout his dominions with much severity. The Turkish Sultan whom Timur thus overcame was, as said, Báyazíd surnamed Ilderim, and this latter title means "the Thunderbolt," for Ilderim in Turkish has this signification, but Báyazíd was his proper name. His father was called Murád, that most famous Sultan; who was slain by the Christian king Lazarus [of Servia] at the battle [of Kossovo].[2] The Sultan had been struck down by a sword thrust in his bosom, which piercing through came out by the shoulder; and Sultan Báyazíd afterwards avenged the death of his father by slaying in battle with his own hand this king Lazarus. The son of king Lazarus came to terms with Sultan Báyazíd at a later date, and is indeed still alive, and he now is a guest in the house of prince Sulaymán Chelebi, already spoken of, who is the son of Sultan Báyazíd. All these details

I give to make it clear who exactly was this Sultan Murád aforesaid, for with the Sultans of Turkey all go by the name of Murád [or Amurath], though in point of fact each Sultan has besides his own personal name. Then further and likewise Tamerlane is not in truth the proper name for this lord, who indeed is always here called Timur, as we have been wont to speak of him. In the Tartar tongue Timur Beg has the signification "Lord of Iron," for Beg with them means Lord, and iron they call Timur [otherwise Demir].[3] To speak of him as Tamerlane is indeed matter of insult, being a name given him by those who are inimical to him, for Lane [in Persian Leng] means "lamed " as indeed Timur was, of his right leg. So likewise he has lost the two lesser fingers of his right hand, cut off by a blow received long ago when as a youth he was stealing sheep by night, as later we shall come back to and relate more fully.

[But to return to our journey]. We remained sojourning in the city of Arzinján until Thursday the 5th of May, when we took our departure thence, and our way passed over several high mountain ranges bare of forest and all that day it snowed being very cold weather. We stayed the next night at a village called Sháh Bágh [the King's Garden] where there is a small castle, with a river running beside it. All around were to be seen wheat lands, also many villages, with scattered houses here and there. On the following Saturday we slept at the village of Pegarich, where there is a great castle on a peak: and this hamlet has two suburbs, one inhabited by Armenians the other by Turks. We were told that about a year ago. Timur passing through this place gave command that all the churches belonging to the Armenians should be demolished. The Armenians having in view to save their churches from destruction had, as we learnt, presented Timur with 3,000 aspers - each asper being the value of half a silver real - and he had accepted the gift but none the less incontinently had ordered those churches all to be demolished. The next day Sunday, which was the feast of Pentecost we departed thence and came to a village where there was a fine castle crowning a peak near by, and this place was counted as of the district of Arzinján. Monday following we slept in camp in the open and our way all that day lay passing bare high mountains where there was no forest, but streams flowed down all the hill slopes and the land was here wondrously rich with grass, both in the heights and in the lower country. All this country-side is in the occupation of the Turkoman people, who, at this season, migrate down hither coming from their home beyond the border in the Turk country, and they are Moslems. On Tuesday we passed on, and our road that day was through the plains where the meadow lands are well watered by streams.

At midday we had reached the city of Erzerum, which is of the lordship of Timur. It stands in the plain and is encircled by a very broad strong stone wall with many towers; and there is a castle here, but the city is not very populous. We saw also a fine church, for this city formerly belonged to the Armenian kingdom which is Christian, and many Armenians still live here: indeed in the past Erzerum was the richest and greatest city of all those parts. The governor of the town at the present moment is a Turkoman, whose name is Yúsuf 'Alí. The following day Thursday the 22nd of May leaving Erzerum we slept at a village called Partir Javán, which is in the territory of the city of Avnik. This last is a very strong place having its own governor, for the Armenians hold it; but the country round and about belongs to a Chagatay lord whose name is Duladay Beg [of whom we shall speak later]. On Friday we had come to a hamlet called Ischu; we stayed here that night and all Saturday as well: the village folk were Armenians. On Sunday we went on coming to a place called Delilárkent a name which signified "the Village of the

Madmen," for those who inhabit this place are all hermits of the Moslem creed [being Dervishes] who here have the name of Kashísh [or Priests].[4] The Moslem peasants from all the country round come in pilgrimage hither to visit these holy men, and forsooth those who are sick regain their health. These Dervishes have a chief to whom all pay much respect, for they hold him to be a saint. When Timur lately passed through this place he took up his lodging living with this chief Dervish while he stayed here. All the Moslem people of the country round give alms abundantly to these pious men and this their chief is the lord of that village, being too the master of those who embrace the religious life. The common people here consider all of them as saints. These Dervishes shave their beards and their heads and go almost naked. They pass through the street, whether in the cold or the heat, eating as they go, and all the clothing they wear is bits of rag of the torn stuffs that they can pick up. As they walk along night and day with their tambourines they chant hymns. Over the gate of their hermitage is seen a banner of black woollen tassels with a moon-shaped ornament above: below this are arranged in a row the horns of deer and goats and rams, and further it is their custom to carry about with them these horns as trophies when they walk through the streets; and all the houses of the Dervishes have these horns set over them for a sign.

On Monday the 26th of May we left Delilárkent and passed the night encamped in the open having come to the banks of that great river which is known as the Aras [Araxes]. This is a mighty stream that traverses almost the whole of Armenia. Our journey that day had passed through defiles, and among hills that were covered with snow where many streams flowed down from the heights. On Tuesday following we came to sleep at a village called Naw Juy [New Brook] and all day we had continued travelling down the bank of the river Aras, the way being by steep places and very rough. At this village a Kashísh [or Priest] was living who received us with honour, he was the lord of that place, most of the people hereabout being Armenians. On Wednesday following we slept at a village where there was a great castle crowning a peak. We observed that the whole of that mountainside was a mass of salt, and indeed for quite half the day's march we had been passing along the flanks of a range of salt hills. The people from far round and about, at will, all come here to get their salt, profiting thereby, and using no other for their cooking.

We shall now describe the city of Surmari[5] which as we learnt was the first township to be built after the Flood: for to this place we came on Thursday the 29th of May at about midday. This is a very large city: and from here at a distance of about six leagues was to be descried the great mountain [of Ararat] on which the Ark of Noah had rested when the Flood abated. This city stands in a plain which on the one hand borders the river Aras, while on the other part is a very deep valley hemmed in on either side by steep hill sides, but this valley is nowhere broader across than the distance that an arquebus can carry its bolt. Thus, this valley surrounds the city at the back, coming down above and below to the river bank, whereby the city indeed is most strongly placed, and cannot be come to directly except from the river side, or by the entrance gate down in the depth of the valley. At this gate stands a castle with high strong towers, having two doorways one behind the other. Now this city of Surmari was in truth, as already said, the first township to be built on dry ground after the Flood: and those who built it were the sons of Noah. The people here told us that some eighteen years[6] before the present time Toktamish the Tartar Khán [of the Golden Horde] had laid siege to their city, bombarding it night and day for two whole days. Then on the third day they had come to terms with him, it being agreed that they should be left in peace and in the possession of their city, neither he nor his men entering the place, but that they should pay him a certain stipulated sum in tribute. To these terms Toktamish gave his word, but he added the demand that one half the armed men of the town should come out to join his forces and march with him against the Georgians, it being his intention forthwith to do battle with the king of that nation whose name is George. No sooner however in compliance had their warriors come out of the town, than Toktamish gave his men orders again to come up to the city which they entered by storm, and sacked, all the riches found there being carried off for booty. These Tartars then set fire to the houses, breaching the city walls in many places and putting to death an immense number of the citizens. Most of the population of Surmari formerly had been Armenian folk, for it is a city of Armenia, but of late years many Christians had been deported from this place the Moslems having come in and taken possession, as we shall explain later more fully. In Surmari are still to be seen many notable and fine buildings. Everywhere throughout this country of Armenia as we passed they supplied us and our attendants with an abundance of provisions, providing us also with horses for our journey: for indeed the whole country is now at peace under the rule and government of Timur.

The following Friday we left Surmari and travelled on coming to a great castle built on a rock, where we must pass the night. This castle was in the occupation of a Lady, and she was a widow, who owned it, paying however tribute to Timur for the lordship of the same and the lands that lay around. Formerly this castle had been a stronghold of robbers and highwaymen who lived by plundering travellers: but Timur had, when marching past this castle, taken it by storm, and put the chief of the brigands to death who had been the husband of the Lady mentioned above, now his widow.

Timur then had left orders that - lest highwaymen should again harbour and shut themselves in here to practice their evil deeds - every door should be removed from the castle gateways, and never replaced, all ways in remaining open; and then he gave the wardship of the castle into the hands of this Lady. When we were there we found all its gateways still without gates; and the name of the place is Igdir. The castle stands at the foot of the great mountain [called Ararat] where the Ark of Noah came to rest. This mountain, like all the other heights that we had passed over since leaving Trebizond, was entirely bare, having no forests even on the foot-hills. At the castle of Igdir the Lady we have mentioned gave us a very hospitable reception that night, supplying us for all our needs.

The next day Saturday which was the [31st] of May we departed from Igdir and our way led us along the flank of that great mountain where the Ark of Noah had rested. The mountain is indeed extremely high and its summit is ever covered with snow. Throughout all the highlands too the snow had now fallen. The valleys of the mountain were quite bare, no forest growing here, but there was much grass here for pasture, and many streams ran through them. Our way lay round the back of the mountain, and we passed many ruined sites, where we saw foundations of what had been houses, built with stones of very large size. Here round and about rye grew wild, and every season, as they told us, it would sprout again of itself as though it had been sown by hand: though it never came to seed, as the grain did not mature. Also the meadow lands abounded in water-cress as though this too had been laid down for cultivation. In the valleys at the foot of the mountain the Kirmiz worm is found, with which they dye the silk crimson.[7] On the hill slopes we saw extensive ruins of a township that had evidently not been inhabited for ages past, and for a space of a league these remains were to be noticed on all hands. The people told us that these were the ruins of that first city which was founded in the days after the Flood by Noah and his sons.[8] The plain which lay before these ruins was intersected with watercourses: trees grew here and there, below them rose bushes, springs of water bubbling out on every hand. The great mountain [of Ararat] at its summit has a very high and steep peak covered always with snow. Clouds prevented us seeing the summit at most times: and they told us that generally, in summer as in winter, the mountain was hidden in mist, the cause being its great height. We had taken our afternoon rest that day at a beautiful fountain of spring water that we came to issuing forth under a stone archway, and while we were here suddenly the clouds lifted, and the whole mountain range became visible to its summit, but again after a moment the mists returned covering all in. They told us it was rarely that the whole mountain ever was thus displayed. Adjoining the main peak of [Ararat] is the lesser mountain peak [of little Ararat] which is equally steep, and between the two stretches a long saddle, and here it was, as they said, that the Ark came to ground, but as already explained the great peak, the lesser peak and the saddle all three are ever entirely covered with snow.

That same night we came to our lodging in a castle called Báyazíd which is built on a high rock that is very wonderful to see. Below the castle is a second rocky crest over which the houses of the town are built. The place is of considerable size and a great wall flanked by towers encloses the town and joins it with the castle height, from which steps lead down to the houses of the town. The peak on which the castle stands is exceedingly high, yet none the less within the castle precincts there is to be found a copious spring of fresh water. This city was besieged by Timur some six years ago, but the lord of the same shortly came to terms with him agreeing to pay Timur tribute, who on his side promised not to let his Tartars enter the place. Neither was the lord of Báyazíd, either of himself or with his men, bound to join and march with Timur.

On Sunday the 1st of June we arrived at the hour of vespers before a castle that is called Mákú, and the place belonged to a lord who was a Roman Catholic Christian, but whose name was Núr-ad-Dín:[9] and those troops who garrisoned his castle also all were of the Roman Catholic faith. They were indeed Armenians by nationality, speaking the Armenian tongue, but at the same time understanding both Turkish and Persian. At Mákú there is a monastery of Friars of the Order of St Dominic. The castle stands down in the valley in an angle below a high mountain peak: and the houses of the town are built on the hill slope. A great wall with many towers of squared stone, well mortared, enclosed the houses of the town passing up round and about on the mountain side above. Enclosed within this wall and also out beyond it on the upper slope of the hill side were many houses of the citizens, and again this outer suburb was protected by a wall with towers and bastions which are brought round to join up with the inner wall. The entrance to this upper suburb was by a stairway cut in the rock, and over the entrance gate was built a great tower to guard the same. And beyond this second wall again other houses had been built among the rocks of the mountain side. Here stood the habitation with towers encircling it where the lord of this place had his abode, and many of the town folk likewise had their summer houses situated on the mountain side which rose up above beyond the double city walls and outlying suburbs. The rocky heights here so to speak form a pent-house that overhangs the castle and the walls enclosing the township; and these give protection and keep off the rain as it falls, for these rocks above entirely shelter the castle precincts. By this peculiar situation the castle never could be attacked successfully either from without below, or from above. Within the castle court

117

there issued a copious spring of water, which served below to supply the wants of the whole town, irrigating later also the orchards round and about. A very beautiful valley stretches out below Mákú through which a river passes whose waters serve many vineyards and corn lands.

Timur in the past we were told had besieged this castle of Mákú but was unable to capture it: he therefore sought and came to terms with the lord thereof, who agreed to serve Timur with twenty horsemen, these same to join his armies whenever called upon. Soon after this agreement was made Timur had occasion again to pass by Mákú, and the lord aforesaid purposed that his son, a youth of twenty, taking three finely caparisoned horses should go out to meet him: these to be presented as a gift. When Timur now had come to the foot of the castle this youth went forth with those horses to present them on behalf of his father, and Timur receiving the gift graciously had proclamation made that none of his men should do any injury to the castle lands. Next Timur noting that the lord of the castle had so fine a son, it were, he said, indeed a pity the youth should be kept mewed up at home, and he Timur would receive him, carrying him off in his train to become the companion of his grandson. This Prince the grandson of Timur is named Omar Mirza, and he was at that time already established as governor ruling over the whole of Western Persia, in which region Mákú is included. The young man whom Timur thus carried off in his train is at this present moment living with Omar Mirza, and has been raised to be a commander in his army. But they have forced him against his will to become a Moslem, having bestowed on him the name of Siurgatmish, and he now is captain of the guards of Omar Mirza. Outwardly he professes himself a Moslem: but not of free will, for at heart he is still a Catholic.

We were all very cordially entertained at Mákú by the

lord of the castle, who had great consolation in the fact that we were Christians, and he showed us much hospitality. He told us that some fifteen days before our coming the Amír Jahán Sháh Mirza,[10] the nephew of Timur and one high in his favour, had sent to him, namely the governor of Mákú, requesting that he would receive him as his guest, and allow him to deposit all his treasure in that castle for safe keeping. The governor told us he had answered this prince that he could not receive and give him hospitality, but that if he had treasure to deposit in Mákú he would take charge of it gladly. He however must not count on ever getting it back. Very pleasantly and comfortably therefore did we pass the night of the day after our arrival in the Castle of Mákú, and later on indeed at the camp of Omar Mirza we met that son above mentioned of the governor and often had speech with him. The governor further had at home there another son, younger than that other, and in conversation he informed us that this second son of his not being a man of arms like his brother, but learned and a skilled grammarian in the Armenian language, he desired that should God grant us to return home from Samarqand passing by the way of this his castle, he would fain confide this youth to our care to carry him with us to Spain. Then our King, who, he trusted, might favour him, would recommend him to the Pope, beseeching his holiness to ordain him bishop over his father's province.[11] It is indeed a wonder how the Christians of this Castle of Mákú hold their own thus surrounded by the Moslem folk and so far estranged from all Christian succour: they are in fact of the Armenian nation, but of the Roman Catholic belief, and they serve God in the orthodox rite.

On the following Monday the 2nd of June we left Mákú and that night camped in the open being unable to reach any suitable village. During our march that day they pointed out to us a castle lying to our left hand on a hill top, [at some distance standing on the northern bank of the river Aras] which is called Alanjik. This castle is encircled by a wall with towers, and within this circuit lie many vineyards and orchards with corn lands adjacent, also there are numerous springs of water with pasture lands for cattle, set round and about the castle on the height above. [In the year 1387] when Timur had overcome Sultan Ahmad [Jalair] of Persia[12] taking all his lands from him, this prince had found safety in the Castle of Alanjik, where Timur besieged him and his men during the space of three whole years. At the end of this time Sultan Ahmad escaped fleeing to Egypt taking refuge with the Mamlúk Sultan of Cairo, and there at this time he remains. The next day Tuesday we slept at an encampment of the Chagatay Tartars, who were pasturing their flocks in those meadow lands, where there were pitched more than a hundred of their tents. Wednesday again we slept at the tents of another camp of the Chagatays, and these folk supplied us with all necessary food, also horses to carry us forward, just as similarly in the villages and towns that we passed through they had everywhere attended to our service. The country we were now travelling across was very mountainous, but fertile in grass lands, being well watered by numerous streams. All around and about we met with the Chagatays who though nomads are accounted as belonging to the township of Khoy. On Thursday the 5th of June at midday we reached that same city, which lies in a plain, encircled by many orchards and corn lands, these again being surrounded by extensive grazing pastures irrigated by many streams and conduits of water. The city of Khoy itself is defended by a wall of baked bricks, with many towers and barbicans: and at this city the province of Upper Armenia has its limit, the frontier into Persia being passed here, but in Khoy itself the population for the most part is of the Armenian race.

Chapter VIII

Khoy to Sultáníyah

WHEN we had arrived at this city of Khoy we found here already come an ambassador sent to Timur, from [Násir-ad-Dín Faraj the Mamlúk] Sultan of Egypt, who was voyaging with twenty horsemen, and fifteen camels. They carried presents which the Sultan was offering to Timur. Among these presents were counted six ostriches brought hither from Egypt, also a beast called a Jornufa [namely a Giraffe] which was strangely made and after a fashion unknown to us.

This animal has a body as big as a horse but with an extremely long neck. Its forelegs are very much longer than the hind legs, and its hoofs are divided like those of cattle. The length of the foreleg from the shoulder down to the hoof measured, in this present beast, sixteen palms, and from the breast thence up to the top of the head measured likewise sixteen palms: and when the beast raised its head it was a wonder to see the length of the neck, which was very thin and the head somewhat like that of a deer. The hind legs in comparison with the forelegs were short, so that any one seeing the animal casually and for the first time would imagine it to be seated and not standing, and its haunches slope down like those of a buffalo. The belly is white but the rest of the body is of yellow golden hue cross marked with broad white bands. The face, with the nose, resembles that of a deer, and in the upper part it projects somewhat acutely. The eyes are very large, being round, and the ears like those of a horse, while near its ears are seen two small round horns, the bases of which are covered with hair: these horns being like those of the deer when they first begin to grow. The animal reaches so high when it extends its neck that it can

121

overtop any wall, even one with six or seven coping stones in the height, and when it wishes to eat it can stretch up to the branches of any high tree, and only of green leaves is its food. To one who never saw the Giraffe before this beast is indeed a very wondrous sight to behold.

We remained in this city of Khoy the Thursday night after our arrival, also Friday, Saturday and Sunday following, and on this last day which was the 8th of June at noon took our departure onwards. In the city of Khoy no horses for our journey could be procured, hence orders had been sent out to the troops stationed round and about, and thus our need was supplied. Setting out we made our camp that night in the open meadows. Our journey from Trebizond as far as this city of Khoy had stage by stage been through mountain lands where the heights had been covered with snow, but from here onward the climate became warmer, and no more snow was met with. On Monday following by midday we had come to a very populous fine township of the name of Tassuj,[1] which lies in a plain and is surrounded by many orchards, that are irrigated by numerous streams. This place stands on the borders of the salt lake [of Urúmiyah] the circuit of which may measure a hundred miles, and in this lake are three islands one of which is inhabited. We passed on forward that evening and slept at a hamlet called Kúzah Kunán which had been a large place, but most of it now in ruins: they say it was Toktamish, the Tartar Emperor who destroyed this town, he whom Timur afterwards overcame, ejecting him from his sovereignty, whereby he is now powerless to do evil as later we shall more fully explain. At Kúzah Kunán we noticed that many Armenians had taken up settlement to reside there. The following day Tuesday we came to a village called Chauscad, which lies in the plain. It is surrounded by orchards and vineyards, with fruit trees and there is shade all around, while from hills near by came many streams of water irrigating its gardens. Great quantities of fruit are carried thence into Tabriz, and even exported to places beyond. That same night of Tuesday we slept in camp in the open, and all the next day our road went skirting orchards and vineyards, watercourses passing through them, and the road lay through the low lands, most pleasant to travel along by reason of those garden lands.

On Wednesday the 11th of June at the hour of vespers we entered the great city of Tabriz, which lies in a plain between two high ranges of hills that are quite bare of trees. The city is not surrounded by any wall, and the hill range on the left hand comes close up to the town limits. This hill slope [facing south] has a hot aspect, and the streams that flow down from it are unwholesome for drinking. The opposite hill slope lying on the right hand stands back from the town [and facing north] has a cold aspect, while beyond on the summits of a range of hills seen here snow lies all the year round. The streams flowing down from this quarter give excellent drinking water, which same is conducted into Tabriz where conduits pass through the city reaching all the houses. In this mountain range to the south, which can be clearly seen from the town, there appear two peaks which, it is said, were once so close together as to form but one mountain summit, but which year by year are now become two peaks and separating apart more and more. In the opposite hill range to the north of the city, and standing about a league distant therefrom, is a very high hill. Here, as they told us, certain Genoese merchants in past days had bought the land from [the Il-Khán] Sultan Oveys,[2] in order to found there a castle to their own use. But no sooner had this Sultan sold the hill to them than he began to repent his bargain: wherefore when the Genoese set to begin the construction of their stronghold, he sent and told them that in his country it was never customary for merchants to build or buy castles. They indeed could buy as much merchandise as they would, and that same they might export, carrying it away with them into their own country: willingly this they should do, but if they should build for themselves a castle, they must also take this up, carrying away the ground on which it was built elsewhere to some place outside his dominions. The Genoese merchants on hearing this had come to words with him, whereupon as we learnt Sultan Oveys[2] had incontinently ordered that they should all be beheaded.

From the hills that are on the right hand to the south a great river flows down towards Tabriz, but before it reaches the city most of its waters are drawn off in irrigation channels. Many conduits later are drawn from these which entering the town the waters flow along through the streets and squares. Throughout the city there are fine roadways with open spaces well laid out: and round these are seen many great buildings and houses, each with its main doorway facing the square. Such are the caravanserais: and within are constructed separate apartments and shops with offices that are planned for various uses. Leaving these caravanserais you pass into the market streets where goods of all kinds are sold: such as silk stuffs and cotton cloths, crapes, taffetas, raw silk and jewelry: for in these shops wares of every kind may be found. There is indeed an immense concourse of merchants and merchandise here. Thus for instance in certain of the caravanserais those who sell cosmetics and perfumes for women are established and to be met with, the women coming here to these shops to buy the same, for they are wont to use many perfumes and unguents. Now the dress the women wear in the streets is that they go covered in a white sheet, and they wear over their faces a black mask of horse-hair, and thus they are concealed completely so that none may know them. Throughout Tabriz many fine buildings may be seen, the Mosques more especially these being most beautifully adorned with tiles in blue and gold; and here they have glass bowls [for the lamps] even as we had seen in Turkish lands.

They told us that all these fine buildings had been erected in days past when there had been living in Tabriz many famous and rich men who had vied each with his neighbour as to who should build the finest house, each spending willingly his wealth in what he did. Of such buildings we visited especially one, a great palace that stands surrounded by its own wall most beautifully and richly planned, and within this building were twenty thousand rooms and separate apartments. We learnt that this great palace had been built by that monarch [already mentioned above] named Sultan Oveys [Jalair], who had constructed it using the treasure that had come to him in tribute paid during the first years of his reign by the Sultan of Egypt. The place is now known as the Dawlat Khánah [the Government House] a name which might also exactly be rendered as "the House of Fortune." This enormous palace for the most part is still standing intact, and indeed it might have been hoped that likewise all those fine buildings in Tabriz would have been left to stand in their early condition, but unfortunately many have of late been pulled down by order of Mírán Sháh that Prince who is the eldest son of Timur, but the cause will be explained later. Tabriz is indeed a very mighty city rich in goods and abounding in wealth, for commerce daily flourishes here. They say that in former times its population was even greater than it is now, but even at the present day there must be at least 200, 000 householders within the city limits, or perhaps even more. We found that in many of the public squares they sold food all ready cooked and nicely served forth for present eating, being prepared in various ways: and fruit too in abundance is to be had there.

In a street of the city near one of the squares is a certain house where a dead withered tree trunk is to be seen, of which they tell the following. It is a belief among the common people that at some near future time this withered tree will put forth green leaves, and next it shall come to pass that one who is a Christian Bishop will appear in the city, surrounded by many Christian folk, and he will bear in his hand a Cross, and forthwith he will convert all the inhabitants of Tabriz to the True Faith in Christ Jesus. For all this as they told us, a certain great saint of the Moslems, who was a Dervish hermit, had made prophecy publicly not long before, on which occasion the common folk of Tabriz much incensed had rejected [what he spoke as to that tree] despising his prophecy. Further the people had assembled together in numbers, intent on cutting down that withered tree, but three blows with the axe having been struck on it, every one who was a striker had had his arm broken. We were informed that this Moslem saint had but quite recently died; and he had prophesied many other marvellous events as about immediately to come to pass. They reported further that when Timur not long since was passing through Tabriz he sent for this saint to come and see him, who then had repeated to him his prophecy [as to the Christian Bishop] with many other amazing matters. The tree just spoken of stands in that very same street at the present day, and no one now dare touch it.

In many of the roads and open places of the city are seen fountains and troughs for drinking from, and in these last in summer time they are wont to cool the water with pieces of ice, and they stand therein their brass and copper pots from which folk drink. The governor of Tabriz is a relative of Timur and they call him the Daroghah [which is the Mayor]: he was most polite in conduct, paying us all honour. There are, as said, many rich and beautiful Mosques in the city, also bath-houses the most splendid, I think, of any in the whole world. We remained in Tabriz for nine days, and when the time for our departure had come for us to set out on the journey forward they brought us horses for us to ride of those that were the property of Timur himself: indeed not only for us the ambassadors but likewise for all our attendants, with sumpter-beasts for our baggage. It is to be noted that from Tabriz all the distance to Samarqand Timur has established relays of horses kept ready at command so that his messengers may ride on his missions night and day without let or hindrance. The post-houses have been built at intervals of a day's journey apart, or sometimes of half a day's journey. In some post-houses a hundred horses will be found, in others only fifty, while in a few there may be as many as two hundred: and thus the high road all the way to Samarqand is served. We were told that from Tabriz to Cairo they count it to be ten days' journey, and the city of Baghdad lies to the right hand of one going thither.

On Friday the 20th of June, therefore, we left Tabriz at [three of the afternoon, which is] the hour of none, and we slept that night at a castle that is called Sa'ídábád. The next day Saturday we dined at the village of Uján, and the night following we camped in the open. On Sunday in the forenoon we passed Seygan, and we dined at the village of Tunglár where the people were all Turkoman tribesmen. Our journey daily was now through the plains, the hill country being left behind, and the weather had come to be very hot. At each village where we halted they would bring us out food in abundance and serve it to us. Thus their custom was that on our coming to any place forthwith they would beg us to alight, and then seating us upon carpets that were spread on the grass in the shade, from the houses near by they would immediately bring us refreshments, namely bread and sour milk, followed by a soup that they are wont to prepare with rice and dumplings of dough. If we purposed to remain the night at any village, meat would then be cooked for us, seeing that what had gone before was merely as might be a refreshment following the afternoon stage. From Tunglár onwards it now became our custom to travel by night, for at this season, namely the month of June it is impossible to ride during the day hours on account of the great heat: further too by reason, during daylight, of the plague of gad-flies which abound thoughout this region, and indeed from their bites both men and beasts often die. Thus when we had come to this village of Tunglár although the heat of the sun was by no means excessive, yet that day the gad-flies already were become so numerous that the horses could hardly stand the annoyance of their stings, and do what we would to ward off their settling on our beasts these were all bleeding most terribly after that day's march.

Monday the day following at the hour of prime [that is 6 o'clock of the morning] we had come to a village called Miyánah, and this name in Persian has the meaning of "Half-way." Here we remained all day and at nightfall very comfortably riding excellent horses proceeded on our journey traveling the night through: and these horses were provided for our use from the stables kept here for the messengers of Timur's service. On Tuesday at daybreak, that being the feast of Saint John [the 24th of June] we came to a great building [which was a Caravanserai] set here for the accommodation of travellers and for merchants on the road, and there we rested till the hour of vespers. While we were taking our ease here there appeared a messenger from the Prince Mirán Sháh, who is Timur's eldest [surviving] son,[3] and he informed us that the Prince had sent desiring that we should make forthwith all speed and come on to him at his camping ground near by that place where he was stationed with his troops. We therefore being provided with fresh horses from the government stables immediately mounted and as night fell rode on in obedience to his orders. After travelling all night however at dawn of day [as we came near the camping place] another messenger met us, who told us that the Prince had gone back to Sultáníyah, and that we must hasten to follow him thither, as he wished now to receive us at that city. We therefore continued our journey and by midday had come to a post-house where we found left to await us fresh government horses. This place was on the bank of a river, and we took a seasonable midday rest, starting again on our way in the late afternoon.

In the course of the night following we came to a place that is known as Zanján, and the most part of the town here is now uninhabited, but in former times they said this had been one of the greatest cities in all Persia. It stands in a plain lying between two ranges of high hills that are bare of forest. We noticed that the town wall had fallen to disrepair but within its circuit many fine houses and mosques were yet standing, and through its streets passed excellent water conduits, but these all now had gone dry being in disuse. They relate that Zanján was aforetime the city where King Darius had lived, this being the capital of his empire and occupied by him as his chosen and favourite abode. Further it was from here that he set forth at the head of his host when he went to combat Alexander the Great. We remained in Zanján resting the remainder of that night, and the morning of the following day, provided with fresh government horses, we rode on our way. We had been very hospitably entertained in Zanján by the people there who supplied us with all the food we needed, and especially with excellent fruit. On that Thursday the 26th of June, by midday we finally arrived at the great city of Sultáníyah where we found Prince Mirán Sháh the son of Timur awaiting our coming.

Now it is the custom in this country when any have their audience of the Prince that they should present him with some gift; we therefore on this occasion of our visit carried certain cloth-stuffs of wool which are esteemed here, and

129

some other rare objects, and these we now intended to lay before the Prince for our offering. We were brought to him at one of his palaces which stands in a fine orchard, and there were many attendants-in-waiting present. He received us in a tent where his abode was that day established, and very graciously enquired of us as to the health of the King of Spain our master. After some time passed in talking they brought in food, and we all partook of this according to our various customs and modes of eating. Afterwards when the time came for us to take our leave the attendants brought in robes made of kincob [gold brocade][4] in which they dressed each of us ambassadors and we then returned to our lodgings This city of Sultáníyah stands in a plain, and it has no wall round it. In its midst however there is a great castle, built of stone, and this has many strong towers: these and the castle walls being adorned with blue tiles which give an enlaced pattern. In each of these towers there stands a small piece of cannon. Sultáníyah is a very populous city, but not so great as Tabriz; though it is a more important centre of exchange for merchants and their goods. In the months especially of June, July and August each year great caravans of camels with merchandise arrive here - they use this word " Caravan" for what with us would be any large company of beasts of burden. The city then is in a state of great commotion, and immense are the customs dues that accrue to the Treasury. Thus every year Sultáníyah is visited by numerous merchants from Lesser India[5] who bring with them all kinds of spiceries. Hither too are imported the best sorts of the lesser spices that are not to be found on sale in the Syrian markets, such namely as cloves, nutmegs, cinnamon, manna, mace and the rest. These are prime spiceries that never reach the markets of Alexandretta and hence are not to be procured in the warehouses there.

To Sultáníyah further is imported all the silk that is produced in Gílán which is a province that lies along the southern shore of the Caspian and where much of that commodity is produced and manufactured. This Gilán silk is exported from Sultáníyah to Damascus and other parts of Syria, also to Turkey and to Kaffa [in the Crimea] with the neighbouring lands. Further to Sultáníyah is brought all the silk made at Shamákhí [in Shirván] which is a place where much of this article is woven, and Persian merchants travel thither to buy it, also Genoese and Venetians. These countries where silk is made are all so hot that any strangers who go there suffer much from sunstroke, which indeed at times may kill; they say that the stroke goes straight to the heart, causing first vomitings and then death. To the sufferers their shoulders will seem to burn, and they say too that those who escape with their lives ever afterwards are yellow in the face or gray, never regaining their natural complexion. Again from the country round and about Shíráz which lies towards the border of Lesser India, they import to Sultáníyah many kinds of cloths woven of silk or cotton, and taffetas with crape-stuffs of various kinds; while from Yesen and Serpi and the province of Khurásán is brought much cotton both spun and in the raw state, and some woven into cloths of many colours. These the people use here and they are made up for wear. This province of Khurásán is a very great district lying between the lands of Tartary and the lands of India the Less, and very soon we were to pass through a part of it on our journey forward to Samarqand.

    The lands round Shíráz [lie to the southward of Khurásán and beyond is] the great city of Ormuz which of old was counted as of Lesser India, but at the present day is included in the dominions of Timur. From this port there is brought to Sultáníyah great quantity of pearls also many precious stones; for these are carried to Ormuz from Cathay by sea. The ships go up in ten days to this port [of Ormuz by the river Minao] after leaving the waters of the Persian Gulf which is the sea that here borders the lands of Persia. Now all the ships and boats that sail in the Persian Gulf are built having their planks put together without the, use of any iron nails, and in their place use is made of pegs of wood, further they stitch the planks together with twine. Were they not thus to construct them, but to use nails, the iron would be drawn out and the ships immediately fall asunder by reason of the quantity of loadstone that is found in these seas.[6] These ships therefore carry the pearls to Ormuz city, in order that there they may be pierced and strung, also they bring hither the rubies from Cathay where alone they are found of fine quality, further spiceries; and from Ormuz these commodities are dispersed in export to all parts of the western world. Now most of the pearls we have [in Spain] come from the seas of Cathay, and they are invariably brought to Ormuz to be bored and strung, for merchants, whether Christian or Moslem all agree that it is only by the skilled men of this city that the work can be perfectly carried out. The caravans that pass from Sultáníyah to Ormuz accomplish the journey in sixty days. They always tell us in the west at home that the pearl is produced in certain great shells which go by the name of Nacar [or Mother of Pearl]: but travellers who come from Ormuz and Cathay all agree that the pearl is the produce of an oyster, adding that the oysters in which pearls are found are of a very large size and white like paper. Pearls and [this Mother of Pearl] or Nacar with other like shells are imported thus to the cities of Sultáníyah. and Tabriz where they are worked up into rings and ear-rings. Every year therefore at this season aforesaid the merchants from Christian lands, namely from Kaffa and Trebizond, with Moslem merchants from Turkey, Syria and Baghdad all are wont to assemble together meeting at this city of Sultáníyah in order to carry out their business transactions.

    The city of Sultáníyah lies in a plain, and the town is intersected by many water conduits. We saw fine streets and squares where much merchandise was exposed for sale: while in all quarters hostels are to be met with very conveniently disposed for the accommodation of the merchants who come to the city. Beyond Sultáníyah to the eastward begin the great plains which continue on for a long space, and all the country here is well populated. On the right hand [south] is seen a range of high bare hills, with no forest and beyond lies the province known as Kurdistán. These hills are very savage and all the year round the snow lies on them. On the left hand side [north] there is another range of high bare mountains, where the climate is warm, and behind these comes the province that is known as Gílán; and it borders the Caspian which is a great inland sea, that has no communication with the outer ocean. From Sultáníyah over to the Caspian Sea is a distance of six day' journey. There are in the Caspian Sea certain islands, and from there they obtain diamonds. This province of Gílán has so hot a climate that no snow ever falls there: and lemon trees and limes and orange trees grow freely. The city of Sultáníyah is so full of commerce that a great sum in customs is brought in yearly to the Imperial Treasury.

In former years Sultáníyah and Tabriz with the whole kingdom of Western Persia all was under the government of Prince Mírán Sháh the eldest son of Timur, but in recent days he has been deposed from this government for reasons which we may now proceed to state. Prince Mirán Sháh when first he was established as viceroy in Persia had appointed to him a great host of troops and many nobles whom his father had sent to attend on him. When he had come into residence at Tabriz the mania of madness took him to demolish all houses: ordering the mosques and very many great public buildings also to be pulled down: and much of this demolition was in fact carried through. Then leaving Tabriz he came on to Sultáníyah, where he began to order the accomplishment of the like ruin. Next entering the great castle at Sultáníyah, where his father had caused much treasure to be stored, he ordered this forthwith to be distributed among the nobles and his personal attendants. Standing some distance outside the city is an immense [mosque and] palace of many apartments that was built in past times by a certain great lord, whose body was later buried here in a magnificent tomb.[7] Mírán Sháh now gave command to have the whole of this edifice demolished, and by his orders the body of the founder that lay buried there was forthwith thrown out lying on the ground to perish dishonoured. Some say the Prince did all these things by reason of the madness that had overtaken him: but according to another report he was heard at one time saying to himself: "Forsooth I am the son of the greatest man in the whole world, what now can I do in these famous cities, that after my days I may be always remembered?" He therefore began to build, but soon came to note that nothing of what he built was better than what had already been built by others before him. Considering this he was heard to say: "Shall nothing remain of me for a remembrance?" and added "They shall at least remember me for some reason or other": and forthwith commanded that all those buildings of which we have spoken should be demolished, in order that men might say: that though Mírán Sháh forsooth could build nothing, he yet could pull down the finest buildings of the whole world.

At last in Samarqand Timur his father came to know of these matters, and he immediately set out to visit his son. When Mírán Sháh heard that his father had arrived in Sultáníyah, taking a rope he put it about his neck and then coming into his father's presence besought of him forgiveness. Timur indeed was on the point of putting his son to death, but his relatives and the great lords interceding obtained at last pardon for Mírán Sháh, but Timur none the less deprived him of his attendant officers and terminated his viceroyalty in the government of Persia which he had hitherto held. Next calling up his grandson, namely Abu Bakr Mirza a son of Mírán Sháh, Timur spoke to him saying: "Thy father has erred, wherefore do thou now take over his lands and government." His grandson Abu Bakr however answered that standing in the sight of God he could never dare hold what his father had held; he begged his grandfather to forgive Mírán Sháh his father and then after a delay re-instate him in his command. Timur however when he understood that Abu Bakr Mirza would not comply with his wish called for another of his grandsons, and this prince was [Khalíl Sultán] the son of Mírán Sháh [by his second wife]. He now eagerly consented to assume his father's government with the command of the troops in Persia; for he indeed was ever the rival of his brothers and in opposition to his father, and would fain have compassed their destruction: a matter that will be touched on more fully later. Now it was very shortly after these happenings that Timur had overcome the Sultan of Cairo taking possession of Egypt with Aleppo and Baghdad. The overlordship of these countries he therefore bestowed on his grandson Abu Bakr who had, as we have said, declined to be made viceroy of Persia in his father's room, and Mírán Sháh in company with Abu Bakr Mirza now passed over into Mespotamia where the latter was instilled governor-general. But his father Mírán Sháh is by him treated with every respect and he too resides there.[8]

At the time when all these mad doings of Mírán Sháh were taking place his wife the Princess Khánzádeh very secretly had left him, and travelling day and night come to the court of her father-in-law Timur whom she informed of what his son Mírán Sháh had been doing, and was about to do. She reported that her husband intended to rebel and seize on the sovereignty. Timur took the matter in hand [as already said] and received his daughter-in-law honourably, keeping her with him, and indeed the Princess Khánzádeh never afterwards returned to her husband. She is the mother of his son who is the Prince Khalíl Sultán [mentioned above as now established as the viceroy of Persia]. The Prince Mírán Sháh his father [whom we, as described, had just visited and seen] is a man of advanced age, being about forty years old, big and fat, and he suffers much from the gout.

Chapter IX

Sultáníyah to Níshápúr

ON Sunday the 29th of June we took our departure and left the city of Sultáníyah, where we had sojourned during three days, being now provided with excellent horses from the government stables, and that night we slept at a village that is called Sáin Qal'ah. The next morning passing on we came at midday to a very large hamlet known as Abhar, and that same evening reached the village of Sagzíábád where we slept: this is a large place surrounded by many well irrigated orchards. The following day Wednesday we came to a castle that had been but recently left in ruins and depopulated. They related to us that Timur with his host had passed through this place, it might be about a month before our coming, and because he had failed to find here a proper supply of corn and no straw or even hay for feeding the cattle and horses of his host, he had allowed his men to supply the lack from the standing crops which were then ripe. After which the camp-followers of the army, when Timur had passed on, immediately had turned to rob and plunder all that was left in the place, for which reason it had been abandoned by its inhabitants. We however now found here encamped a company of men who had charge of over a hundred horses, of those as already explained that are kept for the government service. Travelling from Sultáníyah to this place indeed we had already passed two stations where there had been no government horses ready for us or procurable for our journey onwards: but on that Thursday the 3rd of July good horses were immediately provided for our use and we set forth from the castle aforesaid arriving about midday at the town which is called Shahraqán[1] where we were given excellent lodgings and such food as we needed.

While resting here a message was brought us from a certain noble, whose name was Bábá Sheykh and it was to the effect that the great Timur his master had laid an injunction on him to entertain us ambassadors in passing with due and honourable hospitality. He therefore now sent us an invitation that we should presently come and visit him at the city where he was living. For the moment however we delayed and remained at our ease in this town of Shahraqán where we stayed for that Thursday and Friday till Saturday, on which day we were supplied with fresh horses from the government stables. Leaving at sundown we travelled through the night and the following forenoon when we arrived by midday on Sunday the 6th of July at a town that is called Tehrán, where we found the lord Bábá Sheykh awaiting our coming. Indeed he had proceeded forth to meet us, and now led us in to the city where they lodged us in the hostelry that it was customary for Timur himself to occupy when he was come into these parts, and it was the finest house in all the town. Monday the day following Bábá Sheykh sent early inviting us to come to him, and as we were arriving near to his house he himself sallied forth bringing us in doors, when he bestowed us on a dais and took his seat beside us. Next he sent messengers to call those ambassadors of the Sultan of Cairo who were travelling along with us thither, saying they too must come and visit him: being charged with the embassy from Egypt with gifts for Timur brought for presentation. A great feast was then prepared for our entertainment: and among the rest of the viands was a horse, roasted whole including its head. As soon as we had partaken of his hospitality Bábá Sheykh informed us that next day we must travel on from Tehrán to a certain place where a great Mirza, who was son-in-law to Timur, was in camp, and to whom by Timur's orders we were enjoined to pay our respects. Then, as we were about to take our leave of him, Bábá Sheykh commanded that they should robe me Ruy González in a dress of kincob [gold brocade] together with a hat, and this he did saying I should accept these as a mark of the esteem which his master Timur cherished for the King our master.

The town of Tehrán is a very large place: it is surrounded by no town wall: and it is a delightful abode being a city furnished with every convenience. The climate however they say is not healthy, and the heat here is very great in summer. The territory in which it lies is known by the name of Ray, that being a district of very considerable extent, and most productive; it is of the government of that son-in-law of Timur mentioned above whom we were now about to visit. Our journey from Sultáníyah to Tehrán had been across the plains, these are everywhere well populated, and the climate here is pleasantly warm. On Tuesday following at nightfall we left Tehrán and after travelling about two leagues we saw on our right hand the buildings of a great city entirely abandoned and in ruin. Many of its towers however were still standing, and we noticed the remains of some of its mosques. This was the City of Ray,[2] which was in the past the largest town in all these parts but now it was entirely uninhabited. On the Wednesday following we came to a village in the mountains that is called Lanaza for our road now had left the plains and we were travelling across the hills to reach the place where that Prince who was Timur's son-in-law was encamped. We left Lanaza in the afternoon and that night slept in the open.

On Thursday the 10th of July at the hour of midday mass, we were met by a troop of horsemen who told us that their master the Prince was now near by in camp with his Horde [the Tartars of his command] and he desired that we should halt to await the coming up of our colleague the ambassador of the Sultan of Egypt in order that we might both together be ushered to his presence. We therefore halted for a time and as soon as the people from Cairo had joined us we came on in two detachments riding up to near the place where the Horde was encamped. All dismounting here they forthwith set up a tent for us to wait in till the Prince should be ready to receive us. In less than an hour he sent for us to come to him, and we found him seated under a pavilion set up outside his camp. He then caused us all to be seated before him, and treating us very courteously ordered food to be served; and after we had partaken of this he dismissed us to go to our camp, saying that the next day we should return to feast with him. No sooner had we got back to our tents than forthwith they sent in great quantity of victuals, such as bread and flour together with several live sheep for slaughter. On the following day we came to feast with the Prince, and great was the abundance of cooked meats, prepared after their mode and custom, namely roast horse flesh and boiled tripe of the same, and at this feast a great company was present. After we had all partaken the Prince gave us to understand that we should, by the expressed wish of Timor, now display to him, the Prince, those presents of which we were the bearers to the lord Timor. Further we were informed that the said presents were now to be taken from us and forwarded by dispatch to his Highness. We therefore complied and as soon as the Prince had viewed our gifts he ordered some of his men with escort of camels immediately to take charge of the same, to bring them without delay to that camp of rest where Timur might now be come to [on his march home to Samarqand]

The Prince now gave orders that horses from the government stud should be provided for our onward road; and when finally we took our leave of him he bestowed on each of us ambassadors a robe of kincob, and to me Ruy González in addition he gave a fine horse. This was an ambling hack, a roadster of the breed that with them is greatly esteemed; it was fully caparisoned with saddle and bridle made after the Tartar fashion. Further he bestowed on me a shirt and a hat. The name of the Prince our host was Sulaymán Mirza,[3] and he was one of those nobles who stood highest in the favour of Timur, and he wielded great power. The place where we had found him encamped was on meadow lands that bordered a stream in a valley enclosed by high mountains quite bare of forest. It was a very beautiful place and a pleasant abode at that season of the summer, and the hill range here is known as the mountain of Lar.[4]

The Prince's camp consisted of some three thousand tents. He was Timur's son-in-law by reason of having married the daughter of his Highness. In the camp with him under his charge was a grandson of Timur, named Sultan Ahmad Mirza, who was in bad health. This youth as soon as he heard about the gerfalcons which we were bringing as a gift from our King for presentation to Timur forthwith sent word to Sulaymán Mirza beseeching him to demand of us in his behalf one of those falcons; asserting that his grandfather would certainly not grudge him this as a gift. Sulaymán Mirza knowing well that it would be perfectly agreeable to Timur that the youth should keep one of those falcons sent to us to forward the request. We on this represented to Sulaymán Mirza that in these matters what had been entrusted to us for presentation to Timur was a gift of extraordinary rareness, such that none but his Highness might receive. The answer however came back that this young prince was a great Bahádur of the blood royal, and further being sick and in bad case he, Sulaymán Mirza, would ask us to comply with this request, asserting that the same would undoubtedly please Timur his grandfather. They further related to us how this young noble, on the day when Timur his grandfather was giving battle [at Angora to Báyazíd] the Sultan of Turkey, had been stationed with the body-guard standing round his Highness. At a certain moment Timur ordered these guards to charge the enemy,

141

and the youth had loudly complained that his grandfather in negligence had not given him leave to go with them but had left him standing idle. His grandfather had given him no answer, and in rage at this refusal to listen to him the young man had thrown off his helmet, and bare-headed had rushed into the battle where he had fought helmetless all that day.

On Saturday the 12th of July we took our departure from Sulaymán Mirza's camp. That day both Gómez de Salazar and [Fray Alfonso Paez] the Master in Theology were feeling ill, and I myself, Ruy González also had lately been unwell [of the fever] though now I was come to be somewhat better. Many of our fellow Spaniards our attendants were also now very unwell, and Sulaymán Mirza in consultation pointed out that seeing the long journey before us these sick folk ought not to go forward lest they should die on the march. He advised that we should leave all those sick [of the fever] with him to recover their health, and this we concluded to do, seven of our men staying behind, among whom were numbered two of the squires whom I, Ruy González had brought to attend me, one other squire who had accompanied the Master in Theology, and a boy who had come with Gómez de Salazar. These, with others making seven sick men in all, were now sent back to Tehrán to await us when we should return [and later we took them up] though as will he found two of their number had in the interval died of the sickness. On the day we set out from the encampment of the Horde we slept that night in the open on the bank of a river: and the evening of next day Sunday likewise we were in camp beside another river, and Monday which was the 14th of July at midday we reached the castle which is known as Fírúzkúh. It was here we had news that Timur had passed by this fort only some twelve days previously on his homeward journey to Samarqand. He had left orders that we should follow on without delay, adding that he intended to receive us immediately on his arrival at Samarqand, but not before; and this was because he wished us to come to him in his great capital city of Samarqand. Samarqand indeed was the first of all the cities that he had conquered, and the one that he had since ennobled above all others, by his buildings making it the treasure house of his conquests.

As regards Fírúzkúh, Timur during his passage through these lands had cause to besiege the castle and had left it in a ruined condition, which had befallen only some fifteen days prior to our arrival. The cause of these happenings was that up to that former date Fírúzkúh had been held in garrison by [Iskandar Sheykh] one of Timur's commanders to whom he had always shown much favour, he having granted him the lordship of that castle with the adjacent lands.[5] But lately for some action Timur had seen reason to be displeased with him, and had ordered him to be arrested and sent prisoner to Samarqand, under charge of a certain captain whom Timur had detailed for this duty. When however this captain had appeared before the walls of Fírúzkúh the men of the garrison had sallied out and taking him prisoner had brought him into the castle under guard. Timur hearing of these doings had forthwith appeared in person before its gates, during thirty days he had closely invested the stronghold, and the garrison finding that they could no longer hold the castle had made their escape by night, having given up their rebel commander to Timur. It is said that Fírúzkúh was so strong a place that none could carry it by assault, if the garrison were in sufficient number, for the fortress crowns a height that rises above the plain entirely detached from the neighbouring hills. At the foot of the castle in the plain it is encircled by a wall defended by towers, and within this wall is the township; above this lower town wall is another higher up the slope, and again a third wall higher up still which is defended by its towers. Between these last two walls there

143

were houses for the townsfolk, and above rose the bastions of the central fort with curtains very strongly built and flanked by many towers. Thus it is that though Fírúzkúh is within but a single fortress it is defended by three separate fortifications each one rising above the one below. Further in the fortress is found a copious spring of water gushing forth, sufficient to supply all its people, while the whole of the hill on which the fortifications are set, is almost encircled below by a river, crossed by drawbridges that alone give access to the lower walls of the fort and the township.

On Tuesday the 15th of July we left Fírúzkúh before dawn of day and slept that night in the open, doing the same the next night of Wednesday, for during both those days we passed by no inhabited villages, the road being very rough crossing steep mountain passes. The weather these days was hot, and we lacked for drinking water, very little being to be had. During [the afternoon of] Thursday we finally came to [Ahuván], a large town which stands on the bank of a stream, and it was defended by two castles which however had both been lately dismantled.[6] Then travelling forward on that same Thursday, which was the 17th of July, by fall of night we had come to a city that is called Dámghán which stands in the plain, and is surrounded by an earthen rampart, with a castle on the one side. This city of Dámghán is of the province of Media and is the last of the chief towns of Western Persia that we passed through. That day there arose upon us a hot wind that blew most fiercely, and the air was such as seemed to come from the mouth of hell. Then one of those gerfalcons [that we were carrying to present to Timur] was suddenly so overcome by this heat that it died being as it were suffocated for want of breath.

Outside Dámghán at the distance of a bowshot we noticed two towers, built as tall as the height to which one might cast up a stone, which were entirely constructed from men's skulls set in clay. Besides these there were other two similar towers, but these appeared already fallen to the ground in decay. These skulls were those of certain Tartars of the Aq Quyunlu clan [already mentioned in a previous chapter],[7] who originally had been natives of the lands lying between Asia Minor and the Syrian border where Timur had passed through after conquering Sívás on his road down to Damascus, which city as related he had partially ruined. He had encountered by chance these folk on his path and they had given him battle, when being overcome they had all been made prisoners of war. After this Timur had deported the whole tribe to people the country round Dámghán which was at that time without any settled population. When the men had all been assembled here, in company with their families, they continued to live the life of nomads in the open country, even as they had lived in their former homes. But they had not afterwards settled down in peace, and soon began to desire to return to their lands in the west. Having first ravaged and then plundered all that country side, they set out from Dámghán to march back into the Syrian border. It however happened that Timur with his army was in this neighbourhood at the time, who coming to Dámghán fell on the Aq Quyunlu and slaughtered a great number of them. He had then commanded that these four towers should be built up with their heads, in layers, a layer of skulls being set alternately above the layer of clay bricks. Further Timur made proclamation throughout his army that whosoever should take one of the Aq Quyunlu prisoner should forthwith put him to death, no matter any promise of quarter that had been given. This therefore was done, and wheresoever later the army passed they put to death forthwith any of these folk whom they met. Thus you would come on ten of the Aq Quyunlu killed in one place, and again twenty of them dead in another, or it might be but two or three here or there. They told us that in this way more than 60,000 of this folk had thus been massacred. The people of Dámghán reported to us that very frequently flames, as of burning lamps, might be noticed flickering on the top of these towers of Tartar skulls.

We halted in Dámghán till the evening of the next day Friday, and then being supplied with government horses we departed travelling all that night. On Saturday morning we had come to a small village, where on account of the great heat we took refuge for the day-time and at nightfall again set out riding through the darkness till dawn of Sunday morning. That Sunday the 20th of July at [six o'clock] the hour of prime we had reached a large town called Bostám, and here we found a certain Tartar noble whose name was Ennacora awaiting our arrival. He had come hither to meet us by command of Timur, thus to show us honour. Forthwith he caused us to be provided with a suitable lodging, and he next himself very kindly came to visit us, for we were all at the time suffering much from indisposition. Seeing this state, and that we were not in condition to accept his invitation to come and feast with him, he caused us to be amply provided at our hostelry with meats and fruits. Later, after he deemed that we had thus refreshed ourselves with food, he sent begging us to come to him. This was in accordance with the commands that Timur had laid on him, namely to entertain us at the palace, and bestow on us the robes of honour which his Highness had ordered should be presented to us. We however were forced to send saying that unfortunately we found ourselves much indisposed, feeling so ill [with the fever] that we could not rise from bed to come to him, wherefore would he of his kindness hold us to be excused. But he sent again to us urging our attendance, and so pressed us that in the end Fray Alfonso the Master in Theology had to go, and him they forthwith on arrival invested with two robes of honour. Now the custom on these occasions is for the lieutenant of Timur, who may be charged with the bestowal of these robes, to make a great feast, when after partaking of meat, the guest is solemnly endued and vested; then he, to show his gratitude and respect for the honour his Highness does him, rises up and bends the knee thrice kneeling on the ground.

No sooner had our Master in Theology accomplished this ceremony than the lord Ennacora sent providing fresh government horses for us ambassadors and our people to mount, insisting that we should ride forward on our journey. Indeed he begged us now to set off immediately, and this he did in accordance with the injunction received from Timur that we should follow and come up with him as soon as possible, riding day and night without stop. We however sent to Ennacora saying that he must see how sick we were, and that we were unable to journey that day, and we besought him to let us rest in our lodgings for two days at the very least. The answer none the less came that he dared not let us rest even for a moment, for should Timur come to know of it this would assuredly cost him, Ennacora, his head. Do or say what we would therefore we had to go, though we were most loath being so weak [with fever] that we were more dead than alive when it came to mounting on horseback. To accommodate us in our sad state the good Ennacora provided that our saddles were each furnished at the saddle-bow in front with a small plank on which cushions were strapped, and on these we could lean and ease our weariness. Thus accommodated we now mounted and set off riding all that day and all the following night, when we arrived at dawn to rest at a deserted village of those parts. The next day Monday we had come to a certain great building that has been erected on the high-way here for the service of travellers. In all this region no villages or settlements are to be found during the space of two days' march along the road, and this is by reason of the excessive heat and drought of that countryside. The only water met with in this region is what has been laid to this Caravanserai, as it is called, by an underground conduit a whole day's march in length from the hills.

The next day Tuesday the 22nd of July we came to a town which is called Jájarm, and the heat that day was very great. Jájarm stands in a plain at the foot of some bare mountains, and from these they have tunnelled conduits to bring water to the town. Standing in the midst of the city there is a castle crowning a low hillock artificially built up on clay foundations, and the town itself has no wall round it. During the past winter much snow had fallen, and this, when the summer heat had set in, had melted and flooded the water conduits. A freshet had recently come down, and half the town had been destroyed by the waters, which too had overwhelmed the castle. Further the floods had drowned out all the cornlands. Our road thither that previous day had been over a level plain, and on this there are neither stones nor boulders. All this country-side is very hot and the ground is everywhere scored with gulleys, though very few streams are met with. As soon as we had arrived at Jájarm they served us with an abundance of food, but immediately providing fresh horses we were forced to mount again and ride on. With us came that Tartar lord Ennacora whom Timur had sent to meet us and who treated us with every respect, causing us at all points to be supplied with provisions and everything that we needed. It was too through his orders that daily along the way we were provided stage by stage with fresh mounts from the government studs as we passed by, and thus they hastened our going.

All along this route [as has been already noticed] Timur causes horses to be kept stationed ready for use at post-stages, in one place there may be a hundred in another two hundred horses, and this is the case right up to Samarqand. These are kept for the service of the special messengers or envoys sent to distant places by Timor, or for the use of such envoys as may be coming to him, and such as come and such as go may ride these horses day and night without halt. These government studs are stationed both in those desert or uninhabited regions along the route, and in places where there is a settled population, further for this service there have been built caravanserais at divers intervals, where there are stables for the horses with hostelries: the same being supplied with needful provender provisioned from the towns and villages adjacent. These government horses are cared for by men appointed to see to them, who are as we say postillions, being known here under the name of Yamchis. When any envoy sent by Timur, or any messenger carrying despatches to him arrives at one of these post-houses forthwith they unsaddle the horses that have come in, and saddle fresh beasts of those they keep. Then forward with the envoy will ride a postillion or may be two of those Yamchis, aforesaid, who are in charge of their horses, and these on arrival at the next post-house return thence with the beasts that they have brought thus far. After this fashion the messenger will pass along continuously: but should ever the horse that envoy is riding tire on the road, and by chance should he meet with any other horse whatever in these parts, - for instance should he come on one riding a horseback for his pleasure or business, - the messenger will take that horse, making the rider give it up, the Yamchi in attendance being then held responsible for the animal thus taken on loan, in place of the government horse discarded.

Indeed the universal custom is that any man riding his way, be he ever so great a lord, or any merchant or private citizen, should such an one meet an ambassador going to Timur, or some messenger riding with despatches from his Highness by post, forthwith, on demand, he must set foot to ground and give him up his horse, namely to him who thus comes from Timur or to him who rides to his Highness. No one in this case can refuse, or it will cost him his head, such is the invariable order. After this way indeed may be taken any of the horses of the cavalry stationed here or there on duty, and we too frequently were thus served, taking up the horses of the troopers whom we met on the road, either for ourselves or for the accommodation of our attendants, forcing these men to walk afoot after us to bring their horses back. And it is not only from the like to these that we should have borrowed their horses, but even maybe from the prince Timur's own son, or from one of his wives for even her riding horse might be demanded should the need occur. We were told that on one occasion Timur's eldest son and his attendants had to dismount and give up their horses to certain envoys who were on their road to the Court. Further it was not only on this one high-road [to Samarqand] that his Highness has organized this system of post-horses, for in all other parts of his kingdom and domains similar establishments are kept, in order that he may with all speed have news, by night and day, his messengers passing continuously without let or hindrance. Timur indeed sets much store that those he sends and those who come to him should ride post day and night. So doing they may easily cover fifty leagues in the twenty-four hours, though by thus riding they will kill two horses. But this may be, rather than to take three days over that journey: for he deems speed to be much to his service.

Now Timur had observed that throughout the region round and about Samarqand, also in the rest of Mongolia, the leagues in use were over long. He therefore divided each of these great leagues into two, and he caused small turrets to be set up to mark the league end. It was then established that the Chagatay messengers who carried despatches must cover twelve of these shorter leagues in the day's ride or at least ten. These short leagues go here by the name of Moles, it is said by reason of those turrets being so called set up league by league. The new system was at first only established for use in the country of Mongolia, and when we passed through later on our journey we noticed these turrets marking the league end as we rode along. It is to be understood further that one should count as of two Castilian leagues the length of each of these Mongolian leagues. Verily it is scarcely to be believed, had we not ourselves seen it and thus we can vouch for the truth, what a distance these riders can compass in a day and a night, for they ride their horses to the death, and exceeding the commands of Timur will cover fifteen, nay even twenty, of those great leagues in the twenty-four hours. They spare in nowise their horses and break their wind: then should the horse succumb under the strain, they will proceed to take off the hide of the dead horse and sell the same in the place where they may be passing. By the road-side many were the dead horses we saw during our journey, which had been thus ridden to death and the carcass abandoned: the number indeed a marvel to note.

We left the town [of Jájarm Wednesday morning the morrow of] the day we had arrived there[8] and travelled all that day and all the following night without a halt, for though we would fain have taken some rest our guides did not allow us to halt. The heat all this time, even during the hours of night, was most overpowering, and indeed phenomenal for a strong hot wind blew ceaselessly that seemed to burn us up. Then Gómez de Salazár [of the Royal Guard] our companion ambassador became this night exceedingly ill, so that we thought incontinently he would have died, and during the whole of our journey this day [Wednesday we were athirst and] could come to no water to drink. When night fell we had still to go on, only halting the space to give the horses a feed of barley. The next day [Thursday] we continued to travel passing by no inhabited places and only at late nightfall reached the city that is called Isfaráyin.[9] This is a very large place with many fine buildings both private houses and mosques, but all is now for the most part without inhabitants. We could only remain here for a time to dine: then they gave us fresh horses and we rode on during that night. The next day Friday we came about the hour of midday to an uninhabited village, where from another place a league distant off the road they brought us hither food and what was necessary for our entertainment. Then when it came to the hour of vespers we set off again travelling all that night and our way lay through a great plain. The next day Saturday the 26th of July we had reached the great city that is called Níshápúr.

About a league before coming into Níshápúr the road crossed a district where there were many orchards well irrigated by numerous streams of water, and in this plain we saw a great camp of some four hundred tents. These we found were not of the common sort, but long and low and made of black felt. In occupation of the same were folk known as the Alavari [who are nomad Kurds] they own no other habitations than their tents, for they never take up their abode in any city or village, but live in the open countryside, both summer and winter, pasturing their flocks. These consist of droves of rams, ewes and cows, and the people of this particular tribe possess some twenty thousand camels. They wander over the length and breadth of all this province living under the jurisdiction of Timur, and they give him yearly as his due in tribute three thousand camels, also some fifteen thousand sheep. These they deliver willingly for the privilege of pasturing their flocks on his lands. As soon as we had come up with these nomads their headmen came out to us from the encampment and brought us in. They seated us in the largest of their tents, setting before us bowls of milk and cream with some bread according to the custom of the country. Then we took leave of them and rode into Níshápúr.

Now this day perforce we had had to leave Gómez de Salazar behind in a village we had passed, he having become too ill to sit his horse and ride any further.

The city of Níshápúr lies in a plain, and it is surrounded by many orchards with houses there appertaining. As soon as we had arrived in the city they brought us to a fine lodging, and the chief men of the town attended bringing provisions, namely meat with fruits, such as melons which are here of large size and excellent flavour, further there was no lack of wine. When we had thus partaken of their hospitality they next presented to each of us ambassadors a robe of kincob [gold brocade]. This was all in accordance with the express command of Timur, he having given instructions that in every city that we passed though we should be presented with a horse or in lieu thereof a robe of honour. Now about five leagues before we had come to this city of Níshápúr there had met us a certain lord who was a marshal in the army of Timur and his name was Melialiorga. He informed us that he had been sent hither to meet us by special order of Timur himself that we might be received with all honour, and that everything should be supplied to us that we might need.

When therefore Melialiorga had been informed by us that Gómez de Salazar was not present, having been left behind as already said in a certain village being too ill to mount a horse, he forthwith himself rode to that place to take measures for his comfort. He found our poor companion to be so weak as to be unable to rise from his bed, and a litter forthwith was ordered to be brought, in which Gómez being placed men carried him thus shoulder high stage by stage and from one rest-house to another until they had come with him to us who were anxiously waiting in the city of Níshápúr. On arrival he was immediately accommodated in all comfort, and physicians of reputation, of whom there was no lack, were summoned to attend him, but to no avail for it pleased

God in spite of all we could do that Gómez de Salazar very shortly after this ended his life.

The city of Níshápúr is a large place and it is well supplied with all commodities being a very pleasant abode. It is the capital town of the province of Media, and near here are situated the celebrated Turquoise mines. These gems are also to be found elsewhere in Persia, but those from the mine here are the finest that are to be come by. They are discovered in the earth in a certain place, and also in the bed of the river which flows down from the mountain that rises up at the back of the city. The whole district of Níshápúr is very densely populated, and it is a most delightful place to live in. It is here that the province of Media ends and that the province of Khurásán follows on, which same is a district of very wide extent.[10]

Chapter X

Níshápúr to the Oxus

ON Sunday the 27th of July we left Níshápúr and travelling forward slept at a deserted uninhabited village. The next day Monday we came at nightfall to a large town called Ferrior, from which we found that the inhabitants in greater part had also fled. This was in mistrust of the soldiers of Timur's army; and it was now about twelve days since he and the Tartar host had passed through this place, where in truth very visibly the troops had wrought much havoc. To us ambassadors however such of the inhabitants as remained none the less gave good entertainment, adding as a present for our acceptance the usual robe of kincob [gold brocade]. The country round and about this place is a waste plain, and the climate is here very hot. On Tuesday following by nightfall we had reached a large town known by the name of Asegur but after resting some few hours we set out again while it was still night and travelling on by morrow midday and at the hour of dinner had arrived at a great city which is called Okhakhan. This was Wednesday the 30th July, and in this city we were most honourably entertained, for they feasted us and supplied all our needs, bestowing on us robes of kincob as usual and aforesaid.

It was here that an envoy reached us coming from Prince Sháh Rukh who is Timur's youngest son. The message he brought was an invitation from the Prince that we should be pleased to turn aside going to visit him at the city where he resided which is called Herát. This place is some thirty leagues distant from where we were and to the right from the Samarqand road in the direction of India. The Prince promised us a very honourable reception and that throughout his government we should be everywhere supplied with all that

155

was needed for our comfort and entertainment. We therefore sought counsel with that nobleman [Melialiorga] who had been sent as our conductor, and by his advice returned answer to Sháh Rukh Mirza that the lord Timur had given strict orders that we were to proceed without stopping and come to him with all possible speed [in the city of Samarqand]. Therefore we could not venture to turn aside from our straight road, even though it were to visit him who is the governor of the whole of this province of Khurásán and we begged his highness the Prince of his grace to hold us excused.

Having thus replied to the Prince's message we now proceeded on our way and next arrived at a city which is called Meshed [a name that signifies the Place of Martyrdom, of the Imán Rezá who is known as] the Sultan of Khurásán, he having his tomb in this city. He was in fact the [great great grandson of the great] grandson of the Prophet Mahomet, being descended from the daughter of the Prophet and is regarded by the native Persians as a Saint. He lies buried in the Great Mosque here in a sepulchre that is encased in silver and gilt. Meshed is the chief place of pilgrimage in all these parts, and yearly there come hither people in immense numbers on pious visitation. Any pilgrim who has been here, on returning home to his own country, his neighbours will come up to him and kiss the hem of his garment, for they hold that he has visited a very holy place. On our arrival here they brought us in to visit this sanctuary and the tomb, whereby when travelling later through other parts of Persia it came to be noised abroad that we had been at Meshed and visited this holy place the people would come and kiss the hem of our robes, deeming that we were of those who had acquired merit for having made the pilgrimage to the shrine of the great Saint of Khurásán. It is by the name Sultan Khurásán that this descendant of the Prophet Mahomet is here most commonly known, and the whole province has received its name from him. Khurásán is indeed a country to itself [for it forms no part of Persia Proper], but its language none the less is Persian.[1]

On Thursday the last day of July we came on from Meshed to a great city which is called Buelo [the same is Tús] and of the Khurásán province likewise. This is a most pleasant township, and it has a greater population than any other place that we had come to since leaving Sultáníyah. In this city we halted for the last hours of that day Thursday, for the authorities were engaged in getting together provisions of food for man and beast for our benefit during the next stage, since this would be to cross the desert, where there are neither inhabitants nor habitations for the space of fifty leagues. When therefore we had dined that same evening they brought us fresh horses, which we were to mount and ride crossing this desolate region, and at night-fall we set off leaving [Tús] and rode on till dawn of Friday. All that day too we rode, and also the following night and day, before we came again to any place where we found settled folk. On the Saturday however, which was the [2nd] of August at last towards evening we came to a valley. Here much ground was under cultivation for wheat, and a river [the Tejend Áb][2] ran through the place, on whose banks we found numerous tents pitched where the Chagatays of Timur's Horde were out in camp. These folk were stationed here with their flocks of sheep, and herds of camels with droves of horses, and they had stayed behind the rest of the host to give their beasts pasture on the rich grass: further they all were to be numbered for taxation.

At this place on arriving we were met by another noble of the court, sent to attend us by injunctions of Timur. He was to do us honour in all possible ways, and to see to our being well supplied with food, and with horses for the onward journey. Hence it was that we always found supplies ready to hand at every stage we came to, also beasts to carry us swiftly on our way. This lord who now met us was named Mirabozar, and presenting himself before us he announced that Timur his master had sent him to convey to us his Highness's greetings, adding that he, Mirabozar, was here ready to accompany us onwards to act as our guide and companion serving us in all matters of need. Our guide hitherto [namely the lord Melialiorga] was from this point relieved of his charge, and Miraboiar took his place, as by Timur's orders, but [Melialiorga] and his men still kept on with us, and were supplied day by day at all the stages with rations of food for man and horse as regards himself and his following, and they attended us in all ways that could be to our comfort. Such indeed is the custom of the country, namely, that at every stage on arrival, were it a city or a township or a village, provision had immediately to be forthcoming to victual us and the whole of our company in attendance. Fruit had to be brought with barley for the horses, and this in supply three times as great as there was any need. The head man of the place further had to send a guard to keep watch day and night over us and our goods and our horses: and should aught come to be missed, those of the township or settlement, where at the time we happened to be halting, had fully to make the loss good. Wheresoever we might come and whensoever, no matter at what hour, if those of the settlement or township did not forthwith very quickly bring all that was required, they received merciless blows and beatings, suffering the same in a manner that we marveled to witness.

He who might be at the time our guide would send imperiously for the head men of the city or village or settlement to which we had come, and these would be brought before that lord who had charge of us, and the first words spoken would be seasoned with a very sound beating, bestowed then and there and with no lack of vigour: as was a wonder to witness. Then the men would be informed that it was the express command of Timur, as they must well know, that all envoys on their arrival in any place, should be met and received with honour, and supplied with every possible need: and seeing that we the Frank Ambassadors, whom they saw, had come to them, and that they, the head men, had made as it seemed no suitable reception, thus flouting the known commands of the lord Timur, it was now due for them the head men in the first place to suffer a beating, and in the next place for the people of the township to pay heavily of their goods for this negligence, whereby they would in future have a care to prepare for the arrival of Ambassadors, and make better arrangements for their reception. Thus it was ever that on our arrival at any township or village the [chief of the Tartars of our] escort, or those who were in charge of us, would call for the Reis, as these folk name the head man of the place, and to act as guide [our Tartar lord] would seize on the first person come to in the street making him prisoner. Now these Persians here about are wont to wear on their heads [a sort of turban] made by winding round in folds a long strip of cloth stuff:[3] this a [Tartar] horseman will snatch off and undoing throw it round that man's neck and thus holding will tie him to his horse bringing the poor fellow up to his stirrup. Then giving kicks and blows they drive on forcing the Persian villager to discover the house of him known as the Reis.

Hence it is that the people of that village or town when they see what is going forward, knowing [these Tartars] to be the men of Timor's armies riding on some government errands, forthwith take to flight with all speed as though indeed the Devil were after them. The merchants in shops who are selling their goods immediately set to to close their shutters, taking to flight like the rest or hiding in their houses. As they go they will call out one to another "Elchi" - meaning "the Ambassadors" – for with the arrival of ambassadors they

159

know that a black day is on them. Thus the folk go running away as though the Devil in person were at their heels. It is indeed as though the very host of Satan were present when these [Tartars] arrive in any place, what with the turmoil and commotion of their coming, and the pitiless acts that they do. When they have found the Reis or head man of the place, do not imagine that they speak courteously to him: nay they will insult him and then give him stripes and blows with the mace, making him run before them and fetch out all that the ambassadors may need. Next they make the wretched head-man stand and humbly serve them, not letting him go until he receives their permission.

Now you must understand that we the Spanish Ambassadors and the Ambassadors of the Sultan of Egypt had ridden in company together since we had left [Fírúzkúh] where Timur's son-in-law [Sulaymán Mirza] had entertained us; and throughout, after the fashion just described, during all the time of our journey these [Tartars of the escort] had acted, while providing for our service. But these men always behave thus, without either consideration or pity, when they travel passing through on any other business of the government, for they boast that in carrying out the commands of their lord Timur, they may press to his service, even to kill, all and any, for none may oppose them. Every man must keep silent whatever may be done by him, the messenger, who is carrying out the lord Timur's behest. He may call upon the captain-general himself of the army to serve, or to provide for the service of the government messenger. And indeed it was ever a marvel to us to note how throughout the whole countryside everyone lived in terror of these messengers who were the bearers of Timur's commands.

On the present occasion when we had reached the tents of the Chagatays [by the Tejend river, Mirabozar] our guide promptly made the people bring us out cooked meat with rice, and next milk and sour cream, all of which they set before us adding many melons, which in this country are in abundance and of excellent quality. These Chagatays with whom we were thus guests are a nomad folk living in tents and booths, for indeed they possess no other more permanent habitations, both summer and winter living in the open. In summer they pass to the plains beside the river, where they sow their crops of corn and cotton, and tend the melon beds: and their melons I opine are the very best and biggest that may be found in the whole world. They also raise crops of millet, a grain which forms their chief food, and which they eat boiled in sour milk. In the winter season these Chagatays migrate to lands where the climate is fairly warm. After the like fashion indeed all the host of Timur moves from camp to camp living in the open, summer and winter. But since they fear no enemy they do not need to keep together for safety and the lord Timur will proceed with his own personal horde apart, accompanied by his servants and chief nobles and courtiers, with his wives and female relatives, while the rest of the horde passes elsewhere. Thus do they all spend their lives: for these [Tartars] possess great herds, namely of camels horses and sheep, also of cattle but of cows only few.

When Timur calls his people to war all assemble and march with him, surrounded by their flocks and herds, thus carrying along their possessions with them, in company with their wives and children. These last follow the host, and in the lands which they invade their flocks, namely and particularly the sheep camels and horses, serve to ration the horde. Thus marching at the head of his people Timur has accomplished great deeds and gained many victories, for the [Tartars] are a very valiant folk, fine horsemen, very skilful at shooting with the bow, and exceeding hardy. In camp should they have victuals in plenty they eat their fill: if they have lack milk and meat without baked bread suffices them, and for a long season they can thus march with or without halting to prepare bread stuffs, living on [the meat and milk of] their flocks and herds. They suffer cold and heat and hunger and thirst more patiently than any other nation in the whole. world: when food is abundant they gorge on it gluttonously, but when there is scarcity sour milk tempered with boiling water suffices them, and of this for sustenance there is never a lack. Sour milk, their special food, they prepare after the following fashion. They take and heat a great caldron full of water and before it boils they have made ready a bowl in which they have curds of sour milk, that is like cheese, which they have worked up to a paste with cold water. This is thrown into the boiling caldron, and the whole mass turns to be as sour as vinegar. Next they have kneaded very thin cakes of flour, which they bake and cut up in small pieces, afterwards throwing these into the boiling caldron. Then cooking awhile the fire is next with drawn, and the whole mess served out into bowls. This, which is a kind of soup, without other bread or meat they eat and are satisfied, and for the most part this is their daily food and nothing more. For their cooking fires they use no wood, but only the dried dung of their herds, and it makes the fire for all purposes of roasting and boiling; and this broth of theirs which has just been described goes by the name of Ash [which in the Persian language is Soup].

On the [Sunday] morning following we set out [from the encampment on the Tejend river] under escort of that lord [Mirabozar] whom Timur had sent to meet us, and as we shall explain we travelled without ever halting that day and the following night and the next day throughout never passing by any settlement or village. That first [Sunday] night we slept at a great caravanserai [which was the post-house] in the desert, where they gave the horses we had brought their barley, and here we learnt that the stage from [this caravanserai] to the next resting place was twelve long leagues. Some two hours after night-fall therefore we set out again, fresh good horses being provided at the post house for our use. All through that night we rode, and the heat not abating the air was most oppressive, also nowhere on the road did we come to any water. When morning came, which was Monday, we still continued our journey, and up to the hour of none [namely three o'clock of the afternoon] went on without finding water, good or bad, for man or horse to drink. We had so ridden hard all that last night and this day that the horses were now quite tired out, and barely able to go at a walk. Also by reason of the great heat of the sun that day on the road here over the sands they came near at last to perishing of thirst. We men too were very like to have succumbed for that same want of water, had not a youth in the service of our Master in Theology had a better horse than the rest, who now made haste to ride on ahead before us. Then fortunately at last he discovered a stream where taking off his smock he dipped it in the water and returned quickly bringing the smock to us, who as many as could quenched somewhat of our thirst thereby. Most of us indeed were like to have fainted from that great heat and the lack that we suffered of water to drink; and each man rode his own way. Our escort no longer was keeping up with us, and all struggled on as best might.

At length as the sun was about to set we came to a broad valley where many tents were pitched of the Chagatay folk, and distant beyond we saw the great river which is known as the Murgháb.[4] That ride now accomplished of the night and the two days, had been of the length of at least twenty leagues of those of Castile, and here at last we came to rest and passed the night. The next morning which was Tuesday we took horse again, but only rode for about two leagues when we reached a great building like a hostel, with us, which is called here a caravanserai. This we found to be occupied by the Chagatays who are in charge of the government post-horses, and we dined and rested there that afternoon. At the hour of vespers we mounted again, fresh horses having been provided for us from the stables of this post-house, and two hours after night fall came to the great plains where we found stationed the main encampment of the Chagatays of the Horde. Here at their tents we slept that night. The following day which was Thursday we again started, resting in the afternoon at a village, but that night we passed in camp in the open beside the Murgháb river. Friday the following day in the afternoon we took our rest at the tents of certain of the Chagatays here stationed, and later in the evening rode on, supplied with fresh horses of the government post, and that night slept in camp in the open.

On Saturday which was the 9th of August we halted to dine at a place called Salugar Sukhassa. This had been the property of a certain eminent Kashísh [or Mohammedan Priest] who as we might say had been like a [Moslem] bishop among the [Tartar folk]. The settlement was in a valley by the river bank, and the whole plain round was fully irrigated by watercourses [from the Murgháb]. The country here about was well populated, the valley being full of orchards with many fine vineyards. That [Moslem] Priest who had owned this property had died but recently, and he had left two young sons. To these youths Timur, who had passed through this place it might be some ten days or so back, had graciously granted his protection, but he had now carried them off to Samarqand in his train where they would be brought up at court. Their father, the [Moslem] Priest, had been a man of noble lineage, and the present owner of the settlement was his widow, the mother of these youths. She received us very honourably, coming even to call on us, and ordering needful supplies of victuals with all manner of comforts for our need: and this lady further came to dine in our company. That same evening at a later hour we took our departure, being provided with excellent horses, and riding through the night on the next day Sunday reached certain tents of the Chagatays where we dined and rested that afternoon and slept the night following. On Monday morning at dawn we started again riding all day and passed that night in the open desert.

In all these parts when we came to any tents [of these Tartars] they everywhere provided us with food and all necessaries. This was done even when the people we came to were the Horde of the army of Timur, for they too were obliged to provide us out of their stock with all that we might require. Their men had to serve us as guards by day or by night, being responsible for our goods and our horses. And indeed to supply our convenience we would often turn them out of their tents, which same were very comfortable to occupy; and when the next day's journey was to lie across a span of the desert we would take from them provisions of food for ourselves and barley for our horses with a supply of water, all given us freely and for nothing although the matter might be to them a very heavy charge. On the 12th of August which was Tuesday we came for our dinner and the afternoon rest to a great caravanserai standing in the plain, where [the Tartar] guards are stationed to look after the government post-horses. Later that evening at the hour of vespers we again mounted, and before long came to our night's lodging at a town which is known as Andkhuy. This was the native place of [Mirabozar] the noble whom Timur had sent to be our escort. The city of Andkhuy stands beyond the frontiers of Persia, being already of the Tajik Country,[5] and here the language spoken differs somewhat from the common Persian, though many of the words in use are the same as those common with that tongue. At Andkhuy they received us with all honour and we remained here from Tuesday the day of our arrival till Thursday the 14th of August. We were meanwhile sumptuously entertained, and wine of which much is made here was liberally set before us: further they presented us each with robes of [gold embroidered] kincob, further a horse. The city of Andkhuy lies in a plain and for two leagues all round it are seen orchards and vineyards with many hamlets, for all this land is fully irrigated with water courses.

In the evening of Thursday afore mentioned we left Andkhuy and came on to sleep at certain tents of the Chagatays standing in a plain and on the borders of a stream. This particular tribe of the Chagatays is a very privileged folk, enjoying the special favour of Timur. They are allowed to herd their flocks wheresoever they will, they may seek pasture and sow their crops in all districts, wandering summer and winter without let or hindrance. The clansmen are free of all burdens, and pay no government taxes, but they serve Timur constantly in his armies, personally fighting for him and acting as his guard. You are to understand further that none of these Chagatays, when on the march with the host, ever separate from their women and children or from their herds and flocks. These all march with them as they go to war, migrating from one place to the next. When thus on the way the women who have small children carry them along in little cradles which, as the woman rides on horseback, she lays on the saddle bow in front. Such cradles are conveniently supported by broad straps which pass round the body, and thus the children are carried along. Indeed the women appear to ride as comfortably and lightly thus burdened with their offspring as though they were free of them. The poorer folk have to load their families, with their tents, on their camels, but the children then are worse off than those who travel with their mothers on horse-back, for the camel goes with a much rougher step than the horse.

We were now meeting with those nomads on all hands, as they were wandering seeking pasture; we passing them as we travelled on our way, for the number of these Chagatays is immensely great. They appeared to us to be everywhere as we hurried by, here and there and in the distance. Every second league we would come on others, and the whole day often we were riding through their encampments. In fact we were never free of them, in great numbers too they were camped all round the towns, in all those places where water and pasture were to be met with. All these wandering Chagatay folk appeared to us with faces so burnt by the sun that for ugliness they might well have come straight out of hell itself, and as to their number, as already said, it seemed to us this was infinite. The country side in these parts is a plain and the climate is very hot: hence those of his horde and troops who go with Timur on the march for the most part travel by night. By day they have rest in some spot where both water and pasture are to be found, and then again they will travel on, closely following in Timur's footsteps.

On the occasion above mentioned we had come that afternoon to halt for rest in the tents of certain of those Chagatays, and at nightfall we again mounted and rode on. The next day which was Friday by mid-day we had reached a village where we had our dinner taking our afternoon repose, and that same night found ourselves in a great township of which I have forgotten to note the name.[6] This formerly had been a famous walled city of immense extent, but now the wall had fallen to ruin, and very many of the houses within it were uninhabited, though we noticed that there were many fine buildings and mosques yet standing. We slept here that night of Friday on our arrival and the next day Saturday, after they had bestowed on us a gift of robes of kincob [gold brocade], we took horse again and departed coming that same evening to some tents of the Chagatays where we slept. Sunday, on the morrow they provided us with excellent horses for the road: and that fore noon we set out again, but all that day the wind blew so violently that we were often almost unhorsed. The blast was so hot as to seem to be fire. The road lay over a sandy desert and this hot wind blew the sand over us so that we were at times blinded by it and at last began to lose our way.. Time and again we found that we had gone astray from the road, and finally the lord [Mirabozar] who was escorting us had perforce to send back a man to the Chagatay encampment for one of those folk to come and guide us. Then by God's mercy we at last reached a large village called 'Aliábád where we rested for the afternoon waiting for the going down of the wind, and then at night-fall came on to another village named Oosh: where our horses were given their barley.

That same night we again mounted and rode on, passing many small villages surrounded by their orchards, and by the Monday morning which was the 18th of August had come to the city of Balkh.[7] This city is very large and it is surrounded by a broad rampart of earth which along the top measures thirty paces across. The retaining wall flanking this rampart is now breached in many places, but inside this last the city proper is enclosed by two walls, one within the other, and these protect the settlement. The area between the outer earthen rampart and the first inner wall is not occupied by any houses and no one lives here, the ground being divided up into fields where cotton is grown. In the space between the second and the innermost wall there are houses, but still this part is not very closely crowded. The innermost circle of the city however is densely populated: and unlike the other towns which we had come to in these parts, and which lay open, the two inner walls of Balkh are extremely strong and as yet well preserved. They treated us with much honour in Balkh providing us amply with provisions and excellent wine. Further we were given a horse and a robe of kincob [gold brocade].

We left Balkh on the Tuesday going to our night's lodging in a village on the road. Wednesday we dined taking our afternoon rest in another township and that night slept out in the open. On Thursday the 21st of August we had come to the bank of that great river named the Áb-i-Amú [as the Persians call the Oxus] and this is one of the streams which flows down, it is said, from Paradise.[8] It is here a league in breadth and the current is extremely strong. The river traverses a great plain and its waters are muddy. In the winter season it runs very low for at that time the current up in the mountains is hard frozen and the snows as they fall remain unmelted. But when the month of April is come the stream begins to rise, and for the next tour months the flood continues to increase, after which season the water level goes back the like of what it was before. This flooding is due to the melting of the snows up in the mountains during the summer heats. During this last summer season indeed as they told us, the river had risen so high, going beyond its usual flood level, that a village that stood two thirds of a league distant from its usual bank and strand had been almost swept away by its waters, these having entered among the houses, whereby causing them to fall, much damage being wrought. The Áb-i-Amú takes its rise in the mountain region [to the north] of Lesser India[9] [or Afghanistan] flowing down through the plains of Samarqand finally passing out into the lands of Tartary, from whence the discharge of its waters is into the Caspian Sea; and thus [the Oxus] along its course is the boundary dividing the lordship of Samarqand from the lordship of Khurásán.

Chapter XI

The Oxus to Samarqand

THE lord Timur when he had completed his conquest of the land of Samarqand which lies as we have seen on the further side of the river Oxus, made up his mind to cross over that river and conquer the land of Khurásán to the south. He therefore caused a great bridge of wooden beams supported on boats to be made, whereby to cross, but as soon as he and his host had passed over he had caused the same immediately to be dismantled. Recently as we were told when he was returning home from his late campaigns, and journeying to Samarqand, for the passage of himself and his armies he had given instructions for the reestablishment of this bridge; which we who now had to pass the river were able to make use of for our passage. We were informed however that orders had already been sent by Timur a second time to dismantle the bridge even as he had done on the first occasion. And indeed we found that the bridge no longer stretched quite across to the further bank: however, beginning on the near side for a lengthy portion it stretched out over the waters, whereby our horses and sumpter-beasts could conveniently traverse, but suddenly at the end it failed [and we had to take to the ferry-boats]. It was in this great plain which here borders the Oxus that aforetime Alexander the Great fought his battle with Porus the Indian king whom he entirely defeated.

On Thursday the same day on which we had arrived at the left bank of the Oxus we crossed over to the land beyond, and that evening came on to a great city there which is called Tirmiz. In former times this was included in the lordship of India the Less, [or Afghanistan], but now is counted of the territory of Samarqand, for Timur has taken it for his own. The province of Samarqand begins from the north bank of the Oxus, and the land of this lordship is known as Mongolia, the language spoken here being the Mongolian tongue. This language is not understood to the south of the Oxus, where Persian only is spoken commonly by all folk; and indeed the two tongues have but little in common. Further the script in which those write who live in the land of Samarqand is strange and not read by those who live to the southward of the great river for this is the Mongol script, and Timur keeps with him scribes who can read and write this script for all his purposes.[1] The country here round and about, up to and even beyond Samarqand, is all very well populated, for the land is rich in crops, producing all that is needful to man and beast.

The common custom, as already mentioned, established by Timur in the matter of the passage of the Oxus is this, that as soon as he himself has passed over the river the bridge is ordered to be broken up; then after this, as none can cross by the bridge, boats have perforce to be used to carry folk from the one bank to the other. But none may be given passage from the province of Samarqand to go into the lands to the south of the river unless he have been granted a permit and warrant. This must declare whence he has come and whither he is about to go: and such permit is necessary even though he be a free born native of Samarqand. On the other hand any persons who wish to pass the river going into the Samarqand province may do so unhindered and none need show any warrant for the passage. All the ferry-boats thus have guards stationed in them, set there by order of Timur to oversee and control the passage: and the boatmen demand a good price to be paid for toll on those whom they carry across. The true reason why these guards have thus been set here is that Timur, as formerly explained, has brought to Samarqand in captivity from his wars an immense concourse of folk to people this province of his, causing them to migrate hither from all the conquered provinces. This he has done to

171

re-populate the country of Samarqand and to ennoble the same, and the order above given is that none shall escape him to return home to the place whence they have been brought captive. Indeed as we journeyed along, coming through Persia and Khurásán, we had often met with the officials sent out by Timur; and these were seeking and gathering together all who having lost parents were homeless orphans, also those men or women who were houseless vagrants or without means of livelihood. All such folk were brought together by these officials; and by force, not of their free will, were sent over to the Samarqand territory to increase the population of that province. They are to be seen travelling along the roads, some driving a cow, some riding an ass, others following with a sheep or a couple of ewes or goats. Then as they passed along through the countryside they were fed at the villages by the head-men in accordance with orders sent from Timur. We were told indeed that by this fashion the population of the Samarqand territory had been increased lately by him so as now to number 100,000 souls or perhaps more.

This city of Tirmiz where we now found ourselves is very large and very populous: it has no wall round it nor is it fortified. All about lie many orchards for the district is well irrigated. Except of its great size as already mentioned I shall tell but little detail concerning Tirmiz, and it must suffice to say that from where we entered the town to where finally we came to our lodgings the distance was so great that we were weary of the passage. We passed through streets and squares innumerable, all densely populated, where goods of all kinds were exposed for sale. In Tirmiz as elsewhere we were liberally entertained, all our needs being amply supplied, and further they presented us with a robe of honour made of silken cloth. While yet we were awaiting our instructions there arrived from Timur and sent especially to meet us a messenger on horseback, who brought us gracious words of greeting from his Highness, enquiring as to the road we had come and how we had fared on the journey, and to ascertain if we had been everywhere well treated, and if we were in the enjoyment of good health. In accordance with the usual custom of the country, we knew that we should bestow on this Imperial messenger a present before his departure to return to his Master, and this we did giving him a robe of that kincob [gold brocade]. Further we now presented some pieces of Florentine cloth to Ennacora the nobleman whom Timur had sent and appointed to be our guide [through Khurásán]: and the like was done by the Ambassador of the Sultan of Egypt who as already mentioned was and had throughout been our travelling companion. Further to the second of our guides, [namely Mirabozar] the court official latterly despatched by Timur to attend on us, we also gave a present, in this case a horse. For this is the invariable custom of this country, namely that when any messenger is sent by the lord Timur to any person, it is due and expected of him that he should present that messenger with a gift thus to mark the honour done him, seeing that of right the lord Timur should thus even by deputy have a present offered to him. Further it is to be observed that the value of the present thus offered to his messenger is a measure of the respect in which Timur is held by the giver, and he knows he will be the more held in esteem, by the Lord Timur the more he has bestowed on his envoy.

On Friday the 22nd of August having dined we departed from Tirmiz and came to our camp, where we slept in the open, but near by certain large houses that stood there. The next day Saturday our way lay over the great plain, passing by many populous villages, and at length we came to one where we were to stop as arranged for the night, being here very honourably entertained and supplied in every need. On Sunday the next day we rode on and dined at a large house that had been built for the accommodation of Timur on his passage through these parts: and here they served us with meat and wine and fruit, more especially melons which in this province are abundant and most excellent being of a very large size. It is the custom here when they present you with fruit to bring it all heaped up in a basket and then to cast it down all together before you on the ground in a heap. That Sunday evening we again set out and that night slept in camp on the bank of a river, then Monday following we reached the foot of a range of very high mountains, where at a beautiful house constructed on the plan of a cross at a late hour we dined. This house was built of burnt bricks, being ornamented with tiles that depicted subjects in various coloured patterns. The mountain range beyond this place is very lofty and the pass that traverses it is a narrow cleft where the passage seems to have been cut through by the hand of man, with the mountain wall on either side rising vertical to an immense height. The roadway itself is quite level, passing deep down in the cleft. Here in the midst of surrounding heights stands a village, and the place is known as the Iron Gates.[2] In the whole length of this mountain range there is no other pass to cross it, save this one, which is thus the Guard House of the Imperial city of Samarqand.

It is only by this one pass that all who travel up to Samarqand from India the Less [or Afghanistan] can come: nor can those who go down from the Imperial City voyaging to India travel by any other route. The lord Timur is sole master of these Iron Gates, and the revenue is considerable to the state from the customs imposed on all merchants who come from India going to the city of Samarqand and to the regions beyond. Further as is well known Timur is also lord of those other celebrated Iron Gates that stand near Derbend [to the west of the Caspian Sea] which close off Tartary [to the north] and are not far from the city of Kaffa [in the Crimea]. These Iron Gates at Derbend likewise are a cleft cut in the mountain range [of the Caucasus] which stands between the kingdom of Tartary and the province of Derbend, which last is on the [western] shore of the Caspian and is now included in the kingdom of Persia. Thus those who would come from Tartary to Persia must pass through these Iron Gates of Derbend, just as those who would voyage to Samarqand must pass through those Iron Gates to which we now were come. Between these Gates of Samarqand and those Gates of Derbend indeed is a distance of at least 1,500 leagues of land and of this great territory, as you must know Timur is lord. He is master of both these Iron Gates, and the Iron Gates of Derbend yield him a very considerable yearly tribute from customs, as do those of Samarqand. The city of Derbend is a very large place and it is the capital town of a great district. These Iron Gates of the west, of course are those that are nearer to Spain, and known as the Derbend Iron Gates, while those which lie to the eastward being the furthest from Spain are known as the Iron Gates of Tirmiz, and these last shut out Lesser India [which is Afghanistan].

At this house [on the plan of a cross already mentioned] where we were now resting they made us the gift of a riding horse, and in this district the horses are of very famous breed, being of great spirit. The mountains of this range through which the Iron Gates give passage are quite bare of any growth of forest. We were told that in times past there were actually great barrier gates, cased in iron, which closed the passage way between the mountain cliffs, whereby none could pass without a permit [but no gates were there when we came through], and that day we travelled on and slept in camp on the mountain side. The next day [Wednesday] riding on we had dinner and took our rest in the tents of certain Chagatays who were encamped beside a river. That same evening we went on and shortly after nightfall perceiving nearby another range of hills that we should have to cross we dismounted and slept for some hours in the open. Mounting again soon after midnight we rode till mid-day following, coming to a village where they provided our dinner, and we rested there for that afternoon. It was here in this village that one of the servants of Fray Alfonso Paez the Master in Theology suddenly died, but indeed he had been very ill for a long season past. The next day which was Thursday the 28th of August at the hour of mid-day mass we found ourselves come near a great city which is known as Kesh.[3] It stands in the plain, and on all sides the land is well irrigated by streams and water channels, while round and about the city there are orchards with many homesteads. Beyond stretches the level country where there are many villages and well-peopled hamlets lying among meadows and water lands; indeed it is all a sight most beautiful in this the summer season of the year. On these lands five crops yearly of corn are grown, vines also, and there is much cotton cultivated for the irrigation is abundant. Melon yards here abound with fruit-bearing trees in the adjacent orchards.

The city of Kesh is surrounded by an earthen rampart, having a very deep ditch crossed at the gates by draw-bridges. The lord Timur is himself a native of Kesh and his father [Teragay] also was from here. There are throughout the city many fine houses and mosques, above all a magnificent mosque which Timur has ordered to be built but which as yet is not finished. In this mosque is seen the chapel in which his father's burial place has been made, and beside this is a second chapel now being built in which it is intended that Timur himself shall be interred when the time comes.[4] They told us that when a month or so before the date of our arrival here Timur had entered Kesh [on his way up to Samarqand] he had been much dissatisfied with the appearance of this chapel, objecting that the doorway was too low and ordering that it should be raised: and it was on this alteration the builders were now at work.

In this same mosque too is seen the tomb of Prince Jahángír the eldest son of Timur [he having died in the year 1372]. The whole of this mosque with its chapels is very finely wrought in tiles that are of blue and gold, and you enter it through a great court yard planted with trees round a water tank. Here daily by the special order of Timur the meat of twenty sheep is cooked and distributed in alms, this being done in memory of his father and of his son who lie here in those chapels. As soon as we had ridden into this city of Kesh they brought us to this mosque, and here they served us for dinner with meat dishes and fruit abundantly, next carrying us on to a magnificent palace where lodgings had been provided for us.

On the following morning which was Friday they came and took us to see another great palace that was being built; and this palace they told us had been thus in hand building for the last twenty years, for though continually thus working day after day the builders were still at their work upon it. This palace of which we are now speaking had an entrance passage constructed to be of considerable length with a high portal before it, and in this entrance gallery to right and to left there were archways of brickwork encased and patterned with blue tiles. These archways led each one into a small chamber that was open having no door, the flooring being laid in blue tiles. These little rooms are for those to wait in who are in attendance on Timur when he should come here. At the end of this gallery stands another gate-way, beyond which is a great courtyard paved with white flagstones and surrounded on the four sides by richly wrought arches, and in its centre is a very large water tank. This courtyard indeed may measure some three hundred paces in its width, and beyond it you enter through a very high and spacious gateway the main buildings of the palace. This gateway is throughout beautifully adorned with very fine work in gold and blue tiles, and over the entrance are seen the figures of the Lion and the Sun, these same figures being repeated over the summit of each of the arches round the courtyard, and this emblem of the Lion and the Sun was they told us the armorial bearing of the former lord of Samarqand [whom Timur dispossessed]. We were assured that it had been Timur himself who was the builder of this great palace, but I imagine in truth that some part of it must have been built by that lord of Samarqand who lived before the time of Timur's sovereignty; for the Lion and the Sun which we saw here set up are the emblems of this former sovereign.

The special armorial bearing of Timur is the Three Circlets set thus to shape a triangle which same it is said signifies that he Timur is lord of all Three Quarters of the World. This device Timur has ordered to be set on the coins that he has struck, and on all buildings that he has erected, and it is for that reason, as I opine, that those buildings [bearing the emblem of the Lion and the Sun] were built by a lord who reigned before the time of Timur. These three circlets which, as said, are like the letter 0 thrice repeated to form a triangle, further are the imprint of Timur's seal, and again by his special order are added so as to be seen patent on all the coins struck by those princes who are become tributary to his government.[5]

From this main portal of the courtyard just described you enter a great reception hall which is a room four square, where the walls are panelled with gold and blue tiles, and the ceiling is entirely of gold work. From this room we were taken up into the galleries, and in these likewise everywhere the walls were of gilt tiles. We saw indeed here so many apartments and separate chambers, all of which were adorned in tile work of blue and gold with many other colours, that it would take long to describe them here, and all was so marvellously wrought that even the craftsmen of Paris, who are so noted for their skill, would hold that which is done here to be of very fine workmanship. Next they showed us the various apartments where Timur was wont to be and to occupy when he came here with his wives; all of which were very sumptuously adorned as to floors and walls and ceilings. Many were the various grades of workmen still at work on building and adorning these palaces. We were shown in one that we visited a great banqueting hall which Timur was having built wherein to feast with the princesses, and this was gorgeously adorned, being very spacious, while beyond the same they were laying out a great orchard in which were planted many and divers fruit trees, with others to give shade. These stood round water tanks, beside which there were laid out fine lawns of turf. This orchard was of such extent that a very great company might conveniently assemble here, and in the summer heats enjoy the cool air beside that water in the shade of these trees. But such indeed was the richness and beauty of the adornment displayed in all these palaces that it would be impossible for us to describe the same adequately without much more leisure than we can here give to the matter. The mosque aforesaid and these palaces are a work that Timur has begun and is yet perfecting, all being in the first place wrought to do honour his father's memory who lies buried here, and next, as we have said, because he Timur is a native of this city of Kesh.

Though indeed Timur was born here, yet he was not by descent a citizen of Kesh, being in truth a nomad of the Chagatay clansmen. These are Tartars who originally had their abode in Tartary, but who migrated hither when their countryside was overrun in past times and conquered [by the Mongols under Chingiz Khán]. All this we shall explain to you more in detail presently, and the Chagatays who have been frequently mentioned in our narrative are so named as belonging to this clan. The father of Timur was a man of good family, allied by blood to the clan of Chagatay, but he was a noble of small estate, having only some three or four riders to his back, namely his personal followers. He lived at a village not far from the city of Kesh, for gentle-folk of his sort have ever preferred the country to the town. His son Timur was in the beginning no more than he had been, and only able just to keep himself, having of his following some four or five horsemen. All this that I now tell you is from what was related to us while we were sojourning in Kesh, or later from what we heard while in the cities beyond. According to the stories told us, Timur in his youth was wont to ride out with his four or five companions on foray, and one day they would lift a sheep and on another occasion a cow, taking these by stealth from the flocks of their neighbours. Then when home again Timur would make a feast of his booty, inviting his companions, and others would join for he was a man of heart and very hospitable, dividing what he had with friends. Others now came to join his following until at length he had some three hundred horsemen under his command, and with these he would ride forth through the countryside plundering and robbing all who came his way: but next dividing all he took among those who rode with him. Thus he beset all the highways taking toll of the merchants he came upon.

News of this that was going on soon came to the ears of the Sultan of Samarqand[6] who was overlord of the country where these robberies were taking place, and he gave orders that Timur and his men having been taken should be put to death wheresoever they might be found. At the court, however, of the Sultan there were nobles in attendance who were of the Chagatay clansmen and relations of Timur, and these came to speak for him: so that in the end the lord of Samarqand was persuaded to grant him pardon for his deeds. Further later Timur came to court and finally took up his abode at Samarqand in the service of the Sultan. Of those friends who had pleaded for him with the aforesaid lord of Samarqand in times past, there are two still living at the present hour, and they have become long since Timur's most intimate counsellors; one bears the name of Omar Tobán and the other is Caladay Sheykh, both now become mighty lords and men of immense possessions. Then while Timur was thus living at the court of Samarqand matters fell out to his discredit, such that the Sultan came to regard him evilly; when commands for the death of Timur were issued who however was warned in time by friends. Timur therefore fled, he and his followers again became highwaymen on the roads, where one day they compassed the plundering of an immense caravan of merchants and were possessed of a large sum in booty. Timur then marched south coming to a province that is called Sístán where he plundered the people of their flocks of sheep and of their horse-herds, for this country is extremely rich in cattle.

At this time Timur had with him a following of some five hundred horsemen only; seeing which the men of Sístán came together in force to fight him, and one night that he was engaged carrying off a flock of sheep they all fell on him suddenly and slew a great number of his men. Him too they knocked off his horse, wounding him in the right leg of which wound he has remained lame all his life [whence his name of Timur the Lame]; further he received a wound in his right hand, so that he has lost the little finger and the next finger to it. Thus it was that finally they left him for dead, but he coming to himself crawled as best he could to the tents of some nomads of those parts, where he remained in hiding until he had recovered of his wounds, afterwards returning home, where once more he gathered together round him his band of followers. Now at this season the Sultan of Samarqand had come to be distrusted and evilly looked upon by his subjects, more especially by the chief nobles. The men of the capital city therefore coming together immediately took counsel with Timur urging that he should compass the death of the Sultan, when said they he, Timur, might become their lord. All fell out accordingly, for on a certain day when the Sultan was going out to visit a city in the neighbourhood of Samarqand Timur coming up attacked his following and routed them. The Sultan fled to the mountains nearby where he sought refuge with a man of those parts to whom he promised great riches if he would hide him, and in earnest gave him the costly rings that he wore. Taking these that man, in place of harbouring him, informed Timur of his hiding place, who coming up forthwith put the Sultan to death.

Returning now to Samarqand Timur entered and possessed the city, taking to himself the wife of the late Sultan, whom he married, and she still at the present day is his chief wife, being known as the [Great] Khanum, a title which may be taken to signify the Great Queen, or the Great Empress.[7] Starting now from Samarqand Timur proceeded to conquer all Khurásán, profiting by the discord between two brothers who were the lords of that country, and taking the part of those who were in rebellion against them. Thus it was that Timur came shortly into possession of the lordship of both Samarqand and Khurásán, and this was the origin of his great empire. Of those chiefs who joined Timur from the beginning and were the companions of his early conquests there was one [Chawkú] a Chagatay lord of his lineage, and he was the most valiant of those who rode with him in his wars. To him Timur gave his sister to wife making him a great lord of his court, and to them was born a son whose name is Jahán Sháh Mirza.[8] At this present time this man, his nephew, is the most favoured of all the lords of Timur's court, and he has an immense following of clansmen and possesses extensive lands and much wealth. He is Commander in Chief of the Imperial army being as we should say Constable of the Empire, and except for Timur in person none has higher command in the host, and he is of all the chiefs the most popular among the fighting men who have taken part in the wars.

The original cause of the coming of the Tartars into this province of Samarqand and the reason why they are here known by the name of Chagatay must now be explained to you. In times past [namely in the early part of the 13th century] there was a Tartar chief who abode in a city of Tartary, and his name was Chingiz Khán, a name or title that signifies in their language the "World's Treasure."[9] This man conquered the greater part of the lands [of Western Asia] and at his death left four sons, their names were Tuluy, Ogotay, Juji and Chagatay, who all were the children of one mother. When their father Chingiz Khán died he divided his empire equally among the four, leaving to each his portion, and to his son Chagatay he left the territory which belongs to and lies round the city of Samarqand. Further their father bade his four sons always to be good friends and that there must never be any quarrel among them, for the day when they should come to any difference would be the day of their undoing. Now Chagatay was a bold man of overweening ambition and of great enterprise, and between him and his brothers envy befell, and this led to their undoing, for before long the four brothers were at war each against the other. Then the chief nobles of Samarqand when they saw these happenings rose in revolt against Chagatay and next slew him, slaying also many of his family and followers, and they set up choosing to be their Sultan a man who was a native of the land and the chief noble of that district of Samarqand. But later of the sons of Chagatay, with those who were his tribesmen, many still remained living in the country, and all were rich men holding much property there.

These men soon after the death of their lord Chagatay

resolved to call in the Tartar tribes from without, for it was known that they had kept the name of Chagatay, their former lord, and so from these folk it is that in future days came all those who as we have noted now bear the name of the Chagatays. Timur himself came of this lineage, being descended from one of these Chagatay Tartars, and all Chagatays are accounted to be his tribesmen; and forsooth a good number of the population of the Samarqand neighbourhood have latterly taken to themselves this name, although they are not properly of the Chagatay clan, but they affect so to be by reason of the great renown that those of this lineage bear.

In this city of Kesh we remained that Thursday, of our arrival, and the next day Friday in the afternoon took our departure going on to sleep that night in a village beside the road. Saturday the 30th of August we came to a fine palace which Timur has erected beside a river of these parts, and it stands in the plain, surrounded by a great orchard. It is a most beautiful spot and here we were served our dinner. We then came on and found our night quarters in a very large village, which stands but a league and a half distant from the city of Samarqand and the name of this place is Meser. The Tartar noble [Mirabozar] who up to the present had been our guide, in charge and attendance to show us the way, for the time left us, and though we might easily have ridden on and entered that same night the capital, yet this could no wise be done without the express command of Timur. He [Mirabozar] therefore was about to send one of his men to inform his Highness that we had all arrived: and this was done that night the messenger going to the presence of Timur. The next morning at daybreak this man had returned bringing an order from his Highness directing [Mirabozar] to convey us of the Spanish embassy, as also the Ambassador from the Sultan of Cairo who had been so long our travelling companion, together with our people, to a certain famous orchard nearby this village of Meser, and here we were to remain till instructions were sent as to what we next were to do.

In the forenoon of Sunday the 31st of August therefore we were all conducted to this famous orchard. We found it to be enclosed by a high wall, which in its circuit may measure a full league round, and within it is full of fruit trees of all kinds, save only limes and citron-trees which we noticed to be lacking. Further there are here six great tanks, for throughout the orchard is conducted a great stream of water, passing from end to end: while leading from one tank to the next they have planted five avenues of trees, very lofty and shady which appear as streets, for they are paved to be like platforms. These quarter the orchard in every direction, and off the five main avenues other smaller roads are led to variegate the plan, enabling the whole orchard to be traversed and very conveniently seen in all parts. In the exact centre there is a hill, built up artificially of clay brought hither by hand: it is very high and its summit is a small level space, that is enclosed by a palisade of wooden stakes. Within this enclosure are built several very beautiful palaces, each with its complement of chambers magnificently ornamented in gold and blue, the walls being panelled with tiles of these and other colours. This mound on which the palaces have been built is encircled below by deep ditches that are filled with water, for a runlet from the main stream brings this water which falls into these ditches with a continuous and copious supply. To pass up into this hillock to the level of the palaces they have made two bridges, one on the one part the other opposite, and these bridge-ways are closed with gates. Above lead stairways by which you ascend the height; and thus the palaces are so to speak a fortress apart. Throughout the orchard there are to be seen many deer, which Timur has caused to be caught and brought hither, and there are pheasants here in great abundance. From this orchard you go out to a great vineyard beyond which likewise is surrounded by its wall, and this vineyard is of equal extent to the orchard. Round and about the walls of both the orchard and the vineyard they have planted many tall and beautiful trees which give the whole a very fine effect. The name by which this place is known is Talicia, and in their tongue they also call it Khalvet.[10]

While we were lodged in this garden they provided us with necessary viands in plenty also what was needed to our comfort, and a tent that we carried to serve us was pitched in a meadow irrigated by one of the water courses. Thus we remained awaiting further orders until Thursday the 4th of September when there arrived at the orchard a certain lord who was related by kinship to Timur. This noble informed us that his Highness was at the moment occupied in giving despatch to an embassy from Toktamish [the Khán of the Golden Horde] and for that reason could not as yet receive us, but that we were not to suffer annoyance on that account: wherefore for our entertainment, as for the entertainment of the ambassador from Cairo our fellow traveller, his Highness Timur had now sent us the wherewithal for a banquet that day. Thereupon arrived many sheep which they slaughtered and cutting up proceeded to boil the flesh, also a horse likewise slaughtered whose meat they roasted. Next much rice was cooked after many different fashions, and fruits withal supplied in abundance. Thus they feasted us, and after the banquet was over one came and presented to each of us, as from his Highness, a hat and a robe of kincob [gold brocade] also two riding horses. The days following after the banquet we remained quietly encamped in that orchard, staying there from Sunday the last day of August until Monday the 8th of September, when at length his Highness sent word for us to come to him. It is indeed ever his custom thus to delay and never give audience to any ambassadors who arrive except after a pause of five or six whole days, and the more important the embassy may be the longer is this same period of waiting.

Chapter XII

Samarqand

THUS it was that on Monday the 8th of September we ambassadors left that garden, the place where we had been lodged, and were carried in to the city of Samarqand after crossing the plain. This on all hands is occupied by private gardens and houses between which are streets and squares where goods of all kinds were on sale. By the hour of tierce [nine in the morning] we were come to a great orchard, with a palace therein, where Timur was in residence, and this, as will be understood, lay some distance without the city. As soon as we had arrived they caused us to alight at a certain house that was built outside the palace, and here two of the lords of the court came forward to us saying that we were to give up into their hands such gifts or offerings as we were bringing for presentation to his Highness, seeing that they would arrange and dispose these objects suitably, having them borne by the hands of attendants who would later bring them in and lay them before Timur. As soon as we had given up our gifts into their hands these lords departed: but not before they had likewise said the same to the ambassador of the Sultan of Egypt who was with us, and he too therefore now gave up into their hands the present he had brought.

As soon as our offerings had thus been despatched, other attendants took charge of us holding each ambassador under his arm-pit, and led us forward entering the orchard by a wide and very high gateway, most beautifully ornamented with tile-work in gold and blue. Before this gateway were stationed the imperial door-keepers on guard armed with maces, so that none improperly might dare approach near the gate, although without there had now assembled a very great crowd of folk to see us. On entering what first we noticed was six great elephants, each bearing on its back a small castle of wood-work carrying two standards: and in these castles were their attendants who made the elephants play tricks for our entertainment as we passed by. And thus we went forward and soon came to the men charged with our offerings and gifts which same they were displaying very suitably and bearing aloft in their arms. We ambassadors now passed on standing in front of the bearers of our gifts, and they here made us wait a while, sending on messengers to report that we had come. Then to meet each of us there came forward two of those lords who were in attendance, and they took us as aforesaid under the arms thus to lead us in. Of our company was that Tartar envoy whom Timur had sent [from Angora] to the King of Castile [and who had been our companion throughout our journey hither], but at his present appearance his friends laughed much for he was dressed by us in the manner and fashion of a gentleman of Spain. Thus they brought us all forward till we came to where a certain great lord of the court, a very old man, was seated on a raised dais, he being indeed a nephew of Timur, the son of his sister, and we all made him our obeisances.

Then passing on we came before another dais where we found seated several young princes, the grandsons of his Highness, to whom we likewise paid our respects, and at this point they demanded of us the Letter which we were bringing from our lord the King of Spain to Timur, which being passed over one of these princes received it in his hands who they said was [Khalíl Sultan] the son of Prince Mírán Sháh, the eldest son of Timur [whom we had seen at Sultáníyah]. Those young princes, who were three in number, now got up and forthwith carried away our Letter, bearing it to his Highness and we were told to follow after them. Then coming to the presence beyond, we found Timur and he was seated under what might be called a portal, which same was before the entrance of a most beautiful palace that appeared in the background. He was sitting on the ground, but upon a raised dais before which there was a fountain that threw up a column of water into the air backwards, and in the basin of the fountain there were floating red apples. His Highness had taken his place on what appeared to be small mattresses stuffed thick and covered with embroidered silk cloth, and he was leaning on his elbow against some round cushions that were heaped up behind him. He was dressed in a cloak of plain silk without any embroidery, and he wore on his head a tall white hat on the crown of which was displayed a balas ruby, the same being further ornamented with pearls and precious stones. As soon as we came in sight of his Highness we made him our reverence, bowing and putting the right knee to the ground and crossing our arms over the breast. Then we advanced a step and again bowed, and a third time we did the same, but this occasion kneeling on the ground and remaining in that posture. Then Timur gave command that we should rise to come nearer before him, and the various lords who up to this point had been holding us under the arms now left us for they dared not advance any nearer to his Highness.

There were three nobles here whom we especially noticed standing in Timur's presence in waiting on him, for these were his Highness' chief chamberlains, and their names, as we found later, were Sháh Melik Mirza, Burunday Mirza and Núr-ad-Dín Mirza. These three now came forward, and taking each of us ambassadors by the arm advanced with us to come to stand immediately before the place where Timur sat, and here again they made us kneel. His Highness however commanded us to arise and stand close up to him that he might the better see us, for his sight was no longer good, indeed, he was so infirm and old that his eyelids were falling over his eyes and he could barely raise them to see.[1]

We remark that his Highness never gave us his hand to kiss, for that is not their custom, no one with them should kiss the hand of any great lord which to do would here be deemed unseemly. Timur now enquired of us for the health of the King our Master saying: "How is it with my son your King? How goes it with him? Is his health good?" We suitably answered and then proceeded to set out the message of our embassy at length, his Highness listening carefully to all that we had to say. When we had finished Timur turned and proceeded to converse with certain of the great lords who were seated on the ground at his feet: as they afterwards told one of these personages here present was the son of Toktamish the late Khan of Tartary, while another was the descendant of that [Chagatay] Khan who had formerly ruled over the province of Samarqand, while others were princes of the blood or grandees all of the family of his Highness.

Turning to them therefore Timur said: "See now these Ambassadors whom my son the King of Spain has sent to me. He indeed is the greatest of all the kings of the Franks who reign in that farther quarter of the earth where his people are a great and famous nation. I will send back a message of good will to my son this King of Spain. Indeed it had been enough that he should have sent me his Ambassadors with a Letter merely and no offerings or gifts. It suffices me to know that he is well in health and state, and no gift from him do I ever require." That Letter which our lord the King of Castile had sent by our hands, was at this moment being held up before the eyes of his Highness by the prince one of his grandsons, and [Fray Alfonso] our Master in Theology coming forward with his dragoman forthwith craved permission to have it read, seeing that he was in the position exactly to make known to his Highness the words of his son the King of Spain and he submitted therefore that when his Highness pleased he, Fray Alfonso, might be allowed himself to read the Letter to him. Timur on this took the Letter from the hand of his grandson, but after opening it said that only later he would indeed have it read to him, on which the Master replied that he was at the orders of his Highness. Timur then made it known to us that he intended to send for the Master presently, when at leisure he would receive him in private audience, and then not only the Letter should be read, but all that we ambassadors desired to say should be heard and answered. After this they made us again stand up, and then took us back to be seated on a low dais that was set at the right hand of where Timur was enthroned.

Those lords now conducting us began by placing us in a seat below that of one who it appeared was the ambassador of Chays Khán, the emperor of Cathay. Now this ambassador had lately come to Timur to demand of him the tribute, said to be due to his master, and which Timur year by year had formerly paid. His Highness at this moment noticed that we, the Spanish ambassadors, were being given a seat below that of this envoy from the Chinese Emperor, whereupon he sent word ordering that we should be put above, and that other envoy below. Then no sooner had we been thus seated than one of those lords came forward, as from Timur, and addressing that envoy from Cathay publicly proclaimed that his Highness had sent him to inform this Chinaman that the ambassadors of the King of Spain, the good friend of Timur and his son, must indeed take place above him who was the envoy of a robber and a bad man the enemy of Timur, and that he his envoy must sit below us: and if only God were willing, he Timur would before long see to and dispose matters so that never again would any Chinaman dare come with such an embassy as this man had brought. Thus it came about that later at all times during the feasts and festivities to which his Highness invited us, he always gave command that we should have the upper place. Further on the present occasion, no sooner had his Highness thus disposed as to how we were to be seated, than he ordered our dragoman to interpret and explain to us the injunction given in our behalf. This Emperor of China, as we have said, is called Chays Khán, a title which signifies Emperor of Nine Empires, but the Tartars call him Tanguz, a name given in mockery, for this with them is as who would say the Pig Emperor. He is however the Emperor ruling an immense realm, and of old Timur had been forced to pay him tribute: though now as we learnt he is no longer willing, and will pay nothing to that Emperor.[2]

To return however to what was going forward; no sooner had we thus all been duly seated, namely together with us Spaniards also diverse envoys come from many other countries, with the grandees otherwise present, than the attendants began to bring up viands for the feast. These consisted of a quantity of mutton, roast, boiled and in stews, also horse-meat roasted. What they thus brought before us was laid out severally on very large circular dishes of leather, such as we in Spain call Guadameci [or Cordovan leather],[3] and these had handles whereby the attendants could move them from place to place. Thus when Timur had called for any particular dish, that leather dish would be dragged along the ground to him, for the attendants could not lift them, such was the quantity of meat with which each was charged. When therefore it had been carefully slipped along the ground and brought near his Highness, namely to within some twenty paces, the carvers would come to cut up the viands. These men would kneel down before the great dishes, and all wore aprons for that business with leather sleeves upon their forearms to keep themselves clean of the grease, and thus bestowed they set to work to carve. The slices of meat were next placed in large trencher-like basins, these some of gold and some of silver, while others were of vitrified earthenware, or else of what is known as porcelain, and these last are much esteemed and of very high price.

The joint that is most in favour with the Tartars is the croup of the horse, with the saddle-meat attached but the leg disjointed off, and with portions of the same the servers would fill some ten of those gold and silver bowls or trenchers, in which too they would put pieces of mutton, also of the saddle and buttock, with the ham removed. On these trenchers too they placed knots of the horse-tripe in balls of the size of a fist, with a sheep's head all of a piece. Thus were many trenchers filled, and these then were laid in rows one beside the other, when the cooks bearing bowls of broth appeared, into which salt having been thrown to melt, the broth was poured over each trencher to serve as sauce to the meat. Lastly they took thin cakes of their bread, which doubled fourfold they placed one on each of those charged trenchers.

When all this had been done some of the privileged courtiers of his Highness, with certain other great nobles present, took up those trenchers, two men to each or even three, for one man could never have lifted a charged trencher, placing each in order before Timur and before us the foreign ambassadors and the princes who were present. Then his Highness graciously sent to us of the Spanish embassy two trenchers from those already set before him, thus to show us special honour. Now all these viands in their several dishes were not removed when the second course was brought in to be served, for the remainder of the first course, according to their custom, was merely set on one side to be carried home to our lodgings for later consumption. Indeed should this not be duly done it were a very great mark of disrespect to any guest; and the amount of meat that was placed before us was a wonder to behold. Further the custom, as aforesaid, is that no sooner had any dish been served to us and done with than it was passed back to our servants to be carried away by them: and so ample was this store thus provided for our later consumption that had our servants cared to carry it all home it might have lasted us for the space of at least half a year. As soon as these boiled and roast meats had been eaten they next brought in stews of mutton, and balls of forced meat with many side dishes of diverse sorts. Following we were served with a quantity of fruit, such as melons and peaches and grapes; and with the same they now brought in, for us to drink from, many bowls and goblets of gold and silver that contained mares' milk sweetened with sugar, an excellent beverage that they have custom to use during the summer season.

When thus we had all partaken and were satisfied, they began the display of our presents which as has been already explained were arranged so as to be carried in turn before Timur by his servants. Now these were the gifts we had brought him from our lord the King of Castile, also there were those gifts which the Sultan of Egypt had sent. At last following on these came three hundred horses that went past before Timur the same having been presented to him that, day by one of his nobles. When all this was done we ambassadors were duly taken in charge by the attendants and so brought back to our lodgings. A certain lord was now appointed to be our guardian and guide, who should see to us and provide all that was necessary to our well-being: and he was as we learnt the Chief Doorkeeper of his Highness. He now made arrangements for us Spaniards and for the Egyptian ambassador and they brought us to a house standing in a well watered orchard that lay near by that garden and palace where Timur being in residence had lately received us. Now at the last moment just before we had taken our leave of him his Highness had caused to be brought out and once again displayed those presents which our lord the King had sent him, and which he had lately received and accepted manifesting his great pleasure therein. Of these same presents some pieces of the scarlet cloth he now caused to be cut and divided up among his wives, giving the greater portion to his wife in chief, the Lady who is called the Khanum, who was at that time in residence with him at the palace. But the gifts that the ambassador of the Sultan of Egypt had brought him that day, these he caused to be set aside as also certain other presentations made to him, all being for the moment given back for safe keeping to his servants, to have charge of them for the space of three days, when he would send for them. Such indeed is his usual custom, namely to accept no gift that had not been lying awaiting his pleasure three days under inspection.[4]

The garden with the palace therein where Timur thus granted us our first audience is known by the name of Dilkushá ["Heartsease"], and in the orchard round and about there were pitched many tents the walls of which were of silk stuff or the like. In this garden his Highness remained for some days after we had seen him, namely till the following Friday, when he left moving to another garden where was also a very sumptuous palace, which at the moment was not yet completed but was then still being built, and which is known as the Bágh-i-Chinár [" The Plane Tree Garden"].[5] On the following Monday which was the 15th of September Timur left that palace of the Plane Tree Garden going on to yet another, a place of great beauty, where before its entrance gate was a high portal very finely built of brick ornamented with tiles wrought variously in gold and blue. On this Monday he ordered a great feast to be made to which all three of us ambassadors were invited, together with a numerous company, men and women, of those who were his Highness's relatives: besides others. The garden where this festival took place is very large and it is planted with many fruit-bearing trees with others that are to give shade, and throughout are led avenues and raised paths that are bordered by palings along which the guests might pass on their way. Throughout the garden many tents had been pitched with pavilions of coloured tapestries for shade, and the silk hangings were of diverse patterns, some being quaintly embroidered and others plain in design.

In the centre of this garden there was built a very fine palace the ground plan of which was a cross. The interior was all most richly furnished with hangings on the walls, and within there was a chamber with three arched alcoves[6] which were sleeping places each with a raised dais, the walls and flooring being of coloured tiles. Entering this chamber the largest of the three alcoves was the one facing you, and here stood a screen made of silver and gilt: this being of the height of a man, and broad as to measure three out-stretched arms. In front of this screen was a bed composed of small mattresses some covered with kincob [gold brocade] some with silk stuff worked with gold thread, one mattress being placed above the other on the floor; and this was his Highness's couch.

The walls here about were all hidden being covered by silk hangings of a rose coloured stuff, that was ornamented with spangles of silver plate gilt, each spangle set with an emerald or pearl or other precious stone. Above these wall hangings were strips of silk dependant, and of the width each of a palm across, these coming down to join the hangings below, and ornamented not unlike these last. To the same were attached many coloured silk tassels, and in the draught that blew these waved about here and there after a very pleasant fashion to see. At the entrance of this the chief alcove we are describing, there was a fine archway that was closed by a hanging, made after the same fashion as the rest, and this curtain was fixed from a cross pole like the wood of a lance. From this curtain or hanging depended silken cords with great tassels coming down to the ground. The two remaining alcoves were adorned with hangings after a fashion similar to the one just described, and everywhere the floor was covered with carpets and reed mattings.

In the centre of the palace before the doorway to the alcoves were placed two tables made of gold, standing, each on four legs, and the table top and the legs were all made in one piece of metal. The top of each of these tables might measure five palms in length, the breadth being three palms across. On the one table were set seven golden flasks, and two of them were ornamented outside with great pearls and emeralds and turquoises, set in the metal, while at the mouth there was a balas ruby. Beside these seven flasks there were standing six cups of gold circular in shape, and one of them had set within the rim a very big round pearl of fine orient, while at the centre point of the cup was encrusted a balas ruby of beautiful colour that measured across two finger breadths. Now as regards this feast, which by order of his Highness had been thus prepared, we ambassadors had been duly invited to attend, but when they came to find us at the lodgings where we now were established our dragoman not being there present we delayed for a time awaiting his return. Thus it was that when we did arrive at the palace his Highness had already dined, and he sent us word to say that when next we were bidden to a feast we were to come forthwith and not delay for the absence of any dragoman. On this occasion only would he overlook our not coming in time, for, as his Highness asserted, he had arranged that feast especially for us, and to display to us his court and his palace. Timur indeed on this occasion was very wroth with those lords who were in attendance because we ambassadors had thus arrived too late for the feast, the dragoman not being ready to hand; and further the lords in waiting at the court that day not having seen to it that he, the dragoman, was sent for and fetched in time.

These lords therefore at a later hour sent for our poor dragoman, to whom they spoke thus in their anger: "How now is it by this delay that his Highness is wroth with us and so much annoyed? Why were you not ready in attendance on the Frank Ambassadors? The fault is that you were absent, and to chastise you for the same we now order your nose to be pierced and a cord put through by which you shall be led about the camp, a warning to all!" No sooner was this said than several men seized him, and one holding him by the nose, they were about to pierce it through; but that lord of the court who had in the interval come for us and brought us very late to the presence of his Highness, now intervened, beseeching the others to show mercy and forgive the default of that dragoman. This at length they agreed to, and so that time he escaped from the penalty that was about to have befallen him. Timur after this sent a message to us at our lodgings that since by mischance we had missed being present at his feast, he none the less wished us to be partakers therein and make merry, wherefore he would send us five sheep and two great jars of wine. At this feast there had been present, we were told, a great concourse of lords, and chiefs and all the courtiers personally in attendance on Timur, with many others, and by our absence we had missed seeing that palace with its private rooms and the great orchard where indeed the festival had been arranged. But many of our people were taken over the precincto later and were admitted to the palace, being allowed to view the whole of its magnificence with the gardens.

On the Monday following which was the 22nd of September Timur leaving his palace of Dilkushá went over to another, which like the first stood in a great orchard. This orchard was surrounded by a high wall, four square enclosing it, and at each of the four corners was a very lofty round tower, and the enclosing wall going from tower to tower was very high built, and as strong as the work of the tower. This orchard in its centre had a great palace, built on the plan of a cross, and a very large water-tank had been dug before it. This palace with its large garden was much the finest of any that we had visited hitherto, and in the ornamentation of its buildings in the gold and blue tile work far the most sumptuous. All these palaces with their surrounding gardens, as will be understood, are situated outside the actual city of Samarqand, and this last palace that we have just mentioned was known by the name of the Bágh-i-Naw ["The New Garden"]. In this garden Timur now ordered another feast to be prepared to which we ambassadors were forthwith bidden, together with a great concourse of other guests and here by order of his Highness wine was to be served abundantly and all should drink, since indeed it was to be partaken of by Timur himself on the present occasion. As we were now informed none would dare ever to drink wine either publicly or in private unless by the especial order and licence of Timur.

It is the custom with the Tartars to drink their wine before eating, and they are wont to partake of it then so copiously and quaffing it at such frequent intervals that the men soon get very drunk. No feast we were told is considered a real festival unless the guests have drunk themselves sot. The attendants who serve them with drink kneel before the guests, and as soon as one cup of wine has been emptied another is presented. The whole of the service is to keep on giving cup after cup of wine to the guests: when one server is weary another taking his place and what he has to see to is to fill and give. And you are not to think that one server can serve many guests, for he can at most serve two for keeping them duly, supplied. To any who freely should not thus drink, he would be told that it must be held a despite he thus offers to his highness Timur who is honouring him by his invitation. And the custom yet further is for the cups all to be presented brim full, and none may be returned except empty of all the wine. If any should remain the cup is not received back, but must be taken again and the wine drunk to the dregs. They drink the cupful in one or may be in two draughts, saying in the latter case it is to the good health of his Highness. But he by whom the wine is freely quaffed, will say "By the head of his Highness" and then the whole must be swallowed at a draught with not a drop to be left in the bottom of the cup. The man who drinks very freely and can swallow the most wine is by them called a Bahádur, which is a title and means one who is a valiant drinker. Further he who refuses to drink must be made to drink, and this whether he will or no.

On the day of which we are now speaking Timur had sent to us one of his lords in waiting who brought us as a gift from his Highness a great jar of wine, and the message was that he would have us drink some of this before coming to him, in order that when we should attend his presence we might be right merry. Hence thus we went to him, and he ordered us to be seated, this being after the fashion that has already been described, and thereupon beginning to drink we sat so for a long space of time. Then the viands were brought in, namely roast horse-flesh and boiled mutton, and stews cooked in diverse fashions with the rice thereto prepared in several ways as is their custom. When the feast was ended one of the lords in waiting came forward with a silver bowl in his hand full of small pieces of silver money such as is their current coin, namely Tangas,[7] and of this money he proceeded to throw handfuls over us ambassadors as also over the other guests present, and after he had done this enough for custom, he gathered up all the rest of the coins that remained in the bowl and threw them into the skirt of the cloaks that we ambassadors were wearing, this being a gift to us. Then Timur presented us each with a robe of honour in kincob [gold brocade], when getting up in acknowledgement three times we bowed then kneeling before him as is their custom. On dismissal he told us that the next day we were to come to him again and dine.

On the morrow which was the 23rd of September we heard that Timur had gone over to another palace and garden,

201

which lay adjacent to the one spoken of called Dilkushá, and here again he made a great feast to which more especially were invited many of the chiefs of the army, from stations of the Horde encamped in the neighbourhood of the capital. As mentioned to this festival we had been invited. Both the garden and palace here were very fine, and Timur appeared to be in excellent humour, drinking much wine and making all those of his guests present do the same. There was further an abundance of meat to eat, both of horse-flesh and of mutton as is ever their custom. When the feasting was over his Highness gave command that each of us ambassadors should be presented with a robe of kincob [gold brocade] and we then were allowed to retire going back to our lodging which was situated not far from this palace where Timur had been feasting. At all these banquets the crowd of guests was so great that, as we arrived and would have approached the place where his Highness was seated, it was always quite impossible to make our way forward unless the guards who had been sent to fetch us would force a passage for us to pass. Further the dust round and about was blown up so thick that our faces and clothing became all of one colour and covered by it. These various orchards and palaces above mentioned belonging to his Highness stand close up to the city of Samarqand, while stretching beyond lies the great plain with open fields through which the river [Zarafshán] flows, being diverted into many watercourses.

In the plain here Timur recently had ordered tents to be pitched for his accommodation, and where his wives might come, for he had commanded the assembling of the great Horde, which hitherto and till now had been out in camp in the pastures beyond the orchard lands round and about the city. The whole of the Horde was now to come in, each clan taking up its appointed place: and we now saw them here, pitching the tents, their women folk accompanying them. This was done in order that all [these Chagatays] might have their share in the festivities which were going forward for the celebration of certain royal marriages now about to be declared. From their custom as soon as the camp of his Highness thus had been pitched all these folk of the Horde exactly knew where each clan had its place. From the greatest to the humblest each man knew his allotted position, and took it up, without confusion in most orderly fashion. Thus in the course of the next three or four days we saw near twenty thousand tents pitched in regular streets to encircle the royal camp, and daily more clans came in from the outlying districts. Throughout the Horde thus encamped we saw the butchers and cooks who passed to and fro selling their roast and boiled meats, while others purveyed barley and fruit, while bakers with their ovens alight were kneading the dough and making bread for sale. Thus every craft and art needful for supply was to be found dispersed throughout the camp, and each trade was in its appointed street of the great Horde. And more than this was to be found fully prepared; for there were baths and bathers established in the camp, who pitching their tents had built wooden cabins adjacent each with its iron bath that is supplied with hot water, heated in the caldrons, which, with all the furniture necessary to their craft, they have there. Thus all was duly ordered and each man knew his place to go to beforehand.

As regards our lodgement Timur as already mentioned had ordered a house in a garden to be prepared for our use, this same standing at no great distance from his encampment, and being situate in one of those, orchards that belong to him. On Monday the 29th of September however Timur returned from camp to the city of Samarqand, coming into residence in certain houses, standing near the town gate, which originally he had caused to be built for the accommodation of the mother of his chief wife the Khanum, who, namely her mother, was recently dead and had been buried in the chapel attached to this building. The palace here was very richly furnished and had many separate apartments, though in Samarqand here as a rule they build their houses and the palaces with no great number of separate chambers. However, there were many in this palace, but some not yet finished building, the masons still working at them daily with artificers to complete their decoration. On the day of his coming in Timur now ordered another feast to be prepared, to which same he sent us Spaniards an invitation to be present, and this feast was to celebrate the reception of certain ambassadors who had recently arrived from a land that lay on the borders of Cathay, and which country formerly indeed had been accounted a part of the Chinese Empire.

These ambassadors whom we were taken to see were dressed in a peculiar fashion; for their chief appeared in what might be called a tabard of skins, worn with the fur outside, but the skins of which it was made appeared all very old and tattered. On his head he had a little hat attached by a cord to his breast, and this hat was so much too small in size that with difficulty could he push his head into it, and thus save it from slipping off. All his fellow envoys were dressed in furs, some wearing the fur outside and some with it inside, but to judge by their clothes all might have been taken for so many blacksmiths who had just left serving the forge. They had brought as a present to Timur many marten skins the same to be made up into pelisses, together with sable and white fox skins: and besides these they had brought some falcons as rare gifts. The men were all Christians, after the manner of those of Cathay. As to their mission they had come to beseech Timur to grant and send them for their lord and governor a grandson of that prince Toktamish who has already been mentioned by us, who formerly was the Khan of Tartary, but who now was residing in the camp of the Horde. When we came to his Highness that day we had found Timur engaged in playing at chess, with certain persons who were Sayyids, for it is thus that they call those who by descent are of the family of the Prophet Mahomet; and the gifts which these ambassadors from the Cathay border lands had brought him Timur refused as yet to accept, though they were being now displayed to him and he had examined them narrowly.

On Thursday the 2nd of October his Highness sent commanding us to betake ourselves to a certain garden, where lived that lord to whose charge we were, as before mentioned, consigned and who was the Chief Doorkeeper. On arrival this lord informed us that Timur being perfectly well aware how it was our custom, as with all Franks daily to drink wine, his Highness yet had none the less noticed that we did not willingly ever do so in his presence when it was offered to us after the Tartar fashion. For that reason, as our present host, the Grand Doorkeeper, informed us, it was that his Highness had arranged for us now to be brought to this garden where dinner was about to be served to us and wine provided, that thus we might eat and drink at our ease and as much as accorded to our inclination. We found that for this purpose ten sheep and a horse had been sent by order of Timur to supply the banquet with meat, also a full charge of wine, and on this fare we then dined very sumptuously. At the conclusion of the feast, they presented each of us ambassadors with a robe of kincob [gold embroidery] and a shirt to match, also a hat: further we each received a horse for our riding, all these being the gifts presented to us by the order of the Lord Timur .

Chapter XIII

Samarqand

ON Monday the 6th of October Timur gave orders for a grand feast to be made at his camp in the Horde, and this same is known as the Royal Camp. To this feast his Highness had invited all his wives and the members of his family, namely his sons and grandsons at that time resident with him together with their wives. Further the lords who were of the court all were bidden, as also all those chiefs who were in the various encampments stationed round and about the city, these having been brought in by special command. As regards us ambassadors we were that day taken over to the Horde, and in the great camp we found they had erected an innumerable number of extra tents all very beautiful to see, and for the most part these were erected on the bank beside the river [Zarafshán]. These tents were marvellously fine, all one beside the other very closely pitched, and thither they conducted us through a roadway where all sorts of goods were exposed on sale suitable to the needs of those who might be about later to set forth on the march of the army. As soon as we had come near to where Timur was in residence in the royal tents, they left us for a season to rest in the shade under a spacious awning. This we found to be made of a white linen stuff overset and let in with coloured embroidery, and the awning had wooden poles at the back which supported it by means of cords holding it taut. The like awnings were to be seen in many other parts of the camp and they are fashioned long and high in order to be open to the sun and to catch the breeze.

Nearby this awning where we were seated stood a very large high pavilion, in fact a very huge tent, and it was four square in shape. In height it was the measure of three long lances such as used by a horse soldier, and the side was a hundred paces from angle to angle, it being as said four cornered. The ceiling of the pavilion was made circular to form a dome, and the poles supporting it were twelve in number each as thick round as is the chest of a man breast high. These poles were painted in colours blue and gold and otherwise, and of these twelve great tent poles four were placed at the corners with two others in between on the side. Each pole was made up of three lengths which were firmly jointed together to form the whole. When they had to be set the work people made use of a windlass as big as a cart-wheel thus to hoist them up: further they have shackles of cord bands that are attached in various parts and which serve to ease the strain. From each of these poles at its summit in the dome shaped ceiling there hangs one end of a great curtain in silk cloth that is thereto attached, and these curtains are looped up running from pole to pole, so as to make four archways. Round outside the four walls of the main tent of the pavilion there are low galleries like porticoes, and these likewise form a square, and above they join on to the tent wall of the pavilion. The outer tent walls of these four porticoes just described are supported on twenty-four small wooden masts which are by no means as thick as the twelve poles of the inner pavilion, the whole number of these poles and masts together being thirty-six, which serve to raise up and support the great structure, which is stayed by upwards of five hundred ropes, and these are coloured red.

The inner walls of the pavilion are lined with crimson tapestry very beautifully woven in patterns of diverse designs, further it is hung with silk stuffs of many colours in places worked over with embroidery of gold thread. The ceiling of the pavilion is its mark of greatest beauty for at the four corners are figured four eagles sitting with their wings closed. The exterior walls of the pavilion are made of a silk cloth woven in bands of white and black and yellow that to us appeared made of silk sarsenet. Outside at each corner there is set a very tall staff capped with an apple of burnished copper above which is a crescent. The summit of the pavilion further is square shaped with four tall staves at the corners, each with its apple and crescent. These staves are set at a great height, being also of considerable size, and they form the framework of what is like a turret made of silk cloth, set with what simulates battlements. There is a gangway from below to come up into the turret, for should the force of the wind disarrange any part of the upper works of the pavilion, or cause damage to the poles, men go up thither and walking afoot on the canvas screens repair the fault. From a distance indeed this great tent would appear to be a castle, it is so immensely broad and high. It is a wonder to behold, and magnificent beyond description.[1] Inside within the pavilion there is set a dais, in one part, it is flat and covered over with a carpet on which have been placed three or four mattresses one above the other. This is the seat where his Highness takes his place giving audience. To the left, as you face this, is a second dais also flat and covered with a carpet; it is at some distance apart from the main dais, and beyond it again is a third dais which is lower than the others.

Round and about the pavilion on the ground outside is erected a wall of cloth, as might be otherwise the wall of a town or castle, and the cloth is of many coloured silks in diverse patterns. Along the wall top are battlements, and it is stayed without and within by ropes stretching up from the ground, and on the inner side stand poles which support the same. This encircling canvas wall goes round a space of ground measuring across, may be, some 300 paces, and the wall itself is as high as a man on horse-back may reach up to. There is an arched gateway to it, with double doors without and within, all made of canvas as above described. This entrance gate is very high, and it is capable of being barred and locked. Above the gateway rises a square tower of canvas with battlements, and as forsooth the encircling wall makes grand display of patterns and ornamentation in the stuff of which it is made, so too the gateway-arch and tower just described have even more ornamented work on them than is the case of the walls. This forms the great Enclosure surrounding and shutting in the pavilion. It is known by the name of the Sarápardeh[2] and within its circuit stand many other tents and awnings pitched diversely and at intervals.

Among the rest we noted here a very lofty circular tent of another kind, for this is not stayed with ropes, the wall being supported by poles of the size and thickness of our lances, which are wrought into the canvas wall, as might be to form a netting cross-wise. Above those of the side walls, rise other long poles which hold up the upper part of the tent forming the domed ceiling. The tent walls above and below are held together the one above the other by a series of staying bands, a hand breadth across. These pass down to the ground and are secured by stakes, or tent pegs, and they hold the walls of the tent stretched taut: but indeed it is a marvel to note how such thin stays can hold up so high a canvas wall. Above this wall is made of crimson tapestry, but below the material of the wall is strengthened by a cotton stuffing like that of a coverlet, this being added that the heat of the sun's rays may not pass through. The walls of these tents we are now describing are not ornamented with any pattern work or figures as elsewhere may be seen, their only ornament being bands of white which go all round the back up to about half way of the height, thus engirdling the walls outside. But further these bands are ornamented with spangles of silver gilt, each of the size of an open hand, and in these have been set jewel stones of diverse sorts. Again round the back part of the tent is to be noted half way up a linen band, set over in small loose pleats, as may be the facings of a woman's gown, and these are all embroidered with a pattern in gold thread; and as the wind blows these loose pleats set on the linen band wave to and fro in a manner pleasant to see. This particular tent that we have been describing had a high entrance, shut by doors, and these were made of red tapestry stretched over a framework of small canes.

Nearby again stood another tent but of the kind stayed with ropes. It was very richly made, the stuff being a red tapestry like shag-velvet. Then in a row there were four tents that were connected together by a passage way going from one to the other, by which one could pass as might be through a corridor, and this corridor was covered in above by a ceiling. Within this same great Enclosure we noticed quite a number of other tents, and nearby was another a second Enclosure like the first, and as large in extent, shut in by an encircling wall of silk stuff, woven to look as though it were the pattern on a tile. In this wall there were opened at intervals window frames with shutters, but these window openings could not be passed through from without by any one, for each was guarded by a netting of thin silk tape. In the middle of this second Enclosure stood a tent like that other one, very high and on the model that has been just described, and made of a similar red cloth, ornamented with spangles of silver as was that former tent. All these tents are indeed very tall, rising to the height of three full lance-lengths or even more. High up, in the ceiling of the cupola of the tent we are now describing, is seen the figure of an eagle in silver gilt, it is of a great size and its wings are open. Then a fathom and a half below, on the tent wall they have figured three falcons in silver gilt, one on the one side and the other two beyond: these are very skillfully wrought, they have their wings open as though they were in flight from the eagle, their heads being turned back to look at him, with their wings extended for flying. The eagle is represented as though about to pounce on one of the falcons.

All these birds are extraordinarily well figured, and they are set here as though some special purpose were intended.

In front of the doorway of this tent is erected an awning of many coloured silk cloth: this shades the door, and prevents the sun from shining on any one at the place of entrance: further this awning can be moved about to face this way or that, and so keep the sun's rays from falling within the tent. Of these two great Enclosures with many tents within them as we have described the first Enclosure is that belonging to the chief wife of Timur, who is known as the Great Khánum or Lady, while that second Enclosure belongs to his second wife who is called the Kuchik-Khánum, meaning the Little Lady.[3] Alongside these first two Enclosures there is a third with canvas walls of a different make, with many tents and awnings pitched within the Enclosure circuit, and here too there is a chief tent likewise made very high after the fashion of those already described. Further we noticed many other such Enclosures beyond and about, which same as already said go by the name of Sarápardeh, and we counted of these to the number of eleven in all. Each was of its own colour and design, and in each might be seen one great tent, of the kind set up without tent-ropes to stay it, as has been explained above, each Enclosure having walls of red tapestry similar to those we have already described, with many smaller tents and awnings set about the main central tent. These eleven Enclosures were indeed standing so near one to the other that between their outer walls, from the one to the next, the space was only sufficient for the width of a roadway: and they were indeed, as we came thus to view them, one beyond the other, all of a most noble appearance. All these Enclosures aforesaid were occupied either by the wives of Timur, or by the wives of his grandsons, and these princes and princesses have their abode therein, as does also his Highness likewise, both summer and winter.

On the day of which we are now speaking Timur came out into the royal Enclosure at mid-day and proceeded to his Great Pavilion, whither he sent and had us brought. Here they served us with a feast, and we dined on mutton and horse-flesh, with the usual abundance, and the meal being over we returned back to our lodgings. Next day Tuesday the 7th of October Timur commanded another feast to be prepared in the Horde, to which we ambassadors again were bidden, and this feast was served in one of those Enclosures that we have described. Being sent for by his Highness we were brought thither, and we found him seated in the main tent of the Enclosure. We were again formally introduced, and then partook of the feast, which was ordered after the usual fashion. When the entertainment was over two of the lords of the court who were the intimate attendants of his Highness - their names were Sháh Melik Mirza and Núr-ad-Dín Mirza - that day were permitted to present Timur with a gift, and the several items now were brought before him. Their present was a great number of trenchers in silver, each standing on its tall feet, and on these trenchers were set comfits and cakes of sugar with raisins, almonds and pistachio nuts. Further each trencher was covered over by a piece of silk stuff. On this occasion these trenchers were laid down, nine by nine, such being the custom when any gift is offered to his Highness, for all such must be in groups of nine pieces in any sort of the thing presented. On the present occasion Timur immediately portioned what had been given him as gifts among the courtiers and lords who were present: and to us ambassadors his Highness gave award, bestowing on us two of those trenchers each covered with its silken cloth. As we arose to depart the attendants threw over us and the folk round and about a shower of silver coin, with among the rest small thin patens of gold each with a turquoise set in the centre. With this that festival came to an end and the guests departed home.

On the next day which was Wednesday his Highness had arranged to give another feast to which likewise we were bidden: but that day there arose a great wind blowing fiercely, which caused Timur to keep to the palace indoors and he did not appear at the public reception. He had commanded none the less that those who had come invited should be served with all that had been prepared for the feast: but we two ambassadors, who had been instructed to attend now excused ourselves from remaining to dine and returned home to our lodgings. On Thursday the 9th of October, which was the morrow, the Princess Khánzádeh, the wife of Mírán Sháh Timur's eldest [surviving] son, made a great feast and we were both invited thereto.[4] The feast was held in one of those Enclosures with their tents which the Princess occupied as her abode and these tents were very magnificent. As we approached her pavilion we noticed that here and there on the ground were set many jars of wine, and of this we all partook later abundantly. The Princess on our arrival commanded us to be brought before her, and after being duly presented we were accommodated on a low dais that faced her seat, and this had been set under an awning. Khánzádeh herself with many guests and the other ladies who were in attendance on her, all were seated on a low dais before the door of one of those great tents under an awning. In front of her seat were placed some three or four small mattresses one set above the other, over which she could lean forward at will to take her ease.

This feast to which we were here bidden was given to celebrate the royal wedding of a kinsman where the bride also was her relation. We noticed that Khánzádeh herself was a princess now some forty years of age: she was fair of complexion and fat. At the feast on the ground before her were set many of those jars of wine already mentioned, and there were also other jars that held a beverage which the

Tartars drink called Busa, made from mare's milk sweetened with sugar. Present sitting near the princess were many of the relatives of her highness, and some lords were in attendance, also there were standing in the tent ballad singers who played to their singing an accompaniment on musical instruments. As we came up and were presented the Princess and the company were already drinking wine, and the custom in this case is as follows.

One of the lords, a man of a certain age, of those who are related to Timur in blood, attended by two youths who were also of the family of his Highness, all three would come forward to serve her with the wine cup, likewise serving the other dames there seated her guests. The servers each carried in his hand a white cloth as might be a napkin, while those who had to pour out the wine now filled various small gold cups therewith and set each on a small flat golden platter that was placed ready to hand. The old lord and the two youths who were to serve the wine now came forward, being followed by the attendants who had already poured full the cups that were set each on its platter, and all advancing when they came half way up to the Princess bent the right knee kneeling to the ground before her. This they did three times over, kneeling and rising up again but keeping to the same spot where they had at first knelt. Then the old lord and the youths took a cup each, as set on its little platter from the attendants, and the three came forward near to where the Princess was seated, each with the cup he had brought but holding it with the napkin round it that his hand might not touch the metal. Then again they knelt, but this time immediately in front of the Princess or such one of the ladies as each was serving, and to whom he now gave the cup of wine to drink. This done, each server would get up from his knees holding in his hand the platter, and would return to his former place, but this he did ceremoniously so as to keep facing the dame as he went back. Then at a certain spot he would halt and again kneel, the right knee to the ground, and so wait until each dame had drunk her wine. Then her server would rise from his knee and advance to receive the cup which the lady would place on the gold platter that he carried, who would then retire but again carefully avoid to turn his back to her.

Now you must understand that this method of drinking wine was not carried through and done within a brief space but went on for a long time, and all the dames drank without previously having eaten of the feast. Every now and then one of these ladies as her server was standing before her with the wine cup, would order that he himself should drink of the same, on which the server would put down the platter and drink off the draught of wine. Then turning the cup upside down to show his dame that not a drop had been left in the bottom, would boast of his feats of drinking, and of how much wine he could put away, whereat the ladies would merrily laugh. At this feast that we are now describing the Great Khanum, the chief wife of Timur, was present, and at one time she and these dames would drink wine, and next they would call for that mare's milk beverage of which we have spoken above. After this manner of drinking had gone on for some considerable space of time, the Great Khanum commanded that we the ambassadors should come forward, when with her own hand she offered us the wine cup, and persisted in the attempt to make me Ruy González drink of the same but I would not, though scarcely could she be brought to believe and understand that I never did drink wine. Now when this drinking of theirs had now gone on for some considerable time, many of the men present sitting before the Princess were beginning to show signs of being in their cups, and some indeed were already dead drunk. This state forsooth they deem a sign of manliness, and at none of their feasts do they consider hilarity is attained unless many guests are properly in drink.

Shortly on this the food was brought in, an abundance of roast mutton and horse-flesh, with various meat stews. All began and set to to eat with much talking and joking, where one would snatch a piece of meat from another and all the guests were very merry. This eating of meat, however, lasted but a short while, and then they brought in dishes of rice made up in various fashions, also thin cakes of bread sugared over, and some vegetables. The meat dishes for the most part were served on their separate trenchers, but they also carried the joints in on those leather mats that we have described, and served them to the guests after cutting up. The Princess Khánzádeh is as already said the wife of Prince Mírán Sháh whom she has brought back into favour with his father. She is herself descended from a prince who was the forefather of Timur, and for this reason enjoys great respect at the hands of her father-in-law. Prince Mírán Sháh has a son by her who is now a young man about twenty years of age and his name is Khalíl Sultán. Now on that Thursday the 9th of October Timur commanded a feast to be made in honour of one of his grandsons whose marriage was about to be celebrated.[5] We ambassadors again were invited, the entertainment taking place in one of those Enclosures set about with many fine tents. On this occasion too the Great Khan, Timur's chief wife and the Princess Khánzádeh both again were present with other dames and lords besides much folk in attendance. The amount they did eat this day of mutton and horse-meat was enormous as is their custom, and they drank wine and were exceeding merry. All the ladies likewise partook of the wine, it being served to them after the fashion described at the feast of the previous day.

Further to celebrate this day of the royal wedding his Highness had given command by proclamation throughout the city of Samarqand that all the trading folk of the town, namely those who sold stuffs and those who sold jewels, with the hucksters and merchants for sale of goods of all and every sort, together with the cooks, butchers, bakers, tailors and shoemakers, in short all the craftsmen who were inhabitants of the capital, should betake themselves out for that day to the meadows where the great Horde was encamped. They were at the same time under obligation to bring out their tents to this camping place, and to sell there the goods and produce each of his trade, and thus the city was to remain empty of them all. The order further was given that each trade and craft should next arrange a gala show, where each man should display his skill making an exhibition throughout the Horde for the pleasure of all spectators. Further it was ordered that none were to return to their homes in Samarqand until they had received his Highness's leave and permission. Thus the proclamation took effect, and all the craftsmen and tradesmen migrated from the city to the camp bringing with then their goods and wares to sell. The whole Horde was filled with them, each craft and trade being allotted a street where the men of the same, each separately and in due order, displayed their art. Further in every craft there was set up an exhibition or separate show to display their skill in the matter in hand, and these shows perambulated throughout the whole of the Horde for the entertainment of the people.[6] Again in those quarters where the trades were thus congregated, and at several central points where the diverse exhibition tents were numerous, Timur had commanded that great gallows should be set up. By proclamation at the same time he let it be known that whereas he intended thus to gratify and give enjoyment to all the common-folk at his festival, he also intended to give a warning and example of those who had offended him and done evil deeds, and he would proceed to the public execution of the criminals.

 The first of those to suffer his justice was the Mayor in Chief of Samarqand, a man whose name was Dina, a personage the greatest in all that land of his Empire. Aforetime when Timur had set out on his late expedition, namely six years and eleven months before this present date at which we were come, this man had been appointed to be the chief magistrate, and Timur had left him to be governor of Samarqand. But his Highness since his return had come to know that this man had betrayed his trust using his office to misgovern and oppress the people. He therefore now commanded this Dina the Chief Mayor to be brought before him, and after judgment forthwith he was taken out and without delay hanged; all the wealth that he had so unjustly gathered to himself being forfeited to the state. This act of high justice condemning so great a personage to death, made all men to tremble, and notably he had been one in whom his Highness had reposed much confidence. Then again in regard to a certain man the friend of that Dina and who had sought to intercede with Timur for his pardon, his Highness likewise caused him now to be hanged, thus sharing the fate of his companion. There was also a privileged and very favourite courtier of his Highness, whose name was Burunday Mirza[7] and he too had interceded with Timur seeking to obtain the pardon of the Chief Mayor. To this intent he had offered his Highness to pay in ransom a sum of 400,000 Pesantes, and each of these Pesantes is of the value of a silver real [which may be four shillings]. Forthwith Timur had answered that gladly he would accept the gift, but the moneys had no sooner come into his treasury than he ordered torture to be given to that unhappy man, if possible to get more money from him, and when none could be obtained it was ordered that he be hung on the gallows by the feet head downwards till he died.

Next his Highness had ordered justice to be meted to a certain great lord of the court in whose care had been left three thousand horses of the government stud when Timur had set out on the late campaign. Because on his return those

3,000 were not yet all present that lord was now condemned to the gallows, and it served him for naught that he had promised, if time were granted him, in place of those 3,000 he would soon have 6,000 to bring before his Highness. It was ever after this or a similar fashion that Timur administered justice. For instance he had recently caused certain butchers to be put to death who were caught selling meat at an excessive price. Then, when but just arrived back from his last campaign, he had ordered penalties to be laid on various shoemakers and those who sold sandals and other such like trade folk, and that they should be mulcted of their illicit gains, seeing that they were over charging for their wares. But these various penalties and punishments now caused those traders who, as we have explained, had lately been ordered out from Samarqand city and established in the camp of the Horde, to deem that this had only been done the better to rob them of their livelihood. Now in High Justice as regards the death penalty, it is the custom among these Tartars if the culprit be a person of rank to put him to death by hanging, but if he be but a man of the people they behead him, for they hold decapitation to be a dreadful deed and a matter of much dishonour.

The following Monday which was the 13th of October Timur made another great feast to which as usual we ambassadors were invited. As we presented ourselves with the other bidden guests and came to where that great Pavilion stood, as already described where his Highness was wont to dine in state, we perceived that on either side of the Pavilion two other Enclosures had now been set up with many tents after the fashion that has been described on a previous page. But here there was a notable variation, for each of these two newly established Enclosures with their tents were even more skillfully wrought than those we had as yet seen, and the stuffs used were more costly than in the former case. Thus the enclosing wall of each of these, that had been newly pitched surpassed in magnificence all that we had yet seen: for this wall was made entirely of crimson tapestry embroidered over with patterns in gold thread that was most marvellously beautiful. The outer walls here were far higher than had been the case with the other Enclosures and each gateway far more lofty. Each gate was an archway domed above, and crowning the arch was a high centre piece, the stuffs of which both center piece and arch were made being embroidered over with fine patterns in gold thread. The doors closing the gateway were made with the like tapestry also embroidered in gold thread. The centre piece above the gateway consisted of a square tower with battlements this too made of the same tapestry in all ways similar to that of the rest of the gateway. The walls of the one as of the other Enclosure were all along the summit crowned by battlements of that tapestry stuff embroidered over. In these walls were set at intervals windows with nettings over the openings made with silken cords worked into the tapestry, the window openings having shutters to close them made likewise in tapestry. Within the one Enclosure had been pitched many tents, each magnificently wrought and richly adorned in diverse ways. The second Enclosure was nearby the first and its walls were of white Zaytuni silk stuff plain and unornamented. This Enclosure too had a gateway and windows in the walls like the other; while within were tents of many fashions, and from the one Enclosure to the other you could pass conveniently by a passageway with a closing gate.

These two Enclosures just described and newly made we were not allowed to enter and see this day of the feast which Timur presided over and gave in his great Pavilion: but on the following day we were again brought hither when we were taken over both these new Enclosures and shown the tents and other matters pertaining to them. And further in front of their walls that we have described was erected a second great pavilion, exactly similar to the State Pavilion already so frequently mentioned where Timur was wont ordinarily to make his feast, but this other one was constructed of a white silk stuff which without as within was overlaid with coloured cloths that showed embroidered patterns and worked insets.

This day on arrival at the appointed place for the feast, we were left for a time to sit under an awning placed at some distance from the great Pavilion where we had been entertained on the previous occasion. Further we noticed that in the field lying round the tents and the great Pavilion of his Highness there had now been placed a number of great jars containing wine. These were stood at intervals, between each being the distance that one might cast a stone, and thus they surrounded the field aforesaid where the circuit may have been upwards of half a league in extent. In the field space lying between this line of jars and the great Pavilion no one was allowed to pass, and men on horse-back were on guard here armed with bow and arrows, also they carried maces and if anyone ever approached to come within the line of jars these men would shoot him with their arrows, or strike him down with their maces. We noticed indeed that many thus had been wounded for their inadvertence, and some had been thrown out almost for dead men and were lying at the gates of the Enclosure, for thus those guards were ordered to do no matter who it might be who trespassed. In this field round and beyond a vast number of people had now assembled awaiting the coming forth of his Highness to take his seat in the great Pavilion. Round this and encircling it had been set up many awnings, and under each awning had been placed one of those big wine jars, and the same indeed was of such size as to hold at least the measure of fifteen cantaras of wine, [which is equivalent to about sixty gallons].

As explained above we had sat waiting in this place under the awning for some space when they came and took us thence, for they told us that we should now go and pay our respects to a grandson of Timur, who a day or two before this had arrived in Samarqand from India the Less [namely Afghanistan] where he was Governor General: he having been sent for by Timur to come to him, his grandfather not having seen his face for seven years past. This young prince was the son of Timur's eldest son who had died many years since, whose name had been Jahángír. Timur had loved his son Jahángír very dearly and he now loved this grandson likewise for his father's sake: and the name of the young prince was Pír Muhammad. To his presence we were now taken and we found him in a tent of red tapestry seated on a low dais, round and about which many lords and a great number of folk were standing in attendance on him. As we approached outside the tent two of the lords in waiting came out to us, and taking us under the arms they made us kneel on the ground, and then getting up we advanced a few steps, when we again knelt: and on this we were ushered into the tent. We here made the customary reverence, which was to put the right knee to the ground crossing at the same time our arms over the breast, and bowing with the head. All this we duly performed and stood, when after an interval those lords who had brought us in carried us forth, taking us back to where we had before been seated under the awning. This young prince was as we noticed very sumptuously attired as is the Tartar custom, he was wearing a robe of blue [Chinese] Zaytuni silk embroidered in gold circles; like small wheels, which back and front covered his chest and shoulders and passed down the material of the sleeves. On his head he wore a hat garnished with many great pearls and precious stones, and on the top was displayed a fine clear balas ruby. The people whom we found in attendance on him all paid him the utmost deference.

While we were there the Prince was being entertained with the display of two men who were wrestling. These wrestlers were dressed each in a leathern garment like a sleeveless jerkin, and at first struggling together it seemed as though neither could overcome the other. It was commanded them however to have done, and then one quickly threw his opponent, holding him down for a long space of time and preventing his getting up, for had he been able to get up again it would have been held that his fall was not a defeat. That same day all the foreign ambassadors present came and made their obeisance before this prince Timur's grandson. He was we noted a young man of about twenty-two years of age, swarthy and yellow of skin and he had no beard. He bore the title, we were informed, of Lord of Lesser India but this indeed is not consonant with the true facts, for he who is now native lord and king of India is indeed a Christian, whose exact name is So and So being unknown to me.[8] According to what we heard later the chief and capital city of India is Delhi, and the lord thereof did battle against Timur when some time since he invaded that country. The king of India then possessed an immense army and besides warriors there were over fifty war elephants, fully armed and such as are called tuskers. At the first battle Timur suffered defeat at the hands of the king of India by reason of the charge of these same elephants. On the morrow however Timur returned to give battle and this time he had marshalled a squadron of camels; these he sent forward each bearing a load of dry grass to oppose the elephants. No sooner had the fight begun than fire was set to these loads of inflammable stuff when the camels all in flames did so terrify the elephants that all took to flight. It appears indeed that the elephant especially fears fire, and the reason given is that his eyes are exceedingly small.

Thus on this occasion that lord of India suffered defeat, and Timur next took from him all the country of the upper plains of India the Less which march with the lands of the Empire of Samarqand. The most part of the land of Lesser

India is a rugged and mountainous country, but none the less it is well populated having many great cities and rich hamlets, the soil being very fertile. When the King of India found himself thus worsted in the fight he betook himself to the mountain fastnesses, once more gathering round him his hosts for battle. Timur however had no mind again to give battle, he assembled his host and all his people, then retired returning to the upper plains of the north whither the King of India saw fit not to follow. But this country of the high mountain plains, which Timur then conquered and took from the King of India, [and which is Afghanistan called India the Less], is now under the government of his grandson the young prince of whom we have been speaking. Its southern border extends [down to the shores of the Persian Gulf namely] to Ormuz, which is a very great and rich city. The major part of that India [which is Greater India] the king thereof still keeps in possession, and did not lose when defeated at that battle, which we have spoken of, and this took place some twelve years ago. Since then neither Timur nor the Prince his grandson has ever sought again to invade that country. The people of Greater India are Christians for the most part as is also their king, but they are of the Greek rite, though among them are found other Christians who mark their faces with fire, and have different beliefs from the rest.[9] These latter folk who bear the mark of fire are looked down upon by their neighbours. Among the Indians Jews and Moors also are to be met with, but these live here in subjection to the Christians.

Chapter XIV

Samarqand

WE ambassadors were now taken back [after our presentation, as described in the last chapter, to Prince Pír Muhammad] to that awning where at first we had been seated, and here we awaited the hour of noon when Timur leaving his private tent was to appear in the Great Pavilion. And thither he came and there received us, together with a great crowd of his imperial kinsmen, also many other ambassadors from foreign countries who had arrived to present themselves before him. We and they all now took our seats in due order of precedence in the presence of his Highness under the Great Pavilion, being spectators of the various games that were now exhibited before him. Then too they brought out his elephants, their hides painted with green and red and other colours, each with its castle [or howdah] on its back, and these elephants were made to perform many tricks. Some played on timbrels while the elephants went through their performances and the noise they made was amazing, while also within the pavilion where Timur was seated there were gathered the minstrels who loudly sounded their various musical instruments. Round and about and notably in the presence of his Highness they had stood on the ground as many as three hundred wine jars. Further there were two tripods made of wooden staves painted red, and hung on each was a great leathern sack that was filled with cream and mare's milk. This the attendants having wands in their hands kept on stirring, rocking the milk backwards and forwards, while time and again they threw in many loaves of sugar. This was done in the service of providing drink for the guests that day, both as to the wine and the milk.

All being now in order and arranged, we saw the Great Khanum, his Highness's chief wife, appear coming from one of those neighbouring Enclosures already spoken of which adjoined the Great Pavilion, for she was to be present with her lord at the feast; and she was robed and adorned in the following manner. Her outer robe was of red silk embroidered with gold and it was very ample and had a long train which lay on the ground. This robe was made without sleeves and in it the only openings were that at the neck where her head appeared, and the two armholes for the passage of her arms, and it was made high up to the throat. This garment had no waist and the skirt was exceedingly broad below, the long train being held up by fifteen dames in attendance who walked behind, thus enabling her to proceed forward. The Khanum's face appeared to be entirely covered with white lead or some such cosmetic, and the effect was to make it look as though she were wearing a paper mask. This cosmetic it is their custom for the women to smear on their faces both summer and winter to keep off the sun when they go out, and all the attendants of her Highness had their faces thus protected, as also the other dames of the Court.

The Great Khanum wore before her face a thin white veil, and the rest of her head-dress was very like the crest of a helmet, such as we men wear in jousting in the tilt yard: but this crest of hers was of red stuff and its border hung down in part over her shoulders. In the back part this crest was very lofty and it was ornamented with many great round pearls all of good orient, also with precious stones such as balas rubies and turquoises, the same very finely set. The hem of this head covering showed gold thread embroidery, and set round it she wore a very beautiful garland of pure gold ornamented with great pearls and gems. Further the summit of this crest just described was erected upon a framework which displayed three large balas rubies each about two finger breadths across, and these were clear in colour and glittered in the light, while over all rose a long white plume to the height of an ell, the feathers thereof hanging down so that some almost hid the face coming to below the eyes. This plume was braced together by gold wire, while at the summit appeared a white knot of feathers garnished with pearls and precious stones. As she came forward this mighty head-gear waved backwards and forwards, and the Princess was wearing her hair all loose, hanging down over her shoulders. This was very black in colour for indeed it is the hue they most esteem, black hair with them being held to be more beautiful than that of any other colour, and the women dye their hair to preserve it so. To keep this crest and the other adornments steady on her head the Princess was attended by many dames who walked beside her, some of whom while supporting her kept their hands up to the head-dress; indeed in all she appeared to have round and about her as many as three hundred attendants.

Over the head of the Princess was borne a parasol, a man holding it and the stick was a pole the size of a lance. This parasol was of white silk dome-shaped and round like the top of a tent, with wooden ribs that kept the stuff extended: it was very carefully held over her head as she walked to keep the sun off her face. In front preceding her and the ladies of her suite marched many eunuchs, and these are those who with the Tartars always have charge of their women. Thus the procession advanced entering the Pavilion where Timur was already seated. The Great Khanum now took her place beside his Highness but slightly behind on a low dais, before which had been piled a number of small mattresses one over the other for her to lean over; while the dames who were accompanying her took their places in the background outside beyond the pavilion. Three of her ladies however came in and sat beside her, for these were charged with keeping in its place that great crest which we have described as adorning her head, and which would not have held had not they to right and left steadied it with their hands. As soon as the Great Lady was thus seated the Second Lady, another of his Highness's wives, appeared coming from that other Enclosure of which we have spoken, and she was dressed very similarly in robes of red, with a head-dress formed to be a crest as described above. She too was wearing many jewels, and she advanced escorted with the same ceremony as had been used in the first case, having many ladies to attend her. She now entered the Pavilion coming forward to take her seat in the presence of his Highness on a dais that was somewhat further back than the one where the Great Lady sat. This particular wife of Timur goes by the name of the Kuchik Khanum and she is the second in rank.

Then issuing from another Enclosure and its tents came the third wife of his Highness, the ceremony in every particular being the same, and she too took her seat within the Pavilion but on a somewhat lower dais and at the back: and thus in succession one after another that day nine Princesses of the royal house appeared taking allotted places on their respective seats in the presence of Timur. All of them were similarly robed and bejewelled, and eight of these ladies were the wives of Timur, the ninth being the wife of one of his grandsons. The wives of his Highness bear the following names. The chief wife as already said above is known as the Khanum, and this is as we may say Queen, or Great Lady: she is the daughter of the [Chagatay] Lord of Samarqand of former days. He was besides lord over the whole of Persia, his empire stretching even to Damascus, and his name was Kazan Khán. He was of royal descent as regards his mother, but who his father had been never certainly was known. He was a very valiant commander who had won many battles; and he had promulgated laws and ordinances some of which are still in force to govern the affairs of state throughout the empire of Timur. The second wife is as already said the

Kuchik Khanum, which means the Little Lady: she was the daughter of a king whom they call Tumán Aga, and he ruled over a country that is known as Andarábah. The third wife bears the name of Tukel Khanum, the fourth is Chelpan Mulk Aga, the fifth is Mundasaga [Khanum] and the two next bear respectively the names Vengaraga [Khanum] and Ropa Arbaraga [Khanum]. The eighth and last wife is known as Jawhar Aga which in their tongue signifies the Queen of Hearts.[1] Timur has celebrated his marriage with her but lately, namely, in the month of August that has just gone by: and it is he who gave her this name.

When all these dames were duly seated and everything properly arranged the drinking began and was kept up for a considerable space of time. From the first the various wives of his Highness were served with wine and next with that beverage of mare's milk that is prepared after the fashion above described when we were being entertained in the tents where the princess Khánzádeh made her feast. Timur soon after this called both of us ambassadors to come before him, and taking a cup of wine in his hand presented it to the Master in Theology [my companion Fray Alfonso Paez] commanding him to drink, for he knew well that I Ruy González would not taste of this wine. Now those who are given to drink at the hands of Timur have to do so ceremoniously and after this fashion. They come forward and bending the right knee kneel, once at some distance before approaching: then they rise and step forward nearer to him and kneel with both knees on the ground receiving the offered cup from his hand. Then they stand up and go backwards a little distance, taking care always to face his Highness, and they kneel again and then drink at a draught all that is in the cup, for to leave any wine undrunk would be against good manners. Then having swallowed the draught they rise again and salute placing the hand to the head. When we ambassadors were thus called up for presentation, two of the lords in waiting seized each of us under the arms and did not let us loose until we had been subsequently brought back to our seats.

Now, as regarded our personal attendants and servants they all had been already accommodated under an awning that was placed near by the Pavilion where the feast was in progress. All round and about there were pitched many smaller tents and awnings where sat the various other ambassadors who had come to attend the court of his Highness but who were not deemed of sufficient rank to warrant a seat in the Great Pavilion where Timur himself had his place. There had been set under each of these awnings a great jar of wine for those guests to drink who were accommodated there: and further his Highness now sent two of those especial wine-jars which were in the Pavilion before him, and for his own drinking, despatching them to the awning where our attendants and servants were seated in waiting on us the ambassadors of Spain. Now forthwith before where Timur had taken his place was set up a wooden frame with cords attached which the gymnasts used in the tricks they were proceeding to perform: and next the elephants were brought forward, fourteen in number. Each beast carried a wooden castle on its back, which was covered in with silk facings, and the castle [or howdah] had four green and yellow standards at the corners and in each were five or six men. Further there was a man seated on the neck of the elephant who carried a goad in his hand whereby to guide the beast and make him do his bidding.

These elephants were very black and their skins had no hair except indeed at the tail which is hairy as is that of the camel, where the hairs are of silky texture. These elephants were huge in size, each being of the weight of four or five big bulls. Their bodies are clumsily built: they have no grace of form, and it is as though each were a great sack that had been stuffed out full. At the ankle-joint the leg comes down quite straight, as is the case with the buffalo, but with the elephant the legs, both the pair before and the pair behind, are equally huge of size. The foot is round and plump, with the five toes, each with its black nail not unlike a human toenail. The elephant has no neck to speak of, and the upper rib bones here are of great size in the fore part, so that his head is attached directly on the body, and he cannot put his mouth to the ground for the purpose of eating. The ears are very large, round in shape and the rim is as it were notched. The elephant's eyes are extremely small. Sitting behind the neck his keeper rides astride, and he carries a goad in his hand with which he urges the beast forward making him to go whither he will. The elephant's head is very large, indeed not unlike the packsaddle of an ass in shape, but smaller. In front in the face is a hollow from which the trunk starts and this comes down where the nose would be otherwise. The trunk is formed broad above and tapering below, somewhat in shape like a sleeve, and it reaches right down to the ground. The trunk is perforated throughout and by means of it he drinks at his need, for he puts the end into the water sucking it up into his mouth, as may be said, through his nose.

Further it is with his trunk that he feeds, for he is unable thus to use his mouth, which as noted above he cannot put to the ground. Hence he must fetch up the food to his mouth with his trunk when he would eat, and with it he will catch hold of the grass and pluck it of, cutting it short as with a knife, carrying it to his mouth to which he brings it with a turn of the trunk, and then back again for more, it being thus that he eats. So we see it is with his trunk the elephant purveys all his needs; and hence his trunk is never still but ever kept in motion, coiling and uncoiling like a snake. He can touch his backbone anywhere with his trunk, indeed there is no part of his body that he cannot reach with it. The elephant's mouth is seen to open just below the root of the trunk, where on either side the jaws are like those of a pig or wild boar, and here he carries two tusks, each as big as a man's leg, and as long as both your arms can stretch. When they make their elephants fight they attach a large iron ring on each tusk and fix thereto a sword blade, like the grooved swords we use in war, but theirs are shorter being only as long as the length of a man's arm. The elephant is a most intelligent beast, and quickly does all that his master who guides him commands. His rider sits astride his neck: the rider's legs passing down behind the elephant's ears, where the neck is so short that there is only room for the seat of the man. The rider has in his hand a goad with which he scratches the beast's head, making him walk whither he will: for no sooner has he marked with the goad in which direction he would go than the elephant immediately proceeds thither. And if he would wheel round and go the other way, the elephant quickly will back on his hind legs and turn as a bear would do, for his walk and movements are very like the shuffling gait of a bear.

When the elephant is made to fight his master goes armed, for so too is the case with the elephant as we have explained. His attack is by a series of jumps, not unlike the way a bear would advance, and next using the sword-blades with which his tusks are armed he gives at each step a blow, raising his head to throw it back, and the blows are aimed at any who oppose him. When in the fight his master would urge him on to greater rage, he strikes the beast on the head in front, wounding him there with the point of the goad: and as the elephant feels this wound he gives forth a loud grunt, like a pig's grunt and opening his mouth rushes on goaded by his master. This wound that has been given that day the same night will entirely be healed over, if the animal be left out in the open, but should they put him under the cover of a roof he will forthwith incontinently die of it. His master who rides him will easily make the elephant pick up for him any object off the ground, and this no matter how heavy it be: and to do this he uncurls his trunk, puts it down, picks up what is indicated and turning the trunk back gives it to those who are in the castle on his back. When the men who ride in this castle [or howdah] wish to alight they order the elephant to kneel: this he does by stretching the hind legs back and the front legs forward, lowering himself till his belly rests on the ground: the men in the castle can now come down by slipping over the hind quarters, holding on by ropes attached to the sides of the castle.

On the day of which we are speaking they made the elephants perform many tricks. Thus at one time they made them race against horses, and then they ran pursuing the folk in the crowds assembled round and about. When all the elephants together charged abreast, it seemed as though the solid earth itself shook at their onrush. Indeed there is no animal or horseman or man that can withstand their charge. For what I saw I deem it that in battle every elephant may be counted as the equivalent of one thousand foot soldiers: indeed so it is, for when they are surrounded by a crowd fighting they trample down and crush the men on every hand. When wounded they but fight the better, not perceiving the point of danger. As regards their tusks, as these are long and so set that by nature they only serve to strike a blow upwards, it is the custom to cut them down short, and then arm the base each with a sword blade, as already said, which thus armed enables them to strike the blow downwards. The elephant can go for a whole day, or even two days without feeding: and they say that when engaged in battle they will fight even for three days and require no food.

Upon the feast-day of which we have been speaking Timur and his wives having continued drinking their wine during some time, next it was ordered that the food should be brought in for them to dine. Horses and sheep had been roasted whole, the hair having been removed from the hide of the horse, while with the sheep these were first flayed. The viands when ready were served on great round trays [as already described] of stamped leather [like our Cordovan leather] called Guadamacir, which the attendants dragged over the grass from one part to the other; and such was the quantity of meat to be served that three hundred men and more had to attend the guests as waiters. Great was the shouting they all made, as the meat was finally arranged in the trenchers that were now laid in front of Timur, and as usual the meat was served without bread to be eaten with it. All the while a succession of carts were coming in charged with yet more meat, and next camels loaded up with other viands that were laid in panniers athwart either way, and all was turned out on the ground to be served to the various guests, where indeed it lay in great heaps: yet soon all would be eaten up and gone. When the place was clear of all the roast meat, next they brought in tables, but with no table-cloths, and on these were set bowls filled with the stews; then rice with other sweet-meats followed such as pancakes and sugared bread. By this time night had fallen and they now brought many lanterns to light up the Pavilion where his Highness sat. Then the more all began eating and drinking, namely the dames of the court and the lords, and the crowd without was ever greater as the feasting went on, which indeed we heard was to last the whole night through, for it was the marriage-night of one of Timur's grandsons whose bride was likewise of his kinswomen. When therefore we discovered that the entertainment was like to last till dawn of day, and we found that some who so pleased had already taken their leave, we too retired returning home to our lodgings, and left his Highness with his wives and the princesses to celebrate the marriage-feast to its close.

On Thursday the 16th of October his Highness made yet another entertainment to which we ambassadors were invited. This took place in one of those other Enclosures, being one that was very finely and richly laid out, and the great tent where we assembled was of those not pitched with guy-ropes, but as described above was erected and supported on poles fashioned in the walls, which last were beautifully ornamented. His Highness caused us to be brought inside the tent to sit with him, and he was drinking wine that day as were all those who were his guests. Indeed that they might be overtaken the sooner to enjoy drunkenness they were now we found being served with spirits as well as wine. The meats again this day were in great abundance and the drinking, as said, was such that all when they left the feast were besotted drunk, his Highness at length remaining all alone in the tent where we found him to be in a state of much cheerfulness and contentment. Thus now we took our leave to return to our lodgings, for again the feasting had lasted the whole of the day, but this time ending with the fall of darkness. On the following day, Friday the 17th of October the Great Khanum, his Highness's chief wife gave her feast, and she sent to invite us to be present thereto, the entertainment taking place in a fine Enclosure with many rich tents that was her possession. The guests were numerous, all the Ambassadors come from foreign countries had received invitation, as also the lords and ladies of the court and an immense concourse of folk privileged to attend. The Enclosure where we were now being assembled was beset with many rich tents, the outer walls of the Enclosure being made of white cloth with coloured insets, also bands and lettering and lacings of diverse designs.

That day as soon as we reached the camp coming from our lodgings we were taken in charge by certain great lords who were the kinsmen of his Highness, and they now brought us into that Enclosure, giving us seats in a tent that stood near the entrance gate. This tent had walls of crimson tapestry, with insets of white embroidery laid to its cloth, both without and within. We were forthwith accommodated with a place here inside the tent, and they next brought us meat and wine to serve our wants in due abundance. As soon as we had dined the Great Khanum immediately sent word that we were to be taken and forthwith shown over all her tents that were in that Enclosure and these all were of richest make. Among the rest there was one that was very large and lofty and of the kind that is supported [on poles and] had no guy-ropes, the same being covered outside with a cloth of red silk very beautiful to see. Further it was adorned with rows of silver gilt spangles running from the top to the bottom of the walls. Both without and within this tent was most admirable, the material of its walls being in all parts adorned with inset patterns. There were to it two double doors, the first before the second, and the outer of the two had its double doors of basket work in thin rods painted red, which interlaced. These doors outside were covered with a rose coloured silk stuff loosely woven: and they were made thus that when shut the air could enter through that material; while further any body inside the tent looking out could see those who were outside, though these last yet could not see into the tent to perceive those within.

The inner doorways here were made very high, so high indeed that a man on horseback might easily have entered through them, and these double doors were covered with plates of silver gilt ornamented with patterns in blue enamel work, having insets that were very finely made in gold plate. All this was so beautifully wrought that evidently never in Tartary nor indeed in our western land of Spain could it have been come to. In the one door was figured the image of Saint Peter while in the other was Saint Paul, and each saint had a book in his hands, the entire work being of silver.

They afterwards told us that these doors had been brought hither from Brusa, where Timur had found them when the treasure of the Turkish sultan had come into his hands.[2] In the middle within the tent, facing the doorway was placed a chest or small cabinet which was used as a stand for cups and dishes of plate. This cabinet was entirely made of gold, richly ornamented with enamel work with insets, and in height it would stand to a man's breast. The top was flat and it was enclosed at the back with the like of little battlements in green and blue enamel, which were scalloped. The whole of this cabinet was encrusted with jewels and pearls of large size, and in the centre part between the pearls and precious stones was set a single round jewel the size of a small nut, but it was not of any very excellent colour. To close this cabinet was a small door, and within was kept a set of drinking vessels. These were six flasks made of gold, beautifully chased, set with pearls and precious stones, and beside them stood six round gold cups likewise adorned with pearls and jewels.

In front of this cabinet was standing a small table some two palms in height made of gold this too being ornamented with beautiful stones and many big pearls, while in the top of the table was set a great emerald of very light colour, green;[3] this lay level with the table top and in size it might measure four palms in the length, stretching from end to end of the table, and it was a palm breadth and a half across. Standing and set beside this table was to be noticed a golden tree that simulated an oak, and its trunk was as thick as might be a man's leg, while above the branches spread to right and to left, bearing leaves like oak leaves. This tree reached to the height of a man, and below it was made as though its roots grew from a great dish that lay there. The fruit of this tree consisted in vast numbers of balas rubies, emeralds, turquoises, sapphires and common rubies with many great round pearls of wonderful orient and beauty. These were set all over the tree while numerous little birds, made of gold enamel in many colours were to be seen perching on the branches. Of these some with their wings open seemed ready to fly and some with closed wings seemed as though they had just alighted on the twigs from flight, while some appeared about to eat of the fruits of the tree, and were pecking with their bills at the rubies, turquoises, and other gems or at the pearls which so to speak grew from the branches. Over against this tree but standing back by the wall of the tent was set a screen made of wood covered over with plates of silver gilt, in front of which stood a couch. This was arranged with many mattresses that were covered over with a silk stuff embroidered with oak leaves and flowers and other patterns. Opposite on the other side of the tent there was another like screen with its couch to match, and the floor of the tent here about was laid with very beautiful silk carpets.

After we had thus thoroughly inspected this tent of the Great Khanum we were taken back to that other Enclosure already described by us, namely the one that had the red tapestry walls embroidered over with gold thread, and where Timur was established feasting and drinking wine with his lords and intimate courtiers. As we have said he had on the previous evening celebrated the feast in honour of the marriage of one of his grandsons to a cousin, the grand-daughter likewise of his Highness, and the bride and bridegroom now had come to occupy one of the great tents in that Enclosure. This Enclosure, as you entered it, had on the right hand its Pavilion or main tent, and this was pitched like a booth, its walls being of red tapestry, everywhere embroidered over, and with insets of white and coloured stuffs for further adornment. This Pavilion was surrounded externally by porticoes, which communicated directly with the apartment within, from which the windows opened into the porticoes; these being set at intervals in the tent wall and closed with nettings or with blinds of a stuff similar to the walls, and by these windows those within could look out into the porticoes. The ceilings roofing the porticoes on the inner side closed up to the main wall of the Pavilion, so that from the outside the whole appeared to be of one piece and structure.

Now as soon as we had been brought in thither they gave us seats in the entrance porch of this Pavilion, which passed under a beautiful archway, and this entrance led into a very broad gangway enclosed on either side with canvas walls, while above the high ceiling was in the form of a dome. From this gangway to the right hand you could enter through a doorway into the porticoes already described, and on the left hand access was gained to a magnificent apartment richly beset, while in front at the end of this entrance gangway was the main body of the great Pavilion, with walls wrought in embroideries of gold thread.

The broad entrance gangway of which we have been speaking held in its centre an inner tent of considerable size, of the kind supported without guy-ropes [having numerous poles within the walls] and here it was that Timur was seated with his company drinking wine, and great was the noise of their feasting. It is to be understood that this great series of apartments with the porticoes adjacent was all of one construction adjoined together, and the walls were of that red tapestry which we have mentioned. And the workmanship throughout was so finely wrought and richly ornamented and perfect that to describe it duly in words is impossible, while to appreciate properly its great excellence it must have been seen with the eyes. After we had thus at leisure inspected all these pavilions and tents they led us on and next showed us a house which likewise stood in that Enclosure. It was entirely built of wood, very lofty and you go up to it by a stairway; and it is surrounded on all four sides by porticoes on platforms.

The woodwork of this house is beautifully painted in gold and blue pattern: and it is so constructed that it can be taken down and set up again elsewhere when the need is to remove it, for it is indeed the Mosque in which Timur makes his devotions, and he carries it with him on his journeys and campaigns whithersoever he goes.

That day we went on sight seeing and further they showed us a tent, of the kind stayed by ropes, which were of green colour, and the tent walls without were covered with gray squirrel fur while inside it was lined with a more common fur called vair. In this tent were two bedsteads set according to their customary make. Then we were taken into another tent alongside the last, and this one was of the kind that has no cords [but has poles in the canvas to stay it]. The wall outside was made of a red stuff with insets of cloth of other different colours; while inside the walls were lined below with skins of ermine, which is the most precious fur in the whole world and it is that of the great marten. These ermine skins are so prized that if it be of the first quality a single skin here in Tartary, will fetch from fourteen to fifteen gold ducats, while in the West with us the price may be much more. The lining in this tent above the ermine was of gray squirrel skin. Outside the entrance to this tent was set an awning, so that the sun might not shine into it; and this awning also was lined inside with gray squirrel. By Timur's orders these tents had been made and lined after this fashion in order to keep out the sun's heat in summer and in winter to keep the heat in. We now came from this first Enclosure and were taken to a second, which stood alongside, but connected with the first by a gangway, and the walls here were a white [Chinese] Zaytuni silk.

Here again we were shown many magnificent tents and awnings of diverse kinds made of silk cloths, for throughout the Horde there were all these Enclosures and tents that we have described which more especially belonged to Timur, while besides those that were for his Highness's own use there were also many others which belonged to the lords of the court and the officers in attendance on his Highness. These were all of different make and a wonder to behold, for on every side where one might look the great Enclosures, which as said above they call by the name of Sarápardeh, meet the eye, each with many beautiful tents within their circuit. Thus in this Horde where his Highness was now present there might be reckoned to be from forty to fifty thousand tents, a most magnificent sight to see, while beyond the limits of the Horde in the meadows around were pitched many other tents, each in its orchard or garden, and these grounds all well watered by the streams that flowed everywhere through the countryside round and about Samarqand.

To this great festival that we have been describing Timur had ordered all the great lords and nobles of his Empire to appear and be present, and thus it came about that we saw now in Samarqand the King of Badakhshán, nearby whose capital city are the mines where the balas ruby is found. This monarch was well attended by his lords and courtiers; and we took occasion to present ourselves before him, when after paying our respects we enquired of him as to how the balas ruby was found. He replied graciously and told us that close to the capital city of Badakhshán was a mountain where the mines were situated. Here day by day men go and seek and break into the rocks on that mountain-side to find these precious stones. When the vein is discovered where they lie, this vein is carefully followed, and when the jewel is reached it must be cut out little by little with chisels until all the matrix has been removed. Then grinding the gem on millstones it would further be polished. We were told also that by order of Timur a strong guard had been established at the mines to see to it that his Highness's rights were respected. The capital of Badakhshán lay ten days' march from Samarqand in the direction of India the Less. There was again another great lord at this festival, and he was governor in the name of Timur at the city of Aquivi, which is in the country where the lapis lazuli comes from: and in the rock that gives this stone they also find sapphires. This city of Aquivi is also a like distance from Samarqand, namely ten days' journey in the direction of India the Less, but it lies rather to the southward of Badakhshán.[4]

On Thursday the 23rd of October Timur made another great feast in the Horde to which we were invited and it took place in the Great Pavilion. A mighty concourse of guests was assembled and wine was abundantly served, which was esteemed by all there present to be a matter of special favour shown them. Great was their cheer and joyfulness: the wives of his Highness were all present with him at the feast sitting in the Pavilion, and each of them appeared dressed and adorned as has been already described on a former occasion. This feast lasted all day ending at nightfall. On the Thursday week, which was the 30th of October Timur betook himself from his camp in the Horde back to the city of Samarqand, taking up his residence in a certain place adjacent to the Mosque which he had lately ordered to be built. This Mosque was the place of burial of one of his grandsons, namely Prince Muhammad Sultán[5] who had died in Asia Minor shortly after the battle where Timur conquered the Turkish [Sultan Báyazíd]. Indeed it was this Prince who had taken the Sultan prisoner [at the battle of Angora], but afterwards he had succumbed to his wounds there received. Timur had loved this grandson greatly and in his remembrance had caused this Mosque to be built as his place of burial [after the Prince's body had been brought back home]. To the palace adjacent thereto and but recently constructed Timur came that day, it being his intention to celebrate the consecration of his grandson's tomb by a feast, to which we as usual had been graciously invited. Then as we presented ourselves we were shown over that chapel, which was the place of interment of the Prince, and we found it square in plan and very loftily built. Both outside and in it was magnificently adorned in gold and blue tiles beautifully patterned, and there was much other fine work in gypsum.

Now when this Prince had died in the Turkish country, as above explained his body had been transported home to Samarqand for burial, and the city authorities had received command to erect this Mosque for his tomb. But recently Timur had come in from the Horde to view the building and he had found that the chapel was not to his liking, holding that it was built too low. Immediately he ordered the walls to be demolished, and laid it on the architects that it should be rebuilt within ten days' time, under threat of a terrible forfeit to the workmen. Without delay the rebuilding was set in hand, day and night the work went on, and Timur himself already twice had come into the city to see what progress had been made, on which occasions he had caused himself to be carried in a litter, for at his age he could no longer sit his horse. The chapel had now been completely rebuilt within the appointed ten days' time, and it was a wonder how so great a building could have been put up and completed within so brief a space. As stated above it was in honour and for the memory of his grandson that Timur had now ordered this feast to be made: many were the guests assembled and according to their custom the quantity of roast meat there consumed was immense.

Then after we had all partaken at this commemorative festival, one of the lords present, [whom we have already named] a very privileged courtier, the chamberlain called Sháh Melik Mirza, came up to us ambassadors and leading us forth, brought us into the presence of his Highness, when we were each presented with a robe of kincob [gold cloth]. Also for wearing underneath the same a close fitting jacket such as is worn by the Tartars in cold weather, this last being made of a silk cloth lined with skins, and it had a high collar at the neck made of the fur of two marten skins. At the same time they gave us each a hat to cover our heads withal: and finally we were presented with a wallet in which had been put 1,500 silver pieces, namely the coins they call Tangas each of which is worth two silver reals with us [making a total sum equivalent to over £80]. We therefore now came before his Highness and made him our thanks and obeisance as is customary, when he addressed us saying that we should come back to him the very next day to have speech again with him, and be dismissed, in a good hour, for our return home to our lord the King of Spain whom he told us he regarded in affection now as his very own son.

Chapter XV

Samarqand

IN the matter of the rebuilding of that Mosque for the burial place of his grandson all being completed to his Highness's satisfaction, Timur now turned to another work which he intended for the adornment of the city of Samarqand his capital: and it was to be after this wise. Every year to the city of Samarqand much merchandise of all kinds came from Cathay, India, Tartary, and from many other quarters besides, for in the countries round the Samarqand territory commerce is very flourishing; but there was as yet no place within the city where this merchandise might be suitably stored, displayed and offered for sale. Timur therefore now gave orders that a street should be built to pass right through Samarqand, which should have shops opened on either side of it in which every kind of merchandise should be sold, and this new street was to go from one side of the city through to the other side; traversing the heart of the township. The accomplishment of his order he laid on two of the great lords of his court, letting them know at the same time that if they failed in diligence, for the work was to go on continuously by day as by night, their heads would pay the penalty. These nobles therefore began at speed, causing all the houses to be thrown down along the line that his Highness had indicated for the passage of the new street. No heed was paid to the complaint of persons to whom the property here might belong, and those whose houses thus were demolished suddenly had to quit with no warning, carrying away with them their goods and chattels as best they might.

No sooner had all the houses been thrown down than the master builders came and laid out the broad new street, erecting shops on the one side and opposite, placing before each a high stone bench that was topped with white slabs. Each shop had two chambers, front and back, and the street way was arched over with a domed roof in which were windows to let the light through. As soon as these shops were made ready, forthwith they were occupied by merchants selling goods of all sorts: and at intervals down the street were erected water fountains. The cost of all this work was charged to the town council and workmen did not lack, as many coming forward as were wanted by the overseers. The masons who worked through the day at nightfall went home, their places being taken by as many as had gone, who worked throughout the night hours. Some would be pulling down the houses while others laid out the roadway, others again building anew, and the tumult was such day and night that it seemed all the devils of hell were at work here. Thus in the course of twenty days the whole new street was carried through: a wonder indeed to behold; but those whose houses had been thus demolished had good cause to complain.

Yet scarcely did they dare bring their case before his Highness: then however at last coming together they betook themselves for help to certain Sayyids, and these are the privileged favourites and courtiers of Timur who can talk as they please with him being, as is reputed the descendants of their Prophet Mahomet. These undertook the case, and one day therefore when certain of them were playing at chess with his Highness, they ventured to tell him that since he of his good will had ordered all the houses belonging to those poor people to be laid low, it were but right they should receive compensation for the lands this roadway passed through. It is reported that on hearing this Timur waxed wrathful declaring that all the land of the city of Samarqand was his private property, for that he had bought the same with his own moneys, further that he had the title deeds in his possession, and indeed he would produce them for inspection on the morrow; adding that if aught had been wrongly taken he would compensate for the same forthwith. He spoke this with such command of his rights that those Sayyids were completely abashed. They were now but too thankful that the order had not been given for them all to lose their heads. Having thus fortunately escaped scathless their answer to Timur was that whatsoever his Highness did must indeed be good, and that all he ordered should be carried into effect.

The Mosque which Timur had caused to be built in memory of the mother of his wife the Great Khanum seemed to us the noblest of all those we visited in the city of Samarqand, but no sooner had it been completed than he began to find fault with its entrance gateway, which he now said was much too low and must forthwith be pulled down. Then the workmen began to dig pits to lay the new foundations, when in order that the piers might be rapidly rebuilt his Highness gave out that he himself would take charge to direct the labour for the one pier of the new gateway while he laid it on two of the lords of his court, his special favourites, to see to the foundations on the other part. Thus all should see whether it was he or those other two lords who first might bring this business to its proper conclusion. Now at this season Timur was already weak in health, he could no longer stand for long on his feet, or mount his horse, having always to be carried in a litter. It was therefore in his litter that every morning he had himself brought to the place, and he would stay there the best part of the day urging on the work. He would arrange for much meat to be cooked and brought, and then he would order them to throw portions of the same down to the workmen in the foundations, as though one should cast bones to dogs in a pit, and a wonder to all he even with his own hands did this. Thus he urged on their labour: and at times would have coins thrown to the masons when especially they worked to his satisfaction. Thus the building went on day and night until at last a time came when it had perforce to stop - as was also the case in the matter of making the street [for the new bazaar] - on account of the winter snows which began now constantly to fall.

On Friday the 1st of November we went to present ourselves before his Highness, as he had enjoined on us to do, hoping that he would give us licence to depart on our homeward journey, and we found him lodging in the palace beside the Mosque that had been rebuilt according to his order, and where, as already said, the works were stopped in progress. We stayed waiting his pleasure from the early morning until midday, when his Highness appearing from a tent that was pitched here came forth and took his seat on a dais in the courtyard. Hither they now brought sufficient meats and fruit, of which all present amply partook, but when the meal was over his Highness sent to tell us to go home, for that day we must excuse his not receiving us in farewell audience as he had much other business to transact; namely with his grandson Pír Muhammad, who was the Prince already spoken of as being the King of India, and who was shortly returning to his government from which he had lately come to see his grandfather. It was on this day that his Highness bestowed on the Prince in largess many horses and robes of honour and arms, and gifts the like were given to many of the lords who were in. waiting, and to be of his company on the way back to his kingdom. The next day, which was Saturday, we again went and presented ourselves to attend on his Highness as we had been told to do but he did not appear coming out from his tent, for it was reported that he was ill. We were waiting there till after midday hoping that he would come to his place in the courtyard, and then one of the three Grand Chamberlains, who were of his Privy Council, came forth telling us to go back to our lodgings, for his Highness could not see us, and we returned whence we had come.

On Sunday the following day we again went over to the palace to see whether perchance Timur would grant us audience and give us leave to depart back to Spain. We were waiting there a long time, when at length those three Grand Chamberlains aforesaid again came out, and they now wanted to know who had dared to tell us to come, saying that we were immediately to return to our lodgings for that his Highness could not receive us. Further they then had that Tartar noble brought before them into whose charge we had been given as our attendant, and of him they angrily demanded by whose command we had thus again presented ourselves. Indeed they were exceeding wroth and about to order that in punishment his nose should be bored through, but to excuse himself he asserted that it was not he who had brought us there this day, as in truth he had not even that morning seen us to speak to. Thus he managed to escape without his nose being pierced in punishment, but they beat him none the less very soundly with many sticks. All this was done at the command of the three Grand Chamberlains, for Timur at that time was already very ill, and all those of the court men and women were in a state of great anxiety. Those three Grand Chamberlains indeed, who ruled the affairs of government being of the Privy Council, at that time scarce knew how to act. We were not yet therefore given leave to depart, and the Grand Chamberlains sent word that we were to betake ourselves to our lodgings in peace, where we were to stay till they should send for us again.

Then while we waited patiently in case his Highness should send for us and not daring to go and present ourselves again before him, one of the Chagatays came and told us that those Grand Chamberlains speaking as from Timur himself now had sent to let us know that we must immediately make ready to depart on the homeward journey. We should they said set out the very next day at dawn, departing in company with the

Ambassador of the Sultan of Egypt and the Ambassador from Turkey. Further we learnt that [a certain Tartar lord named] Carvo Tumán Ughlán was appointed to accompany us as our guide as far as Tabriz, who would cause rations to be supplied on the way with all that was needful, as also horses to carry us. The Chagatay said also that the Grand Chamberlains were giving orders for our due entertainment in all the cities and camps that we should pass through on the journey, until we came to Tabriz where Prince Omar the grandson of his Highness would receive us, and then send us on, each ambassador severally to his own country. On receiving this message brought by the Chagatay we immediately made our protest urging that as yet his Highness had not granted us our dismissal nor had he given us any answer to the message we had brought him from our lord the King of Castile, wherefore we said we could not and would not thus go hence. The Chagatay none the less answered us shortly that we had better say no more for everything had been arranged by the Grand Chamberlains. Let us (he said) therefore make all needful preparations for the journey, as likewise (said he), the other ambassadors were already occupied in doing. We however would not, and forthwith repaired to the palace demanding an interview with the Grand Chamberlains.

They received us and we proceeded to remind them how forsooth his Highness had on the previous Thursday given us command to return and see him, saying he would grant us speech and then dismiss us: but now this Chagatay had come telling us as from them - the Grand Chamberlains - that we were to prepare to set out forthwith on the morrow on our homeward voyage, and this had caused us much dismay. The Grand Chamberlains in reply told us that we could not possibly now have audience of his Highness, nor remain any longer at the Court; we must hasten our departure and set out exactly as they had sent the Chagatay to say. This indeed they had had to do and arrange because his Highness was in a very weak state, having already lost all power of speech, and he might be at the very point of death according to what the physicians prognosticated. They plainly said that this haste in dealing thus with us and our mission was necessary from the fact that Timur appeared to be dying, for our own sakes we must be off and away before the news of his death was here made public, and above all before that news reached the provinces through which on our journey we should have to pass.[1] To all we could urge against this view of the case, or put forward against our being thus summarily dismissed with no Letter to our King from his Highness, the Grand Chamberlains gave answer that it was useless further to discuss the matter, that we must and should go immediately, and as for the reply to our King's letter to his Highness it would be the business which that Tartar noble they were sending with us as our guide and companion would fully attend to.

The Ambassadors Receive their Passports

Thus matters undecided stood over from that day Monday [the 4th] till Tuesday fortnight the 18th of November, when the Grand Chamberlains again sent that Chagatay to us. He now brought us four written passports and orders of the government, on four chief cities that we had to pass through on our journey, and the orders stated that on arrival we ambassadors were to be supplied with fresh horses to carry us forward. The Chagatay further informed us that by the expressed commands of the Grand Chamberlains on the very morrow we were to set out and depart. We again replied that we would not start without having first seen Timur or having received from his Highness his written order: but the man answered that whether we would or would not, we must forsooth depart and go. This indeed we had to do, for that day they took us from our lodgings and carried us forth to an orchard outside the city, where we joined company with the ambassador from the Sultan of Cairo. Here therefore we rested that night, with our guard, waiting for the Turkish ambassador, who was to be our companion on the road; and we remained in camp that Tuesday of our coming, with Wednesday, Thursday and Friday following, which last was the 21st of November. Then at length all our company having assembled we took our final departure from Samarqand.

Now therefore that I have narrated in detail all that befell us during our stay in Samarqand, I must describe that city for you, telling of all that is there to be seen in and round and about, and of all that Timur has accomplished there to embellish his capital. Samarqand stands in a plain, and is surrounded by a rampart or wall of earth, with a very deep ditch. The city itself is rather larger than Seville, but lying outside Samarqand are great numbers of houses which form extensive suburbs. These lie spread on all hands for indeed the township is surrounded by orchards and vineyards, extending in some cases to a league and a half or even two leagues beyond Samarqand which stands in their centre. In between these orchards pass streets with open squares; these all are densely populated, and here all kinds of goods are on sale with bread stuffs and meat. Thus it is that the population without the city is more numerous than the population within the walls. Among these orchards outside Samarqand are found the most noble and beautiful houses, and here Timur has his many palaces and pleasure grounds. Round and about the great men of the government also here have their estates and country houses, each standing within its orchard: and so numerous are these gardens and vineyards surrounding Samarqand that a traveller who approaches the city sees only a great mountainous height of trees and the houses embowered among them remain invisible. Through the streets of Samarqand, as through its gardens outside and inside, pass many water-conduits, and in these gardens are the melon-beds and cotton-growing lands.

The melons of this countryside are abundant and very good, and at the season of Christmas there are so many melons and grapes to be had that it is indeed marvellous. Every day camels bring in their loads of melons from the country and it is a wonder how many are sold and eaten in the market. At all the outlying villages the melons being so abundant, at one season the people cure them, drying the same as is done with figs, which thus can be kept for use from one year's end to the next. The melons are cured after this fashion. They slice the fruit up into great pieces, removing the rind, when they are put to shrivel in the sun. As soon as these pieces are quite dry, they bind them one with the other storing them in hampers and thus they keep good for a whole twelvemonth. Beyond the suburbs of Samarqand stretch the great plains where are situated many hamlets these being all well populated, for here the immigrant folk are settled whom Timur has caused to be brought hither from all the foreign lands that he has conquered. The soil of the whole province of Samarqand is most fertile producing great crops of wheat. There are abundant fruit-trees also with rich vineyards: the livestock is magnificent, beasts and poultry all of a fine breed. The sheep are famous for having those fat tails that weigh each some twenty pounds, in fact as much as a man can readily hold in the hand: and of these sheep the flocks are so abundant that even when Timur is in camp here with his armies, [and there is a scarcity] a couple of sheep can be had in the market for the price of a ducat [which is about six shillings]. The prices indeed are so low that for a Meri, which is a coin worth [about three pence] or half a real, you may have a bushel and a half of barley. Baked bread is everywhere plentiful and rice can be had cheap in any quantity.

The richness and abundance of this great capital and its district is such as is indeed a wonder to behold: and it is for this reason that it bears the name of Samarqand: for this name would be more exactly written Semíz-kent, two words which signify " Rich-Town," for *Semíz* [in Turkish] is fat or rich and *Kent* means city or township: in time these two words having been corrupted into the name Samarqand.[2] Further this land of Samarqand is not alone rich in food stuffs but also in manufactures, such as factories of silk both the kinds called Zaytúmí and Kincobs, also crapes, taffetas and the stuffs we call Tercenals in Spain, which are all produced here in great numbers. Further they make up special fur linings for silk garments, and manufacture stuffs in gold and blue with other colours of diverse tints dyed, and besides all these kinds of stuffs there are the spiceries. Thus trade has always been fostered by Timur with the view of making his capital the noblest of cities: and during all his conquests wheresoever he came he carried off the best men of the population to people Samarqand, bringing thither together the master-craftsmen of all nations. Thus from Damascus he carried away with him all the weavers of that city, those who worked at the silk looms. Further the bow-makers who produce those cross-bows which are so famous: likewise armourers: also the craftsmen in glass and porcelain, who are known to be the best in all the world. From Turkey he had brought their gun-smiths who make the arquebus, and all men of other crafts wheresoever he found them, such as the silver-smiths and the masons. These all were in very great numbers, indeed so many had been brought together of craftsmen of all sorts that of every denomination and kind you might find many master workmen established in the capital. Again he had gathered to settle here in Samarqand artillery men, both engineers and bombardiers, besides those who make the ropes by which these engines work. Lastly hemp and flax had been sown and grown for the purpose in the Samarqand lands, where never before this crop had been cultivated.

So great therefore was the population now of all nationalities gathered together in Samarqand that of men with their families the number they said must amount to 150,000 souls. Of the nations brought here together there were to be seen Turks, Arabs and Moors of diverse sects, with Christians who were Greeks and Armenians, Catholics, Jacobites and Nestorians, besides those [Indian] folk who baptize with fire in the forehead, who are indeed Christians but of a faith that is peculiar to their nation. The population of Samarqand was so vast that lodging for them all could not be found in the city limits, nor in the streets, and open spaces of the suburbs and villages outside, and hence they were to be found quartered temporarily for lodgment even in the caves and in tents under the trees of the gardens, which was a matter very wonderful to see. The markets of Samarqand further are amply stored with merchandise imported from distant and foreign countries. From Russia and Tartary come leathers and linens, from Cathay silk stuffs that are the finest in the whole world, and of these the best are those that are plain without embroideries. Thence too is brought musk which is found in no other land but Cathay, with balas rubies and diamonds which are more frequently to be met with in those parts than elsewhere, also pearls, lastly rhubarb with many other spiceries. The goods that are imported to Samarqand from Cathay indeed are of the richest and most precious of all those brought thither from foreign parts, for the craftsmen of Cathay are reputed to be the most skilful by far beyond those of any other nation; and the saying is that they alone have two eyes, that the Franks indeed may have one, while the Moslems are but a blind folk. Thus the Franks and the Chinese in what they make have in the matter of eyes the advantage over the people of all other nationalities.

From India there are brought to Samarqand the lesser spiceries, which indeed are the most costly of the kind, such as nutmegs and cloves and mace with cinnamon both in the flower and as bark, with ginger and manna: all these with many other kinds that are never to be found in the markets of Alexandria. Throughout the city of Samarqand there are open squares where butchers' meat ready cooked, roasted or in stews, is sold, with fowls and game suitably prepared for eating, also bread and excellent fruit both are on sale. All these viands and victuals are there set out in a decent cleanly manner, namely in all those squares and open spaces of the town, and their traffic goes on all day and even all through the night time. Butchers' shops are numerous also those booths where fowls, pheasants and partridges are on sale: and these shops are kept open by night as by day. On the one part of Samarqand stands the Castle which is not built on a height, but is protected by deep ravines on all its sides: and through these water flows which makes the position of the Castle impregnable. It is here that his Highness keeps his treasure, and none from the city without may enter save the governor of the Castle and his men. Within its walls however Timur holds in durance and captivity upwards of a thousand workmen; these labour at making plate-armour and helms, with bows and arrows, and to this business they are kept at work throughout the whole of their time in the service of his Highness.

Some [seven] years gone by, when Timur last left Samarqand and set forth on that campaign whereby he conquered Turkey and plundered Damascus, he gave orders that all the troops who should accompany him might carry along on the march their wives and children, unless indeed by preference any man might wish to leave his household behind at home, in which case he should do so. This order Timur had given because it was then of his intention to remain abroad from his capital for seven whole years, while he should conquer all his enemies: and he had sworn an oath that he would not re-enter this castle of his in Samarqand until that period of seven years had run out. At that time when we were his guests in Samarqand there had arrived certain ambassadors sent by the Emperor of China who came to Timur bearing this message, namely: that all men knew that he, Timur; was in occupation of lands formerly held in fief to China, and hence that tribute for the same yearly had been due from him to the Chinese Emperor: but seeing that for seven years past no tribute had ever been paid, he Timur must now forthwith pay down the sum. The answer of his Highness to these ambassadors was that this was most true, and that he was about to pay what was due: but that he would not burden them, the ambassadors, to take it back to China on their return, for he himself Timur would bring it. This of course was all said in scorn and to despite them, for his Highness had no intention to pay that tribute. Of course during all those seven years past, none had ever been sent, nor had he who was at this time the Emperor of China ever sent any demand for it during those years: this absence of demand being caused by certain events now to be explained that of late had been happening in China.[3]

At the beginning of that period the reigning Emperor of China had died, and he had left three sons among whom his Empire and lands had been divided according to his will. The eldest son not unnaturally had wished to take to himself the whole empire putting out his two brothers, and he had forthwith compassed the death of the younger of the two, but the other brother had fought with him and succeeded finally in completely overcoming him. Then this eldest one, seeing that as matters now stood he could not come to terms with his brother, despaired and putting fire to his camp had perished, he and most of his men in the flames. Thus the one brother who survived was now Emperor, and when the tumult had quieted down and order was restored this new Emperor it was who had sent his ambassadors to Timur demanding that tribute which, he asserted, had been paid in the days of his father. We heard presently that his Highness had issued orders that those Chinese ambassadors should forthwith all of them be hung, but whether this order was actually carried out or whether the Emperor of China finally compassed to safeguard his honour is not known to us. Now from the city of Samarqand it is six months' march to the capital of China, which is called Cambaluc,[4] and this is the largest town in that empire: and of this six months' journey two are passed going across a desert country entirely uninhabited, except by nomad herdsmen who wander over the plains feeding their flocks. During the month of June of this year, immediately before the date of our coming to Samarqand, there had arrived a caravan of eight hundred camels bringing merchandise from China. Then it was that Timur having come home from his western campaigns had received that Chinese Embassy bearing the message sent him by the Emperor of China: and he forthwith had ordered the whole of this caravan, men and goods, to be taken into custody and that none should return to China.

Next from certain of the men who had travelled from Cambaluc with those ambassadors, as from those who had come in charge of the caravan of camels, he proceeded to obtain exact information concerning the many strange peculiarities regarding the country over which that Emperor was lord, with details of the great wealth and number of the Chinese people. There was in particular one [Tartar merchant] who had been allowed to reside in Cambaluc during six whole months. He described that great city as lying not far from the sea coast, and for its size he said it was certainly twenty times larger than Tabriz. If so it must indeed be the greatest city in all the world, for Tabriz measures a great league and more across and therefore this city of Cambaluc must extend to twenty leagues from one side to the other. The man further reported that the Emperor of China was lord of so many warriors that when his host went forth to wage war beyond the limits of his Empire, without counting those who marched with him he could leave 400,000 horse-men behind to guard his realm together with numerous regiments of foot-guards. As that man further reported it was the order current in China that no nobleman should be allowed to appear publicly on horseback unless he kept in his service at his call at least a thousand horsemen; and yet of the like of such nobles the number to be met with was very large. Many were the other wonderful facts that were further related of the capital and country of China. Lastly it was told us that this new Emperor of China had by birth been an idolater, but lately had been converted to the Christian faith.[5]

To return however to matters in hand, at the moment when we had come with our Embassy to Samarqand those seven years already spoken of above were now accomplished during which, as reported, Timur had sworn not to set foot within the Citadel of Samarqand where his treasures were stored. He therefore now proceeded to enter the same again with much pomp and rejoicing, and that all might wonder he caused to be brought before him for inspection the arms and armour that those workmen, his captives, had completed since the time when he set forth and last had been present. Among the rest they brought to show him three thousand new suits of plate armour, which is of the sort stitched on a backing of red canvas. To our thinking this appeared very well wrought, except that the plates are not thick enough, and they do not here know how properly to temper the steel. At the same time an immense number of helms were exhibited, and these each with its suit of plate armour were that day many of them given as presents by his Highness, being distributed among the lords and nobles there in attendance. These helms of theirs are made round and high, some turning back to a point, while in front a piece comes down to guard the face and nose:- which is a plate, two fingers broad, reaching the level of the chin below. This piece can be raised or lowered at will and it serves to ward off a side stroke by a sword. These suits of plate-armour are composed very much as is the custom with us in Spain, but they wear a long skirt, made of a material other than that is plate-armoured, and this comes down so as to appear below, as might be with us a jerkin.

Some fifteen days' march from Samarqand, and in the direction of China, lies a country that is inhabited by Amazons, and these women hold the custom of admitting no men to live with them. At a certain season of the year however with the consent of their elders, the younger mothers take their daughters and proceed with them to the countries thereto lying adjacent. Here the men on their coming invite all to stay in their houses and the maidens go to those men they prefer eating and drinking as of their household, and now living with them. Then after a time the women all return home to their own country. When subsequently daughters are born these they keep at home, but sons that are born to them are despatched away to their fathers in the places where these last may be living. These Amazons, though in neighbouring lands, are not among the people subject to Timur but are counted as a folk of the Chinese Empire, and they are Christians of the Greek rite. They are all of the lineage of those same Amazons who of old fought before Troy, when that city was about to be destroyed by the Greeks. At that time in Troy there were two nations of the Amazon peoples, one of the Turkish family which remained permanently there and the other which migrated to where they now are found.[6]

Good order is maintained in Samarqand with utmost strictness and none dare fight with another or oppress his neighbour by force: indeed as to fighting that Timur makes them do enough but abroad. When journeying in foreign parts his Highness is everywhere accompanied by his justices who administer the law to all both in camp and palace. As to outlying provinces whither the judges are sent they give justice likewise to all and hear plaints. These judges are specially appointed, and the law has to be administered after the following system. Certain justices are maintained to give sentence in criminal matters and bloodshed arising from quarrels, while certain judges deal with money frauds such as may affect the government. Next there are justices who have it in charge to deal with the affairs of the government proctors who reside in the outlying districts and cities, and who come in to lay their cases and complaints before his Highness. Lastly they are those officials who attend to the reception of foreign embassies. Thus in three departments they give justice, and wheresoever the royal camp is set they give audience each justice in his own department; and there are three great tents erected to which are brought all litigants and criminals, where the justices hear and give sentence. But before this last is performed and done they will go and report of all matters to Timur: and then six by six and four by four the judgments are carried into effect.

When any decree has to be drawn up in writing the justices order their scribes to attend and engross it, but the writing is short, and soon finished. No sooner is it engrossed than it is copied into a register-book which the scribes keep and it is signed. Then the decree is given to the attorney who is charged to carry it into effect and he taking a silver seal engraved with its proper device, inks this over and stamps it on the decree at its foot. Then another official will take it and register it in his book, and it is then brought back to the judge who finally affixes his own seal with ink as above described. When three or four of these decrees have thus been sealed and despatched, they take them and seal them with Timur's own official seal which is inscribed with the legend that proclaims these words: "This is the Truth" and this script goes round the three O's arranged in a triangle.[7] So it is that each of those official attorneys has his scribe for engrossing the deed or decree, with his register for taking a copy; and no sooner has he seen on any deed or order the seal of one of the justices and the seal of Timur in corroboration, than he forthwith without delay carries into effect what is therein ordered to be done.

Now therefore having finished my description of the city of Samarqand and related all that befell us of the Spanish Embassy therein and detailed how we were received by his Highness, I will now relate to you how Timur in the past did overcome and utterly rout Toktamish the Khán [of the Golden Horde] in Tartary, a most powerful and valiant prince, who was indeed a far more redoubtable enemy than the Turkish [Sultan Báyazíd]: and next again how after the defeat of Toktamish one arose in his place claiming the over lordship of Tartary, namely the chief called Idiku, who had been at one time the subject and vassal of Timur: but is now the most powerful opponent that his Highness has to contend with as rival for the sovereignty.[8] It was indeed about eleven years ago that Toktamish the Khan of [the Golden Horde] in Tartary, coming to power and having an immense following of horsemen, sallied forth to conquer [from the lands of Kipchák] and invaded Persia. He came down on the province [of Azerbayján] taking possession of Tabriz and occupying all the districts of Upper Armenia. Many cities were sacked, many castles devastated and all the countryside was ravaged by his troops: as we ambassadors saw during our Journey through those parts, especially when we came to the city of Surmari [as has been described in a former chapter].[9] The same was the case with the chief town of the

Sisakán district [lying south of the Gokchah Lake]: together with other lands of Armenia. All this country at that time was already counted as in the lordship of Timur, and well knowing this Toktamish gathering up his booty soon made haste to retire back into Tartary. Timur however receiving news of these doings, marched and in all haste pursued him, though his horsemen were fewer in number than those of Toktamish. Following in their tracks he came up with the Tartar host on the banks of the great river Terek which flows near by Tartary, and Timur immediately made effort striving to seize the ford, it being his intention to pass over.

In all those parts this ford was the sole passage by which that river could be crossed. When however Timur reached the river bank, he found that Toktamish had already passed to the further side, who learning that Timur was at his heels immediately hastened to guard and hold the ford which he now caused to be further protected on his side by wooden beams. On coming up Timur finding that Toktamish was in possession of the passage, halted, sending envoys to Toktamish demanding why he acted thus, and assuring him that he Timur had not come to make war on him, being indeed his good friend, and calling on God to witness that he Timur on his part had never intended any aggression against him. Toktamish however would listen to none of his message, knowing well the guile of Timur. The next day therefore Timur broke up his camp and proceeded to march up the river bank on the south side, seeing which Toktamish did likewise and marched his host along the northern bank keeping pace opposite him. Thus the one following the other both hosts took the way upstream, and at night camped each over against the other with the river in between. This business went on and was repeated during three days, neither army outstripping the other, but on the third night as soon as his camp was formed Timur issued orders that all the women who marched with his soldiers should don helmets with the men's war-gear to play the part of soldiers, while the men should mount and forthwith ride back with him to the ford, each horseman taking with him a second mount led by the bridle. Thus the camp was left in charge of the women disguised as warriors, with their slaves and their captives under guard, while Timur went back by a forced march the three days' journey to where the river could be crossed. On coming to the ford the army halted that night, and the following day passed the river, next marching back along the opposite bank when at the hour of tierce [namely nine of the morning] they fell on the camp of Toktamish and completely routed him, plundering all his possessions of which great was his store: but Toktamish himself escaped.

This was a great and famous battle for Toktamish had under his command an immense host. Timur ever counted this the most notable of his victories; indeed it was a greater one than that where the Turkish Sultan Báyazíd was overcome. However Toktamish after this disaster once more assembled his forces hoping to surprise and fall on Timur unawares, but the latter again forestalled him, marching into the Tartar lands, where he was victorious as before. This second defeat overwhelmed Toktamish and he lost heart, taking flight once more. His people were entirely dismayed saying that he had changed his luck and was undone seeing that he could gain no victory. The Tartar chiefs now fell to quarrelling each with the other, and their discord continued until at last a certain man called Idiku, who formerly had been in the army and service of Timur, arose grasping the chief power. He it is who is now at the head of the Tartar folk in opposition to his Highness, and the Tartars have acknowledged him for their commander. They have thrown off all allegiance to Timur, and Idiku with guile has sought to compass his death, hoping that when Timur was thus disposed of he, Idiku, would be emperor not only of Tartary but would succeed to the sovereignty in Samarqand. This ambition on the part of Idiku Timur well knows, and he has sought, but failed, more than once to capture him and put him to death. Thus till now Idiku has escaped his toils, for he is a man of power and craft, but the two are open enemies. Timur at the head of his forces on a recent occasion had surprised Idiku in camp, who in fear of defeat had not awaited to offer opposition, but had fled. Yet Idiku is now a great chief, having under his command more than 200,000 horsemen of his Horde.

Toktamish and Timur have recently become friends, and together have sought to compass the overthrow of Idiku. With intent to beguile, Timur lately sent messengers to Idiku saying that he, Timur, was now on his side, that he loved him and had pardoned him all his misdeeds if indeed any there had been; further to prove he was his friend, and to make public acknowledgement that he Timur and Idiku were indeed of one kindred and lineage, he would send him one of his grandsons who should marry with a daughter of the family of Idiku. To all this it is said Idiku made reply that having in the past lived for twenty years in the service of Timur, he knew perfectly to what he might safely give credit: he understood the ways of Timur so well that it was not thus he was to be beguiled. He clearly perceived that what had been said was but to ensnare him, that if Timur wanted him as a friend he must yield up to him half his power and in future fight side by side with him sword in hand and in equal alliance. Thus matters have been left undecided. Further Toktamish had a son living in those parts whom Idiku had expelled from his lands, and recently Toktamish having taken shelter with Timur was now living in the vicinity of Samarqand. This son of Toktamish therefore went off to Kaffa the city which the Genoese hold [in the Crimea] on the borders of Tartary, and from that quarter, he began to make war on Idiku with such help [as the Genoese gave him]. Idiku however marched on Kaffa, ravaging all those lands round and about, whereupon the people of Kaffa coming to terms made peace with Idiku and that son of Toktamish had to depart. He has now sought shelter with his father and is living in the territories of Timur. Thus matters stand, Toktamish and his sons are harboured by Timur; and meantime Idiku is engaged very piously in compassing to convert his Tartar folk to the Moslem religion. He is working day after day thereat, for up to now they have not been of this faith, having indeed accepted no particular form of religious belief though at last forsooth they will all be of the sect of the Prophet Mahomet.

As regards the Tartar army which every day and all day waits on the orders of Timur following his Highness wheresoever he goes, this is organized after the following fashion. The host is divided into Captaincies: and there are captains of one hundred and of one thousand and of ten thousand men. Over the whole force is a single commander-in-chief, as with us may be the Constable of Castile. When any warlike expedition is on foot those captains each are called on, and by the number sent for it is known how great the force assembled is to be. At the present day the commander-in-chief of Timur's armies is [the prince his nephew mentioned on a former page][10] Jahán Sháh Mirza. He [and more particularly his father] in the past gave notable support to Timur when he made war on that Khán of Samarqand [called the Amír Husayn in the year 1366] and brought him to his death. Timur has ever since shown Prince Jahán Sháh great favour, bestowing rich lands on him, so that now he is a mighty lord. It is the custom of Timur to give in charge his stud of horses and his great flocks of sheep each to some one of his nobles who must see to their wants, giving pasture in the lands they personally possess. One noble thus may have in charge a thousand head of cattle and another ten thousand. If when the time comes for Timur to regain possession of his own it should appear that the number falls short or that their condition anywise be wanting, his Highness will seize whatsoever that lord may possess and very probably in addition put him to death, for such is his rule and ordinance.

Chapter XVI

Samarqand to Tabriz

Now having finished telling of all these matters we shall relate the events of the return journey and all that befell us on the road home. On starting from Samarqand our caravan was joined in the first place by the Ambassador of the Sultan of Egypt, and by several other persons, one of whom was the brother of a certain great nobleman of Turkey, and his name was Alaman Oglan, then next there was a man who had come from Sívás [in Asia Minor] and another person from the city of Altologo[1] and again one from yet another city of those parts called Palatia [on the Ægean Sea]. Further yet another man from Altologo: and we all now were to travel in company together, for those Chamberlains of Timur understanding the condition to which his Highness was now brought were in haste to despatch us. Our journey was not at first by the way we had come, for on leaving Samarqand we immediately turned westward going in the direction of Tartary. It was Friday, the 21st of November, when we set out leaving Samarqand and our journey lay through the plain alone a good road and through a populous country. We marched thus for six days passing through their villages, and we were everywhere supplied with provisions and well lodged.

On Thursday the 27th of November we had reached that great city of Bukhárá that stands in the middle of an immense plain, being enclosed by walls of sun-dried bricks, with a deep ditch full of water on the outside. At one part of the city there was a castle likewise constructed with sun-baked bricks, for in this country there are no stones for building the masonry of walls, and beside this castle flowed a river. Outside the city of Bukhárá lies a great suburb having many fine buildings. This place is well supplied with provisions both of meat and bread stuffs and wine, with every other commodity: and the merchants here are very rich. In Bukhárá all that we needed was given us, and they presented us each a riding horse. For the rest it is not now my purpose to detail all the events of this our homeward march, and I need only name the cities we passed through, for in our outward journey I have described all our experiences sufficiently fully not to need repeating them in this place. In the city of Bukhárá we rested for seven days and during this time much snow fell: then on Friday the 5th of December we set out again, and during three days' march made our way through a well populated plain where there were villages on every hand, reaching at length the bank of the great river the Áb-i-Ámú [as they name the Oxus], which as you have heard we had crossed higher up above this point on our journey to Samarqand. Coming to a village on the riverside we now laid in provisions of meat for ourselves and barley for our horses to serve us for crossing the desert beyond the Oxus which we learnt would extend for six days' march. We stayed at this village making our preparations during two days, and then on Wednesday the 10th of December embarking in the ferry-boats crossed the broad stream of that mighty river.

Its banks on the further side consist in great sandy plains, and the wind here continually drives the sands backwards and forwards from one spot to another. Thus the dunes are ever in motion, being here blown down by the wind and heaped up there at another place. The sand is very fine and as it is moved about it makes the like of waves as might be seen on a cloth of Camelot: further when the sun shines clear no one can look down on it but must hold his eyes off the glitter. The way across these sands can only be traversed by those who know the signs that have been set up as guide posts, and these desert guides are commonly known [as already noted] by the name of Yamchis, and a Yamchi was our leader on this occasion, but even he many times almost lost his way in the desert. There is no water to be met with in this land except at the interval of the day's march, when you will come to a well-shaft dug down in the sand, and protected by a dome that rises above a surrounding wall of fire-baked bricks; and but for this protecting wall the sand would soon blind the well. The water in these wells is the store from the rains or the snow that has fallen. As we went, upon the last day of our march across this desert tract, we could find no well, so had to ride on continuously that day and all the night following. It was only the next day by the hour of mass at noon that we came to a well, and here we ate our food and watered our beasts who were in great need of refreshment. On Sunday the 14th of December we at last reached a village where we rested that day and Monday and Tuesday following, setting out again Wednesday to traverse a second span of desert the passage of which lasted five days full going. This was crossing a plain, and here the wells were more abundant than in the tract we had formerly passed. Half way over this second desert waste we had to pass a low hill of sand, and the heat here was quite overpowering [in spite of its being the month of December]. Further all the last three days of our passage across were very wearisome and long, for we had to keep on by night as well as by day, only halting when it was necessary to take food and to give our horses their barley.

 On Sunday the 21st of December we came to a great town called Bávard,[2] and this lies within the government of the Khurásán province. Bávard stands at the foot of mountains that were at this season covered with snow: the climate is very cold: the city has no wall and it lies out in the plain. They provided us here with fresh horses and provisions for the way; we enjoyed their hospitality and remained here that Sunday of our coming, also Monday, Tuesday and Wednesday following. On Thursday the 25th of December Christmas day, which was the first day of the year of our Lord 1405, we left Bávard passing on through high mountain lands, everywhere covered with snow, and this part of our journey lasted five days, crossing a country almost entirely uninhabited, the weather being now very cold. Then on Thursday the 1st of January we came to a city lying in the open plain beyond the hill country, the name of which is Khabushán; it is unwalled, and here we halted that Thursday and the Friday following. Khabushán is the first town in the province of Media. On Saturday the 3rd of January we set out again and our way now lay over the plains. In that district the weather already was warm, no snow remained on the ground, nor did it freeze at night. We travelled on that Saturday and Sunday and on Monday the 5th of January reached the town of Jájarm, having come by two villages lying on the roadside thither. Jájarm has no wall round it; and as will be remembered we had already passed there on our outward journey to Samarqand, [whereby we here rejoined our former route]. In Jájarm we stayed the night of our arrival and all next day Tuesday. On Wednesday we set out and all that day travelled through the plains finding no inhabited places. That night we slept at an empty building of considerable size that stood near a ruined castle; for both this house and this castle had been abandoned and lay desolate.

Thursday again we went on finding no inhabited homestead, but that evening we came at last to a populous village. All this day and the day before, our way had skirted beside a range of red hills, on whose summits no snow was seen lying, and during both these days it was quite hot in the countryside round and about. Friday we proceeded on our journey and that day also found no habitations, but on Saturday by the hour of vespers we had reached Bostám the great town we had been in on our outward march. Leaving this on Sunday following we came on to Dámghán, and when we were still about a league distant from that city, a strong cold wind got up and blew hard although the day was perfectly fine. The cold now became suddenly intense, giving us cause much to wonder, both man and beast suffering greatly therefrom. When we had finally reached Dámghán we made enquiries as to that terrible wind, and they told us in explanation that in the great mountain overhanging the city there was a spring of water, and if any foul or filthy animal matter came to fall into that water the wind would immediately and wondrously begin to blow a gale, and it would not go down until that impurity had been removed from the spring. As a consequence on the next day after our coming men from the town went up with poles and pot-hooks to clean out the fountain, after which the wind suddenly ceased to blow.[3] This town too it will be remembered we had passed through on the outward journey, and here we now halted for two days to rest. On Wednesday the 15th of January we again set out, but at a point beyond Dámghán did not take the road we had come by before, which passed by the castle of Fírúzkúh, for that road had lain through high mountains, which now were deep in snow. At this place that other road branched off on our right hand, and we now took the way which went to the left, and thence proceeded along down through the plains.[4]

The next night we slept in a great empty uninhabited house and Thursday the day following travelled on through an uninhabited country Friday being the like, and Saturday at the hour of vespers reached a great city which is called Semnán. This lies on the frontier of Media and to the west thereof is Persia. Semnán stands in the plain under a high range of mountains, it is a very populous town but is protected by no surrounding wall. We remained there till the following Monday, when we journeyed on and slept that night at a small village, coming Tuesday night to a certain castle, and that day we found much snow on our road. Thence we went on travelling through plains that lay between ranges of mountains from whose slopes many streams came down, but we noticed that in all these the water was salt in taste: and thus Thursday went by. Friday which was the 23rd of January we reached the city which is called Veramín, [this we had passed on the outward way] and the township is of very considerable extent but most of its houses are no longer inhabited. There was no wall surrounding it, and the district in which it stands goes by the name of Ray. Here there was living that great noble who was son-in-law to Timur, having married one of his daughters: and we came here also to know another great lord. His name was Bábá Sheykh and Timur's son-in-law was called Sulaymán Mirza. These were the two lords who had taken charge of our sick folk when we had passed through this place on the outward journey, and we found our people safe and now sound in health, except only for two of their number who had died of the sickness. All had been well treated and cared for, their wants amply supplied by their hosts, the nobles above mentioned.

On Sunday the following day we took dinner with Timur's son-in-law, while on Monday we had the like entertainment from Bábá Sheykh. Then on Tuesday following they supplied us with horses and we all took our departure together from them, going on that night to sleep at a castle on the road. Thursday the 29th of January we came to the city of Shahraqán passing the night there, and this was the town we had stayed at on our outward journey. From this point however we diverged [northwards] from the route we had taken [from Sultáníyah to Shahraqán] on our outward march, and during four days, Friday Saturday Sunday and Monday, travelled on continuously, but our way was much hampered by the snow that had fallen. Finally on Tuesday the 3rd of February we reached a great town that was called Qazvín. Here the major part of the houses are indeed now in ruin, though their number formerly had been very great, for this city of Qazvín was the largest of any that we had met with in those parts, Tabriz and Samarqand alone excepted. Here we found that much snow had fallen, the streets were quite blocked by it, and the people all were occupied in making roads through the drifts for the passage of traffic. So much snow had come down that great was the peril lest it should stave in the roofs of the houses, and the householders were busy with poles and shovels throwing it off down into the yards below. In Qazvín we slept Tuesday the night of our arrival and remained there till after the following Friday, being held back by the great snowfall on the road beyond. They gave us hospitable entertainment for this time, amply supplying our needs and requirements.

It is indeed thus the custom everywhere to harbour ambassadors going to or coming from Timur, likewise any of the princes of his family who may be travelling. During a sojourn of three days and nights, should they need to stay that time all are entertained, and of these last, namely any person of the immediate relationship of his Highness, it is usual to supply him and his following with food and lodging for nine days, but the expense is then borne by the commune in which their stay is made. On the following Saturday at length we found we could set forth again, but thirty men had to go with us on foot with shovels to open a road for us by their labour. These men all came out from Qazvín for this work, but as soon as we had reached the first hamlet settlement outside they went back home, and the men of the hamlet were obliged to take on the work, turning out to beat down a way for us to pass. The snow had now fallen so abundantly that the hill slopes and the plain both were covered very deeply, all seemed level ground and no road could be seen.

Snow-blindness affected the eyes of men and beasts, none could see looking over the snow, and indeed until the surface had frozen hard it was almost impossible to make our way across the plain. So deep was the snow in places that coming to a town or village we could not recognize where it lay, all being covered over. In this condition we made our journey coming on to the city of Sultáníyah which is the chief town of that populous district and amply supplied with food stuffs. Here we arrived on Friday the 13th of February and stayed till the Saturday of the week following which was the 21st of the same month. I need say little concerning Sultáníyah as the place has been sufficiently described by us at the time when we were passing through it on our outward journey: it is indeed a very great and noble city of the land of Persia, and though it is not protected by any wall there stands here on the level plain near by the city [as described on a former page] a very magnificent castle.

Our long delay of eight days in Sultáníyah was caused while awaiting the orders that now reached us, and we learnt that we must go thence and pay our respects to the Governor General of Western Persia, who [as already mentioned in a previous chapter] is a grandson of Timur whose name is Omar Mirza. The Prince was at this moment established in camp on the plains of Qarabágh, where with his army he was spending the winter season. The quickest way to reach this place would have been to turn aside and go north from Sultáníyah, but the road thence passes over high ranges of mountains and these were now deep in fresh fallen snow. We were delaying therefore those many days hoping for the snow to melt, and let us pass, but the frost continuing they advised us it were better to proceed straight on to Tabriz and thence set out for Qarabágh, where the mountain road would be shorter and the snow less deep. This therefore we now arranged to do and on Saturday the 21st of February left Sultáníyah and slept that night at the town of Zanján, which we had passed through on our outward journey.

Sunday following we slept at a great roadside caravanserai: and on Tuesday reached the village of Miyanah: Wednesday we came on and slept at the village of Tungalar [or Tucelar] and the following day reached the village of Uján. Finally on Saturday the last day of the month of February we entered the city of Tabriz, where lodgings were assigned to us in certain houses of the Armenians, who were Christian folk, and here they supplied the customary rations of food. On the Tuesday following, which was the 3rd of March, horses for our party were as we learnt in readiness for us to set out to go to Prince Omar who, as said, was with his host encamped in the Qarabágh plains at winter-quarters.

These are certain immense plains providing excellent pasture during that season, for the climate there is very mild, snow seldom falling or should it do so melting rapidly. It is for this amenity that Prince Omar is wont to go there for the winter months of each year: and thither now it was incumbent on us to seek him out and pay our respects. It was not however till Thursday the 5th of March that we finally got away from Tabriz, and of our company was the Ambassador from the Egyptian Sultan, as likewise the Envoy from Turkey. Thus we all together now set out for the Qarabágh plains and make this visit of respect to Prince Omar. On the road thither we had for guide and companion that same Tartar lord who had brought us all the way from Samarqand, and who had seen to it everywhere throughout the journey that we were amply provided with all that was needed of rations. Those who thus have charge of foreign ambassadors are by the Tartars called Chagaul. On this occasion I and my companion [the Master in Theology] travelled with but few of our Spanish servants, for we were warned to leave most of our attendants at the lodgings in Tabriz to await our return. Now after we had all been travelling together after this wise for two days' journey we were met by a special messenger sent by Prince Omar with command that we should immediately turn back to await further instructions in Tabriz. We were there to take our ease, he said, for some days, when the Prince would let us know when and where he could receive us: it was added in courteous guise that we who had come so long a journey must be weary and need a time to repose ourselves. Thus therefore we all forthwith retraced our steps to Tabriz, Prince Omar having given orders for us to be well supplied with good rations - or as they term them here Alafa[5] even as we do.

In this city of Tabriz we now remained waiting instructions and it was not till Wednesday the 18th of March that these came, when again we must journey to Qarabágh. On Thursday the 19th of March therefore we set out, and after crossing several high ranges of mountains lying to the north of Tabriz came to a valley that was full of orchards and many villages, with rich vineyards; for the climate here was mild, and fruit is grown in great abundance. Across through this valley runs the great river [Aras]. Our journey onward through the lands of these villages with their orchards lasted for four whole days, and at the end of this time we came to the great plains. Here the inhabitants are a settled population in very considerable numbers, for much rice with crops of white and dark millet both are grown here: indeed all the provinces round and about are supplied with rice from these harvests. No wheat or barley is grown here, but the rice is so abundant that they feed their horses on it. All over these plains the nomads who form the Horde of Prince Omar were encamped in tents with their herds. On Wednesday the 25th of March we were making our way through the concourse of these Tartar folk, and had come to within ten or twelve leagues of the place where, as we were told, Prince Omar had his residence, when we suddenly were met by men coming our way who advised us that the Prince's camp was in an uproar, so that it would be better if we turned back. We enquired the cause of this uproar and they informed us that Prince Jahán Sháh [the Commander-in-Chief] had just before made an attempt on the life of Prince Omar. The men of the Horde had however risen and led by the Tartar lords and chiefs had fallen on Prince Jahán Sháh taking him prisoner, and on this Prince Omar had ordered him to be beheaded. The men of Jahán Sháh's regiments had then revolted and were now fighting those of Prince Omar's Horde and many on either side had fallen. Prince Omar they proceeded to tell us had already betaken himself across the river [Kur] with horsemen of his own squadrons, having ordered the bridge of boats behind him to be broken up. Men were passing from one side to the other, and none knew what was about to happen, all the troops were in great commotion of discord.

On hearing all this we ambassadors together held council, and finally agreed that as we were there so near we should go on and see for ourselves how matters really stood: thus we proceeded forward again. On Thursday next day the 26th of March we had arrived at the great camp where Prince Omar in the midst of his Horde was stationed, and we halted awaiting his orders, hoping for our reception. But the whole concourse of the troops were in a mighty confusion: on all hands they were coming in, the Tartar folk driving their flocks before them. Then while we were thus waiting one of the Chagatays came to us with a message from Prince Omar, to the effect telling us that his Highness was now much beset with business, that he could not at present receive us, and that he begged we would all forthwith return to Tabriz there to await instructions. This Chagatay added that he was commissioned to accompany us thither and see that all our needs were provided for, in accordance with the wish of his Highness. Forthwith therefore we re-mounted and set off back on our journey. It will be understood that Prince Omar had been at this season lying in camp with his Horde in the plains on the [south bank of the Kur], his army here numbering perhaps 45,000 horsemen; though this was not all his following for many regiments were stationed elsewhere in places round and about. As has been said it had been the custom, aforetime for Timur himself to come to these plains, where he would establish his winter-quarters, and indeed he had but lately ordered a city [called Baylagán] to be built here, where already there was in residence a population of 20,000 settled folk.[6]

This Prince Jahán Sháh [as mentioned above had been lately Commander-in-Chief of Timur's armies] being a nephew of his Highness, a son of one of his sisters. He had now been summarily beheaded by order of Prince Omar, though he was truly the most powerful chief of the Tartar armies, and honoured of all men, as so nearly allied to the family of Timur. He had been the possessor of many broad lands and many were the men who rode daily in his following. In times gone by when Timur had first named his grandson this same Prince Omar to be governor general in Western Persia, he had commissioned this nephew of his, Jahán Sháh, to be the young Prince's governor, to control his household, and to manage his government. Thus heretofore all that Jahán Sháh might have ordered was carried out into effect as though his Highness had himself given the command, and the reason why now Jahán Sháh had been put to death, as we have related, and so suddenly, was explained to us, but in two different ways. On the one hand it was said that Prince Omar had had him killed simply because he was afraid of him; for Timur his grandfather being now dead, he feared lest Jahán Sháh should seek his life, since he, Jahán Sháh, had at his back not only the troops of the empire all under his command, but also all the Chagatay clan who were of his own following and who would obey him blindly. Thus probably, as Prince Omar reasoned, he would rebel, and all men would say that Timur being dead, he, Jahán Sháh, was the man to take his place.

This was the first report: the other account given us was that Jahán Sháh, on having certain news that Timur was dead, had armed himself and accompanied by many of his followers all bearing arms had come to the great tent where the Council was to be held. Here he had met a certain Mulla, that is a Doctor of their Religion, who was a personage very intimate with Prince Omar, and who had the superintendence of affairs in his camp. Jahán Sháh hated this man, by reason that at one time a woman, whom he Jahán Sháh loved, had been taken from him by Prince Omar and given in marriage to this Mulla. For this as for other reasons he therefore detested this personage, and finding him now thus present in the great tent incontinently he had slain him. Then, the deed thus done, he had left that tent and gone straight to the one where Prince Omar was residing, holding yet his naked sword in his hand and followed by all his men with their swords drawn. At the Prince's tent the guards seeing them thus coming fell to their arms and immediately took station at the Prince's doorway - his Highness being within - while at the same time the rumour ran through the Horde that Idiku the Khan of the Tartars and King George of Georgia both were upon them making a surprise attack. In the midst of this commotion Jahán Sháh had managed to overpower the main guard at the tent of Prince Omar, and had set his own men to hold the post, while in the confusion entering the royal tent, it was said, he had purposed to put Prince Omar to death. He however had found many attendants on guard in the Prince's anteroom who all were ready to defend him.

There was more especially a certain great Tartar noble who had recently entered into the antechamber with all his followers well armed. This man stopping now enquired what he might be doing there, saying that he would report the matter to the Prince. Jahán Sháh turning to him besought him to tell his Highness to have no fear, for all he Jahán Sháh had done was to kill his personal enemy that Mulla. The noble, aforesaid, going within thus reported, but found Prince Omar in straits of terror, not knowing well what to do. He therefore comforted his Highness telling him to have no anxiety, for that if the Prince would but give his command he himself would settle with Jahán Sháh. Whereupon coming back he fell on him of a sudden, and with a single blow of his sword cut off Jahán Sháh's head. No sooner was Jahán Sháh thus dead, than all his followers sought their safety in flight. Prince Omar taking up Jahán Sháh's head had it forthwith carried to Baghdad, presenting it to his father Mírán Sháh and to Prince Abu Bakr his brother. To them Prince Omar also wrote saying that they would now have the head of their enemy before them, adding that since his grandfather was now certainly dead, it was incumbent on them both to come and join their forces with his, when he Prince Omar with his nobles and grandees would give in allegiance to Mírán Sháh as Emperor in rightful succession to Timur. It was however told us later that when Mírán Sháh saw the head of Jahán Sháh [his cousin] thus sent him, he began to tremble fearing treachery on the part of his son Prince Omar, and he sought to avoid this meeting which had been arranged to take place in the Plains of Vian at no great distance outside Tabriz.

Now in regard to the events, as afterwards reported to us, that were at this time happening in the city of Samarqand, no sooner was Timur dead and he had died [at Otrar beyond the Jaxartes, as already said][7] than the great lords and his chamberlains did their utmost to keep the fact unknown till they could send a guard for safety on the great treasure [in the castle of Samarqand] and take the state in charge. It however was found impossible to keep the secret, and very soon all men knew, from the servants in attendance, that Timur indeed was dead. At the time of his death there was present in the capital his grandson Prince Khalíl Sultán, again a son of Mírán Sháh, and he as soon as he received the news [from Otrar] of his grandfather's death, assembling all his men and, summoning the nobles of his party, fell on those three privy chamberlains of Timur [already spoken of in a previous chapter who now returning from Otrar] had already taken into their charge the household and the treasury of his late Highness. Of these three grand chamberlains, one they forthwith slew, and he was by name Butudo, being a son of Jahán Sháh whom Prince Omar had so recently beheaded in Tabriz as already said: and on this the other two chamberlains fled seeking shelter in the city of Herát with Prince Sháh Rukh the youngest son of Timur, he being as we have said governor-general of the Khurásán province.[8] Then as soon as Prince Khalíl had killed Butudo, and the other two chamberlains had gone off, he betook himself to the castle of Samarqand and possessed himself of all his grandfather's treasure which he found there, whereby becoming master of the capital. This done he proceeded to make the necessary arrangements for the funeral and burial of Timur his grandfather, and to his father Mírán Sháh sent messengers begging him immediately to come and join him in Samarqand. He would then, he said, hand over the treasure to his father, who should be received and acknowledged by all as rightful heir of the Empire in the room of Timur. The treasure, Prince Khalíl wrote, was immense, and the Chagatay clan surely would rally to him if they knew it was in his possession, for indeed the Tartars are a money worshipping folk.

Thus Mírán Sháh was to be made Emperor: but Prince Khalíl's messengers had been told to warn Mírán Sháh that his wife, the Princess Khánzádeh, might very probably now intrigue against him, though she had in the past striven to make peace between him and his father Timur. She was as has been said the mother of Prince Khalíl in whose palace at Samarqand she was now living: but she would most probably be opposed to Mírán Sháh, her husband, because of her constant fear and dislike of him. Further it was her ambition that her son Khalíl should be Emperor, indeed she was continually now urging him to take for himself that title. At Samarqand we had known this Prince Khalíl very well: he was a young man then about twenty-two years of age, fair-skinned and fat like his father Mírán Sháh whom he resembled in face. Prince Khalíl indeed had paid us very great attention while we were staying at court in attendance on his grandfather. Now as regards the news at last made public of the death of Timur, it should be remembered that twice before this time his Highness had falsely put about the rumour that he was dead, in order to probe who would then rebel against the provisions of his will for the succession. Twice before, beguiled by the report, some had gone out in rebellion, who had immediately been put to death, whereby though the news now come was in fact true, many believed that Timur could not be dead. Thus while we were still waiting on in Tabriz making ready to depart home, rumour declared that Timur was alive and at the very moment marching at the head of his host being intent to invade Egypt and conquer the Sultan of Cairo.

To proceed: when Mírán Sháh received in Baghdad the certain news of the death of his father, he had at the same time received the head of Jahán Sháh [the late Commander-in-Chief] which his son Prince Omar now sent him, together with the urgent invitation begging him to come forthwith to the meeting in the Plain of Vian [some ten leagues to the west of Tabriz] where matters were to be settled for his succession. Mírán Sháh therefore took his departure from Baghdad and marched on Tabriz, his son Abu Bakr accompanying him. Before however he reached the meeting place, news was brought him that Prince Omar had already assembled together at Vian a great force superior to what his father commanded, and further had sent his orders to the troops stationed in the cities of Sultáníyah and Tabriz that they should stand to their arms and be ready to march forth immediately at the moment of call. Mírán Sháh learning of these warlike preparations began to fear what Prince Omar might be intending to do. He halted on his march, sending envoys to discover what was the true intention of Prince Omar, who gave reply assuring him that all this mustering of troops on his part was merely to safeguard the frontiers of the province and on his father's succession as Emperor to establish peace. When this answer was brought to Mírán Sháh his son Abu Bakr who was yet with him proposed that he should proceed on alone to meet his brother, Prince Omar, whom it was his purpose to bring to reason. He told his father it was his intention indeed forthwith to seize him and carry him back to the camp of Mírán Sháh whether he would or no: but his father refused to sanction this course, saying that all men would find scandal in the deed.

Now as we have written before, Omar and Abu Bakr were full brothers, on the mother's as on the father's side, and the Princess their mother, who was in the camp with her husband Mírán Sháh, now set forth alone and travelled coming to the camp of Prince Omar of whom she obtained interview. She accused her son Omar of intending to thwart the wishes of all true men, for all must hold that Mírán Sháh had without doubt full right to succeed to the throne of Timur his father. To her Prince Omar promptly replied: God forbid that any other course should be followed, that he was ready to acknowledge the rights of Mírán Sháh and that all should be done as she commanded. The Princess his mother therefore now went back to the camp of Mírán Sháh, assuring her husband that this solemn promise had been given, hearing which Mírán Sháh agreed that his son Abu Bakr should proceed and visit Prince Omar in his camp, when all matters could be arranged between them, as to how and when Mírán Sháh should be proclaimed Emperor. Affairs being thus amicably settled, Abu Bakr with his body guard, but unattended by any other troops, rode in to meet his brother Prince Omar, who becoming aware of his heedless unsuspicion determined to make him prisoner. When Abu Bakr therefore had entered the camp and was approaching the great tent, Prince Omar issued to meet him and taking him cordially by the hand conducted him in. No sooner was he thus fallen into his power than he had Abu Bakr arrested prisoner, on news of which the five hundred horsemen of Abu Bakr's body-guard who had come with him, immediately fled back to the camp of his father Mírán Sháh. Prince Omar having thus his brother in his power despatched him for custody to the castle at Sultáníyah where he was put in irons. Prince Omar next marched on his father's camp hoping thus to get him too into his toils, but Mírán Sháh having news had already taken to flight, making his way by a forced march round to the province of Ray, where he found shelter with Sulaymán Mírzá, his brother-in-law, and there met various lords and chieftains of the Chagatay clan.

The Princess, the mother of Omar and Abu Bakr, having news of what was taking place, and learning how her elder son had thrown his brother into prison, therefore journeyed forth again coming to her son Prince Omar, and with garments rent and bosom bare, weeping many tears, she now admonished him saying: "My son did not I your mother bear both you and him? Is he not your own full brother? And yet you would murder him: him whom all men love." To which Prince Omar replied comforting and assuring her that he had only arrested Abu Bakr because he was a heedless madman, saying and doing what should not be said or done, and that all he Prince Omar desired was for his father forthwith to be proclaimed Emperor. Very contrary however to all this was Prince Omar's real intention, which same he proceeded now to carry into effect, having thus got his brother into his power. Now Omar being an over-bearing man, all the Chagatay nobles respected and loved him; his fine promises to the Princess his mother were but with intent to beguile his father Mírán Sháh, and in order to get him into his power.

Forthwith it became known that Mírán Sháh had left Ray and was making his way towards Samarqand: Prince Omar therefore set out to follow him, but he soon saw that he could not compass to come up with him to make him his prisoner. Prince Omar turned off therefore seeking now to come to terms with his uncle Sháh Rukh, his father's brother, with whom he offered to make common cause against Mírán Sháh. The pact agreed to was that Prince Omar and Sháh Rukh together and conjointly should divide the Empire: and as to Mírán Sháh since he must pass through the Herát province on his road to Samarqand, he might easily be taken prisoner on his passage Sháh Rukh giving the orders. Mírán Sháh now realized that his brother and his son having come to terms, must be in league against him. He determined therefore to halt and remain where he was, namely at the place his camp had reached in traversing Khurásán, as he dared not now continue his march on to Samarqand. Next he sent his messengers seeking to treat for peace with Prince Omar: but the terms offered to him were never such as he could safely accept, and matters thus remained in suspense. We further learnt that Prince Omar having his brother Abu Bakr in his power took from him his wife, who was the daughter of the lord of the city of Mardín [in Upper Mesopotamia], but afterwards he sent back this Princess to her father.

Chapter XVII

Tabriz to Seville

WE were still awaiting in Tabriz the commands of Prince Omar, and about this time he was moved to send us ambassadors a letter, in which his Highness assured us that we had no cause for anxiety in the delay which was postponing our departure homeward. We were informed that very soon all matters of dispute between him and his father Mírán Sháh would be adjusted, and immediately on this happening he would summon us to his presence for a farewell audience when we should take leave of him. Nevertheless shortly after this gracious letter had been brought us, namely on Tuesday the [28th] of April, the day of the Feast of Saint Peter Martyr, we Spaniards being at our lodgings in Tabriz there appeared before our door the governor of the city and his secretary with a crowd of attendants. Coming in these men seized and took in charge all our swords and other arms that we had about us, when ordering to be closed the outer gates the governor proceeded to inform us that it was Prince Omar who had sent him with charge to impound all our goods and possessions, which same they were now about to take into custody. We on this gave as answer that we must submit to what they should do since we were completely in their power: but they should remember that our Master the King of Spain had sent us as his envoys to his late Highness the Lord Timur on a mission of friendship, and that up to the present we had ever been treated in a very different fashion to this that was proceeding. His Highness the great Timur however was alas dead: and forsooth they might now do as seemed good in their eyes. To this the governor replied that what Prince Omar had ordered to be done was that we might be the better guarded, adding that in nowise should we be harmed.

His men however had no will to act courteously, nay rather they from the first intended to plunder us, and they now carried off all our possessions, namely wearing apparel, money, our saddles and our horses, everything in fact, leaving us with nothing but the clothes we had on. They then marched us off to another house where they left us and set a guard at the door. Next they took action in the same way with the Ambassador of the Sultan of Egypt, as also with the Ambassador from the Turk, both of whom were still travelling with us, and of all the possessions they thus carried off by force from us and them, they stole later the better part. Some twenty days after these events we received another letter from Prince Omar in which he assured us that we had no need to be vexed by what he had sent orders for his men to do: that now we might be in comfort and rejoice for he had established terms of complete amity with his father; further that very shortly he was coming to stay at a castle some five leagues distant from Tabriz called Assarec, and as soon as he was there he would send for us, give us audience and despatch us on our homeward way. There was however as we learnt no truth in all this, for he had not come to any accommodation with his father. He was causing all such news to be published and these rumours to be spread abroad, with intent of quieting the public mind, and to forestall rebellion. The chiefs of the Chagatay clan, and the commanders of his troops he ever thus kept in ignorance of what he purposed to do and whither he was going. None could know the truth, and every man reported differently as to what had been done or was going to be done. Whither and when the army was about to march was unknown: for indeed these folk are all very disingenuous and crafty, and they ever avoid telling the plain truth.

Thus we were left awaiting on events, and expecting daily to hear that Prince Omar had arrived at the castle of Assarec. It was about this time that the King of Georgia of whom we have already spoken [and whose name was George VII] came out in rebellion. He invaded the country round and about Ani and Erzerum, which is of Greater Armenia, and extended his raid down even to Tabriz, plundering and burning many villages and hamlets, spreading terror on all hands. The Moslems of Tabriz held that Prince Omar must of his duty march to their defence, but he failed to come. But next he sent in his place, giving him command in Tabriz, a certain great noble [of whom we have already spoken] a very old man, him whose name was Omar Toban, who at the head of some 5,000 horse had hitherto been stationed on the Georgian frontier of those parts. From the country round Tabriz troops were hurriedly collected, these numbering some 15,000 horse, and forthwith proudly marched through the streets of that city, where they made a very fine display. Then these all took their departure for the frontier in the region of the Alatáq plains, which are of Greater Armenia. No sooner had king George heard of their approach than he marched out with 5,000 of his horsemen to encounter them: and coming fell on them at night. Taking them thus by surprise, he slew most of these men, while such as escaped fled back to Tabriz, where the terror and confusion of the Moslem folk became very great.[1] The cry arose that the Kafirs were conquering the Moslems, for they call us Christians Kafirs [which is Infidels], implying that we are an unbelieving folk with no divine law, and they call themselves Moslems, for that name in their tongue signifies the folk who live under the divine law of Almighty God. In Tabriz it was now said that the fault of the disaster did not rest with the troops, but with Prince Omar, and that it lay at his door, for he was luckless, lacking that good fortune which hitherto had always attended Timur his grandfather.

It was now Prince Omar at last realized that he could neither compass to get his father Mírán Sháh into his power, nor by treaty come to any accommodation with him; he therefore marched back to the city of Sultáníyah [on his way to Tabriz and the castle of Assarec]. Here he had his brother Abu Bakr still a prisoner, and he now gave instructions that as soon as he was away Abu Bakr should be done to death by poison. Prince Omar then left Sultáníyah setting out for Assarec in order to hold a review of his troops, and to give us ambassadors our final audience before despatching us on our homeward journey. While he was thus on his way and approaching Tabriz, news was brought him that on a certain Tuesday, which was the 14th of July of that year, his brother Abu Bakr had made his escape from his prison, having slain his jailer. Further Abu Bakr had seized on the treasure that was in the castle of Sultáníyah, carrying it off with him. Prince Omar on this immediately turned back, and on arrival at Sultáníyah hastily despatched troops to overtake his brother, but his horsemen failed to come up with the fugitives.

What had taken place was this:- Prince Omar had commissioned the captain of his guard, whom he had left in charge of his brother, to bring about his death by a poison, and a potion was left prepared for that purpose. The secret of this however got to be known to some of Abu Bakr's friends and they warned the prince lest harm should befall. He on this took counsel how he might make his escape, promising a rich reward to all who gave aid, and the plot thus was set on foot. Horses and arms were prepared for the morrow, and the prince was secretly provided with a sword wherewith to fall on his jailer, when his friends being ready would come to his aid, and free him from his prison. The plot perfectly succeeded, as arranged on the following morning. The captain of the guard who was his keeper entered the prison accompanied by three men on whom he had reliance. He immediately made known to Abu Bakr that Prince Omar his brother had just sent word to state that he had at length come to terms with their father Mírán Sháh; and it was added that very soon he, Prince Omar, would release his brother from that prison when, bestowing great riches on him, he would assign him a position in the state such as perfectly to content him: and Abu Bakr therefore might now rejoice and take his ease, and fear nothing. The captain then went on to say that this good news which he now brought to Abu Bakr in truth warranted that the latter should deign to drink wine with him afterwards dining with him.

Now it is the custom of these folk to drink before they eat, and the captain had with him the wine cup, with the poisoned wine, that was to cause death. He thereupon presented this cup kneeling before the Prince and offering it to him, as is their mode, and begging that he would graciously receive it at his hands. The Prince however first excusing himself under some pretence, immediately put his hand to his hidden sword and struck the jailer such a blow on the head that it killed him. He then attacked and promptly despatched those three men who were in attendance on guard, when all in the castle fell to a state of alarm and confusion. The conspirators, namely those who had promised aid to the Prince, now rushed in to his assistance, and forthwith struck off his fetters: which were indeed of silver chains. He then could mount his horse and accompanied by his friends all proceeded on horseback to the square, where they were joined by others in the plot. Taking command the Prince sent for the official in whose charge was the treasury, and him they slew. The uproar now became general, the people flocking to Abu Bakr, who issued his orders that stout horses, wheresoever found, should be seized, whether from merchants or from private persons, by which means he soon found himself at the head of some five hundred horsemen. He now went back to the castle, where the treasure was forthcoming, and this he proceeded to distribute liberally among his followers letting each man take as much as he could carry. Of the remainder he burdened a hundred camels and carrying these with him set out to join his father Mírán Sháh.

On arrival at his camp father and son greatly rejoiced to be together and Mírán Sháh acquainted Abu Bakr with what had happened, and the latter learnt how his uncle Sháh Rukh was withstanding them and keeping them from coming to Samarqand. Abu Bakr on this, that same night of his arrival, set off again with all his following, being joined by many of his father's friends, and making his way straight to where his uncle Sháh Rukh was lying in camp fell on him suddenly overcoming all resistance. He thereupon brought Sháh Rukh his uncle back with him to his father's camp, who, in company with most of his men, now seeing that Abu Bakr was once more in power and a free man, joined his standard as shortly did many others from outlying parts of the country. Further after these things became known, daily many would come in, having deserted from the party of Prince Omar. The latter at length realized that Abu Bakr his brother was now beyond his power, freed from his prison, and he finally made up his mind to seek an accommodation with his father, Mírán Sháh, who with his son Abu Bakr was now marching unopposed on the way to Samarqand. Now at this season Prince Omar had already gone back to his army lying in camp in the Plains of Vian, which as already said are situated ten leagues distant [to the westward] of Tabriz. Prince Omar next sent word to the cities of Tabriz and Sultáníyah that it was his intention to hold a funeral feast to the honoured memory of his grandfather Timur, for the which intent they were to send him in supplies, namely sheep, horses, bread and wine. Further they must provide 3,000 robes of kincob [gold brocade] and other such stuffs, which it would be his intention to bestow on various of his lords.

It was at this date that Prince Omar at length issued his orders that our goods and possessions which, as related, had been seized should all be returned. In consequence two of the Chagatays were sent to us with our goods on Thursday the 13th of August, and they further brought us a letter from Prince Omar in which we were invited to come and see him. On Friday the following day therefore we left Tabriz sleeping that night in camp, and by the morning we were present with his Highness in the Plains of Vian where he was in residence, and they assigned us our quarters by a stream where we pitched our tents. On Saturday next day, the Feast of the Assumption of the Blessed Virgin Mary, Prince Omar issuing from his tents went to a great pavilion, and here sent for us to come to his audience. Thither we now proceeded and making him our obeisance, he received us very graciously, giving us good words; after which we were taken to an awning near the pavilion where they served us with dinner. The next day Sunday his Highness sent for us again to the pavilion, where a great feast was made, and a Mulla preached before the Prince, lauding the memory of his grandfathe. What they all did eat that day was immense in quantity; and here we took occasion to present Prince Omar with our gifts, namely stuffs in cloth of wool and silk, also a [Spanish] sword very richly ornamented, which he appeared much to prize. It is his custom never to receive any persons who do not come with a gift, and the first thing enquired of us on this occasion when we arrived at his camp was whether we had brought anything to present to him, and they demanded that we should show them what it was we had brought. On Tuesday the [18th] of August Prince Omar bestowed on us various pieces of cloth as his gift, and appointed to us [a Chagatay] one of his men who should attend on us, as likewise on our fellow ambassador the envoy from the Turkish Sultan, to act as our guide during the journey forward. In regard to the ambassadors of the Sultan of Egypt these men the Prince ordered should yet be detained, and as we heard they were next day thrown into prison.

It was that same Tuesday that we and the Turks thus took our departure from the camp of Prince Omar and next day Wednesday reached Tabriz again, where we and the Turkish Envoys took counsel together as to how and by what way we should arrange our journey, for we now hoped to set forth without any further delay. On the evening of the Friday however we having made everything ready to leave Tabriz, the Daroghah, or as one might say the city Mayor, appeared accompanied by the police and his secretaries with much folk in attendance armed with maces and clubs, and the Mayor demanded that we should bring out and show him all our baggage, further this was said with such an air of authority that we were fain to comply. Then no sooner did he see certain stuffs of the Zaytúní silk and the Chinese kincob with the scarlet cloth and the like that we had in store, than he impounded these bales, saying that his Highness had need of them, seeing that in the province there was utter lack of any of all such good ware. Then he added the Prince would pay us the just price in detaining these goods, and on this he and his men mounted and made off. On this we having sought the counsel of our Turkish colleagues, thought it prudent no longer to delay, for these men told us that the like had been done to them, and that they had had to suffer the plundering of much of their baggage. Thinking therefore that to wait on for redress would only mean further and worse ill-treatment, we decided to submit. We determined to start on the morrow, and thus it was that on Saturday the 22nd of August before daybreak that we Spaniards with our colleagues the Turkish Envoys made our way out of Tabriz city, where as related in these later pages, we had been detained in all during five months and twenty-two days, counting from the 1st of February which had been the day of our arrival.

This 22nd of August therefore we set out, having that Chagatay already spoken of as our guide, and we joined company with a caravan numbering some two hundred sumpter-horses carrying merchandise, bound for the country of the Turks, the ultimate destination of the caravan being Brusa. With these men we made our way for good company, all being in fear of bandits, and we marched that day Saturday of our departure, also Sunday and Monday following when at dawn we reached the city of Khoy, where too we had halted on the outward journey going to Samarqand. At this city of Khoy the land of Persia ends and Greater Armenia begins. No sooner had we come thither than we heard bad news, namely of a certain Turkoman chief whose name was Qara Yúsuf,[2] who had aforetime been a vassal of Timur but now had come out in rebellion. At the head of ten thousand horsemen he had recently been plundering and ravaging all that country round and about Khoy, but at the moment he was gone to Arzinján, to which city it was his intention to lay siege. This news caused us to change the route we had purposed following, namely to return by the same road we had taken on the outward journey, going from Khoy straight to Mákú. Instead of this we now turned off by a road to the left hand, taking a direction that led south [west]. Thus we left Khoy on Tuesday at the hour of vespers, travelling all that night and the next day Wednesday we halted in some meadows, but only a sufficient time to give our horses their barley. Then passing on that afternoon and night on Thursday by the hour of vespers, we had come to a village where there was a small castle, the people of the place being Armenians, for this was already in the Armenian country, though they were subjects of Prince Omar. Beyond this village to the south began a territory occupied by a Moslem folk of the Turkish race, and their country is known as Turkistan. These people lord it over the surrounding districts, but they live at peace among the Armenians for the most part, and the region is rich in corn lands and pastures.

On our arrival here we received news that Qara Yúsuf the Turkoman had raised the siege of Arzinján departing thence, and his troops now were said to be holding the road that we had intended to take the next day. We therefore sent forward one of our men to spy and see whether that Turkoman chief was already come into these parts, and late the next day Friday the man returned to us, saying that the road was open. We now immediately set forth on our journey and that night camped in some fields near by a large village, for all that day on our road we had passed many populous villages inhabited by the Armenians. In many of these villages there were fine churches, and we noticed that in the churchyards the tombstones and graves were ornamented with crosses standing up as high as a man could reach, which were most beautifully carved. While travelling the road we were now following we soon had news that Qara Yúsuf was come near, and that his men were out plundering the country-side, we again therefore turned aside taking our way to the left hand and marched till midday in this new direction, though we knew that the longer we followed on this path the more we were straying from our right route. We none the less had to keep on thus all the following Sunday, passing across a totally uninhabited tract and Monday it was the same. The entire lack of inhabitants in this part of Armenia, you must know, is due to the fact that the Christians have lost their power throughout most of Greater Armenia by reason of the civil war that recently has raged between three royal brothers. On Tuesday which was the 1st of September at [nine of the morning which is] the hour of tierce we finally had come to a large town, but here too most of the houses were empty of their inhabitants. The name of this town was Alashkert.[3] The city walls which had been very broad and very strong were all in ruin, and the castle finely built of masonry set in mortar was all open, breached in many places, though a few poor folk were still inhabiting its chambers, and still there were many fine buildings to be seen throughout the city, for the houses were everywhere of good masonry.

Here we now took our midday dinner, and the while the people related to us how it had come about that this great place had thus been ruined as we now saw. In this country of Greater Armenia there had been formerly a famous and very powerful king, the lord of the whole land, who at the time of his death had left three sons: and he had by his will divided Armenia among the three after this fashion. To his eldest son he had left this city of Alashkert with adjacent lands: to his next son he had left Ani city, with its province, and to his third son Erzerum: these cities aforesaid being the three capital towns of Armenia. The eldest son seeing that he possessed Alashkert the strongest place in all the land, forthwith tried to dispossess his two brothers of their inheritance, and open war broke out between the three. The war being at its worst, each party now sought an ally to aid him against his rivals: and the brother who was lord of Erzerum brought in that lawless Moslem folk, namely those Turkomans [already frequently mentioned]. Then the lord of Ani for aid and to do the like joined him of Erzerum and they two fell on their elder brother the lord of Alashkert, each with allies from among the Turkomans. Seeing and fearing these Turkomans the lord of Alashkert took counsel with himself and to do likewise for foreign aid called in that Moslem folk who were his neighbours, namely the Turks of the border. These Turks however had their language in common with the Turkomans already spoken of who were the allies of the other two brothers, and they of one tongue making common cause, came to an understanding to take for themselves that city of Alashkert, putting its lord to death and laying it in ruin. This done they slew both the other brothers, devastating their cities of Ani and Erzerum with the adjacent lands. Thus it was that the

Moslems had come in and now held all Armenia: for when they had conquered the cities, they put to death most of the Christian Armenians who were the inhabitants, and their places had not since been occupied.[4]

When we were thus come to Alashkert we had sure information that Qara Yúsuf the Turkoman was on that very road by which we now proposed to pass, he and all his host, we therefore again changed our plan and now purposed to turn off [north] making our way direct to Ani; and lucky indeed for us it was that we did so. With this intention on leaving Alashkert we journeyed during four days and four nights through an uninhabited barren region, and on Saturday the 5th of September at last reached Ani city in safety.[5] Then on the Monday that followed we betook ourselves up to the castle of Ani to pay our respects to the governor. He was the son of that Chagatay noble [mentioned on a previous page when describing our outward journey] under the name of Duladay Beg, and to him Timur had granted the territory [of Avnik] in lordship at the time of his conquest [of Georgia and Armenia].[6] The present governor of Ani, the son of Duladay Beg, was therefore stationed here as his father's lieutenant; and on presenting ourselves before him we offered as a present a robe of kincob [gold brocade] as it is usual and customary to do, explaining to him the difficult position in which we were placed. He assured us that Qara Yúsuf was still in the Arzinján lands, his men occupying the road that we had intended to pass, and that they were raiding that country-side. This being so we must needs go by another route; but he added that to serve our Master the King of Spain, and to honour the memory of Timur to whose court we had been sent, he would provide us with a sure guide: and at the same time would forward our colleagues the Turkish Envoys on their homeward way but by another road. We found the castle of Ani to be a place of great strength being set crowning a height that was encircled by three concentric walls very strongly built. Within the castle court was an abundant spring of water, and it was well provisioned and provided with all means for defence.

On Tuesday the 8th of September therefore we left Ani, in charge of a Chagatay who was commissioned by the governor to carry us in safety through the Georgian territories, and with this purpose we left the direct road to Arzinján which goes off on the left hand, along a part of which we had formerly passed on our outward journey. That night we slept at a village belonging to the governor of Ani, and the next day at dawn began to go up a steep mountain pass over a crest, and on the further side of this came to a castle set on a high peak the name of which was Tartum.[7] This is a place very celebrated, for Timur had laid siege to it, capturing it and imposing his tribute, though it lies well within the confines of Georgia. Passing by this castle we came forward and slept at a village about a league beyond it: and then for the next two days our road lay across the rugged mountain passes of the country of Georgia. On Friday which was the [11th] of September we reached a castle of the name of Vicer, held by a Moslem governor who was a Mulla, and a Mulla with them is a doctor of laws and forsooth a learned person. This Mulla received us very courteously and we dined with him: he told us how all the country round about was in confusion by reason of the raids of Qara Yúsuf, indeed the population for the most part had come in under the castle walls, with their herds, to obtain shelter from rapine. When we left Vicer our guide gave us to understand that we must needs now go aside from our road to pay our respects to a certain lord who held the city of Ispir; since he, our guide, carried letters for him from his master the governor of Ani. We therefore proceeded thitherward, crossing many mountain passes, for indeed all the way from Tartum our way had been across successive ranges of mountains.

The name of this lord of Ispir was Piahacabea, and his lands were very fertile and rich, in spite of this province being an extremely hilly country. Thus on that Saturday, the next day after we had come into Ispir, we went up and paid the governor our respects offering him a gift of two robes of kincob [gold cloth], and we afterwards dined with him. In the afternoon he provided us with a guide who should see us across his frontier into the country of the Emperor of Trebizond: and setting forth again we slept that night at a village below the next mountain pass. On Sunday the following morning we began to go up a very steep road to the crest, the first four leagues of the way going through a region bare without forest, and the pass was so rocky and beset that both men and beasts scarcely could go forward, save with utmost labour. Thus on that day's journey we crossed the frontiers of the lands of Georgia and entered the territory known as Arraquiel. Of the people of Georgia we shall notice they are a fine race of men, very handsome in face and gallant in bearing. They are Christians of the Greek rite in matters of religion, but their language is not Greek being an idiom peculiar to themselves. On Monday which was the day following we passed on and dined that afternoon at a village of the Arraquiel district, and proceeding forward slept at the next village. The Moslem lord of Ispir city and district is also lord of the Arraquiel district, and he has come to be so after this fashion. The men of the Arraquiel district in the past became discontented with their lord, one who bore the name of Arraquiel, like the district that was his. These folk therefore sent privily to that neighbouring lord of Ispir, with whom they compassed to betray their master, promising that he, of Ispir, should be made their ruler in the other's place. And so it all fell out, for they delivered up Arraquiel to the lord of Ispir, whom he imprisoned, setting in his place to rule the Arraquiel lands a Moslem governor, but at the same time appointing a Christian lord-deputy to act as his assistant.

All this country-side of Arraquiel is very mountainous, with mere path-ways that cross the passes, and these so rocky and steep that burdened horses cannot travel them. In some places they have had to build bridges of beams from rock to rock to traverse the hill crests. No sumpter-beasts are here in use, but men who are porters have to carry all burdens on their shoulders. There is but little corn grown in this region, and the people are of a barbarous race. As we passed through we were in some danger from them, for though they are Armenians and profess to be Christians all are robbers and brigands; indeed they forced us, before we were let free to pass, to give a present of our goods as toll for right of passage. We were four days journeying through their country and then came to the sea-shore, at a place on the coast [of the Black Sea] that lies six days' journey east of Trebizond, and here journeying along a wretched road soon reached the little port of Susurmena [or Surmeneh]. The land is of the district of Trebizond, it lies along the sea coast and is very mountainous, the hill sides everywhere being covered by forests. The trees as they stand support many creepers, most of which are grapevines, and of the wild grapes a wine is made, but no vineyards are tended by these people. The population live in hamlets each of which bears the name of Curio, the same consisting of well masoned cottages, a few together standing in one place and elsewhere others. The paths we had to follow going through this country were so abominable, that it cost us the lives of near all the beasts of burden we had with us for our baggage.

On Thursday the 17th of September we came at last to Trebizond, and on our arrival there were informed of a ship having just that morning set sail thence for Pera, with a cargo of hazelnuts. The wind fortunately for us proved contrary and we soon had news that she had put back and had come into the port of Platana, the little harbour lying some six miles to the west of Trebizond. We therefore immediately provisioned ourselves for the sea voyage, and taking a boat, were rowed over thither and found the ship on board which we now came. She was commanded by a Genoese captain, whose name was Messer Nicoloso Cojan, who agreed to give us passage, and we made our voyage with him thence to Pera in twenty-five days. It was on Thursday the 22nd of October that we were come to Constantinople once more, as the night set in. On entering the port of Pera we found that three carracks, of the Genoese, had just arrived from Kaffa, and were about to sail with destination home, to Genoa, and in one of these we now took passage after provisioning ourselves for the voyage. The carracks sailed on Wednesday the 4th of November, and that same evening put into Gallipoli where we received on board a cargo of cotton bales, and sailing again Saturday came in due course to the island of Chios. Monday the of November we again put to sea, and [Crossing the Ægean] arrived off the island of Sapiencia and Cape St Angelo [in the Morea] where we were come to the districts of which the Venetians hold lordship. Sailing from here on Monday the last day of November we were shortly in sight of the island of Sicily[8] and made for the port of the city [of Messina] where we came to anchor.

Wednesday the 2nd of December we thence set sail [for Genoa], but falling in with bad weather put into the port of Gaeta, which is in the Kingdom of Naples, and lay here five days. Then putting to sea again we fell in with another storm which caused us to turn back to Gaeta for shelter, and there remained till Tuesday the 22nd of December. Setting sail once more, a heavy squall drove us across to the island of Corsica, and there we stayed to celebrate the Feast of Christmas. Putting to sea once more the tempest again took us, whereby we ran for shelter to a port that is called Gumbin. Thence on the Saturday following we set sail and shortly found ourselves off the harbour of Veane: from which road-stead on Sunday the 3rd of January [1406] we at last came to the port of Genoa. The Genoese coast for full six leagues before coming to that city is everywhere set with houses standing in beautiful orchards and fine gardens, the same is indeed a very pleasant sight to see. The city itself is extremely populous, being full of magnificent palaces, and above almost every house of the town there stands a tower. We stayed in Genoa some days and then went over to Savona where we saw [Benedict XIII whose surname is Luna the Spanish Anti]-Pope with whom we had business, but next returned. From Genoa finally on Monday the 1st of February we set sail in a ship of which the captain was Messer Biemboso Barbero, but our voyage again was beset with storm and contrary winds, worse even than what we had suffered heretofore: so that it lasted from that first day of February when we put out from Genoa till Sunday the [7th] of March when we landed at San Lucar: and went up to the city of Seville. It was after this that on a Monday the [22nd] of March, in the year of Our Lord one thousand four hundred and six that we Ambassadors finally reached Alcalá de Henares where we found our lord King Henry III of Castile.[9]

Laus Deo and thus ends the Chronicle of the great Timur, and the Itinerary of the voyage made by the Spanish Ambassadors sent to, him by that most serene King Henry, surnamed the Invalid, together with the true account of all the notable events and marvellous sights met with in the East.

Printed [for the first time] in Seville, at the house of Andrea Piscioni in the year 1582. [338]

Notes

Introduction

1. The two Genealogical Tables for present and future reference stand as follows:

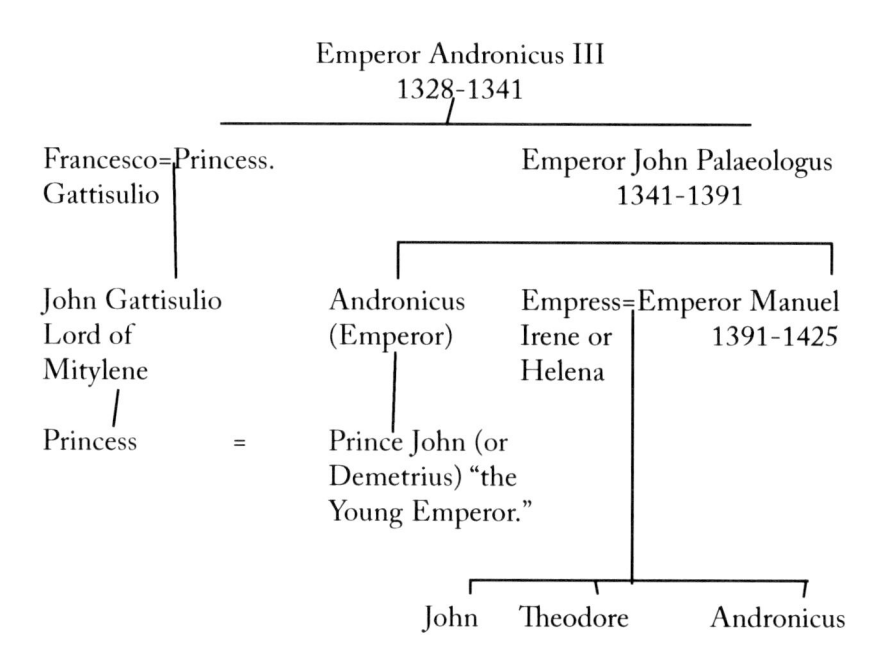

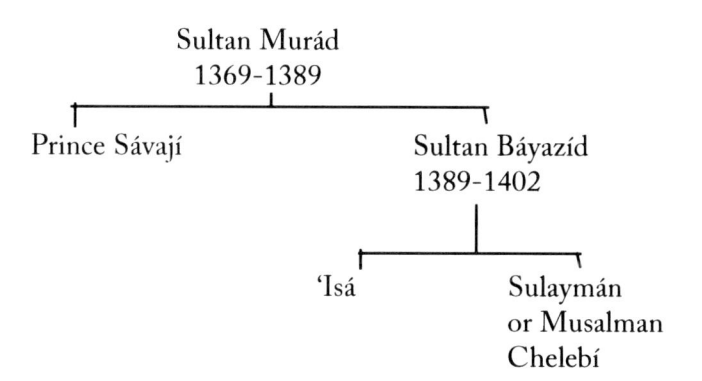

```
                    Emperor Andronicus III
                         1328-1341
    ┌──────────────────────┴──────────────────────┐
Francesco=Princess.                    Emperor John Palaeologus
Gattisulio                                    1341-1391
    │                           ┌──────────────────┴──────────────┐
John Gattisulio           Andronicus        Empress=Emperor Manuel
Lord of                   (Emperor)         Irene or      1391-1425
Mitylene                      │             Helena
    │                         │
Princess       =        Prince John (or
                        Demetrius) "the
                        Young Emperor."
                              ┌───────────────┼───────────────┐
                            John          Theodore        Andronicus
```

Further:

```
                    Sultan Murád
                      1369-1389
            ┌─────────────┴─────────────┐
      Prince Sávají              Sultan Báyazíd
                                    1389-1402
                                ┌───────┴────────┐
                              'Isá           Sulaymán
                                             or Musalman
                                             Chelebí
```

2. A history of Timur was composed in Persian a score of years after his death by Sharaf-ad-Dín 'Alí of Yezd, and is the best account of that conqueror and his campaigns. Petis de la Croix translated this into French - *Histoire de Timur Bec* - published at Delft in 1723. This and other Persian historians Major David Price has used for his account of Timur in the third volume of his *Chronological Retrospect of Mahommedan History* (London, 1811).

3. Argote de Molina (the editor of Clavijo) in the *Discurso* which he prefixed to the Editio Princeps of 1582 states that with the presents of jewels Timur sent to King Henry two Christian maidens found captives in the seraglio of the defeated Turkish Sultan Báyazíd, their names being Maria and Angelina. Angelina is said to have been of Greek parentage. Maria was the daughter of a certain Count John and granddaughter of the King of Hungary. Both had probably been prisoners with the Turks since the disastrous overthrow of the Christian forces at the battle of Nicopolis (see Introduction, p. xxxi). In charge of the Spanish ambassadors the two ladies arrived safely in Spain and in due course married Spanish noblemen, perhaps dowered by the King: and both find mention in Spanish ballads of the time. In the case of Maria the Hungarian, a lady of surpassing beauty, Argote de Molina quotes a ballad, apparently otherwise unknown, which gives words as spoken by Don Payo Gómez de Soto Mayor who is represented as courting her at Jódar, and who subsequently became her husband. Jódar lies six leagues from Jaen to the north of Granada, and from Seville where they had landed the two returning ambassadors, one of them this Payo de Soto Mayor, were conveying the ladies to the court of King Henry. As a matter of fact he and she had been travelling together, seeing each other every day since leaving Angora, so it was the fountain that must have brought matters to a head.

    En la fontana de Jódar
    Vi a la niña de ojos bellos,
    E finqué ferido dellos
    Sin tener, de vida, un hora.

Beside that fountain at Jódar
The maid with beauteous eyes I saw:
I died by the wound they gave me
And not one hour could I survive.

Angelina the Grecian damsel married at Seville Don Diego González de Contreras who was afterwards Regidor of Segovia. Argote de Molina has much to say of the Contreras family in another of his works, *Historia de la Nobleza del Andaluzia* (Seville, 1583) and quotes a contemporary poem by Francisco Imperial who seems not to be sure of her nationality.

Ora sea Tarta o Griega.
En cuanto la pude ver,
Su disposición no niega
Grandioso nombre ser.

Whether Tartar or Grecian maid
Was unknown for all I could see:
But her presence left no doubt
That her birth was of high degree.

4. The topography of Constantinople is fully treated in the two works of A. Van Millingen: *Byzantine Constantinople and the Walls* (London, 1899) and *Byzantine Churches of Constantinople* (London, 1912).

5. For the geography of the route from Trebizond to Samarqand I may refer readers to my *Lands of the Eastern Caliphate* (Cambridge, 1905) also to the *Nuzhat-al-Qulûb* which gives the geography of Western Asia in the first quarter of the 13th century. Its author Hamd Allah Mustawfí must have died a few years before Clavijo was born. For the English *Translation* (also the Persian *Text)* see E. J. W. Gibb Memorial, First Series, XXIII 1 (1915) and 2 (1919), London, Luzac and Co.

6. Genealogical Table of the House of Timur

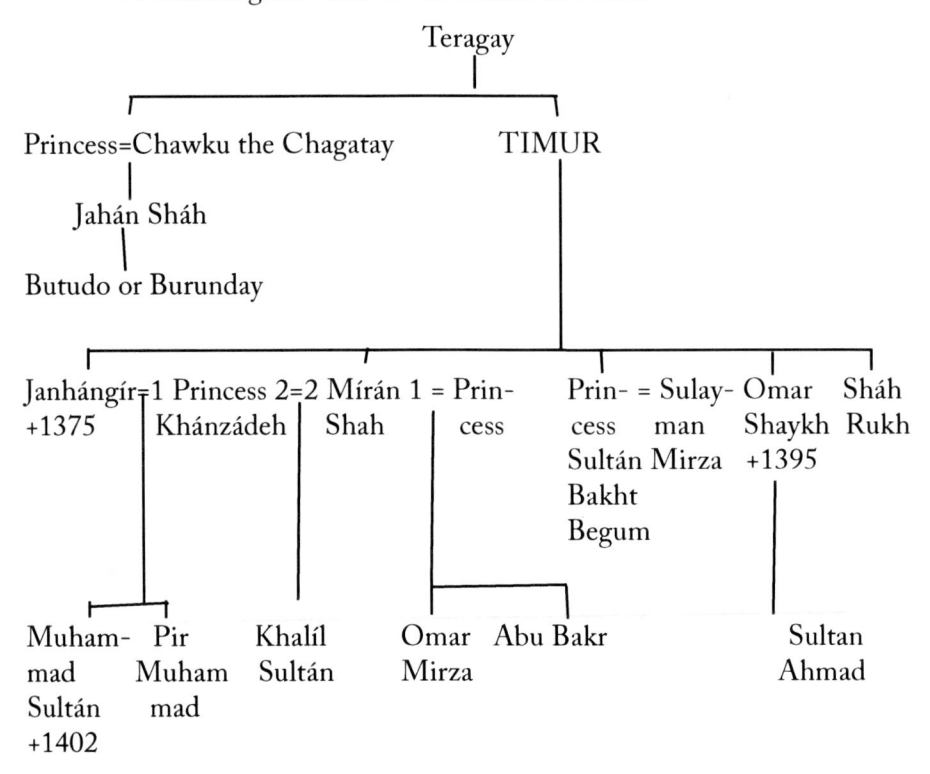

```
                            Teragay
                               |
        ┌──────────────────────┴───────────┐
Princess=Chawku the Chagatay            TIMUR
        |
    Jahán Sháh
        |
Butudo or Burunday
```

```
┌──────────┬──────────────┬────────────┬──────────────────────┬──────────────┬──────────┐
Janhángír=1 Princess 2=2 Mírán 1 = Prin-   Prin- = Sulay- Omar      Sháh
+1375      Khánzádeh    Shah      cess    cess    man    Shaykh   Rukh
                         |         |      Sultán Mirza  +1395
                         |         |      Bakht
                         |         |      Begum
   ┌────┐                |    ┌────┴────┐                  |
Muham- Pir            Khalíl  Omar   Abu Bakr            Sultan
mad    Muham-         Sultán  Mirza                      Ahmad
Sultán mad
+1402
```

7. At the present day Mirza *after* the personal name is equivalent to Prince, but before the name (e.g. Mirza Sulaymán) only implies that the personage is a gentleman of some education. This is the usage introduced by the Safavi kings in the 16th century and after. In Clavijo's days however Sulaymán Mirza was not necessarily a prince of the blood, for he names several other Mirzas (prefixed) who were not of royal descent.

8. See Nicolas Antonio, *Biblioteca Hispana Vetus*, where the account of our author appears under the name of *Rodericus Gundisalvi a Clavijo* (Vol. 11, p. 130 of the Roman edition of 1696). In the article devoted to him in *Hijos de Madrid* by José Antonio Álvarez of Baena (Vol. IV, p. 302, Madrid, 1791) it is incorrectly asserted that of the three members of the embassy sent to Timur Clavijo alone came home; whereas as will be seen the Master in Theology survived the perils of the way.

9. The precious 15th century MS. is catalogued under the press mark Bb. 72/9218 and is briefly noticed by B. J. Galliardo in his *Ensayo de una Biblioteca Española de libros raros y curiosos*, Madrid, 1866; see Vol.11, Appendix, p. 66. The copy made by Molina in the 16th century is numbered 18,050 in the catalogue of the Madrid National Library.

10. The French title page reads:

Ruy Gonzales de Clavijo
Itineraire de l'Ambassade Espagnole
à Samarcande en 1403-1406

and it was printed in Volume XXVIII of the *Sbornik* or Miscellany for Russian Language and Literature of the Imperial Academy of St Petersburg, 1882.

Chapter I

1. This title-sheet is not found in the 15th century MS. only in the copy made by, or for, Argote de Molina.

2. The name Timur is said to have been given to him by a certain holy Moslem shaykh to whom his father brought the child and who happened at the time to be reading a verse of the Quran (ch. lxvii, v. 16) which closes with the word "*Tamur*" - in the Arabic meaning "it shall shake": which was taken as an omen naming the boy. Tamerlane, Tímúr-i-Lang, the second word in Persian meaning "the Lame" was the name afterwards given him by his enemies, in disrespect, because of a limp caused by a wound received in early days at the siege of Sístán City. Clavijo at first generally writes of him as Timur Bec, but later in his narrative when he comes to be living at Samarqand generally refers to him as El Señor: occasionally as the Emperor. The Chagatay (or Jaghatay) were the imperial clan of which Timur was chief. All the nobles, officials and messengers of his court were Chagatays and Clavijo, as will be seen, generally refers to any officer as a Chagatay.

3. See below : Chapter X, note 5, p. 330 on "Tagiquinia."

4. In the text given as "Mahomet Alcagi," where it is uncertain whether the last word stands for Al-Qází "the judge" or perhaps, and more likely, for Al-Hájjí "the Mecca Pilgrim." The paragraph of the text here begins with the word "*con*," in error, as though the Ambassador and the Hájjí were two separate people, which is not consonant with what follows.

5. Among them Angelina and Maria, see above, Introduction, note 3, p. 308.

6. See Introduction, p. xxxvi. A. Jall, *Archéologie Navale* I, 453 and II, 211, gives descriptions of the Carrack, also of the Galliot the vessel in which the Spaniards took ship at Pera.

7. Malaga was at this date the chief port of the Moorish kingdom of Granada.

8. The celebrated physician Avicenna (Ibn Síná, A.D. 980 to 1037) was born at a village near Balkh on the Oxus, lived in Persia all his days and died at Hamadán. There seems to be here a confusion between him and one Ibn Sídah a philosopher of Moslem Spain who died in A.D. 1067.

9. The Torre Orlanda was older than the time of Charlemagne, dating from the days of the Emperor Augustus, having been built, to serve as his sepulchre, by Munatius Plancus celebrated as the founder of the city of Lyons.

10. Joanna, Queen of Naples and Provence who died in 1382, leaving no issue, willed Naples to her cousin the Duke of Durazzo, who succeeded as king Charles III: and his queen was Margaret daughter of Mary, Queen Joanna's only sister. Their son Ladislas became king of Naples, on the death of Charles III in 1387. Queen Joanna, by her will, had left Provence to the Duke of Anjou, Louis I, son of king John of France (Valois), and in 1385 Louis's son Duke Louis II succeeded him. In 1390 Louis II, who had declared war on Ladislas, expelled him from Naples, of which kingdom he took possession ruling there as king till 1401. At that date Ladislas recovered Naples, in turn expelling Louis II, and after this reigned in peace till his death in 1414. His sister, the wife of Duke William of Hapsburg, succeeded to his kingdom of Naples, being known as Queen Joanna II, and there she reigned till her death in 1435.

11. This cape at the eastern horn of the Gulf of Naples is now called Punto della Campanella.

12. San Pedro González, otherwise San Telmo, is the patron saint of Tuy in Galicia. He is the storm-saviour of mariners. He died at Eastertide in 1248: he was canonized in 1254 and his tomb is shown in the Tuy Cathedral. See Florez, *España Sagrada* XXIII, p. 143.

13. The Arabs when in possession of Sicily spoke and wrote of Etna as El-Jebel "the Mountain." The Sicilians ever since, forgetting the meaning of the Arabic word added again "Mountain," and Etna at the present day is still called Mongibello.

14. Now known as Gerakounia or Phalkonera, lying half way in the passage across the Ægean.

Chapter II

1. The Knights Hospitallers of St John of Jerusalem held Rhodes from 1309 to 1522, when the Turks turned them out. The ninth Grand Master in Rhodes (out of nineteen) was "Philibert de Naillac, of the Tougac of France, elected in 1396, died in June 1421" (see *Rhodes of the Knights*, by F. de Belarbre, p. 19). Naillac had fought at the disastrous battle of Nicopolis in 1396 (see Introduction, p. xxxi), but fortunately had escaped being taken prisoner. Marshal Boucicault who was also present and was taken prisoner at this celebrated defeat had to be ransomed with the Duke of Nevers his Commander. Boucicault was then over thirty years of age and after returning to France was sent by King Charles VI in 1399 in aid of the Emperor Manuel at Constantinople (see Introduction, pp. xxxii-xxxiii). France in the year 1396 had seized on Genoa, and in 1401 Boucicault was made Governor of the town to the entire satisfaction of the Genoese. He took command of their galleys and in 1403 sailed against Cyprus joining forces with the Knights of St John. They raided the coasts of Cilicia and plundered Beyrut. Marshal Boucicault is more than once mentioned in the pages of Clavijo. At a later date the Marshal, with his French garrison, was expelled from Genoa. This was in 1410; in 1415 he fought at Agincourt, was taken a prisoner to England where he died in 1421. See Du Pilham, *Histoire du Maréchal Boucicault* (La Hay, 1699); *Decline and Fall* (Bury) VII, pp. 37 and 65. Here and elsewhere subsequently Clavijo writes of "el Reyno de Alexandria," and "Alexandria" referring to Alexandretta or Iskandarún, on the coast of northern Syria. Sreznevski in his Index (and apparently in the Russian translation) gives this as Alexandria of Egypt, which it cannot be.

2. "El Soldan de Babylonia," in the text, namely the Burjí Mamlúk Sultan Násir-ad-Dín Faraj (1393 to 1405). Cairo was known to Europe, very generally, as Babylon from the old Roman castle bearing that name, the walls of which are still standing a short distance to the south of Cairo. Hence with Clavijo Babylonia generally stands for Egypt, but not invariably, for when we have "Babylonia y Baldas" (Baghdad) it is Mesopotamian Babylonia. Timur after sacking Damascus in 1401 had marched back to Anatolia, taking Baghdad on his road. After the battle of Angora

in 1402, with Sultan Báyazíd in his train, he had set out on his return to Samarqand, intent next on conquering China. Both the Ottoman Turks and the Mamluks of Egypt being new his vassals, there was no need to conquer Egypt.

3. In text printed as "Lango." The island of Kos was known to the Latins as Stanchio ('Ες ταν κω).

4. Palatia is the ancient Miletus visited by St Paul (Acts xx 15). An embassy from here went to Samarqand to visit Timur, as mentioned later, see p. 268.

5. El Forno may be Pharmakussa to the eastward of Leros, or it might be Pharin lying to the north of Patmos.

6. Cape St Mary now known as Baba Burun at the corner of the mainland north of Mitylene. This island, the Lesbos of the ancients, took its name Mitylene from the capital town more commonly called Kastro, in the strait over against the mainland. Mytilene or Mitylene island was also known as Stalimene which Clavijo writes Estalimen and otherwise Escalines.

7. She was sister to the Emperor John Palæologus, father of the Emperor Manuel. See Genealogical Table, p. 307; Ducange, *Familiæ Augustæ Byzantinæ* (Paris, 1680), p. 239.

8. See the Genealogical Table, p. 310.

9. The text reads "el Turco Murat" in error.

10. Gallipoli had been in the hands of the Turks since 1358, and here Sultans Murád and Báyazíd stationed the fleet of galleys which secured the passage of the Hellespont and enabled the Turks at will to blockade Constantinople.

11. Text "ellos visten silicio Negro": for which read "cilicio."

12. In fact not more than three miles.

13. "El Cabo de los Caminos," now called Qum Qalʻah.

14. Now called Sidd-al-Bahr: "the Sea Barrier."

15. " Torre del Vituperio."

16. After the overthrow of the Turks at Angora, with the capture and subsequent death of Sultan Báyazíd, his sons waged civil war each against the other. From 1403 to 1410 Prince Sulaymán often called Musulmán Chelebi (this last a title the equivalent of "Master") was for the most part commonly recognised as Sultan: though a faction had always stood out for his elder brother Prince ʻIsá, whose recent death Clavijo has recorded.

Chapter III

1. Of the Palace of the Blachernæ not a wall exists above ground, but its approximate site is well known, occupying the hill in the northern quarter of Constantinople, overlooking the city and the Golden Horn. See *Byzantine Constantinople : The Walls*, by Van Millingen, p. 28.

2. Ducange *(Familiæ Augustæ Byzantinæ*, p. 242) gives a woodcut reproducing a miniature in a MS. of Dionysius the Areopagite, which represents, to left, the Emperor Manuel, to right, the Empress Irene (or Helena) and below their three elder sons, of whom John, born 1390, is apparently of the age here spoken of. For Messer Ilario Doria the Emperor's son-in-law see Ducange, *op cit.*, p. 245.

3. Of the Church of St John the Baptist in Petra no trace now exists, but its site is marked by a building once occupied by the Envoys of Moldavia to the Porte, and known as the Bogdan Serai. "Petra" is the rock near by, known to the Turks as Kesmeh Kaya. Van Millingen, *Byzantine Churches*, p. 282.

4. The word in the text used here and often later, is "Chapitel," and this the Dictionary of the Spanish Academy gives merely with the signification "capital of a column" in the architectural sense. That Clavijo uses it to mean a cupola or dome is proved by the passage in his description of Santa Sophia (see later, p. 48-9) where he refers to the ceiling of the great dome over the nave as "un chapitel redondo e muy alto." All the churches described by Clavijo were basilicas in form with an oblong or square shaped nave. At the east end was the apse, and this plan is evidently what is indicated by the term "quadra redonda" used by Clavijo. He further speaks of "three naves" by which we may understand a narthex and two side aisles to the main nave. To judge by the existing churches of Santa Sophia and St John of the Studion, the orientation of the Constantinople basilicas was almost exactly south-east.

5. The Church of St Mary Peribleptos ("Admired of all Observers ") has entirely disappeared, its site being occupied by the present Armenian church of St George, known to the Turks as Sulu Monastir. Van Millingen, *Churches*, p. 268.

6. The text reads "ninety" but this is evidently a typographical mistake: CC in the original manuscript having been read as XC.

7. J. Ebersolt *(Constantinople Byzantine,* p. 136) states that this was the tomb of the Emperor Nicephorus III Botoniates (1078 to 1081) who was the second founder of the church, after the time of Romanus III Argyrus (1028 to 1034).

8. With the exception of the mosque of Santa Sophia the only Byzantine church still standing in Constantinople, of those visited by Clavijo, is the Church of St John the Baptist of the Studion monastery. This of course is now become a mosque, and is known to the Turks as the Mír Akhor Jámi'si. It stands at no great distance from the Golden Gate, within the city wall. This basilica is one of the few buildings in Constantinople that is older in date than Santa Sophia, it having been erected in the year 463 by the patrician Studius (Van Millingen, *Churches,* pp. 35 and 56). It is noteworthy that the present plan does not agree with the description left by Clavijo; for a total of 18 columns only can be counted in the present Mosque, as shown in the plan (here reproduced) given by Van Millingen.

9. In the text "Otro dia" "The next day," which was Wednesday, but this appears to be in error; for on Sunday the 28th October they had their audience of the Emperor; Monday 29th he sent his officers to return an answer to their mission: Tuesday 30th they started sight-seeing: Wednesday 31st, as stated (with the reason) in the following chapter, they stayed up at Pera: Thursday 1st November sight-seeing again. But apparently on that Tuesday 30th of October they must have done an almost miraculous amount of sight-seeing. What probably happened in fact was that during this first week they had a general look round: and during the following five months of their stay in Pera, added needful details from subsequent visits to the Churches of Stambul.

10. The Byzantine Hippodrome is the present Turkish Át Meidán (Horse Plain), but the area of the ancient Hippodrome occupied nearly twice the present limits of the Meidán. The Obelisk brought from Egypt and placed in the Hippodrome by Theodosius the Great (to whom the Greek Inscription that Clavijo could not read refers) is 60 feet high, and rests on the pedestal supported

317

by four bronze cubes. The Serpent Column (bearing the Serpent's heads in position) originally came from Delphi, and dates from the year of the victory of the Greeks over Xerxes (B.C. 479). It was set up in the Hippodrome by the Emperor Constantine the Great.

11. This column and its statue were destroyed by lightning in 1492, forty years after the Turks had come in, and a rough sketch of it is preserved among the MSS. of the Library in the Seraglio at Constantinople. Copied from Mordtman a woodcut of this is given by Ebersolt, *Constantinople Byzantine*, p. 30, and see *The Church of Sancta Sophia*, by W. R. Lethaby and H. Swainson, p. 180.

12. These twelve pilasters are: the four main supports of the central dome: next the four piers, two under the east and two under the west semi-dome; lastly the four piers, two in the north wall and two in the south wall of the lateral aisles, these corresponding to the four great central pilasters first mentioned.

13. This is the Ambo, a raised platform ascended by steps from the sides east and west, for which see Lethaby and Swainson, Figure 7, p. 54, *op. cit.*

14. Argote de Molina in his text prints "noventa pasos" but the Madrid MS. (folio 27, second column *recto*) has "ochenta." In the line above we have "el altar menor" which seems certainly a mistake for "mayor" as rectified by Argote. As regards 90 paces (or indeed 80 as given in the MS.) for the width of the gallery, as Sreznevski points out (p. 431), this must be a mistake, and he suggests "veinte" as the right reading, which is adopted in the translation.

Chapter IV

1. The Mangana was the Constantinople Arsenal with workshops for ship-building and war stores. Of the church of St George which stood here nothing now remains, for all this region is occupied by the Seraglio, but its position is known, namely about half way between Santa Sophia and Seraglio Point and close to the seashore. Van Millingen, *Walls*, pp. 250, 251.

2. According to Sreznevski (p. 430) this Empress was the wife of Constantine X, Monomachus (1042-1054) who founded the Church of St George.

3. The gate of Kynegos (the Hunter) on the Golden Horn is now probably the Petri Qapusi, and near it was the Convent of the Petrion, called Omnipotens or Pantocrator (as mentioned by Clavijo a few lines later) where ladies of high rank, become politically troublesome, were sent to be interned. Of this building some remains exist. Van Millingen, *Walls*, pp. 200-202 and 207; Ducange, Constantinopolis Christiana iv. p. 81,

4. See above, p. 19.

5. In the text " Santa Maria de la Cherne," this last a mistake for " Blachernæ," doubtless. This was the famous church of the Theotokos (the Mother of God), where the Girdle of the Blessed Virgin was kept. Its position in the Blachernæ quarter is known, but no trace of it exists. The Castle here nearby must be identified with the State Prison called the Tower of Anemas, the greater part of which is still standing. Van Millingen, *Walls*, pp. 152, 162, 164, 197, and *Churches*, p. 193.

6. Of the great Church of St Mary of the Hodegetria ("Guide of the Way ") nothing remains. It stood near the sea-shore to the east of Santa Sophia; to which church with others the Picture painted by St Luke - the Eikon. of the Theotokos - was taken in procession. Van Millingen, *Churches*, p. 227, and *Walls*, p. 258.

7 See Introduction, p. xxxi-xxxii, with the Genealogical Table, p. 307. It will be noticed that throughout this account the proper names of the Emperors and others are for the most part omitted. Clavijo's Chirmanoli is for Kyr (the Lord) Manuel.

8. This son of Andronicus, whom Clavijo here names Demetrius,

referring to him elsewhere and otherwise as the "Young Emperor," is more generally known as John. See Gibbon, *Decline and Fall* (Bury) vii, p. 41.

9. The particular cistern - for of cisterns Constantinople had many - which Clavijo visited cannot be identified with certainty: but it probably was the Cistern of Philoxenus near the Hippodrome, now known as the Bin Bir Derek, "the Cistern of 1001 Columns." Who was Clavijo's "Mahomete" is unknown.

10. The great church of the Holy Apostles was pulled down by Sultan Muhammad the Conqueror who used its materials for building the mosque (called after him), which now occupies its site. The site is near the Aqueduct of Valens (still standing) which brought water to Constantinople, and the church was famous for its grandeur and its roof covered with tiles of gilded bronze. Van Millingen, *Walls*, pp. 35, 41.

11. This proves that at least half a century before the Ottoman conquest the Greeks spoke of their city as Ἐις την πολιν, which the Turks changed to Stambul.

12. This is the well-known Genoese Tower of Galata built in 1348, now used as a watch-tower against fire. In the middle ages it was known as the Tower of Christ, and is not to be confused with another Tower of Galata on the sea-shore below, where the great chain was anchored. This chain - supported on floats - at its southern end was fixed in the Stambul shore, and closed the harbour of the Golden Horn. Van Millingen, *Walls*, p. 228.

13. On the recovery of Constantinople from the Latins in 1261, the Genoese were granted Pera as a fief of the Empire by the Emperor Michael Palæologus. Holding Pera the Genoese came into possession of all the Black Sea trade.

14. This was the tomb of Philip Count of Artois, Constable of France, who was taken prisoner by Báyazd at the battle of Nicopolis, and died June 1397 (see Ducange, *Constantinopolis Christiana* iv., p. 123). The Monastery of St Francis no longer exists, its site being now occupied by the Mosque of Sultan Valideh, built on its foundations in 1659, and which stands below the Galata Tower near the northern end of the modern Outer Bridge.

Chapter V

1. The text has "a hora de tercia" and tierce would be nine in the forenoon of Thursday the following day. This however must be a mistake, not agreeing with what follows. Further Therapia is but 10 miles by water from Constantinople which was left at midday Wednesday, and it would hardly, with a fair wind, have taken the galliot 21 hours to make that distance. Probably for "tercia" we should read "nona," three o'clock of the afternoon of that same Wednesday.

2. In the text "El Guirol de la Grecia y el Guirol de la Turquia." Ruins of later built castles still guard the entrance to the Bosporus: and "Guirol" is evidently "Qaraol" the Turkish for a Guard or Watch, more generally now applied to a man than as here to a tower.

3. Finogia is Kirpen Island in the Bay of Kefken, where lies the port of Kirpen the ancient Calpe described by Xenophon.

4. This is a misunderstanding. If "Ponto" be for "Bender," that is Persian for "a harbour" and very commonly so used in Turkish: while if "Raquia" be "Eregli" that is for Heraclea (Pontica) which was not the name of an Emperor.

5. The name Leona appears to be a clerical error for Puliman, the modern name for the Turkish village representing the ancient Polemonium.

Chapter VI

1. The Empire of Trebizond resulted from the capture of Constantinople in 1204 by the Latins. It flourished concurrently with the re-established Empire of the Palæologi after 1261: and survived the fall of Constantinople in 1453, by eight years, succumbing to Sultan Muhammad the Conqueror in 1461. At the time of Clavijo's visit a namesake of the Constantinople emperor, namely Manuel II (Comnenus) was reigning. He of course naturally was the enemy of the Turk, and now paid tribute to Timur. His narrow territory stretched along the coast from some distance west of Treboli to a point at the south eastern corner of the Black Sea.

2. It will he noticed that only five fasts are mentioned.

3. " Guadamacir," otherwise " Guadamecil " (variously spelt) is the name given in Spain to what we know as Cordovan leather. It came from Morocco, being originally called "Ghadamesi," from the town of Ghadames where it was first manufactured. This leather is mentioned in the Poem of the Cid: 12th century. (See Dozy and Engelmann, *Glossaire des Mots Espagnoles dérivés de l'Arabe*, s.v. *Guadamaci.)* "Sofra" is Persian "Sufrah," a table-cloth, a word still commonly so used. The unleavened thin cake of bread as here described is common and everywhere eaten throughout Persia at the present day.

4. Chagatay (or Jaghatay, already mentioned, Ch. I, note 2, p. 312) was the name of the third of the sons of Chingiz Khán: and Timur was descended from a Mongol lord who had been his Vizier. Throughout Clavijo's narrative (as already said) Chagatay is commonly used to indicate a Mongol or Tartar, either a lord of the family or clan of Timur, or a Government Messenger and Imperial Official.

5. In text "Sutimi (later 'Setuni') azul": that is blue Zaytúní (silk) made at or imported from the Chinese port and city of Zaytún so often spoken of by Marco Polo and the Arab geographers. See Yule, *Marco Polo* (1874) II, p. 224, and Mustawfi, *Nuzhat*, p. 255. It is supposed that this word Zaytúní, through the Spanish form Setuni is the origin in English and French of Satin.

6. The spelling given in the text is "Xevali," which might stand for Sheykh 'Alí. 'Alí of Yezd, apparently, does not mention him.

Chapter VII

1. What was commonly known as the silver Real was worth just under sevenpence; but the "Real de a ocho (reales)" the Piece of Eight was the dollar worth about four shillings. According to Pegolotti the Asper was worth just over half a crown of our money. See Yule, *Cathay* (1866), p. 298.

2. The text has "el conde Lazaro," but King is generally given as equivalent to the Servian title Kral. The battle of Kossovo took place in 1389 when Sultan Murád completely crushed the Servians and their allies. As matter of fact it was not Lazarus who killed Murád but a Servian warrior named Milosh Kobilovich who, starting from a heap of dead, stabbed the Sultan when he was viewing the battlefield, inflicting a wound in the stomach of which Murád expired next day. Lazarus was however put to death by order of the dying Sultan. His son Stephen was granted peace by Báyazíd, and lived afterwards to become a pensioner of the Turk.

3. This is popular etymology, for though Timur or Demir means "iron" Timur was his proper name. See chapter I, note 2, p. 312.

4. Partir Javan is Javán Qal'ah now known as Hasan Qal'ah, and Delilárkent is the present Deli Bábá. "Kashish" is Persian for a Priest, here used for a Dervish.

5. Clavijo is one of the few to give a description of Surmari, a very important city during the middle ages; but of which all that remains today is represented by the insignificant Turkish village of Surmalu standing on the right, south, bank of the Araxes, 10 miles below the junction of the Arpa Chay and about 40 miles west respectively from Eriván and Mount Ararat (see Map, in Vol. I of H. F. B. Lynch, *Armenia Travels and Studies)*. Surmari, Sulmari, or Surmali, the Armenian Surb Mari, that is Saint Mary, is frequently mentioned by the Armenian historians (see J. Saint-Martin, *Mémoire sur l'Arménie II*, pp. 101, 226; M. F. Brosset, *Histoire de Stephanos Orbelian*. p. 222; Injijean, *Description of Ancient Armenia*, p. 444). According to Ibn-al-Athir (Tornberg X, p. 25), Surmari was stormed and left in ruins by Alp Arslán in 1064 and the same fate befell the city at the hands of the Mongols in 1239 (M. F. Brosset, *Kirakos de Gantzac*, p. 129) and lastly by Timur in 1387 (*Timur Bec* I, p. 412). The situation of the modern village of Surmalu lying between rocky ravines is

323

described by Dubois de Montpereux *(Voyage autour du Caucase* III, pp. 419 and 446) and Ibn-al-Athír in the 11th century states that it had "a fine castle surrounded by many gardens with running brooks." Our author spells the name Calmarin. It should be noted that this is not the place visited by William of Rubruck and lying at the foot of Ararat called by him Cemanum, which stands for the Arabic Thamanín – "the City of the Eighty." Further our author's Naujua (which is probably for Naw Juy) cannot be identified with Nakhjeván, which Rubruck writes Naxua, the Arabic form being Nashawa, and which lies on the northern (left) bank of the Araxes as fully described by the Moslem geographers.

6. Toktamish who died in 1046 was Khán of the Golden Horde of Kipchak, a notable opponent and rival of Timur who in the end overcame him. The text here reads "eight years," but the date when Toktamish invaded Armenia and Azerbayján was in fact A.H. 787 or A.D. 1386.

7. Which is cramoisie. See *Nuzhat*, p. 89: s.v. Marand.

8. These remains are supposed to be the ruins of the ancient Artaxata.

9. Núr-ad-Dín "the Light of the (Moslem) Religion" is a curious name for a Christian, but doubtless it had been imposed on this Christian governor by Timur, as later he did in the case of the governor's son.

10. When Timur appointed his young grandson Omar Mirza to be vice-roy of Persia, the Amír Jahán Sháh was sent as his governor to take charge of the youthful prince for whose acts Timur held him responsible. Compare the Genealogical Table, Introduction, note 6, p. 310; *Timur Bec* IV 147.

11. On the return journey, however, the ambassadors did not pass through Mákú.

12. At the date (1384) of Timur's first invasion of Western Persia, that country which then included Kurdistán and lower Mesopotamia (Baghdád) was ruled by Sultan Ahmad the Il-Khán, who unable to resist the Tartars fled for refuge to Sultan Barqúq at Cairo. He was finally able to resume his government in 1405 after the date of Timur's death when affairs in Samarqand were in confusion, Persia having then relapsed to its former conditions and rulers.

Chapter VIII

1. In the text given as "Caza" almost certainly a misreading for "Taza" which would be for Tassúj (otherwise Tarúj) a well-known city of these parts (*Nuzhat*, p. 83). The name Kúzah Kunán, the next stage (*Nuzhat*, p. 82) means "the Potteries." When printing from the copy of the original Spanish MS. the letters C and T appear constantly to have been mistaken one for the other, thus a few lines below we find Coramix for Toctamix, Toktamish.

2. Sultan Oveys the Jalair Íl-Khán who died in 1374 was the father of Sultan Ahmad mentioned in Chapter VII, note 12 p.324.

3. See Introduction, pp. xlvi-xlvii.

4. Text "Camocan," which is Cammocca. See Yule, *Hobson Jobson* (1886) 368, *Cathay* (1866) 295; Dozy and Engelmann, *Glossaire* 246.

5. India Menor according to Clavijo and his contemporaries was all the country between Persia and (Greater) India which includes the present Afghanistán Beluchistán and Makrán. But Clavijo writes in very general terms for he only spoke from hearsay.

6. This is the well-known story put about to explain why ships in eastern waters were built without the use of iron. See Yule. *Cathay* (1866), pp. 57 and 217.

7. This is the great green dome still the most prominent building in Sultáníyáh. It was originally built for his burial place by the Mongol prince Uljaytú, a descendant of Chingiz who died in 1316. It was probably his body that Mirán Sháh ejected. A hundred years later this great Mosque was restored by Sháh Muhummad Khudá Bandah (the father of Sháh 'Abbás the Great) and in a much ruined condition its dome still towers over the plain of Sultáníyáh. See E. G. Browne, *A Year among the Persians*, p. 75; E. B. Eastwick, *A Diplomat in Persia* I, p. 208.

8. Mírán Sháh's mad doings and his deposition from the government of Western Persia took place in the year 1399, from which date onwards he resided in Baghdad. That he was in Sultáníyáh when Clavijo came was doubtless because he had lately come there to greet his father Timur on his passage through

Persia a few weeks previous to the date of Clavijo's arrival (*Timur Bec* III, pp. 189-198, 207). The princess Khánzádeh, a niece of the Khwárezm Sultan had been married in the first instance to Jahángír, the eldest son of Timur. After his death she became the wife of Mirán Sháh his brother. Clavijo as will be seen later was her guest at a feast in Samarqand. *Timur Bec* I, p. 244, and see the Genealogical Table, Introduction, note 6, p. 310.

Chapter IX

1. In the text printed as Xaharcan and later as Xaharica. What town or village this indicates is uncertain, for no place appears on the map of any very like name. It cannot be the important junction point of Súmíqán (more than once mentioned in the *Nuzhat*) as this stood west of Sagzíábád; but Xaharcan might be Sunqurábád also mentioned in the *Nuzhat* which occupies approximately the position indicated by Clavijo. In Persian place names *ábád* and *án* are common terminations, and by Clavijo often confounded or confused. Thus Ceguesana must stand for Sagzíábád, the final *d* being dropped as is common in Spanish pronunciation (while the *n* for *v* is counterchanged with *b*), and Zanján becomes Sanga. Thus possibly Xaharcan may be for Shahrábád, a very common name (meaning Townlet), and there is in fact a Shahrábád on the map at the place indicated. For Súmíqán and its variants see *Nuzhat*, English translation, p. 168, and the Persian text, p. 59.

2. Ray (Rages of the Book of Tobit) was the capital city of northern Persia during the Caliphate. In the year 1220 it had in the days of Chingiz Khán been plundered and burnt by his Mongols, and its supremacy soon after passed to Tehran, which at a later date became the capital of all Persia under the Qajar dynasty.

3. This name is variously spelt in the text. He is generally known as the Amir Sulayman Shah. About this time he had been made governor of the Ray district. *Timur Bec* IV, p. 170.

4. In the text misprinted as Car: the famous valley and trout stream on the southern flank of Mount Demavend. Sultan Ahmad Mirza here mentioned was a youth of seventeen, the son of the deceased Prince Omar Shaykh the second of Timur's sons. *Timur Bec* IV, pp. 170 and 302.

5. See *Timur Bec* IV, pp. 148 and 155.

6. The name of the place is not given, but the village of Ahuván (where there are ruins of an ancient town) is at the junction for the mountain roads coming in from the north where they meet the great highroad of the plain. See E. B. Eastwick, *A Diplomat in Persia* II, p. 150.

7. See pp. 106-7.

8. They had slept at Jájarm (see above, p. 148) and the text in error says they set of again the same day Tuesday, whereas it was Wednesday morning the 23rd of October. Some lines later "Martes" Tuesday is put where we must read Thursday, since Friday follows.

9. Isfaráyin the chief city of the Isfaráyin district, which forms the northern half of the great Juvayn Plain extending from Jájarm to Nayshápúr, was a place of much importance before the Mongol invasion and the subsequent wars. All trace of the city has now disappeared from the map. The name was often pronounced Asbarayn which Clavijo gives not incorrectly as "Zabrain." It lay half way between Jájarin and Nayshápúr, thirty-six hours' march from either town: Jájarm and Nayshápúr having some 150 miles of road between them. Sreznevski incorrectly suggests that Clavijo's Zabrain stands for modern Zafarain, a village which lies barely 40 miles to the west of Nayshápúr on the (lower) post road. See *Lands of the Eastern Caliphate*, pp. 381 and 393, also the nearly contemporary account given by Mustawfí, *Nuzhat*, p. 148.

10. At this date and later during the period of the Safavi kings the province of Khurásán included all that is now reckoned as Western Afghanistán, and its political capital was Herát, where Sháh Rukh, Timur's youngest son was at this period established as his father's viceroy.

Chapter X

1. Some of the place names in this section of the text appear corrupt beyond identification. It is impossible to say what towns the names Ferrior, Asegur or Okhakhan stand for. Clavijo implies that the province of Khurásán took its name from Khurásán the proper and personal name of the Imám Rezá which is of course absurd. His tomb at Meshed is still the greatest place of pilgrimage in Persia, visited by all pious Shi'ahs, and second only in importance to Kerbelá on the Euphrates where his ancestor the martyr Husayn (grandson of the Prophet) was done to death. Half a day's journey from Meshed "Buelo" must stand for the city of Tús, which in the Arab geographers is variously known, as the population came to shift, by the names of Tabarán and Sanábád.

2. The Tejend Áb, the Meshed River, after passing that city flows on in the direction of Herat (S.E.) and half way thither is met by the Herát River coming down thence. The two joined then flow northwards past Serrakhs, near which township Clavijo crossed the Tejend, and then some distance to the north of Serrakhs the Tejend is lost in the sands of the desert.

3. The Spanish word used in the text is "Alfareme" (of Arabic origin) which Dozy and Engelmann (*Glossaire*, p. 109) explain as "une sorte de coiffure" and we shall see from a later passage in Clavijo's narrative it was used to mean generally, a man's head gear or a turban.

4. The course of the river Murgháb roughly speaking lies parallel with that of the Tejend after this last has been joined by the Herát River. Both streams rise in the mountain ranges of Afghanistán to the east of Herát, the river Murgháb flows westward for the first part of its course: then at a right angle turns north, and reaching finally the Merv Oasis is soon afterwards lost in the desert sands to the northward of Merv. Between the Murgháb and the Tejend River to the eastward, intervenes the waterless desert of the Qara Qum sands, everywhere over 80 miles across. Clavijo and his party crossing the Tejend near Serrakhs must have struck the Murghib a day's march or more south of Merv, probably near Yuletán. Of the great city of Merv, so famous under the Abbasid Caliphs, no

buildings could have remained habitable at the date of Clavijo's visit. It had not recovered from the destruction wrought by the Tartars of Chingiz Khan in the earlier years of the 13th century. For a description of the desert between Serrakhs and Merv, and beyond to the Oxus see *Glimpses of Life and Manners in Persia*, by Lady Sheil (1856), p. 360, where the late Sir William Taylour Thomson has described his journey from Tehran to Khiva in 1842.

5. In the text "Tagiquinia" (see above, p. 1), namely the Land of the Tájiks, or Persians, as opposed to the Land of the Turks. In other words, Írán, Persia, *versus* Túrán of the Tartar folk.

6. Probably this is Shaburqán lying between Andakhuy and Balkh *(Lands of the Eastern Caliphate*, p. 426). This city had suffered much in the Mongol invasion of Chingiz Khan.

7. The ruins of Balkh "the Mother of Cities" are to be seen near the modern shrine of Mizár-i-Sharíf, which the Turcomans imagine to mark the tomb of the Caliph 'Ali (son-in-law of the Prophet), who in point of fact was buried at Kúfah in Mesopotamia. See Vambery, *Travels in Central Asia*, p. 232.

8. The Persians call the Oxus by the name of Amú or Amúyah, the Greek name, Oxus, being derived from one of its upper affluents the Wakhsh: Áb-i-Amú, or Amú Dariyá as the name generally appears, meaning the Amú-Water, or River. The question whether during the middle ages the Oxus flowed to the Caspian is a matter of debate: the Oxus and the Jaxartes at the present time flow into different parts of the Aral Sea. What Clavijo writes is of course mere hearsay, but it tends to confirm the testimony of the Persian geographer Háfiz Abrú, who, writing in the year 1417, clearly states that the Oxus in his day flowed into the Caspian. For the discussion of this matter see *Lands of the Eastern Caliphate*, pp. 455 to 458.

9. Text in error "del aldina menor."

Chapter XI

1. For Mongol we should here read Chagatay Turkí. Persian is of course written in the slightly modified Arabic character: Chagatay Turkí generally used a different script, now known as Uighúr. Timur spoke Turkí, understood Persian, but of the Mongol language he was apparently ignorant.

2. These celebrated Iron Gates were first described by the Buddhist pilgrim Hwen Thsang, who visited them in A.D. 629 on his way from China to India (see J. Wood, *The Oxus,* and Sir H. Yule's Introduction thereto, p. lxix). These Iron Gates are frequently mentioned by the Arab and Persian geographers of the middle ages being called (in Arabic) Báb-al-Hadíd and (in Persian) Derbend Áhanín. For a description of the present appearance of the Pass see Mayef in the *Geographical Magazine* for 1876, p. 328. The Iron Gates near the Caspian, at the eastern end of the Caucasus range, are close to the town called Derbend: and these were known to the Arabs as the Báb-al-Abwáb "the Gate of Gates." See *Lands of the Eastern Caliphate*, p. 180.

3. The town of Kesh by the end of the 15th century had already come to be known as Shahr-i-Sabz "the Green City." At present the township consists of the neighbouring settlements called

Kitáb and Shahr (literally "Book" and "Town"). A. S. Beveridge, *Babur Nama in English* 1, p. 83, and Schuyler, *Turkestan* II, p. 64.

4. When, however, in 1405 Timur died at Otrar his body was brought back to Samarqand and buried in the mosque now known as the Gúr Amír, where it rests under a huge block said to be of Jade. Schuyler, *Turkestan* 1, p. 252.

5. These three circlets forming a triangle appear on many of the silver pieces struck by Timur, see for instance Plate 1, No. 36, and text p.16 of Vol. VII of the *Catalogue of Oriental Coins in the British Museum.* Whether the emblem of the Lion and the Sun really was the armorial bearing of the former Sultan of Samarqand is uncertain. The Sun in the Sign of the Zodiac Leo, the highest sign, is found on the coins of the Seljuks of Rúm (Asia Minor) as early as the 12th century and it reappears on the moneys issued by Gházán, Uljaytú and Abú Sa'íd, the Íl Kháns of Persia, between 1295 and 1335. Yule, *Marco Polo* (1875), I, p. 343.

6. The Khan or Sultan of Samarqand here spoken of was probably the Amír Husayn, who ruled there from 1360 to 1369, and held sway both in Transoxiana and Khurásán. On the death of Chingiz, in 1227, his vast dominions were divided between his four sons and Chagatay became Lord of Transoxiana with Bukhárá and Samarqand for capitals. A long succession of Chagatay Kháns, his descendants, ruled here for the next century and a half, temporarily often displaced by Kháns of minor local dynasties. Thus from 1342 to 1346 Kázán the Chagatay was Khan, and he was then displaced by Kazaqán a local chief whose grandson was Husayn Khan. His chief capital was Balkh, from which centre he controlled Samarqand to the north and Herat to the south. Husayn Khán gave his sister in marriage to Timur in early days his ally, who afterwards quarrelled with him and as a result Husayn Khán was put to death in 1369 *(Timur Bec* 1, pp.1, 28, 192). For Omar Tabán mentioned below, see Price, *Mohammedan History III*, p. 491.

7. Timur's chief wife, the Great Khánúm, the mother of Sháh Rukh, was known also as Serai Mulk Mihrebán, having been a daughter of the Chagatay Khán Kázán (see previous note). She was found in and taken from the Harem of Husayn Khán at his defeat in 1369, and apparently had not been taken to wife by him. The confusion made by Clavijo may be due to the fact as stated that this Khán's sister had married Timur (see previous note). *Timur Bec* I, pp. 193, 290.

8. See above, Chapter VII, note 10, p. 326. For Chawkú the father of Jahán Sháh see D. Price, *Mahommedan History* III, p. 404.

9. The text has "que es llamada [for "llamado"] Dorgancho," as though Dorgancho (which is in fact Chingiz) were ("La Citudad") the name of the town of his birth. The names of three out of the four sons of Chingiz are phenomenally misprinted, namely Gabuy (Tuluy), Esbeque (Ogotay) and Charcas (Juji).

10. The name printed in the text is "Calbet": this may represent Qulbah a meadow land very famous close to the capital and also the name of a hamlet near by Samarqand (A. S. Beveridge, *Babur Nama in English* 1, p. 80). If "Calbet" is taken to represent "Khalvet" (as adopted in the translation) this would mean "the Privacy " (Garden): but a third alternative is that "Calbet" is for Gul-Bágh "the Rose Garden." What "Talicia" stands for is uncertain.

Chapter XII

1. Timur was at this time in his seventieth year.
2. In 1227 on the death of the great Chingiz, his son Tuluy took the appanage of the Home-clans of Mongolia, residing at Karakorum. His son Kubilai who succeeded as Great Khan (or Qaán) (1257 to 1294) conquered China, and living at Pekin had Marco Polo in his service. As Great Khan the descendants of Chagatay at Samarqand paid him tribute. The successors of Kubilai degenerated, and in 1370 the Mongol dynasty of China, by the Chinese called the Yuen, were replaced by the native Chinese dynasty of the Ming. The founder was the Emperor Hongwou who died in 1399, being succeeded after an interregnum of disorder by his son Chingtsu who became officially the Emperor Yunglo, reigning from 1403 to 1425. He is the potentate whom Clavijo names Chayscan otherwise Tanguz Khan, as too 'Ali of Yezd names him. He sought ineffectually to get Timur to pay him the old tribute. Relations between Timur and China becoming strained the Tartar conqueror in the spring of 1405 was about to set out to add Cathay to his other dominions when death overtook him at Otrar at the crossing of the Jaxartes. Tanguz, Tunguz or Donguz means Pig in Chagatay Turkish. "Chayscan" or "Chuyscan" may well be a typographical mistake for "Chuycon," the Chinese "Chingtsu," the emperor's personal name. *Timur Dec* II, p. 120, D. C. Boulger, *History of China* (1898) 1, pp. 356, 431, 441.
3. For this Cordovan leather see above, Chapter VI, note 3, p. 322.
4. 'Ali of Yezd describes the reception on this occasion of the various ambassadors from Egypt and Spain, but he naturally gives precedence to those of the Moslem power. It will be remembered that when Clavijo reached Khoy he had found there the ambassador from Cairo who had in charge a giraffe and six ostriches sent as gifts to Timur. 'Ali of Yezd gives the name of the Egyptian envoy as Manghalí Bugay, who had been chamberlain to the late Mamluk Sultan Barqúq. He had managed safely to convoy the giraffe with nine ostriches to Samarqand, where he duly presented them as his master's gift. The ostriches whether six or nine had doubtless been brought in crates on camel back, but the giraffe must have walked

all the way from Cairo to Samarqand, a distance of more than 3,000 miles. *Timur Bec* IV, pp. 180, 184, 194.

5. The Garden of Dilkushá and the Garden of the Plane-tree are both described by the Emperor Bábar writing at the close of this 15th century, the former lying at some distance to the east of the Turquoise Gate of the city. See Beveridge, *Babar Nama* I, p. 78.

6. In Spanish "Alhania," a word of Arabic origin, for which see Dozy and Engelmann, *Glossaire*, p. 135.

7. The Tanga or Tanka was a thin silver coin current throughout Tartary. In a subsequent passage Clavijo states that a Tanga was worth about two Castilian silver reals, it was equivalent therefore to rather over a shilling of our money.

Chapter XIII

1. For these huge pavilions, and the tents in Kibitka form spoken of subsequently, see *Marco Polo* (1875) 1, pp. 244, 390, 394, and *William of Rubruck* (Rockhill, Hakluyt Society), p. 54.

2. Sarápardeh means in Persian a Curtain or Veil, but in its technical sense is the Enclosure (curtained round) where the monarch sits in state or where his women abide protected from the public gaze. In this sense it is often used by 'Ali of Yezd. *Timur Bec* IV, p. 183.

3. As will be more fully explained in the next chapter, at this date Timur was the husband of eight wives, double the number allowed by Moslem law, but a matter for which doubtless he granted himself a dispensation as in the case of drinking wine. The two Khanums were his chief wives, and the Little Khanum was niece to the other, being the daughter of her brother the Amír Músá, their father having been Kázán Khán, a former Sultan of Samarqand. *Timur Bec* 1, pp. 124, 125, 298.

4. See above, Chapter VIII, note 8, p. 353. The princess Khánzádeh was now living at Samarqand apart from her husband, and at her father-in-law's court.

5. According to 'Ali of Yezd these feastings, at which the Spanish envoys were now taking part, had been arranged by Timur to celebrate the nuptials of six of his grandsons, namely Ulugh Beg and Ibráhím Sultán the sons of Sháh Rukh, of Prince Aidgel the son of Mírán Sháh, and of Ahmad, Sayyid Ahmad and Bikrah all three the sons of the late Mirza Omar Shaykh (Timur Bec IV, p. 189). The date for this feast given above is Thursday the 9th, but this was the date of Khánzádeh's feast which according to what follows took place one day before. Timur's great feast therefore probably was on Friday the 10th, if indeed he gave this festival on a Friday, when he should have been at Mosque.

6. For these shows see the description by 'Ali of Yezd. *Timur Bec* IV, pp. 185-189.

7. See pp. 220 and 315. The name is variously spelt, Burodo, Borundo, or Butudo. He was Timur's nephew.

8. For Zaytúní see above, Chapter VI, note 5, p. 322.

9. This account would appear to be derived from some echo of the Prester John legend.

Chapter XIV

1. If, as Sreznevski suggests, Jawhar Aga is the true reading for the name that Clavijo gives Yauguyaga, this would simply mean "Jewel Lady." The wives numbered five, six and seven bear Tartar names that it has been impossible to identify in Clavijo's transliteration. Chelpan Mulk Khánum and Tukel Khánum both are mentioned by 'Ali of Yezd, and it was for the latter lady, as a bride, that Timur laid out the celebrated garden of Dilkushá where the Spanish embassy had first been received. The Great Khánum and the Little Khánum have both been spoken of in a former note (see Chapter XIII, note 3, p. 335) and Clavijo is mistaken when stating that the father of Kúchik Khánum was Túmán Aga, for this was the Little Lady's own name: her father being the Amír Músá. *Timur Bec* I, pp.125, 298; II, p. 425 ; IV, p. 80.

2. Timur entered and sacked Brusa, which was at that time the Ottoman capital, immediately after his victory at Angora. These doors originally must have come to Brusa from Constantinople, probably erected there by the Greeks before the Turkish occupation.

3. Possibly transparent jade, hardly a true emerald of this size.

4. What place Aquivi stands for is uncertain.

5. Prince Muhummad Sultán had died of his wounds, at Qara Hissar, soon after the battle of Angora in 1402. He was the son of Timur's eldest son Jahángír (who had died in 1375), and of the Princess Khánzádeh, who afterwards married Prince Mírán Sháh her brother-in-law. *Timur Bec* IV pp. 68, 82, 301.

Chapter XV

1. The report of Timur's death at this date was premature: he recovered, spending December with January following in his preparations for the invasion of China.

2. Popular etymology, but compare E. Bretschneider, *Mediæval Researches* (1888), Vol. I, notes pp. 76-78.

3. See above, Chapter XII, note 2, p. 333. It was these events that led to Timur's threatened invasion of China, and only his sudden death at Otrar saved that country from a repetition of the conquests as effected by the Mongols in the time of Kubilai Khán.

4. Cambaluc, Khán Báligh "the city of (the Great) Khán" founded by Kubilai Khán, as described by Marco Polo, is now Pekin "the Northern Capital." See Mustawfi, *Nuzhat*, note to p. 250.

5. The emperor of China certainly never embraced Christianity, and this doubtless is again an echo of the Prester John legend.

6. For the Amazons see Lane, *Arabian Nights,* chapter xxv, note 23, and *Marco Polo* (1874) II, p. 397. Mustawfi *Nuzhat*, p. 266) describes a City of Women in Maghrib.

7. See above, Chapter XI, p. 178, and note 5, p. 331.

8. Toktamish, Golden Horde, lord of the Kipchák steppe, which lies round the northern shores of the Caspian and extending westward, has been more than once mentioned by Clavijo. He traced his descent direct from Jújí, the eldest of the four sons of Chingiz: and had inherited the chiefship of the Blue and the White Hordes which in 1378 came to be united with the Golden Horde. In the past Toktamish had been much favoured by Timur, but he had of late set himself up as his rival. Toktamish was promptly defeated in two campaigns (1391 and 1395), the latter of the two fought on the banks of the Terek, a river flowing into the Caspian 120 miles to the north of Derbend. This is the campaign to be described by Clavijo. In point of fact Toktamish had made his invasion of Armenia and Azerbayján in 1385, which therefore had no connection with his defeat on the Terek in 1395. After this crowning disaster, all real power in the Golden Horde passed to

Idiku, chief of the Nogay Tartars, who set up one puppet Khán after another to nominal chiefship. This Idiku had formerly been a captain in Timur's armies, and his subsequent history is given by Clavijo. The dis-possessed Toktamish survived till 1406, a year after the death of Timur, at whose court from time to time he had found refuge, being hospitably entertained. *Timur Bec* II, p. 342.

9. See above p. 112.

10. See above, pp.182-3.

Chapter XVI

1. Altologo is probably the town known as Altobosco during the middle ages, lying between Ephesus and Smyrna, and said to be the site of the ancient Colophon. See J. H. Zedler. *Universal Lexicon*, Halle, 1733, I, p. 1595.

2. Bávard, now Abiverd: the next town mentioned Khabushán is now known as Kúchán in the plain at the source of the Meshed river.

3. The same wonder is chronicled by Mustawfi in the *Nuzhat*, p. 271.

4. The lower road along the plain at the foot of the mountains is the present post road from Tehran to Meshed, going by Semnán.

5. In the text "Alafa," the Arabic "Al-'Áfiyah," a word that has passed into the Spanish language; originally it signifies "a benefit that is bestowed" (see Dozy and Engelmann, *Glossaire*, p. 53, s.v. Alafa). The famous winter quarters in the plains of Qarabágh lay west of the junction of the two rivers Kur and Aras (Cyrus and Araxes) of which district the capital city was at this time Baylaqán. At the end of the previous November on leaving Samarqand the Spanish ambassadors, it will be remembered, had been granted no farewell audience of Timur who was at the time very unwell, sick unto death as his chamberlains feared. Timur, as already noted, later had recovered, he had spent December assembling his armies for the invasion of China and had set off on his march to cross Central Asia in January. Early in February he had passed over the Jaxartes on the ice, coming to Otrar, but again his malady overtook him, this time fatally, and he had expired on the 17th of that month. A disputed succession was inevitable. From Samarqand to Qarabágh by the shortest road is nearly 3,000 miles, which the Tartar post riders (as described by Clavijo in a former chapter, see pp. 150-1) could probably cover within twenty days. This would bring us to the 7th of March when Clavijo and his people were stopped and turned back, the critical news just brought being the cause. To understand the following complicated narrative the Genealogical Table given in the note to the Introduction, p. 309, should be consulted, with the summary given, pp. xlvi-xlvii, of the chief events that followed the death of Timur.

6. The city of Baylaqám was rebuilt by Timur and became the capital of the province of Qarabágh. It was connected by a canal with the river Kur to the north. *Timur Bec* IV, p. 118.

7. Text in error "que murió en la ciudad de Samarcante."

8. As to these personages and events compare the Genealogical Table, p. 310, and the Introduction, p. xlvii.

Chapter XVII

1. It is remarkable that this raid of the Georgians into Armenia and Ázerbayján is passed unnoticed in the contemporary Armenian and other Christian chronicles. Sreznevski suggests that Clavijo may here be confounding King George of Georgia with the celebrated Qara Yúsuf, the Turcoman chief who, at this time, took occasion of raiding the frontier during the period of the disputed succession, of which Clavijo is giving his account. See next note.

2. In the text incorrectly given as Qara Othman - "Caraotoman." This Qara Yúsuf was the Turkoman chief of the Qara Quyúnlú (Black Sheep) Clan, who temporarily rose to be master of all Western Persia. In April 1407 (a year after Clavijo's return to Spain) Prince Omar was defeated by these Turkomans in a great battle, and subsequently died of his wounds. In the course of the next year Qara Yúsuf overcame the army of Mírán Sháh and his son Abu Bakr. Abu Bakr escaped from the battle unhurt, but his father Mírán Sháh lost his life, and Abu Bakr after taking refuge in the province of Kirmán was killed in a skirmish in December of that same year 1408. D. Price, *Mahommedan History III*, pp. 497, 505, 509.

3. The exact position of Alashkert remains to be identified. Mustawfi (in 1330) describes it as a fortress with a market town, the revenues paid to the state amounting to 7,000 gold dinars. He spells the name Valasjird and Yáqút (a century earlier) says it stood at no great distance from Akhlát the capital city of the Lake Van district. Alashkert must have stood on the upper reach of the Eastern Euphrates, probably a little to the north east of Minazkert. *Nuzhat*, p. 101.

4. Armenian historians make no special mention of this king and his three sons, but presumably it was Leo V, the last of the Rubenian dynasty, of whom Clavijo tells the story. See *History of Armenia*, by N.Y. Gregor, p. 18 2.

5. Ani, which the Greeks called Anion (Clavijo writes Aumian), was the ancient capital of Armenia standing on the north bank of the river Aras, due north of Alashkert. The road that Clavijo followed therefore must, at some point near Delilarkent, have crossed his outward going road.

341

6. See above, Chapter VII, p. 112, and *Timur Bec IV*, p. 151. Duladay Beg had been a favoured intimate at the court of Timur.

7. Tartum (its exact position unknown) lies on the borders of Georgia and is spoken of by 'Ali of Yezd, who describes the siege. *Timur Bec III*, p. 409.

8. The 15th century MS. of the Madrid National Library ends here. What follows is from Argote de Molina's copy of the MS., of which no trace is forthcoming.

9. It is curious that in both cases the dates in this passage are given incorrectly. The text has "Domingo primero dia de Marzo," but the 1st of March was a Monday. Then their home coming to Alcalá is said to have taken place on "Lunes veinte y quarto dias del mes de Marzo," but the 24th of March fell on Wednesday. The next paragraph, beginning *Laus Deo*, is the colophon added in his edition by Argote de Molina, and is not found in the MS. he copied.

Appendix

The inscription on Clavijo's tomb, López Estrada 1943, p.lxxix:

"Aqui yace el honrado caballero Rui González de Clavijo, que Dios perdone, camerero de los Reyes D.Enrique de buena memoria, e del Rey Su fixo, al qual el dicho Señor Rey ovo enviado por su embaxador al Tamorlan, et fino dos de abril, año del Señor de MCCCCXII años."

Pero López de Ayala on Ambassadors and Embassies from the *Libro Rimado de Palacio*:

> Nueve cosas yo fallo con quales tú verás
> el grant poder del rey en qué lo conosçrás:
> las tres de muchas luengas tierras las entendrás
> las seis son en el regno, segunt aquí verás.

> Si sus enbaxadores enbia bien ordenados,
> cavalleros muy buenos, doctores bien letrados,
> con buen apostamiento e bien aconpañados,
> de los que a ellos veen luego serán notados.

> Algun prínçipe muy grande dizen, çierto sera
> el que tal enbaxada onrada enbiará;
> el que nunca le vio luego le notará,
> e su fama muy grande non la olvidará.

> La segunda, si veen su carta mensajera
> en nota bien fermosa, palabra verdadera,
> en buena forma escripta, en con fermosa çera,
> çerrada, bien seellada, con día, mes y era.

> Si veen su moneda, que es bien fabricada,
> de oro e de plata, redonda, bien cuñada,
> rica de buena ley, en toda bien guardada,
> ésta es la terçera señal dél muy granada.

Index

Ægean xxxii, xxxv, 268, 302, 312
'Aliábád 168
Áb-i-Amú (Viadme, Biamo) 169, 269, 331
Abhar (Huar) 137
Abiverd xliv, 340
Abu Bakr (Aboaquer) xxx, xlvii, 135, 281-6, 290, 291-2, 342
Afghanistan 169, 170, 174, 175, 222, 224
Afghanistán – Lesser India 326, 329, 330
Agincourt 313
Ahmed Julair, Sultan of Persia 120
Ahúván 144, 328
Akhlát 342
Alafa 340
Alanjik (Alinga) 120
Alanza (Alangogaza) 94
Alashkert (Alesquiner) 296-8, 346-8, 395
Alatáq (Alara) 107, 289
Alavari Kurds (Alabares) 152
Alcalá de Henares xlviii, 303, 364
Alcazaba 5
Aleppo xxxiv, 2, 135
Alexander the Great 129, 170
Alexandretta (Alexandria) 19, 20, 21, 22, 29, 54, 130, 313
Alexis Comnenus xxxviii
Alexius, Prince (Quelex) 85

Alfareme 330
Alfonso Paez xxxv, xlvi, xlviii, 3, 142, 176, 229
Algeciras 4
Alhania 338
'Aliábád (Alibed), 168
'Ali, Caliph, his tomb, 356
'Ali of Yezd 308, 324, 337, 339, 341, 346
Alp Arslán 325
Altologo or Altobosco, 268, 343
Amalfi 12
Amasera (Samastro) 79, 80
Amazons xxx, 260, 338
Ambassadors xvi, xviii, xxx, xlix, and *passim*
 - Chinese 192, 257-8
 - Egyptian 138, 160, 29
 - Spanish at Ankara
 -Tatar 204, 205
 -Turkish 293
Ambo in Santa Sophia, 319
Amú Daryá, 333
Andarábah (Andricojo), 229
Andkhuy (Ancoy, Andkhoy) 165, 166
Andronicus III, Emperor xxxii, 27, 37
Andronicus, Prince and Emperor Elect, 55, 60-62
Anemas Tower xxviii, xxxii, 55, 319
Angelina, the Greek Maiden xii, 308-309, 312
Angora (Ankara), battle of xxvii, xxviii, xxxiv, xxxv, 2, 3, 24, 28, 35, 82, 99, 102, 108-9, 141, 189, 242, 309, 314, 339

345

Ani (Aumian) xxx, 289, 297-9, 342
Antioch 41, 113
Antipsara 26
Apostles xxviii, 53, 64, 88, 321
Aqueduct xxviii, 64, 321
Aquivi 242, 341
Aq Quyunlu Tartars (Tartaros Blancos, White Sheep Clan) 106, 145
Aragon xxxv, xlix, 5, 6, 7
Ararat 113, 115,116, 325,326
Aras, Araxes (Corras) xxxvii, 112, 113, 120, 277, 324, 325, 340, 343
Araxes xxxvii, 112, 324, 325, 340
Argote de Molina ix, x, xiv, xlix, 308, 309, 311, 318, 343
Armenia *passim* incl. xxx, 1, 107, 112, 114, 120, 262-3, 289, 295-8, 325-6, 342, 345
Armenians xxiv, xxviii, 34, 87, 102, 107, 110-4, 117, 119-22, 255, 295-6, 317, 301
Armenian church rites 87
Armenian king, 297
Armour, Turkish xxx; armourers, 254, 246, 259; plate armour 259-60
Arraquiel 300, 301
Artaxata 324
Arzamir 83
Arzinján (Arsinga) xxviii, xxxviii, 1, 93-4, 96, 98, 99, 102-11, 295, 296, 298-299
Asbarayn 331
Asegur 155, 332

Ash, soup (Hax) 162
Asinara 7
Asper xxi, 103, 110, 325
Assarec or Sarec 288, 290
Athos monastery (Monteston) 32, 33
Augustus, Emperor 313
Aumian (Ani, Anion), ancient capital of Armenia 345
Avicenna 6, 312
Avnik (Aunique) 1, 111, 298
Awnings 206, 209, 211, 221, 230, 241
Azoff 71, 77
Azulejos xlii
Báb-al-Abwáb 334
Báb-al-Hadid 334
Baba Burun (Cape St Mary) 315
Bábá Sheykh (Babayeque Baxambec – Babylon i.e. Cairo) xxviii, 138, 273
Babylon and Babylonia, namely Cairo and Egypt 314
Badakhshan, King of (Balaxia), xxix, 241-2
Baghdad (Baldac, Baldas) xxxiv, xlvii, 2, 127, 132, 135, 281, 283, 314, 315, 328
Bágh-i-Chinár 196
Bágh-i-Naw 200
Balas rubies 196, 198, 222, 226, 237, 255
Balas ruby mines 241
Balkh (Vaeq) iii, xxix, xli, 168, 169, 312, 333. 335
Bandah, the father of Shah Abbas 328

346

Barqúq, Sultan 326, 337
Bartan river (Parten) 79
Bávard (Baubarte, Abiverd) xxx, 270-271, 343
Báyazíd, Castle (Vasit Calaside) 116
Báyazíd, Sultan (Ilderim – the 'Thunderbolt) xxxi-xxxiv, xlviii, 2, 24-25, 28, 34-35, 61, 65, 68, 79, 82, 99, 102, 104, 107-110, 116, 141, 242, 262, 264, 308, 315, 325
Baylagán (Baylaqán) 279, 343
Baylaqán 343
Bázayíd xxxi
Beasts, Isle of (Isla de las Bestias) 23
Bender Eregli (Heraclea Pontica) 78-79
Benedict XIII 303
Beyrut 21, 57, 314
Bin Bir Derek ("Cistern of a Thousand Columns") 321
Blachernæ xxvii, xxviii, 37, 38, 55, 63, 316, 319
Black Friars 16
Black Sea xxiv, xxvii, xxviii, xxxi, xxxvi, xxxvii, xxxix, 69-78, 301, 321, 323
Black Sea Storms 70-77
Black Sheep (Qara Quyúnlú) xxx, 345
Blame, Tower of (Torre del Vituperio) 34
Bogdan Serai 316
Bonifacio, Castle and straits 7
Bosporus xxxvii, 65, 69, 70, 76, 77, 78, 321

Bostám (Vascal Bastan) 146, 271
Boucicault xxvii, xxxii, xxxiii, 28, 29, 54, 313
Bread, consecrated (Greek) 87-8
Bread, Persian 95
Brusa xxxi, 36, 237
Brusa, gates from in Timur's camp 337
Buelo (Tus?) 157, 332
Bukhárá xxx, 268, 269, 333
Burunday 190, 218
Busa 214
Butudo 282, 336
Byzantine Constantinople 309, 316
Cabasica, Cyril (Arbosita, Quirileo) xxviii, 90-94
Cabrera 7, 16
Cadaca 90-91
Cadiz ii, xxvii, xxx, xxxvi, 1, 3, 4
Cairo 127, 135, 314, 327, 338
Cairo, Sultan of 19-20, 120, 135, 184, 283
Cairo, Ambassadors of the Sultan of 138-9, 184, 186, 252, 337
Calabria 15, 16
Caladay Sheykh 181
Calbet (?Gul-Bagh) 335-6
Calmarin 326
Camag, City and castle 103-104
Cambaluc (Pekin) 258-259, 342
Camocan 328
Capri 12
Car (Lar) 141
Caravan 103, 130, 132, 181, 260
 – from China with 800 camels 258

347

- to Turkey with 200 horses 295
Caravanserai 128, 128, 148, 149, 162, 163, 165, 276
Carrack xxxvi, xlv, 4, 5, 8, 12-15, 17, 18, 64, 69, 71-76, 311
Cartagena ii, xxxv, 5
Carvo Tumán Ughlán 250
Caspian Sea (Mar de Bacu) 133, 169, 174
Castile, see Introduction *passim*, 1, 2, 19, 74, 78, 163, 189, 191, 195, 250, 266, 303
Castle of Greece 70
Castle of Turkey 70
Cathay xxix, 131, 132,
 - Ambassador from 192
 - Ambassadors from the borders of 204-5
 - gems 131-2
 - merchandise from 245, 255
Caza 326
Cemanum 324
Cerigo (Cetul) 16, 17
Cetul 16
Chagatay *passim*
Chagatay clan, 179, 184, 279, 282, 285, 288
Chagatay Turkish 337
Chagatay, son of Chingiz Khán 183, 323, 335, 337
Chagatays xxix, 120, 157, 160, 160-7, 175, 179, 184, 203, 249, 278, 293, 311
Chagaul (Xagarve) 276
Chapanli Turks (Chapenies) 94
Chapar (Persian establishment of post-riders) xl

Chapitel or Cupola 317
Charcas 333
Charles III of Naples 313
Charles VI xxi, xxxi, 314
Chastel Morate, nephew of Boucicault 54
Chauscad 122
Chawkú, Chagatay lord 182, 335
Chays Khán 192, 193
Chelebi "Master" a title 315
Chelebi, 78, 82, 109
Chelpan Mulk Aga (Cholpamalaga), Timur's wife 229, 337
Cherne, Santa Maria de la 320
Chess 205, 246
China or porcelain 193, 253
China xvii, xix, xxix, xxx, xliv, 193-260, 314, 332, 334, 338, 340
Chinese xvii, xix, 222, 240, 257, 258, 260, 294, 322, 334
 - ambassadors 192, 257-8
 - caravan with 800 camels 258
 - Christians 204
 - exports 255-6
Chingiz Khán (Dorgancho) 179, 183, 323, 330, 333
Chingtsu Emperor 337
Chios (Xio) ii, xxvii, 22, 25, 32, 302
Chirmanoli (Manuel II) 60, 320
Christians xi, xxviii, xxxi, xl, 96, 102,
 - forcibly brought to Samarqand 255

- called kafirs by the Muslims 289
Christians, Armenian 119, 296, 301
  - forced conversion, churches destroyed 102-3
  - deported by Timur 107
  - by the Muslims 114; 119, 296, 301
  - Chinese 204
  - Greek 102, 103, 260, 300
  - Indian 224, 255
Churches, *passim*; see Contents and Constantinople
Cinolis (Quinoli) 81
Circlets, three, Timur's emblem 178, 334
Cisterns xxviii, 51, 62, 320
Clavijo, Ruy González de, *passim* – see Introduction and Contents
Colophon 343
Columbus xxxiv
Constantia, Queen of Naples 11-12
Constantine 42, 318, 319
Constantine the Great 318
Constantine X Monomachus 319
Constantinople *passim*, esp. Introduction, 27-88, 103, 107-109, 302 and Notes 309-337
  - Anemas Tower xxviii, xxxii, 55, 319
  - Apostles, Church of the Holy 63-4, 320
  - Aqueduct of Valens xxviii, 64, 321
  - At Meidan 317
  - Bin Bir Derek (see also Cisterns) 321
  - Blachernae Palace 37, 38, 55, 63, 316
  - Bogdan Serai 316
  - Cisterns xxviii, 51, 62, 321
  - Genoese Tower of Galata 320
  - Golden Horn 37, 53, 63-66, 77, 317, 320, 321
  - Hippodrome 44-6, 317
  - Justinian, Emperor, statue of 47
  - Kynegos Gate 55, 319
  - Obelisk 45-6, 317
  - Omnipotens or Pantocrator Monastery 57, 59, 319
  - Pera suburb, *passim*, see Pera
  - Painting of the Blessed Virgin by St Luke xxviii, xxxvii, 67, 320
  - Relics
  - - of saints xiv, 37, 39, 56-9, 67
  - - of the True Cross 42, 59, 67
  - St Francis, Monastery 66-68, 320
  - St George of the Armenians (Sulu Monastir) 316
  - St George at the Mangana 53, 319
  - St John the Baptist in Petra 38-42, 56, 316
  - St John the Baptist in Studion xxxvi, 43, 316, 317
  - St Mary of Blachernae 55, 319
  - St Mary Hodegetria (Dessetria) 59-60, 319

349

- St Mary Peribleptos 40-1, 316
- St Paul, Monastery 66. 68
- Santa Sophia xxvii, xxxvi, 47-8, 51-2, 60, 88, 317, 319, 321
- Serpent Column 46, 318
- Skutari 65-6
- Walls of the City 66

Coramix (Toktamish) 328
Cordovan leather (Guadamacir) 95, 193, 234, 323, 337
Corsica ii, 7, 302
Cuaraca, castle 26
Curio, hamlets 301
Cyzicus (Quinisicos) 35
Damascus xvi, xxxiv, 2, 21, 131, 145, 228
   - besieged and sacked by Timur 107
   - craftsmen carried off to Samarqand 254;
   - looted 256, 315
Dámghán (Damogan) xxviii, xxx, xxxix, 271-2
   - Towers of skulls 144-146
Dardanelles (Boca de Romania) xxvii, xxxii, 26, 30, 33-5, 108, 109
Darius xxviii, 129
Dawlat Khanah (Tolbatgana), Government House 125
Daroghah 126, 294
Dawlat Khanah (Tolbatgana), Government House 125
Delhi (Delieste) xxi, 223

Delilárkent , "Village of Madmen" xxviii, 111, 112, 325
Demetrius or John Palaeologus 62, 88, 320
Derbend xxix, 1, the Iron Gates 174-175; 334, 342
Dervishes xxviii, 112
Dilkushá, garden (Dilicaxa)196, 199, 202, 338, 341
Dina, Mayor of Samarqand hanged by Timur 218
Don Henry ix, 1, 2
Doorkeeper, Chief 195, 205
Dorgancho 335
Dorileh, castle 91
Dos Castellos 80
Dragon, a miracle 41-2, 80,
Drinking, Tatar customs xxix, 100, 214-5, 222-30, 339
Drinking, Clavijo does not drink 100, 229
Dubeque, near ancient Troy 34
Duladay Beg, Chagatay noble 111, 298, 346
Egypt xi, xxvii, xxxiii, xxxviii, xlii, xlvii, 20, 121, 315,319
Egypt, Ambassadors 138-9, 160, 173, 188, 196, 268, 288, 293
Egypt, Sultan of xxxiii, xxxviii, xlvii, 106,121, 125, 195,250
Elchi, cry meaning "The Ambassadors" 159
Elephant xliii, 189, 223, 230-233
Enclosures xxix, xlii, 209-212, 220-221, 228, 235-240, 336

"End of the Roads", site of the Greek camp at Troy 33
Ennacora, Tartar lord 146, 147, 148, 173
Eregli (Pontoraquia, Heraclea Pontica) 78, 79, 322
Ermin fur xliii, 240
Erzerúm (Asseron) xxviii, 1, 111, 289, 297, 298
Estombol 64
Etna (Mongible) 16, 313
Eunuchs 227
Examillo, castle 35
Exchange, in Pera 64
Falcons (see Gerfalcons)
Faro lighthouse 15
Ferrior 155, 332
Finogia (Kirpen) 70, 71, 78, 322
Fírúzkúh, castle xxviii, xxxix, 142-144, 160, 272
Fol (Viopoli), castle 84
Formentera 5
Forno, El 24, 315
Fusta, or Barque xxxvi
Gad-flies, near Tabriz 128
Gaeta ii, xxvii, 8-12, 302
Galata 66, 321
Galliot *passim* incl. xxxvi, 312
Gallipoli ii, xxvii, 32-5, 61, 302, 315
Gattilusio (Catalus), John, Lord of Mytilene and Francis xxxiv, 27-29
Genealogical Tables
Genoa xv, xxx, xlv, 28, 31, 37, 64, 67, 77, 302, 303, 314
Genoese *passim* incl. xii, xiv, xxvii, xxxiv, xxxvii, xlv, 7, 19-22, 25, 27, 29-34, 54, 64-87, 103, 107, 109, 123-124, 131, 265, 266, 302, 303, 314, 321
Genoese Castle at Tabriz 123-4
Genoese defeat at Modon 54
Genoese Tower 320
George, King of Georgia (Rey Sorso) 114, 280, 288-9
Georgia (Gargania) xxxiii, xxxiv, xxxv, 1, 289, 298, 299, 300, 342, 345
Gerakounia (Phalkonera) 313
Gerfalcons xxviii, xxxv, 17, 141, 144, 204,
-made of silver gilt 210
Ghadamesi 323
Gibraltar xxxv, 4
Gilán 130, 131, 133
Giraffe xxvii, xxviii, xxix, xxxix, described 121-122; 337-8
Golden Horde 113, 186, 262, 326, described 342
Golden Horn 37, 53, 63-66, 77, 317, 320, 321
Gómez de Salazar xvi, xxxv, xxxvi, 3, 142, 153, 154
Greece xxxiii, 16, 32, 34, 35, 69, 70, 108
Greek Church 22, 103; rites 86-9
Guadalquivir xxxv, xlv, 64
Guadamacir 95, 234, 323
Guirol, ruined castles (Qaraol) 322
Gúr Amír 334
Háfiz Abrú 333
Hajji Muhammad, the Tatar envoy 3,

351

– wears European clothes as a disguise, 75; 189
Hanging preferable to decapitation 219
Hasan Qal'ah 325
Helena, St, mother of Constantine 42
Helmets 97, 264
Henry III of Castile and Leon, xxvii, xxxiv, xxxv, xlviii, xlix, 303
Henry IV of Castile and Leon xlviii
Henry IV of England xxxiii
Heraclea Pontica 78
Herát (Helac, Hore. Heley) x, xxii, xlvii, 155, 282, 286, 331, 332,
Herat River 335
Hijos de Madrid 310
Hippodrome xxvii, 44-6, 317, 318, 319, 321
Hissar, Qara 341
Hongwou, Emperor 337
Horde, *passim* incl. xxviii, xxix, xlii, xliv, 113, 139-142, 157, 164-5, 186, 202-206, 212, 217, 219, 240-3, 262, 265, 277-8, 280, 324, 342
Horse meat and tripe xxxix, 131, 193, 216
Hospitaliers, Knights 18-21, 23, 314
Husayn, Amir 266, 335
Husayn, Imam 332
Husayn Khan 335
Ibiza 5, 6
Ibn-al-Athír 325, 326
Ibn Síná or Ibn Sídah 311

Idiku, (Ediguy, Edenguy) Tatar Chief xxx, 262, 264-6, 280, 342
Igdir, castle 115
Ilario Doria 317
Ilderim (Sultan Bayazid) 2, 109
Illness of the Spaniards and deaths, 142, 176, 273
Imám Rezá xxix, xl, 330
Imbros 30
India, Greater and Lesser, iv, xix, xx, xxix, xxxiii, xxxiv, 1, 131, 155, 170, 174-5, 222-4, 242, 245, 248, 256, 326, 332
India, invaded by Timur 223-4
India, Christian King of 224
Ineboli (Ninopoli) 80, 81
Ipsara and Antipsara 26
Irene, Empress 37, 317
Iron Gates of Samarqand and Derbend xxix, 174-5, 334
Iron nails, not used in ships, 132
'Isa, Prince – eldest son of Bayazid – 25, 316
Ischia 12
Ischu 111
Isfandiyár 81-82, 98
Isfaráyin (Zabrain) xxviii, 151, 331
Iskandarún (Alexandretta) 314
Iskandar Sheykh 143
Ispir (Aspir) 299-301
Jahángír, Prince (Janguir) xlvi, xlvii, 177, 222, 329, 341
Jahán Sháh, Prince, eldest son of Timur (Iazan Miraxa Janza Mirassa) xlv, xlvii, 119, 182, 266, 278-83, 326, 335

Jájarm (Jajaro) xxviii, xliv, 148, 151, 271, 331
Jalair, Ahmad Sultan 120, 125, 328
Janus, King of Cyprus 12
Javán Qal'ah 325
Jawhar Aga (Yauguyaga) 229, 341
Jaxartes xliv, 281, 333, 337, 343
Jebel, "the Mountain" i.e. Etna 313
Jerusalem 19, 20, 22, 42, 314
Joanna, Queen of Naples, 12, 313
John (or Demetrius) the Young Emperor 27-9, 60-2, 85, 86, 321
John Palæologus xxviii, xxxi, xxxii, 31, 55, 61, 62, 315
John, Prince, son of Emperor Manuel II, 317
Jornufa (Giraffe) 121
Juji, eldest son of Chingiz Khan (Charcas) 183, 335, 342
Justinian, Emperor, statue of 47
Kaffa (Zefa) xviii, 77, 131, 132, 174, 265, 266, 302
Kafirs, or Infidels 289
Kalymnos (Calamo) 18, 23
Kandeli, castle (Candeloro) 20
Kashísh, Priest or Dervish 112, 113, 164, 325
Kastamuni (Castamea) 81
Kastro (Mytilene) 26, 29, 315
Kazan, Khans of Samarqand (Ahincan) 228, 335, 339
Kerasund (Guirifonda) 83
Kerbelá 332
Kesh (Quex) xii, xvii, xviii, xxix, xli, xlii, 176, 177, 179, 180, 184, 334
Khabushán (Cabria) 271, 343
Khalíl Sultan, Prince (Caril Sultan) xxx, xlvii, 135, 136, 189, 216, 282, 283
Khalvet, garden (Calbet) 186, 335
Khanum, Great, Timur's chief wife xxix, xxx, xlvi, 182, 196, 203-4, 335, 339, 341
- Her dress 226-7
- Her feasting described 215-6, 235-6
- Her mother's mosque 247
- Her mother's palace 204
- Her tents 211, 238
- Kuchik, "Little Lady", 211, 228, 229
Khanums, Timur's eight wives listed 228-9
Khánzádeh, Princess (Hausada) wife of Miran Shah, Timur's eldest son xxix, 135-6,
gives a feast 213-6, 229, 282, 329, 339, 341
Khoy (Hoy) iii, xxviii, xxxviii, xxxix, 102, 120-2, 295, 337
Khurásán xliv, 1, 131, 154, 156-7, 169, 170-3, 182, 270, 282, 286, 331, 332, 335
Kibitka xlii, 339
Kincob (Camocan) Gold brocade xli, 130, 139, 140, 153, 155, 166, 167, 168, 173, 186, 197, 201, 202, 205, 244, 292, 298, 300
- Chinese 294
Kirmiz worm (crimson) 115

Kirpen (Carpi) 71, 74, 75, 321
Kolominos, island 35
Koros, (Horchi) page attending the Emperor 85, 86
Kos (Lango) 18, 23, 314
Kossovo 109, 325
Kral, or King 325
Kubilai Khán xlii, 342
Kur (Cyrus) river, 278, 279, 343
Kurdistán 133, 326
Kurds 152
Kureli (Corila) river 84
Kúzah Kunán (Cusacana) 122, 328
Kynegos Gate 55
Ladislas King of Naples (Lanzalago) xxvii, 7, 11-3, 313
Lanaza 139
Lands of the Eastern Caliphate 310, 331, 333, 334
Lango (Kos) 18, 315
Lapislazuli mines (El Azul) 242
Lar (Car) 141
Lazarus, King of Servia 109, 325
Leona 83, 321
Leo V, King of Armenia 345
Leros (Berro) 24, 315
Lion and Sun emblem, 178
Lipari 13, 14
Loadstone 132
Longosardo, castle 7
Louis II, King of Naples 11, 313
Louis of Capua 11
Madrea, island 24
Majorca ii, 7
Mákú xxviii, 117, 118, 119, 295, 326

Malaga and Velez Malaga 4, 5, 312
Mambre, island 33
Mangana, arsenal xxvii, 53, 320
Manghali Bugay, Egyptian envoy 337
Manuel II, Emperor of Constantinople (Chirmanoli) xxxi, xxxii, xxxiii, xxxiv, xxxvii, 27-9, 31, 37, 55, 60-2, 67, 79, 85, 107, 313-9, 323
Manuel II, Emperor of Trebizond (Germanoli) xxxviii, 84, 93, 99, 300
Marco Polo x, xx, xxxvi, xlii, 323, 335, 337, 339, 342
Mardín 1, 286
Mares' milk, 195, 214, 215, 225, 229
Margaret, Queen of Naples 12, 313
Maria, the Hungarian maiden 308, 309, 312
Marmora island xxvii, xxxi, xxxii, 35, 63, 64, 65
Mastic gum 25
Media 1, 144, 154, 271, 272
Melaseno 83
Melialiorga 153, 156, 158
Melons, abundant and excellent 153, 161, 174, 195; dried and cured 253
Meri, coin xxi, 253
Merv xxix, xli, xliv, 332, 333
Meser 184, 185
Meshed (Maxaque) xxix, xxxix, xli, 156, 157, 332, 343

Mesopotamia 2, 286, 314, 326
Messina ii, xxvii, xlix, 15, 16, 302
Michael Palæologus 321
Miletus 315
Milosh Kobilovich 325
Minazkert 345
Minerva, Cape 12
Ming dynasty in China 337
Mirabozar, Lord, escort of the envoys 158, 160, 162, 165, 168, 173, 184
Mírán Sháh, (Mirassa Miaxa, Miaxa Mirassa) Timur's eldest son, *passim*, incl. xxviii, xxxix, xlvi, xlvii, 125, 133-6, 189, 213, 216, 281-92, 328-9, 339, 341, 345
Mirza, title, *passim* see n.7 p.310
Mír Akhor, mosque xxxvi, 318
Mitylene xxvii, xxxiv, 26-27, 29, 315
Miyanah (Miana) 128, 276
Mizar-i-Sharif 333
Modon 16, 54
Mola di Gaeta 10
Moles, breakwaters 22
Moles, measure of distance 150
Mollenos, island 26
Mongible (Etna) 16
Mongolian leagues 151; language and script 171
Monomachus, Constantine X 320
Monte Cassino 7
Moslems *passim* incl. xxx, 103, 111, 114, 126, 255, 289, 298
Mosques *passim* incl. xxix, xxx, xxxvi, 318, 321, 328, 334, 339
- Arzinjan, churches converted into 102-3
- destroyed by Miran Shah 133-4
- Gur Amir 245
- Isfarayin 152
- Kesh 176-7, 179
- Meshed 156
- portable 240
- ruined in Tehran 139
- Samarqand 242-8
- Tabriz 124, 126, 133
- Zanjan 129
Mother of Pearl (Nacar) 132
Muhammad the Conqueror xxxiii, 321, 323
Muhammad Sultan, Prince, his tomb 242
Mundasaga Khanun, Timur's fifth wife 229
Murád, Sultan (Amirate or Murate) xi, xxviii, xxxii, 31, 61, 109, 110, 315, 325
Murgháb xxix, xli, 163, 164, 332
Muscovy xxxiii
Nacar (Mother-of-pearl) 132
Naillac, Philibert de 314
Nakhjeván 326
Naples 7, 11, 12, 302, 313
Nashawa 326
Násir-ad-Dín Faraj, Sultan of Egypt 121, 314
Naw Juy (Naujua) 112, 326
Nevers, Duke of xxxi, 313
Nicephorus III Botoniates, Emperor 318

Nicolas Antonio, Clavijo's biographer, xlviii, 310
Nicopolis, battle of xi, xxvii, xxxi, xxxii, 68, 308, 314, 321
Nikaria, island 24
Nios, island 17
Níshápúr (Nixaor) xxviii, xxix, xxxvi, 137, 152-5
Nisyros, island 18
Noah, the Ark on Ararat 113, 115, 116
Nogay Tatars 342
Núr-ad-Dín the Christian 117
Núr-ad-Dín Mirza 190, 212
Nuzhat-al-Qulúb 310
Ogotay (Esbeque), son of Chingiz Khan 183, 335
Okhakhan (Ojajan) 155, 332
Omar, Prince, Timur's grandson *passim* incl. xlvii, 118-9, 181, 250, 275-95, 324, 328, 330, 345
Omar Tobán (Homar Toban), Timur's counsellor 181, 289
Oosh 168
Orlando's Tower 8, 9
Ormuz 131-2, 224
Ostriches xxxix, 121, 337
Otrar xliv, 281, 282, 334, 347, 343
Oveys, Sultan 123-125, 328
Oxus *passim* incl. xix, xxvii, xxix, xxx, xli, xliv, 155, 169-71, 269, 311, 333, 334
Palatia (Miletus) 23, 24, 268, 315
Palima, castle (Pilomazuca) 90
Paris, son of Priam 17

Paris, workmen of xxii, xlii, 178
Partir Javán 111, 325
Patmos (Tatanis) 24, 315
Pavilion xxix, xlii, 212, 219-21, 225-30, 234, 238-9, 242
Payo de Sotomayor 2
Pearls *passim*; trade at Ormuz 131-2
Pedro IV of Aragon 6
Pegarich (Pagarrix)110
Pekin (Beijing) see Cambaluc 337, 342
Pera *passim* incl. xxvii, xxviii, xxxvii, 19, 36-7, 53-6, 63-78, 84, 103, 107, 109, 301-2, 311, 317, 320, 364, 365
Persia *passim*
Persian Gulf 131, 132, 224
Persians ill-used by Tartars, 158-9
Pesante, coin 218
Petis de la Croix xxii, 308
Phalkonera 313
Pharmakussa (Pharin) 315
Philibert de Naillac 314
Philip, Count of Artois x, 320
Philoxenus, cistern of 321
Piahacabea 300
Piece of Eight, or dollar 325
Pig, Emperor 193, 337
Pir Muhammad (Pyr Mahomed), Prince, Timur's grandson xlvi, 222, 225, 248
Pitalibet 101
Platana 84, 302
Polemonium (Puliman) 322
Ponto 79, 322

Pontora 79
Pontoraquia (Bender Eregli)   78
Ponza 7
Porcelain dishes 193, 254
Porus, King of India 170
Prester John, legend xi, xx, 340, 342
Priam, King 17, 30
Price, Major David 308, 335
Proceda, island 12
Protevestati, Lord Treasurer 86
Punto della Campanella 313
Pyxites, river (Pexic) 89
Qarabágh plains xxxv, xxxvii, xliv, 21, 78, 94, 105, 275, 276-7, 343, 344
Qaraol of Greece and Turkey (Guirol) 69, 322
Qara Hissar 341
Qara Othman (Caraotoman) 345
Qara Qum xli, 332
Qara Quyunlu 345
Qara Yusuf, Chief of the Black Sheep Turcomans, xxx, 295-9, 345
Qazvín xxx, 273, 274
Qipchaq xxxiii
Qulbah 333
Qum Qal'ah 315
Raquia 79, 322
Ray, Rhages (Xariprey) xlvii, 139, 285
Real, silver coin xxi, 103, 110, 218, 244, 253, 325
Redea 35
Reggio, Passage of 16
Retrospect of Mahommedan History 308

Reza, the Imam xxix, xl, 156, 332
Rhodes and Knights of ii, xv, xxvii, xxxvi, 1, 18, 19, 21-4, 29, 313
Rio, castle 79
Roland, Tower of 8
Romania, Passage of (Dardanelles) 26, 30
Romanus III, Emperor 40, 41, 318
Ropa Arbaraga Khanum, Timur's eighth wife 229
Ruby mines xxix, 241; see also Balas
Ruy González *passim* incl. ix, 1, 3, 100, 101, 139, 140, 142, 215, 229
Sakaria, river 78
Salazar, Gómez de (Zalazar) xvi, xxxv, xxxvi, 3, 142, his death 153-4
Salonika 28-9
Salt-pans in Ibiza 6
Salugar Sukhassa (Sujassa) 164
Samarqand *passim* incl.
 - Arms manufactured, stored at 256, 259-60
 - Bágh-i-Chinár (Plane Tree Garden) 196, 334
 - Bágh-i-Naw 200
 - Castle or citadel, 256, 259
 - Description of the city 245-266
 - Dilkusha Garden 196, 199, 202, 334, 336
 - Gúr Amír 242-3, 334

357

- Law and order 260-1
- New bazaar, how built 247
- Palaces 200, 202 204
- Population 172, 252
- Sultan of 180-1, 331
- Wealth of and manufacturing at 254-5

Samos 24
Samsún (Simiso) 82
Sanábád 332
Sánchez de Palazuelos 2
Sanfoca, castle 84
Santa Maria xvi, xlviii, 3, 59, 319
Santa Sophia xxvii, xxxvi, 47-8, 51-2, 60, 88, 317, 319, 321
Santo Nicio, castle 83
Santorin 17
Sapphire mines, 241-2
Sarápardeh (Zalaparda, Calaparda) curtain or enclosure 209, 211, 241, 339
Sardinia 7
Sarec (Assarec), castle 288-90
Satin 323
Satorado, castle 35
Sávaji xxxii, 61
Savona xxx, xlv, 303
Sayyids 205, 246, 247, 339
Sekellio (Sequello), castle 70, 78
Sekilos, island 17
Seljuks of Rum 334
Selymbria xxxii, 28
Semíz-Kent, "Rich Town", a name for Samarqand 254
Semnán (Cenan) 272, 343
Serpent Column xxvii, 46, 319
Serpi 131
Serrakhs xxiv, xli, 332, 333

Servia 109
Seville *passim* incl. Intro., 4, 64, 252, 287, 303, 309
Seygan (Santguelana) 127
Shahraqán (Xahariea, Xaharcan) xxx, 138, 273
Sháh Bágh 110
Sháh Melik (Xamelique) 190, 212, 244
Sháh Rukh, Prince (Haroc Mirassa, Xaharoc) xlvi, xlvii, 155, 156, 282, 286, 292, 331, 335, 339
Shahr-i-Sabz (Kesh) 334
Shamákhí (Xamahi) 131
Sheep *passim*, fat-tailed 253
Ships, without iron nails 132
Shiráz (Xiras) x, 131
Shirván 131
Sicily 14-6, 312
Sidd-al-Bahr 315
Silk *passim* xvii, 9
- carpets 238
- Chinese 96, 220, 222, 240, 294, 323
- in churches 38, 53, 56
- crimson 115, 226
- elephants' howdahs 230
- furnishings 98, 190, 196-7, 207-12, 220-1, 236-41
- gift fromSpain 293
- manufactured at Samaqand 255
- parasol 227
- trade 124, 130-1
- weavers carried off from Damascus 254
- winter clothes

358

Sinope (Sinopoli) 81, 82, 98
Sisakán (Susakania) 263
Sístán (Cisten) 181, 312
Siurgatmish (Sorgatmix) 118
Sívás (Sebastria) xxviii, 102, 105-8, 145, 268
Skulls, towers of xxviii, 144-5
Snow, *passim*; snow-blindness 274-5
Sour milk, food of the Tartars 127, 161-2
Spiceries (spice trade) 130, 132 254-6
St Agatha, veil of 13
St Elmo's Fires 14
St John, Knights Hospitallers of ii, xv, xxvii, xxxvi, 1, 18, 19, 21-4, 29, 313
St Luke, ikon of the Virgin by xxviii, xxxvii, 67, 320
St Mary, Cape 26, 34, 315; see also Santa Maria and description of Constantinople for Churches
Stalimene 29, 314
Stambul xxxvii, 317, 321
Stanchio (Lango) 23, 314
Stephen, King of Servia and Saint 67, 325
Stromboli 13
Studion xxvii, xxxvi, 43, 317, 318
Studius the Patrician 318
Sulaymán Chelebi, Prince (Muzalman Ahalali Mizal Mathalabi) 78, 82, 109
Sulaymán Mirza (Culemaxa, Zuleman, Cumalexa Mirassa) xlvii, 141, 142, 160, 273, 185, 310, 325
Sulmari, or Surmari (Salmarin, Colmarin) 273, 275, 284-5, 290, 292
Sultan Ahmad Jalair (Zolten Amad), 120
Sultan Ahmad, Prince (Zoletan Hamet Mirassa), 141, 326, 328
Sultáníyah *passim* incl. xxviii, xxxix, 1, 94, 121, 129-39, 157, 189
Sunqurábád 328
Surmari xxv, 113, 114, 262, 323
Susurmena 301
Sunstroke, 131
Suyurghatmish 1
Sweetmeats, served at feasts 212
Syria xxvii, xxviii, xxxiii, xxxiv, xlvii, 19-22, 103, 106-7, 131-2, 313
Tabarán 332
Tabriz *passim* incl. Introduction, 123-7, 130, 132-3, 250, 258, 262, 268, 274-8, 281-4, 287-94
Taharten, Prince (Zaratan) xxviii, 98, 99, 102-7
Tájiks 1; Tajik country, Tagiquinia 165; 331
Talicia, garden 186, 336
Tamerlane (Timur) i, iv, v, ix, xii, xiii, xv, xxii, xxxiii, 1, 110, 311
Tana (Sea of Azov) 71, 77
Tanga, coin xxi, 201, 224, 338
Tangier 4

Tanguz, mocking name for the Emperor of China 93, 337
Tartars *passim* incl.
 - Black Sheep Turcomans (Qara Quyunlu) 341
 - - clothing 244
 - - drinking habits 200
 - - eating 194
 - - great herds 161
 White (Aq Quyunlu) 106, 107, 145
Tartary 131, 169, 174-5, 179, 183, 191, 204, 236, 240, 245, 255, 262-5, 268, 337
Tartum (Tarcon), castle 299 -300, 346
Tassuj or Taruj (Caza), 122, 328
Tauris iii
Tehrán xxxix, 138, 139, 142
Tejend, river xli, 157, 160, 162, 332
Tenedos 30-3
Tents *passim* incl. 211-21, 228-45, in gardens 255
Teragay xli, 176
Terek , river 263, 342
Terracina 8
Theodosius, Emperor 46, 318
Theotokos, Church of 320
Therapia, tower 69, 322
Three Circlets, emblem 178, 334
Tiles, coloured xlii, 124, 130, 174, 177-8, 185, 196-7,
Timur *passim* – see Contents
Timur Bec, Histoire de, Notes *passim*
Tireboli (Tripil) 84
Tirmiz (Termit, Tremit) xxix, xli, xliv, 170, 172-3, 175

Toktamish (Tetani, Coramix, Totamix, Tortamix) xxx, 113-4, 122, 186, 191, 204, 262-6, 326, 328, 338, 342
Tower of skulls 145-6, 345
Transoxiana xxxvii, xli, xlvii, 333
Trebizond iii, xxiv, xxvii-xxviii, xxx, xxxvi-xxxviii, xlv, 54, 69, 76, 84-9, 93, 98, 115, 122, 132, 300-2, 310, 323
Tree of the Bishop 126
Trenchers of silver 212
Trilla Bay of 36
Tripe 140, 194
Tripoli of Syria iv, 20
Troy, ruins of, ii, xxvii, 30, 33, 34, 260
Truxi, Lord of 68
Tucelar 276
Tukel Khanum (Dilcoltagana), Timur's 3rd wife 229, 341
Tuluy (Gabuy), son of Chinghiz Khan 183, 335, 337
Tuman Aga 341
Tungalar (Tucelar) 276
Tunglár 127-8
Turks *passim*
Turkey *passim* incl. xxxi, xliv, 2, 22-6, 29, 30, 33, 69, 70, 82, 103, 108-10, 131-2, 141, 250, 254, 256, 268, 276
Turkistan 295
Turkoman 111, 127, 295, 296, 298, 342
Turquoise 59, 198, 212, 226, 237-8
 - mines xxix, xxxix, 154
Tús 157, 332
Tuy 313

Uighhúr script 334
Uján (Hujan, Ugan) 127, 276
Unieh (Hinio) 82
Urúmiyah Lake xxxviii, 122
Van Millingen xxiii; Notes *passim*
Venetian xxi, 16, 32, 54, 71, 77
Venice xxxiii, 16, 31, 32, 77
Vengaraga Khanum, Timur's 6th wife, 229
Veramín (Vatami) 273
Vian plains xxx, 281, 283, 284, 292, 293
Vicer, castle 299
Vituperio, Torre de 34, 315
Volcano 13
Wakhsh 331
Waterspout 13
Well of the Wind, at Damghan xxx, 272
White Sheep Tartars 106, 107, 145
William of Hapsburg 12
Wine-drinking customs 97, 213-4, 229-30
Wrestlers and wrestling 223
Xaharcan or Xaharica 330
Xanto, Cape 25
Xetea 34
Yam and Yamehi xl, 149, 269
Yauguyaga (Jawhar Aga), Timur's 8th wife 229, 341
Yesen, in Khurasan 131
Yezd, Sharaf-ad-Dín 'Alí of, Notes, *passim*
Yunglo, Emperor 337
Yúsuf, Qara, Turcoman chief, xxx, 111, 295, 296, 298, 299, 345

Zabrain or Zafarain 331
Zampia Palæologina, Princess, 38
Zanján (Sanga) xxviii, 129, 275, 328
Zarafshán river, xviii, xliv, 202, 206
Zaytúní silk, 96, 220, 222, 240, 294, 323 294, 323
Zegan (Sigana) 90

Sanlucar de
Barrameda

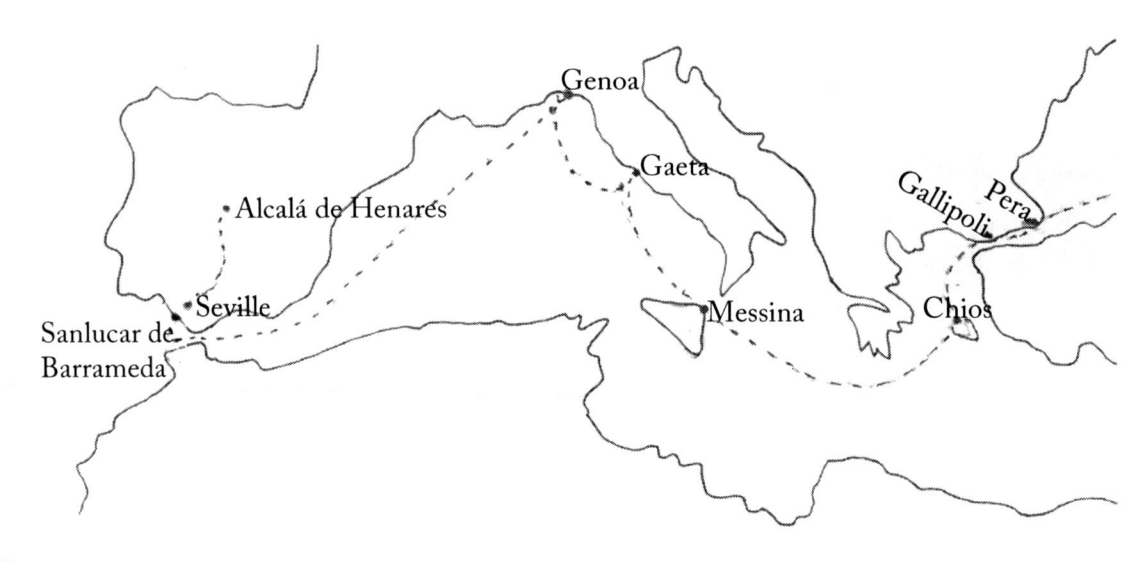

Seville

Alcalá de Henares

Genoa

Gaeta

Messina

Gallipoli

Pera

Chios

The Route Back

Pera

Trebizond
Platana
Aunique
Khoy

Caspian Sea

Aral Sea

Bukhara
Samarqand

Sultaniya
Tehran
Damogan